Gendered Voices

THE MIDDLE AGES SERIES

Ruth Mazo Karras, General Editor
Edward Peters, Founding Editor
A complete list of books in the series
is available from the publisher.

Gendered Voices

Medieval Saints and Their Interpreters

Edited by Catherine M. Mooney

Foreword by
CAROLINE WALKER BYNUM

PENN

University of Pennsylvania Press

Philadelphia

Copyright © 1999 University of Pennsylvania Press
All rights reserved
Printed in the United States of America on acid-free paper

10 9 8 7 6 5 4 3 2 1

Published by
University of Pennsylvania Press
Philadelphia, Pennsylvania 19104-4011

Library of Congress Cataloging-in-Publication Data

Gendered voices : medieval saints and their interpreters / edited by
Catherine M. Mooney ; foreword by Caroline Walker Bynum.
     p.   cm. — (Middle Ages series)
   Includes bibliographical references and index.
   ISBN 0-8122-3485-5 (alk. paper). — ISBN 0-8122-1687-3
(pbk. : alk. paper)
   1. Christian hagiography.   2. Church history—Middle Ages,
600–1500—Historiography.   I. Mooney, Catherine M.   II. Series.
BX4662.G46   1999
270.3′092′2—DC21   98-54774
                                                              CIP

For

Paul Meyvaert and Ann Freeman

Distinguished medievalists and generous friends

Contents

Foreword

Caroline Walker Bynum

The saints are odd subjects for historical research. They are, as the current jargon has it, "socially constructed." Whether we speak of officially designated *sancti* or of those revered locally without papal canonization, there is no saint without an audience. Fashioned and authenticated in a complex relationship between clerical authorities and the adherents who spread the holy person's reputation for virtues and miracles, the saint herself or himself is lost to view almost from the beginning. Moreover, the virtue of the saints is such that they are self-effacing and secretive, brave when God trumpets through them but often otherwise modest and inarticulate, bracketing rather than naming their ineffable experience of the Other. Hence the saints are not typical. And there are not, of course, very many of them.

Nonetheless, for almost four hundred years, hagiography or the study of the saints has been a microcosm of the study of European history. It is possible to argue convincingly that modern "scientific history"—that is, history based on careful authentication and criticism of the documentary record—was created in the seventeenth century by two Catholic religious societies, the Bollandists of Belgium and the Maurists of France, who developed the fields of codicology, paleography, and diplomatics in the course of writing the histories of the saints. In the last half century, many of the fashions and innovations in history writing have been reflected in hagiography. The enthusiasm of the 1960s and '70s for both anthropology and quantification led not merely, as might have been predicted, to new studies of popular mentalities and demography but also, quite astonishingly, to large statistical analyses of the population of holy men and women. The years 1981–82 saw the appearance of no fewer than three studies that undertook, with learning and audacity, the task of quantifying the saints according to social class, gender, type of charismatic authority, etc.[1] The 1970s and '80s also saw the flowering of women's history, and a determination to ferret out evidence for women's lives in often unlikely places led to creative new study of texts by and about religious women. Such texts had long been known and had sometimes embarrassed their editors deeply. Formerly examined only as philological evidence concerning early forms of the European vernaculars, they were now suddenly read for their content: everything from the incidental evidence they might provide about domestic and urban life to their audacious, sometimes stunningly erotic, sometimes antinomian poetry and theology.

In the late 1980s things began to change. The large syntheses in both women's history and in hagiography fragmented. Micro-history and literary criticism moved to the fore. Scholars such as Sharon Farmer and Thomas Head began to focus in great detail on the world of single cults. Aviad Kleinberg challenged the value of generalizing or quantifying from such chronologically diverse and at the same time formulaic material as *vitae* and canonization processes.[2] What John Toews, among others, called the "linguistic turn" raised insistently the problem of "voice" and "perspective." In Anglo-American history writing, the pressure came from so-called French theory, in Germany from a tradition of literary scholarship that saw genre as all-powerful.[3] Some sensitive and alert medievalists began to wonder whether the hagiographical and mystical treatises by and about women that had seemed our best hope for recovering their particular and intimate experiences might not be too opaque, too constructed by high-status male authors to give any window on women's lives.

It is to this problem that Catherine Mooney and her collaborators address this wonderful set of essays. Their efforts demonstrate that, once again, hagiography is at the forefront of historical scholarship and methodology. For these studies of a small group of atypical texts about atypical figures not only illuminate the past with a fierce and probing light but also raise, with nuance and power, fundamental issues of interpretation and method. Undaunted by the difficulty of the task, the eight historians who contribute to this volume consider the problem of "voice" in a complex array of texts—texts in which women and men collaborate, texts in which men use or misuse women's texts or experiences, texts in which women themselves write or dictate, sometimes appropriating, sometimes rebelling against or ignoring religious stereotypes and expectations. The eight essays ask: how do we discern individual voices? how are these voices gendered? how much of what survives is determined by genre, by social or religious stereotypes, by individual experience?

Such questions are formidably challenging. Sorting out the voice of the hagiographer from that of the saint is difficult even where gender difference is not an issue. Simone Roisin remarked long ago that mystical phenomena become more external and somatized the further an author is from the personal experience recounted, and we have examples from the high Middle Ages of women-authored accounts (such as Gertrude the Great's *Herald of Divine Love*) where the female saint is interiorized in her own words, externalized in the words of her sisters.[4] Moreover, theology, canon law, and politics shape genre as much as gender does; when admirers of saints praise virtues more than miracles, or vice versa, they may be responding less to the saint's life or to gender expectations than to changing requirements for what it takes to gain canonization or cult. What is exciting about these essays on "gendered voices" is their engagement with the full complexities of both "gender" and "voice."

Even more exciting, however, is their confidence. For the eight authors of this collection, empowered in part by their philological skills, in part by their deep historical knowledge, listen hopefully, certain of catching genuine echoes of the whispering voices of the past. They know that texts can be authenticated, strands of transmission sorted out, better and worse readings of manuscripts established. They know also that any text tells us first and foremost about itself but that we see very little in any text if it is the only one we read; the more we know, the more context we have; texts do tell us about the world from which they come. Hence these eight essays, fragments in 1990s style of a grand picture we are not yet ready to draw, make a whole far greater than their individual parts. As Catherine Mooney's introduction spells out, trends in the history of spirituality emerge from them.

Brother A., scribe of Angela of Foligno (d. 1309), described his own efforts to record her words by saying: "I had so little grasp of their meaning that I thought of myself as a sieve or sifter which does not retain the precious and refined flour but only the most coarse."[5] As these essays make clear, even a claim not to understand can shape, manipulate, obscure, clarify, or empower. Any sifter changes what it sifts. But we may be certain that the eight historians who have made this volume have studied the flour as well as the sieve, and that their own sifting has given us an understanding of the past, insight into our methods of sifting it, and a new confidence that such sifting is worth doing.

Abbreviations

AASS	*Acta sanctorum . . . editio novissima*, ed. J. Bollandus and G. Henschenius
AB	*Analecta Bollandiana*
AF	*Analecta franciscana*
AFH	*Archivum franciscanum historicum*
AFP	*Archivum fratrum praedicatorum*
ALKG	*Archiv für Literatur- und Kirchengeschichte des Mittelalters*
CCCM	*Corpus christianorum: Continuatio medievalis* (Turnhout, 1953–)
MGH, SS	*Monumenta Germaniae historica: Scriptores* (Berlin, 1826–)
PL	*Patrologia cursus completus: series latina*, ed. J.-P. Migne

I

Voice, Gender, and the Portrayal of Sanctity

Catherine M. Mooney

AMONG THE ISSUES explored in this collection of essays are three inter-related methodological questions that face scholars of medieval sanctity. The first concerns the attempt to distinguish the voices and the points of view of saints, on the one hand, from those of their interpreters, on the other. Are there general tendencies that demarcate the ways in which medieval saints speak of themselves from the ways in which they are represented by their admirers and collaborators? Since all but one of the essays in this volume regard female saints and their male interpreters, the question is focused particularly on female self-representations and male representations of female sanctity. Our individual attempts to search out the voices of the saints and their interpreters have varied significantly according to the texts at our disposal. Some authors (Newman, Mooney, Hollywood, Scott) listen to and compare the voices of holy women in their own individually authored texts with the voices of the men who admired them in texts authored by those men. Others (Clark, Coakley, Tobin, Elliott) seek to discern women's and men's voices in texts collaboratively authored by a saint and one or more of the saint's admirers. In yet another variant, some contributors (particularly Coakley, Tobin, and Elliott) search also for traces of women's experiences preserved within what appear to be entirely male-authored texts that discuss the women.

The second and related question that we address is whether or not the voices one hears in these texts are "gendered." Since each essay concerns at least one woman and one man—a saint and the saint's interpreter of the opposite sex—we can ask to what extent women's experiences of sanctity and ideas about it, on the one hand, and men's experiences of sanctity and ideas about it, on the other, are influenced and therefore distinguished from each other by their respective experiences of themselves as females and males in societies that attached very particular meanings to being women and to being men. More particularly, because holy women figure prominently in all of the essays, this volume explores especially whether holy women qua women perceived and represented their sanctity in ways significantly different from the ways their male contemporaries perceived and represented female sanctity.

In a final and related question, we ask to what extent portrayals of sanctity are influenced not so much by gender as by genre. This consideration goes well beyond the most obvious distinction separating the ways in which a holy person would speak about herself and the ways in which an admiring hagiographer would praise her in an account intended to edify and impress others. The hagiographical texts that chronicle and idealize the lives of the saints whom we consider represent exceptionally disparate genres, including poetry, theological treatises, papal bulls, letters, visionary tracts, prayers, and inquisitorial records. Each author therefore must grapple with the ways in which the varying purposes of distinct genres influence or even determine the self-representations and representations of sanctity propagated within those texts.

Each of the essays in this volume represents original research on these interrelated themes of voice, gender, and the representation of sanctity, seven through exploration of individual medieval holy women and their male interpreters and collaborators and one, in an intriguing reversal of this scenario, in a discussion of a medieval holy man and the role his pious female collaborator and her notes about him played within his own autobiographical text.

How We Got Here: The Portrayal of Medieval Women in Male-Authored *Vitae*

The driving and defining force behind all these themes has been the vibrant research conducted since the 1970s in the field of women's history. For medievalists, religious women's history in particular has proved a galvanizing force, invigorating hagiographic scholarship, opening complex avenues of inquiry for historians of gender, and transforming treatments of medieval ecclesiastical and religious institutions, theology, heresy, spirituality, and popular religiosity.[1] The very process of restoring religious women to the historical record has prompted historians to take a new look at the question of voice, the extent to which voices may be gendered, and the way representations of sanctity are often determined by their specific textual expression.

How did this happen? It came as no surprise to anyone that the answers to some of the earliest questions about medieval religious women—who were they? where did they live? what did they do?—were most readily found in texts that happened to have been penned by medieval men, clerics in fact, the men whose privileged access to the world of letters left them as the authors of a vastly disproportionate share of all surviving medieval documents. Most medieval holy women, in fact, are known to us solely through texts written by men. *Vitae*, the written lives of the saints, constitute the single most available and important genre about male and female saints. Since we can safely assume that male-authored texts about male saints do reveal men's thinking about male sanctity—even if the male saint in question would not always have agreed with his hagiographer's representation of him—the question of gender does not arise in the *same* way (although arise it does) as in the case of male-authored texts purporting to represent female sanctity. Given the patriarchal and misogynistic cast of medieval society and, in particular, the medieval Church, many scholars have increasingly expressed skepticism regarding these sources, noting that male-authored depictions of holy women, however sincerely intentioned, are likely to reveal far more about men's idealized notions of female sanctity and its embodiment in women's lives than they reveal about the female saints themselves.

Our approach, however, is not to dismiss such documents out of hand as suspect sources for understanding medieval women. We seek rather to find new ways of interpreting these documents to understand better how the gender of medieval authors influences the ways in which they either self-represent or represent others, others who also are "gendered" in very specific ways. Our aim is to use these documents to understand better both saints and their admirers, both men and women, both writers and their subjects.

By considering the relatively rare cases of women who wrote (Newman, Mooney, Hollywood, Scott) or managed to leave a discernible imprint within other texts, we can begin to conjecture knowledgeably about the ways in which women's self-representations diverged from those of their male contemporaries. In the cases of those male writers who incorporated—or claimed to have incorporated—the words of a medieval woman into their texts (as discussed by Newman, Clark, Coakley, Tobin, Elliott), close scrutiny of each author's relationship with his female subject will help us understand better the dynamics driving male authorial representations of medieval holy women. Although the essays in this collection are not specifically about women who left no writings of their own or for whom no vestiges of their voices or personal agency can be clearly discerned in other texts, their insights about the relationships between male writers and holy women represent an important contribution to the scholarly quest to develop strategies for reading with a sharper eye male-authored portrayals of such women.

The Essays: A Brief Overview

Beyond this larger and longer-term goal, however, these essays represent significant new research regarding these specific saints, their medieval collaborators and interpreters, and the array of texts associated with them. The following overview of the essays sets forth in succinct terms the parameters of each contributor's study and so sets the stage for a subsequent discussion of some of the most salient insights, patterns, and themes that emerge across the essays as a whole.

The subject of Barbara Newman's essay is the nature of Hildegard of Bingen's inspiration and authority and the ways in which the meaning of her prophetic speech evolved from Hildegard's own writings through those of subsequent hagiographers. Newman examines the *vita* of Hildegard jointly authored by Gottfried of St. Disibod; Theoderic of Echternach, who finished the *vita* after Gottfried died; and Hildegard herself, from whose memoir Theoderic drew selected quotations. Newman complements her analysis with a discussion of two contrasting hagiographic depictions of Hildegard that emerged in the later Middle Ages.

Anne Clark examines the series of texts chronicling the visionary experiences that Elisabeth of Schönau recounted to her brother Ekbert. Ekbert recorded them for posterity in a newly developing style of religious writing that combined traditional hagiography with the literature of personal revelation. Because Clark can track the chronological appearance and various redactions of these visionary diaries, thematic texts, and letters, she is able to analyze the evolving dynamics of Elisabeth's and Ekbert's relationship.

The centrally important Franciscan theme of imitation, both imitation of Christ and imitation of Mary, is Catherine Mooney's focus in her essay comparing Clare of Assisi's writings with those of her myriad male interpreters, including her principal hagiographer, popes, and prominent Franciscan writers. Mooney elaborates her analysis by comparing the treatment of these same themes of *imitatio Christi* and *imitatio Mariae* in texts by and about Clare's better-known, more prolific, and more written about friend, Francis of Assisi. She is therefore able to compare and contrast saintly self-portrayals with portrayals of saints, and depictions regarding a holy woman with those regarding a holy man.

Both genre and gender explain the striking differences separating Beatrice of Nazareth's vernacular mystical treatise "Seven Manners of Loving God" from the Latin *vita* about Beatrice by an anonymous hagiographer, as Amy Hollywood shows. A close analysis of several passages in particular shows how the hagiographer liberally reinterprets his subject and, in the process, presents a strikingly different portrait of female sanctity, even when he claims merely to be translating her own words.

John Coakley examines a wide array of texts regarding the beguine Christine of Stommeln in order to compare her confessor Peter of Dacia's view of her with her own view of herself. The texts include correspondence between the two, Peter's account of his visits with her, his theological ruminations about her, and narratives collaboratively authored by Christine with a parish priest and a schoolmaster, who each recorded experiences she shared with them about herself. Peter's editorial control over all of these texts is key to understanding their various depictions of Christine.

Frank Tobin explores the extent to which we can discern Elsbeth Stagel's contribution to Henry Suso's autobiographical *vita*. Suso not only claimed to have used Stagel's notes in writing his life story, but also included her as an important figure within his text. Cognizant of the extent to which the hagiographical genre can influence or even distort information regarding the historical reality of saints and their collaborators, Tobin judiciously reviews the evidence for an actual literary partnership between Suso and Stagel. An apparent reversal of the female saint/male interpreter scenarios discussed by other contributors to this volume, this case resembles them also insofar as a male writer presents his readers with information he alleges to have come from a pious woman.

Karen Scott compares Catherine of Siena's self-portrayal in her letters with Raymond of Capua's representation of Catherine in his *vita*, composed some fifteen years after her death. Although Scott finds that Catherine's and Raymond's representations of Catherine overlap in important respects, she shows too how they diverge sharply in others. Scott argues that Catherine's words should be given priority over Raymond's and that, for those topics about which Catherine kept mostly silent, one should be cautious not to harmonize or confuse Raymond's perspective with that of Catherine.

Dyan Elliott scrutinizes the extensive Latin writings about Dorothea of Montau—four *vitae*, two collections of her revelations, and the acts of her canonization. The *vitae* and revelations were all recorded by John Marienwerder, who also carefully monitored the progress of her canonization proceedings. Elliott's focus, however, is not on Dorothea alone, but rather on John's invention of Dorothea and his own quest for self-authorization.

Portrayals of Sanctity: Common Patterns and Themes

Despite the significant span of time separating these women and men and the diversity of texts associated with them, a number of common patterns emerge that unite these individuals. These points of intersection highlight some of the major themes in depictions of female sanctity apparent across the two and a half centuries covered by the lives of these saints, beginning in about 1140 with Hildegard of Bingen's first recorded words and closing about 1400 when, close on the heels of the death of Dorothea of Montau, her patron and hagiographer concluded his vast corpus about her. Although the motifs here highlighted regard specifically these eight saints and their interpreters, with certain themes illustrated by only several figures from among the eight, scholars of medieval sanctity will nonetheless immediately recognize features of these saints in others not discussed in this volume.

Two related categories are useful for discussing characteristics common to the saints and their interpreters scrutinized in these essays. The first category comprehends questions regarding the textualization of these hagiographic accounts, and the second encompasses themes which capture notably divergent emphases characteristic of women's descriptions of female sanctity on the one hand, and men's on the other. Close attention to questions regarding the texts, including genre, authorial intention, the compositional process, editorial style, and similar matters, reveals a host of attributes common to documents as disparate as *vitae*, letters, personal revelations, inquisitorial records, theological commentaries, and personal prayers. Our project to examine rigorously and thoroughly the often complex details of textual composition, transmission, language, and vocabulary has allowed us to speculate with confidence and sometimes in surprising new ways about texts collaboratively authored by holy women and men and, further, about the suggestively distinctive accents of women's and men's voices within them. These analyses, coupled with our examinations of texts tied exclusively to either women or men, lay a foundation for the second category discussed below regarding tendencies differentiating the ways the women in these essays speak of themselves from the ways their male associates speak about them.

Textual considerations in hagiographic accounts about medieval women. Among the insights regarding the composition of hagiographic texts is the well-known fact that men, and clerics in particular, exercised nearly complete control over the textualization of women's utterances. Women's words almost invariably reach us only after having passed through the filters of their male confessors, patrons, and scribes. As these essays show, although the filters are varied, their effects share common features. Whether authored by women or men, most texts regarding women bear the indisputable signs of men's controlling influence. Most women's stories would never have been recorded, much less survived the centuries, had they not been sanctioned by the male clerical elite. The strong-willed and brilliant Hildegard of Bingen, although surely one of the most gifted individuals of the twelfth century, quite likely would never have produced her vast corpus had her ecclesiastical superiors not first put their stamp of approval on her earliest and, at that moment at least, tentative attempt to record her experiences. What is true for Hildegard, in this respect, is a fortiori true, as these essays show, of other medieval women.

Women's relatively less extensive formal education goes a long way toward explaining their initial reluctance to speak and their dependence upon the clerics for a sense of self-confidence as writers or dictating authors. The vernacular accounts dictated by Elisabeth of Schönau, Christine of Stommeln, Elsbeth Stagel, and Dorothea of Montau, to the extent that these reach us at all, do so almost only in the learned Latin, the dominant idiom of religious truth, of their male scribes, confessors, and promoters. These men, as Elliott remarks, gave such women a "home of literacy"—a home, it should be noted, that was often in a real sense foreign or strange to them.

Most clerical writers, however, were much more than scribes and simple translators, even when they claimed to be only that. Careful com-

parison of Beatrice of Nazareth's Dutch treatise with the Latin "translation" her hagiographer claimed to have made of it shows just how fan-
cifully he embellished and transformed her text. One necessarily wonders
about so many other self-described "scribes" who, in the "women's texts"
they have bequeathed to us, claimed to have transcribed into Latin only
what the women they admired dictated to them, adding not a whisper of
their own.[2] In a preponderance of these cases we are not so fortunate as we
are in the case of Beatrice and her hagiographer, for customarily no text
authored by the female protagonist in question has survived against which
we might check the claims of her male scribe or hagiographer.

Men also frequently exercised critical control over the very shape
women's stories took through the men's assiduous questioning of the
women. Mooney points to evidence that the sisters who testified in the
canonization process on behalf of Clare of Assisi were often responding to
quite pointed questions addressed to them by the ecclesiastical inquisitors
charged with overseeing their testimony. The women's testimony, whatever it may have been when orally delivered, would then be recorded,
abbreviated, or omitted entirely according to the judgment of the supervising males. Elliott, in her detailed discussion of medieval confessional
practice, makes this same case in far stronger terms. She pays particular
attention to John Marienwerder's role as confessor (and interrogator) of
Dorothea of Montau and his virtually absolute control over her behavior
and speech while she was sequestered in an anchoress's cell the last fourteen
months of her life. John's manipulation of Dorothea's memory, his redaction of her revelations, his orchestration of the canonization proceedings,
and his complete narrative control not only dominate our perceptions of
Dorothea, but ultimately set the terms of Dorothea's own spiritual self-
understanding.[3]

The breadth and magnitude of such editorial control can be stun-
ning. Coakley shows how Peter of Dacia, as the ultimate editor of all of
the myriad texts concerning Christine of Stommeln, exercised paramount
control over them, so much so that the Christine we hear in these texts—
even in her ostensibly dictated autobiographical reports—although certainly shaped in part by the historical Christine, is in fact a collaborative
literary persona. In a slightly different fashion but yielding a similar result,
Tobin examines Henry Suso's editing style by comparing several passages
from Suso's earlier works with subsequent revisions of those same passages included in Suso's later works. Based on this analysis, it appears that
if Suso indeed used Stagel's notes in composing his *vita*, he likely took

great liberties with them. Suso's Stagel, then, who plays such a central role within his *vita*, emerges as a decidedly fictional figure built upon a factual core. Close scrutiny of other male-authored or edited texts shows the unmistakable—albeit sometimes frustratingly elusive—transformations of women's stories. Ekbert of Schönau's continual re-working of his sister's visionary corpus allows Clark to track his interventions and re-workings of passages that in earlier redactions could be more reliably tied to Elisabeth's own views.[4]

Male manipulation of female texts and saintly portrayals endured long after the saints and their original interpreters had completed their texts and died. Newman shows how two contrasting views of Hildegard in the late medieval period can be traced to two other influential hagiographers besides Gottfried and Theoderic, the authors who completed her *vita*. Guibert of Gembloux's efforts to promote Hildegard and her cult helped establish her as the Mother of Mystics, the first in a long line of female visionaries, while the reformist and anti-heretical Gebeno of Eberbach kept Hildegard's public persona alive in his widely read selected anthology of her writing. Hildegard's fame in the late medieval period owed much more to the influence of these men than it did to a reading of her far more extensive writings. Similarly, careful attention to the evolving representations of Clare and Francis of Assisi reveals that Clare's intimate bond with Francis and his early followers, an association bothersome to many later friars, was consistently downplayed in their textual and iconographic depictions of the two.

Divergent emphases in male and female accounts of female sanctity. Our individual findings about specific saints and their interpreters point to other themes about which women and men and saints and hagiographers appear to differ. Although common parlance labels women and men as members of opposite sexes, the contrast between them is hardly antithetical. In fact, the common heritage shared by female saints with their male interpreters is vast. They typically occupied the same geographical space and chronological time; they were devout Christians; most were members of religious orders, many evincing similar rules and spiritualities; they heard much the same by way of biblical interpretations, liturgical celebrations, sermons, and pious literature; they imbibed together the same cultural messages regarding masculinity, femininity, and the proper roles for each sex regarding leadership, oral and written expression, and the pursuit of holiness.

The very vastness of the common ground they shared and the fact that no absolute dichotomies can be drawn between women and men makes the marked differences between them all the more striking. Among the many features distinguishing women's and men's voices, five in particular highlight the fact that, while the mother language of the saints and their interpreters may be the same, their accents most certainly are not. The reasons for these discrepancies, as the essays show, can vary considerably, ranging from considerations of the gender of the saints and their interpreters and the genres in which they wrote to the specific theological biases or even petty self-interested agendas motivating some authors' reflections. The first three themes, integrally related to one another, include women's relatively more assertive self-understandings of their religious roles, men's tendency to understand these women as mystical and mysterious, and men's propensity to employ nuptial imagery in their discussions of holy women. The representation of women's religious experience as somatic and the particular prototypes and exempla put forward as appropriate for women's imitation also point to differences separating women's and men's ideas regarding female sanctity.

In those cases where women appear to speak in their own voices, they speak of themselves in decidedly more active and assertive terms than do their male promoters. Comparing the voices of Hildegard, Gottfried, and Theoderic in the *vita* they jointly coauthored reveals that, while Hildegard considered herself to be God's prophet, Gottfried remolded her as an aristocratic abbess and foundress and Theoderic, interested less in Hildegard's message than in the type of saint she represented, portrayed her as a bridal mystic. Despite Ekbert of Schönau's role as the final arbiter in the textualization of his sister Elisabeth's utterances, Elisabeth emerges not only as the subject of these texts, but also as an influential and increasingly self-confident agent in their production. Like Hildegard before her, she welcomed her role as author of a book and she used her position as God's prophet to alter her brother's and others' view of her. Catherine of Siena presented herself as a lively, assertive, and self-assured apostle continually intervening in the affairs of her world, traits largely missing from Raymond of Capua's account of the saint. Although Clare of Assisi accentuated her and her sisters' active *following* of Christ's footprints, both her hagiographer and a pope described her as *being* "the footprint of the Mother of God," a phrase evocative of imitation but casting Clare in a decidedly more passive position.

Male hagiographers, moreover, were wont to see their female subjects as mysterious and otherworldly, a fact not surprising since they were writing about saints. Nevertheless, male hagiographers were more likely to conceal or diminish a saint's this-worldly activities if the saint in question was a woman. Fear of offending a Church or public opposed to feminine assertiveness likely influenced their choices, but other agendas, ranging from their unconsidered assumptions about women and female sanctity to their own self-interest, also played a part. These women were "others" in the eyes of their male admirers, and this otherliness included the women's proximity to the supernatural realm, a holy intimacy the men admired but felt incapable of imitating.[5] Of course, depicting women as otherworldly and possessed of arcane knowledge was a double-edged sword: the effect of Theoderic of Echternach's and Gebeno of Eberbach's representations of Hildegard as unfathomable and obscure, for example, may have served simultaneously to enhance her stature and to relieve readers of any responsibility to study her writings seriously. Catherine of Siena and Raymond of Capua each tell us of her mystical encounters, but while Catherine reported such incidents only in the context of her life as an apostle, prayerfully interceding on behalf of her Church and her neighbors, Raymond treated her mysticism both at greater length and as a subject in and of itself. The intense fascination Peter of Dacia expressed regarding Christine of Stommeln's ecstatic experiences of rapture, although not ultimately at odds with her more sparing accounts of mystical experience, is a vehicle for him to make his own theological statement: Christine, for Peter, is an example of grace completing nature. Another aspiring theologian, John Marienwerder, finding himself stuck in a dead-end job, uses his brief relationship with the spiritually gifted Dorothea of Montau in his quest for self-authorization—a quest intrinsically bound up with his aspirations to have Dorothea recognized as a saint. Dorothea's *vitae* and revelations, in his hands, create an impression of occlusion and mystification and are, in Elliott's words, "a masterstroke of clerical self-authorization." John is at once self-effacing and self-aggrandizing: his professed inability to understand the mystic's idiom of love mirrors her incapacity to grasp the ineffable, and his artful description of this idiom as "barbaric" to his understanding serves as a sly reminder to the reader that without his learned Latin the illiterate mystic's vernacular story would not have been written.

The use of nuptial imagery within these texts suggests a third theme differentiating female from male writing. One might expect, given the fact that medieval people often thought of God in masculine terms, that nuptial imagery would appear with greater frequency in holy women's than in holy men's self-representations, but this is not so in the case of two saints discussed in this volume. Clare of Assisi certainly thought of herself as God's mother, sister, and bride. More surprising, perhaps, is the fact that Francis of Assisi described himself and his brothers as God's mother, exhorted both men and women to be Christ's spouse, and was described by his brothers as the spouse of Christ. The very fluidity with which medieval people employed gendered imagery to speak of their relationships with the divine requires that close attention be paid to the gender of both the writers who used such language and the subjects whom they described.

In contrast to the case of Clare and Francis, the prevalence of nuptial imagery in male hagiographic texts describing women's relationship with God appears to reflect a particularly male concern that is not similarly echoed in many women's self-representations. Hildegard of Bingen regarded herself as a prophet speaking *for* God; her hagiographer Theoderic of Echternach, however, was more intrigued by her relationship *with* God, a relationship he depicted by drawing on the bridal imagery of the Song of Songs. In Hildegard's own vast corpus, she seldom invoked the Song of Songs and expressed little if any interest in its nuptial mysticism. Beatrice of Nazareth, on the other hand, did use the language of Lover and Beloved in the Song of Songs, but it is interesting to note that she describes the soul as eventually relinquishing its bridal role to assume the more mature role as God's housewife. Peter of Dacia's accounts about Christine of Stommeln are suffused with nuptial imagery: she is Christ's bride and he, Peter, the wedding guest invited to observe their nuptials. Elsewhere, Peter presents himself as the bridegroom's rejected wife; late in their relationship when he comes to understand his relationship with Christine in more mutual terms, Peter speaks of himself as Christine's bridegroom along with Christ. In contrast to Peter's versatile use of nuptial imagery, however, Christine rarely speaks of herself as God's bride in any of the texts she ostensibly dictated to others. John Marienwerder similarly cast his confessee Dorothea of Montau in the bridal role, describing his own relationship with her with clearly romantic undertones: so close is their confessional union that the two are, as it were, married to one another. How Dorothea—who had herself been married in life—would have reacted to this construction of her relationship with a priest whom she met only in the final years of her life is impossible to know. The effect that men's obvious proclivity to understand women as brides of God had on the women about whom they wrote, especially those under their spiritual tutelage, is a subject ripe for further investigation.

An oft-noted feature of medieval women's religious experience is its bodily expression. Medieval texts regularly describe holy women, much more than holy men, as fasting, swooning, swelling, bleeding, or otherwise manifesting their interior spiritual dispositions through concrete physical signs. Women, as scholars agree, are embodied physicality in a way that men, more often identified with mind and spirit, are not.[6] Still contested, however, is the extent to which women and men shared an understanding of women's embodied religious experience. Two examples from among these studies suggest that they may not always have agreed. Catherine of Siena's intense interest in the world around her stands in marked contrast to Raymond of Capua's focused emphasis on her paranormal bodily experiences—her scars, swoons, stigmata, struggles with demons who almost kill her, apparent deaths, and mystical death. As Scott suggests, humility and self-effacement could certainly explain Catherine's relative and sometimes absolute silence regarding these experiences. Raymond's theologically and politically motivated need to present his readers with a woman "dead" to herself, withdrawn from the world, and thus entirely receptive to God (her own accounts of apostolic activity notwithstanding), figures as another powerful explanatory principle. The Catherine he fashioned was certainly more likely to be canonized. Amy Hollywood's essay comparing Beatrice of Nazareth's spiritual treatise with her hagiographer's "translation" of the treatise suggests a more striking divergence in the two authors' perspectives on the female body. In his *vita*, the hagiographer personalizes Beatrice's impersonal description of the loving soul's insane desire for ecstatic union with divine love by identifying that soul with Beatrice herself. He further transforms Beatrice's account of an interior spiritual experience by supplying an external narrative replete with stories of asceticism, miracles, visions, and otherworldly journeys absent from her mystical treatise. Hollywood points to his focus on the suffering body as the site of female sanctity and argues that Beatrice's own reluctance to speak about bodily asceticism or devotions centered on Christ's suffering indicates her resistance to the kinds of female religiosity commonly prescribed in hagiographical texts.

One final theme setting female self-portrayals apart from portrayals of them by their male admirers regards the prototypes and exempla put forward for women's imitation. Saints are not only presented as models to others for imitation, but also are often themselves described typologically as patterned after figures such as earlier saints, biblical personages, or even God. While the female saints discussed in these essays tend to pattern themselves after male exemplars, their male hagiographers are likely to enhance or sometimes replace these male models with female exemplars. Both Hildegard of Bingen and Elisabeth of Schönau regarded themselves as standing in a long line of God's heroes. Hildegard compared herself with a host of biblical figures, including Joshua, Joseph, Job, Jeremiah, Susanna, Moses, and St. John the Evangelist. Her hagiographer, Theoderic, did not similarly emphasize Hildegard's biblical self-comparisons, and he elaborated them by adding the feminine role models of Leah, Rachel, and Deborah to interpret Hildegard's role. Similarly, Ekbert of Schönau compared his sister Elisabeth to biblical women to convince his readers that even a "weak woman" could be a prophet, although Elisabeth herself failed to cite any biblical women, invoking instead the names of Moses, Jeremiah, and Paul; she even employed patently male-gendered expressions such as "act manfully" to explain her activity. Clare of Assisi consistently spoke of herself and her sisters as followers and imitators of Christ, placing herself squarely in the tradition of her early mentor (and example) Francis of Assisi. Many of her interpreters, however, gratuitously elaborated her account by depicting Clare as an imitator of the Virgin Mary, a motif she never emphasized. In a further attempt to delineate clear boundaries between themselves and their female counterparts, male Franciscans increasingly suggested in their writings and art that Clare, more than Francis, should serve as the sisters' model for imitation. An interesting variation on the theme of women's imitation comes from Henry Suso's autobiographical discussion of his female devotee Elsbeth Stagel. There, Suso presents himself as her model, a representation we are unfortunately unable to check against Stagel's no longer extant notes. Suso concludes his autobiography by presenting Elsbeth, years after his sagacious spiritual guidance of her on the path to sanctity, as herself a model for imitation. Suso, the male saint and mentor, here provides an interesting contrast with the male hagiographers mentioned above who seem bent on binding women to women and increasing their distance from male models.

A final feature of these essays regards not a trait common to them but rather the steady and striking shift traced in depictions of female sanctity from the twelfth through the fourteenth centuries. The earliest women discussed in this volume are high-status Benedictine nuns; the last are humbler laywomen affiliated with groups such as the beguines and *mantellate*, religious associations that still puzzle historians. The suggestive hints of women's mystical and mysterious character appearing in texts about the earliest women have become, by the close of the medieval period, a major *leitmotif* of women's sanctity. The lives of these later women revolve ever more around raptures, visions, and other paramystical phenomena. In contrast to the relatively more stolid, privileged, and stable lifestyles of the earliest women, the later women appear more passionate, socially diverse, and unstable. This "instability" of later medieval women's lives typified multiple aspects of their experience, at least if we can believe the texts: these women frequently changed their states of life, from married to celibate or from one religious order or affiliation to another; they moved between vigorous social involvement and reclusive enclosure; some people would suspect them of heresy even as others venerated them as beacons of orthodoxy. The mental and emotional states of many of these women is represented as erratic, and in their spiritual lives they often swung wildly between excruciating doubt and an overwhelming sense of certitude.[7] As these essays show, the shifting models of female sanctity also had dramatic effects on women's relationships with their male confessors and scribes, the men we can thank (and sometimes blame) for our images of these women. The efforts of these male clerics to control and canalize the danger they sensed in these women—women they both admired and often feared—frequently appear at least as overwrought as the very women they represent.

There are, of course, notable exceptions. In fact, all the themes described above point to common patterns prevalent among hagiographic treatments of female sanctity, but they do not fully explain or establish any of them. For a more nuanced understanding of these themes, the reader will have to turn to the essays themselves. There, the tight focus on the questions of voice, gender, and the diverse portrayals of sanctity begins a discussion we hope will continue. Indeed, it will be only after many additional close studies of individual saints and their interpreters that we will be able to speak with confidence about the many tendencies that distinguish saints' writings from those of their interpreters and, especially germane to this collection, that differentiate female from male portrayals of female sanctity.

2

Hildegard and Her Hagiographers

The Remaking of Female Sainthood

Barbara Newman

ALTHOUGH THE *Vita S. Hildegardis*, a work begun during the seer's life-time (1098–1179) and completed by the mid-1180s, has long been mined for its biographical data, its full importance as hagiography has yet to be recognized.[1] For this extraordinary *vita* is not only the first "autohagiog-raphy" of the Middle Ages,[2] but the first and only *vita* that lets us compare a holy woman's self-portrait directly with male representations of her, set down by not one but two hagiographers for the eyes of the newly vigi-lant saintmakers in Rome. Because of the diverse perspectives of its three authors, beginning with Hildegard herself, it allows us to watch a process of saintmaking unfold before our very eyes. In it we can observe both the development from a holy woman's personal (albeit highly stylized) recol-lections to a formal hagiographic account, and the gradual paradigm shift from an older to a newer model of female sanctity.[3] By the same token, the subtly contrasting representations of Hildegard already apparent in her *Vita* point forward to two divergent strands in her later medieval recep-tion. On the one hand, we see the authorized prophet, the "sibyl of the Rhine,"[4] whose books were said to have been "canonized" by a pope; and on the other, the prototypical "feminine mystic," remembered and praised not so much for her outspoken public message as for her ineffable private raptures.

The tangle of collective authorship in the *Vita* is a splendid instance of cultural creativity evoked by historical flukes. Hildegard's longevity had placed her in the unfortunate position of outliving her most likely biographers. Her lifelong friend and secretary Volmar, who would surely have undertaken the task, died in 1173, six years before the abbess herself.[5] His successor Gottfried, a monk of St. Disibod and provost at the Rupertsberg from 1174 to 1176, took the bold but not unprecedented step of beginning a *vita* while his saint was still alive, no doubt expecting her imminent demise—but it was he who predeceased her. Finally, the Belgian monk Guibert of Gembloux, who in 1175 had written to Hildegard with detailed and starstruck queries about her visions,[6] responded to her urgent plea for secretarial help two years later. Arriving at the Rupertsberg in 1177, he quickly began collecting materials for a *vita* and must have seemed to Hildegard's nuns to have been sent by God for that very purpose. But his work too was destined to remain unfinished. Guibert's truncated *vita* continues only through 1141, ending just as Hildegard's public life begins.[7] The heroic scale of the fragment suggests that if Guibert had finished his work, it would have been one of the most massive of medieval saints' lives on a par with the biographies of Francis of Assisi. It was not that Guibert died young; he achieved an even more impressive longevity than the seer herself. But in 1180 he had to yield to his abbot's urgent demand that he return to Gembloux, taking his own unfinished *vita* with him but leaving his dossier of sources (including Gottfried's work) with the nuns.[8] So Hildegard's friends, thrice foiled in their efforts to secure a biography, cast about once more and lit upon Theoderic, the librarian and chronicler of Echternach.[9] But this monk proved an unlikely choice for the job: he had never met Hildegard, seemed bewildered by her writings, and had so little pertinent knowledge that he could not even say who had buried her or where.[10] Utterly dependent on Guibert's dossier, he cobbled his sources together with enough topoi to produce a respectable *vita*, albeit one of the oddest in the medieval repertoire.

The core of the *Vita* is a first person memoir written or dictated by Hildegard herself, recounting key events in her life from birth through 1170. It was probably in that year that the abbess, then 72 and seriously ill, responded to a letter from Volmar requesting some kind of spiritual testament for her friends. As I have argued elsewhere, Hildegard may have composed this narrative (which does not survive independently of the extant *Vita*) for the express purpose of helping Volmar prepare her biography.[11] But her unexpected recovery and his own subsequent death forestalled that intention. Gottfried, Volmar's successor, seems to have inherited the memoir and reworked it into a standard third person narrative, supplemented by Hildegard's oral memory and various documents available at the Rupertsberg. His account of her life, with an explanatory preface by Theoderic, now survives as Book I of the *Vita*, while her own narrative is incorporated piecemeal into Books II and III. Although these two accounts differ in detail, Gottfried follows Hildegard closely in his choice of incidents to include or omit through 1155, the point where his composition ends.

Theoderic, in turn, appears to have received Gottfried's unfinished *vita* as well as Hildegard's memoir, both preserved in Guibert's dossier, when he was commissioned by her friends to complete her biography. But he had little information to help him where these two sources were silent. His solution to this problem was to retell Gottfried's story in Hildegard's original words, interspersing them with his own rapt commentary to create a sort of narrative palimpsest. Unable to supply any new historical particulars, he filled the remaining gaps in the *Vita* with letters and a few miscellaneous "visions" that bear little relation to the account of Hildegard's life, presumably because he found these texts already intermingled with her memoirs in Guibert's dossier. Theoderic's construction thus reveals a literary procedure strikingly different from Gottfried's. Whereas the older monk had begun a spare, action-packed story of Hildegard's external life, replete with miracles, economic transactions, and legal arrangements concerning the Rupertsberg, Theoderic abandoned this narrative mode and opted for a pattern of visionary texts alternating with hagiographic glosses. Even though his choice seems to have been dictated as much by lack of information as by stylistic or spiritual concerns, his continuation dramatically changed the course of Gottfried's *vita*. Because of his curious compositional technique, the *Vita* as a whole reads more like a miscellany of "Hildegardiana" than a standard saint's life. Yet it would set a precedent for some of the most significant trends in mystical hagiography of the next two centuries, and its pronouncements had an enormous if indirect influence on the seer's posthumous reception.

From Seer to Prophet

Despite the complicated origins of the *Vita S. Hildegardis*, its three authors seem at first to achieve a remarkable unity of tone. Both Gottfried and Theoderic echo Hildegard's self-representation as a humble and embattled figure who, tried physically by illness and spiritually by human and demonic foes, remains prophetically assured and larger than life. On closer reading, however, it is possible to distinguish the three voices and discern behind each of them a different model of sanctity. Hildegard saw herself primarily as a prophet and modeled her self-understanding on biblical heroes, while Gottfried adapted the hagiographic type of the aristocratic abbess and foundress, emphasizing the official "authorization" of Hildegard's visions in order to heighten the prestige of the Rupertsberg.[12] Theoderic, whose redaction gave the *Vita* its final form, folded both these types into the newer model of the feminine bridal mystic, valiant in the active life but supremely gifted in the contemplative—a type that would come to full flower in the *vitae* written by Jacques de Vitry and Thomas of Cantimpré a generation later.[13] To highlight these differences, I will concentrate on one key aspect of Hildegard's portrayal in the *Vita*: the nature of her inspiration and authority, and the consequent meaning of her prophetic speech. Both vision and prophecy would become central to later medieval representations of holy women. But in the *Vita S. Hildegardis*, the stylization of these themes is still fluid; they have not yet attained the rigor of stereotypes.

For Hildegard herself, the unfolding of her visionary gift was *the* story of the first half of her life. This development took place in distinct stages, beginning in early childhood and culminating at the midpoint of her life when the seer became a prophet, the timid recluse a commanding leader. It is easy to forget the deep malaise Hildegard recalls as characterizing her early years, when she had as yet no categories to explain her peculiar visionary bent. It was simply a part of her physical and psychological being: "In my first formation, when God quickened me with the breath of life in my mother's womb, he affixed this vision in my soul. . . . and in my third year I saw a light so great that my soul trembled, but because of my infancy I could say nothing about these things."[14] Far from experiencing these early visions as a vocation, the young girl felt them to be an embarrassment. Her visions marked her as different from other people and made her childish for her age. She does not say that they either relieved or exacerbated her chronic illness, but the two were inseparable insofar as visions and sickness together defined her earliest memories. In her own mind, her experiences of "seeing" and suffering built a spiritual wall around her as thick as the physical wall of her enclosure, so that she felt terrified of other people and ashamed of her condition, not daring to speak of it. If at times she could not keep from predicting the future, she would weep and blush as her vision faded. This state of affairs continued through her early life as a recluse and nun, which she summarizes with the terse comment: "After

[Jutta's] death I continued to see things (*ita permansi videns*) until the fortieth year of my life." [15]

The significance of this "fortieth year" is probably biblical rather than historical: it was for forty years that Moses wandered in the desert before seeing the Promised Land. Strangely, although Hildegard eulogizes her teacher Jutta, she says nothing of her subsequent election as *magistra* or superior. But on a particular day in 1141, when she "was forty-two years and seven months old," her hitherto private and vexing quirk of visions for the first time linked itself with her profession as a nun, and its object became clear to her. What she would "see" henceforth would be the goal of every monastic: the spiritual understanding, or true meaning, of the Scriptures. Her vision thus became an intellectual gift, a sense of illumination leading her first to inspired exegesis and soon also to musical composition. In this moment of transformation, this coming-together of an intensely personal with a deeply communal experience, Hildegard perceived her "prophetic call," the famous "pressure" that drove her in spite of inner and outer resistance to "speak and write," that is, to take on the role of a prophet. Hereafter she would become as boldly extroverted as she had been shyly introverted before. This was the central turning point of her life and she wrote two very similar accounts of it, both quoted in the *Vita*: the first from the *Scivias* preface (1141), the second composed about thirty years later as part of her memoirs.

When I was forty-two years and seven months old, the heavens were opened and a fiery light of great brilliance came and suffused my whole brain and my whole heart and breast like a flame, yet not burning but warming, as when the rays of the sun fall upon some object and warm it. And suddenly I arrived at a spiritual understanding of books (*intellectum expositionis librorum . . . sapiebam*), i.e., the Psalter, the Gospel, and other catholic volumes of the Old and New Testament. But I had no ability to interpret the texts grammatically, to divide the syllables of words or to construe the cases and tenses. [16]

Then in the same vision I was compelled by a great pressure of suffering to reveal openly what I had seen and heard. But I was very fearful and ashamed to tell what I had hidden in silence for so long. . . . In the same vision I came to understand the gospels, the writings of the prophets and other saints, and of certain philosophers without any human instruction, and I expounded some of them even though I had scarcely any literary knowledge, as the woman who had taught me was not educated. I also composed and sang chant with melody in praise of God and the saints without instruction from anyone, although I had never studied either musical notation or singing. [17]

In both accounts Hildegard stresses her ignorance of grammar and music, a point that has been much discussed and often misunderstood. Her disclaimer has nothing at all to do with the breadth of her reading. It indicates, first, that she was an autodidact—a fact abundantly clear from the eccentricities of her style—and second, more important, it stakes her claim to prophetic authority.

But if Hildegard had little "human instruction"—or at any rate, little that she could acknowledge[18]—she was very far from lacking human validation. This slow but vitally necessary process, which could easily have gone astray and led to her silencing, took at least seven years and was undoubtedly fraught with more hesitations than the telescoped accounts in the *Vita* suggest. Hildegard calls to mind only a few moments in the process. She confided her secret first "to a certain monk, my teacher"—obviously Volmar—who understood that the visions "were from God" and collaborated with her "in great desire" to record them. Volmar then "told his abbot," Kuno of St. Disibod, but Hildegard does not record his response. Nor does she mention her impassioned plea for validation to Bernard of Clairvaux circa 1147, or his brief but encouraging reply.[19] Some time later— she does not say when or how—"these things were brought to the attention of the church of Mainz and discussed." From her own perspective, the judgment of the bishop and clergy (perhaps including her brother Hugo)[20] was the crucial one: "they all said that [the visions and writings] were from God and from the prophecy by which the prophets prophesied of old."[21]

Afterward, as she gratefully notes, her work was read by Pope Eugene "when he was in Trier" (1147/48) and he wrote a letter of blessing and approval, bidding her continue her labor of writing.[22] But for Hildegard this was icing on the cake. The support that mattered most was that of her archbishop, Heinrich of Mainz,[23] and her key phrase is "ex prophetia, quam olim prophete prophetaverant." Once she understood herself as a *prophet*, Hildegard arrived at a total revaluation of what had seemed to be the greatest obstacles in her path.[24] Every mark of human inability now became a proof of divine enablement. Most strikingly, the visionary experience that had marked her as eccentric all through her childhood and youth—the sign of her individual selfhood—became the condition that allowed her to transcend individuality altogether, drowning her merely human voice in the peal of a "trumpet sounded by the Living Light."[25]

Gottfried tells essentially the same tale with a different coloring. Instead of development or change, he sees only continuity in Hildegard's inner experience, and there is no hint in his words of any discomfort or uncertainty about her visions. Nor does he present her experience of 1141 as a radical break with her past. Rather, "the time came for her life and teaching to be exposed for the benefit of many," so she received the call to write. Gottfried does not here or at any point invoke the charism of prophecy, so important for Hildegard's self-understanding, and he ascribes her resistance to "feminine modesty" rather than the deeper kind of fear and shame she herself recalls. What matters far more to him is her official validation, which, to be effective and proper, had to pass step by step through the ecclesiastical chain of command. Volmar, whose support was central to Hildegard's narrative, becomes simply the mediator through whom she approaches Abbot Kuno, and it is he who reaches a decision[26]—but not before calling a council of the seniors, as the Benedictine Rule requires; recognizing the hand of God in a miracle; and seeking further counsel from the archbishop. The emphasis falls on careful deliberation and discernment at every stage, since the point is no longer to soothe the visionary's fears but to assure readers that the Church gave its plenary approval to her message. Kuno's part is highlighted, as Monika Klaes suggests, because Gottfried wanted to reflect as much glory as possible on his own abbey; but the starring role belongs to Pope Eugene.

Though Gottfried's account of the events at Trier is well known, its broader historical significance is usually overlooked. As Herbert Grundmann has argued, Eugene's commendation of the *Scivias* seems to be the first case on record of a pope's formal approbation of a potentially controversial theological work—a practice that would become increasingly common in the thirteenth century.[27] According to Gottfried, Heinrich of Mainz brought Hildegard's case to the pope's attention while he was staying in nearby Trier (Nov. 1147–Feb. 1148) after the Council of Rheims. (The monk was in error here: Eugene's sojourn in Trier actually preceded the Council of Rheims [21 Mar.–7 Apr. 1148], at which Bernard would play a major role in the condemnation of Gilbert of Poitiers.)[28] Being a discreet man, Eugene sent a delegation to the Disibodenberg to investigate the matter. The legates spoke with Hildegard and returned to Trier with a manuscript of her still unfinished *Scivias*, from which the pope personally read in the presence of the assembled cardinals. The reading "stirred the minds and voices of all to rejoicing and praise of the Creator." Gottfried further asserts that Bernard of Clairvaux was present and intervened on Hildegard's behalf, admonishing the pope (a Cistercian and his protégé) not to let so brilliant a light remain hidden beneath a bushel. Accepting this advice, Eugene wrote to Hildegard and gave her "license" (rather

than a "command" as she herself said) to continue writing, and he likewise honored the monks of St. Disibod with a letter of congratulation.[29]
Bernard was indeed with the papal court in Trier and already knew about
Hildegard's visions from the letter she had sent him, probably in January
1147, while he was preaching the Second Crusade in the Rhineland and
working miracles in the sight of adoring crowds.[30] His involvement in the
Scivias affair seems plausible enough, given this recent correspondence, his
close relationship with Eugene, and his well-known interest in securing
official pronouncements on controversial books.

The influence of Gottfried's account was profound and lasting, albeit
indirect. Among the handful of monasteries that commemorated Hildegard's feast day was the Cistercian house of Eberbach.[31] A monk of that
abbey, Gebeno, in 1220 visited the Rupertsberg, studied Hildegard's *Vita*
and writings, and anthologized her prophecies in a book he called the
Speculum futurorum temporum (*Mirror of Future Times*) or *Pentachronon*.
This work was read so avidly that it survives in hundreds of manuscripts,
far surpassing either the *Vita* or Hildegard's own books in popularity. Gebeno's aims in compiling these prophecies were reformist and antiheretical,
but to inspire confidence in them, he had to prove the seer's credibility beyond the shadow of a doubt. Gottfried's account gave him exactly what he
needed. "It should be known, moreover," Gebeno writes, "that St. Hildegard's books were received and canonized by Pope Eugene at the Council
of Trier in the presence of many French and German bishops and of St.
Bernard, abbot of Clairvaux."[32] This brief, authoritative notice goes beyond Gottfried in its audacious wording—*canonizati sunt*. Conveniently
fudged is the fact that when Eugene saw the *Scivias* in 1148, Hildegard had
not yet written its final section, which contains the apocalyptic prophecies
so dear to Gebeno—much less the later prophecies in her *Liber divinorum
operum* (*Book of Divine Works*) and certain letters.

Bolder still is a remark in the *vita* of St. Gerlac, a hermit (d. ca. 1165)
whom Hildegard had once honored with a gift. Gerlac's biographer, writing around 1225, knew Gebeno's work and perhaps also the *Vita S. Hildegardis*: he says of the seer that "although she was not trained in any literature except the Psalms of David, she produced great volumes, instructed
by the Holy Spirit, concerning the divine oracles and mysteries that were
revealed to her. These were canonized by Pope Eugene at the mediation of
St. Bernard, abbot of Clairvaux, and numbered among the sacred writings
(*inter sacras scripturas*)."[33] *Canonizata*, a strong word to be sure, may have
been introduced by analogy with the newly formalized process for the ele-

vation of saints. This claim, based on the prominence accorded to Pope
Eugene's approval in the *Vita*, was to become a standard report on Hildegard throughout the Middle Ages: if she herself was not "canonized," her
books were. The statement is repeated by Albert von Stade (d. after 1264)
and William of St.-Amour.[34] By 1270, when the English Franciscan John
Peckham wanted to undermine Hildegard's authority because her predic-
tions were being cited against the friars, he had to confront the widespread
belief that St. Bernard had collected her prophecies and Pope Eugene had
confirmed them—an authorization so strong that he could counter it only
by resorting to flat denial and misogyny. The report "is plainly a lie," he
fumes, "for the apostolic see is not wont to confirm doubtful matters—
especially as this woman is known to have handed down many errors in her
other reckless scribblings. So until anything persuades me to the contrary,
I believe that Hildegard's prophecy proceeded from the devil's cunning."[35]

From Prophet to "Mystic"

Hildegard, who modeled her literary persona on the prophets,[36] often
compared herself with biblical heroes in typical hagiographic style. Like
Joshua and the patriarch Joseph, she was attacked by envious foes; like
Job and Jeremiah, she was afflicted with painful illness. Like Susanna she
was falsely accused; like Jonah she was punished by God when she tried
to resist his command.[37] In one passage she cites a long litany of biblical figures from Abel to Zacchaeus to illustrate the eternal war of flesh
and spirit, and concludes by aligning herself squarely with the spirit.[38] But
her most revealing self-comparisons revolve around Moses and St. John
the Evangelist, the greatest prophets of the Old and New Testaments respectively. Twice she compares her migration from St. Disibod with the
Exodus, likening her detractors to those rebellious Israelites who "mur-
mured against" Moses: "In the same way God allowed me to be afflicted
by the common people, my relatives, and some who were staying with
me . . . for just as the children of Israel afflicted Moses, they too shook
their heads over me and said, 'What use is it for noble and rich girls to
move from a place where they lacked nothing into such penury?'"[39] Later
on, describing the conversion of a "wealthy philosopher" from opponent
to supporter of the Rupertsberg, Hildegard writes that the foe became
a friend "once God had choked off the injustice in his heart—just as he
drowned Pharaoh in the Red Sea."[40] Hildegard's perspective is not un-

usual for a hagiographic heroine—or any twelfth-century monastic. Life is a spiritual combat in which the righteous, imitating the saints of old, face constant assault from demons and the human agents of their will.

Of all Hildegard's biblical self-comparisons, only one can be construed as "mystical" in the sense characteristic of later medieval saints. In her letter to Guibert of Gembloux (1175), the seer famously insisted on the non-ecstatic character of her visions, claiming that they did not interfere in any way with her ordinary sense perception.[41] But on one unique occasion, she did experience ecstasy:

Just after this time I saw a mystical and marvelous vision, so that my whole frame was shaken and the sensation of my body was extinguished, for my knowledge had been transformed into another mode as if I no longer knew myself. And from the inspiration of God, drops as of gentle rain splashed into the knowledge of my soul—just as the Holy Spirit inspired John the Evangelist when he sucked the most profound revelation from the breast of Jesus, when his mind was so touched by the holy divinity that he could reveal the hidden mysteries and works: *In the beginning was the Word*, etc.[42]

Hildegard goes on to say that this revelation would become the starting point for her new book, the *Liber divinorum operum*, which has at its heart an exegesis of the Johannine prologue. Here too, the *Vita* is concerned with authorization: the abbess is entitled to expound this most sacred text because she draws inspiration from the same source as the evangelist himself.

Struck by this passage, Theoderic quotes it in his prologue to Book II, where he also alludes to Moses—not the harried leader with whose trials Hildegard identified, but the initiate into celestial mysteries, who like her "dwelt in the heavenly tabernacle and transcended every cloud of carnality."[43] For this hagiographer, the decisive category for understanding Hildegard was not biblical prophecy but bridal mysticism. Although he does laud her as a prophet, he is less concerned with her ability to speak *for* God than her privileged relationship *with* God, which is significantly gendered. Thus, no matter how impressive the comparisons with Moses and St. John, Theoderic also felt the need to mine Scripture for feminine role models. I have shown elsewhere that Hildegard was not very interested in that form of validation: when she needed female models she preferred divine or allegorical ones (Lady Wisdom, Mother Church, the Virtues) rather than human figures.[44] In her memoirs, when she wanted to stress her filial love for her favorite nun, Richardis, she alluded to the love of

Paul and Timothy, not (for example) Naomi and Ruth or Elizabeth and Mary.[45] Theoderic, on the other hand, likens his saint to Leah and Rachel, standard types of the active and contemplative lives, and more elaborately to the prophetess Deborah, who he says (quoting Origen) "offers no small comfort to the female sex."[46] But most of all, he finds the Song of Songs convenient and casts Hildegard in the bridal role, although she herself— despite her admiration for Bernard—was not especially drawn to that book or the nuptial mysticism it inspired. Theoderic, however, was convinced that the king had led her into his wine cellar to drink of the torrent of his pleasure, and surely she had cried out to her bridegroom, "Draw me after you, we will run in the fragrance of your ointments."[47] Somewhere between Gottfried's hagiographic generation and Theoderic's, the tide in female sanctity had definitively turned.

The most glaring contrast between Theoderic's piety and Hildegard's appears in his sole effort to explicate one of her writings. Near the beginning of Book II, he cites a long text which he titles "Prima Visio," though it consists of two apparently unrelated passages, neither of them a "vision" in the strict sense. The first deals with the "five tones of righteousness," a musical metaphor for the epochs of salvation history; the second is Hildegard's record of her life from birth up to Pope Eugene's letter. Theoderic introduces the passage by announcing how well it illustrates Cant. 5: 4: "My beloved put his hand through the opening, and my womb trembled at his touch." As Klaes has shown, this verse—the most sexually explicit in the Song of Songs—was applied by Rupert of Deutz to one of his own mystical experiences, which were of a markedly erotic character; elsewhere the verse was rarely used in such a sense.[48] Theoderic no doubt understood Rupert better than he understood Hildegard: how else to explain this tour de force of interpretation?

So from this beautiful vision of the blessed virgin, and from her account of the fear she felt at the approach of the Holy Spirit, and of the pope's blessing and the permission to write that she received from him, we clearly gather that her *beloved* heavenly bridegroom, Jesus Christ, truly *put his hand*, i.e., the activity and inspiration of the Holy Spirit, *through the opening*, i.e., through his secret grace, and her *womb*, i.e., her mind, *trembled at his touch*, i.e., at the infusion of his grace, from the extraordinary vigor of the Spirit and the weight that she felt within. What could be more suitable, more fitting?[49]

Such a procrustean reading shows that Theoderic was more concerned to represent Hildegard as a certain *kind* of saint, a "bridal mystic," than he was with the content of her message. In fact, he seemed to delight in representing her words as unfathomable, even when the texts themselves are straightforward. Hildegard's discourse on the conflict of flesh and spirit, for example, presents no great difficulties of interpretation. In a familiar exegetical fashion she contrasts Cain with Abel, Jacob with Esau, the penitent Zacchaeus with the rich youth who went away sorrowful. Had Theoderic read such a passage in any other exegete, his intellectual powers would not have been overtaxed. But Hildegard was not "any other exegete": by definition, anything she had written *had* to be deep, mysterious, and obscure. Thus he comments on this passage as if it were filled with the thorniest philosophical conundrums, recalling Augustine's counsel to the novice Bible reader in *De doctrina christiana* (*On Christian Education*): "It would no doubt be of great value to probe the obscurity of such a subtle discourse. . . . For it would exercise our mind so that it might be broadened by effort, and what the lazy mind could not grasp, the practiced mind would. But now we must hasten on to other matters."[50] Theoderic was employing the topos of the "fastidious reader," pretending to abridge his material in order to spare the audience: not all would be capable of such arduous mental exercise. In a similar vein the hagiographer thanks God at the end of Book II that he has safely "navigated so vast a sea of visions."[51] Klaes rightly discerns a certain "half-heartedness and reserve" in such comments, ascribing them to Theoderic's lack of acquaintance with Hildegard,[52] and we may also suspect some impatience with his role as a literary hack.

But there is more at stake in the rumor of Hildegard's obscurity. A prophet is not without honor unless she is understood. As long as the abbess could be seen as grandiloquent, vague, and beyond the grasp of common readers, her authority was unimpeachable; but at the same time she was in no danger of being taken too seriously as a writer. An authorized prophet walked a fine line, for the same credentials that gave her an audience set her at such a distance from them that her books became more daunting than inviting. In other words, just as Hildegard received an infusion of the Holy Spirit to interpret John, potential readers required the same grace to interpret *her*, and those who lacked it might do best to admire from afar. So, if Gottfried's enduring legacy was the account of her "canonization" as a prophet, Theoderic's was her reputation for opacity. Gebeno of Eberbach acknowledged this in the prologue to his *Pentachronon*: "Many people dislike and shrink from reading St. Hildegard's books because she speaks obscurely and in an unusual style, not understanding that this is a proof of true prophecy. For all the prophets have a habit of speaking obscurely. . . . The fact that she speaks in an unusual style is like-

wise a proof of the true finger of God, the Holy Spirit."[53] Kathryn Kerby-
Fulton notes that this remark was copied, highlighted, and annotated
more than any other in insular manuscripts of Hildegard.[54] Trithemius
of Sponheim, the fifteenth-century abbot and occultist who revived her
reputation, liked to remark that "in all her writings the Blessed Hildegard
proceeds very mystically and obscurely" so that only the "religious and devout" can understand them.[55]

It might of course be objected that Hildegard really *is* obscure—and
has not grown any easier with the passing centuries. Anyone who has tried
to read her theological trilogy from cover to cover must plead "no contest"
to that charge. Yet when Theoderic implies that his failure to understand
Hildegard is a compliment to her, and Gebeno apologizes for her obscurity even as he culls a selection for "fastidious readers," they are launching
a new hagiographic topos, one that led a whole series of male biographers
to profess themselves mystified by the arcane wisdom of holy women.
I will cite only two examples of this hiatus between women's spiritual
teaching and its more cautious clerical interpreters. Beatrice of Nazareth's
thirteenth-century hagiographer ends his work, which he has presented
from the outset as a "translation" of her own vernacular diary, by admit-
ting that he has in fact censored much of her material.[56] Like Theoderic,
he says he wanted to spare readers who might be confused by the "excessive depth" and "very subtle reasoning" (*subtilissima ratio*) of his author:

Do not let my long-drawn-out narrative account beget weariness in you, since . . .
in many places I have omitted no small part of those things which might have
evaded the reader's understanding by their excessive depth (*nimia profunditate*).
Even if they were intelligible to the more perfect, they would have been more
tedious than edifying, would have done more harm than good to those with minds
less practiced in these matters. . . . I have touched briefly on the very extensive and
interminable material so that in a few words I have given to the wise—for whom
it suffices to have touched a few points—the occasion of investigating the greater
mysteries of charity, and I have satisfied the fastidious with a kindly short compen-
dium.[57]

Consideration for the average reader is doubtless a virtue, as trade
publishers are quick to remind academic authors. Yet when a hagiographer
worries that a book so edifying as Beatrice's discourse on charity might do
readers "more harm than good," there is reason to think he was not merely
concerned about ennui. The real danger was heresy. Beatrice's monastery
of Nazareth lay in the diocese of Cambrai, where the notorious inquisitor
Robert le Bougre had established his headquarters, and during her lifetime

he put a beguine to death "on account of her true love," as Hadewijch of Brabant wrote in her *List of the Perfect*.[58] In 1273, just as the *Vita Beatricis* was being written, Gilbert of Tournai complained to the pope in his *Collectio de scandalis ecclesiae* (*On the Scandals of the Church*) about beguines who "blossom forth in subtleties and rejoice in novelties," daring to interpret Scripture for themselves in the vernacular.[59] In such a climate, Beatrice's abbess and her biographer must have decided how her reputation could best be served. First, a sanitized *vita* must be composed in Latin, with all the "excessive" and "tedious" theology excised and the "subtle reasoning" dumbed down to the level of simple God-fearing clerics. That done, her original journal must be well hidden or destroyed lest it fall into their "fastidious" hands.[60]

A similar move can be seen slightly later in the book of Angela of Foligno. The "brother scribe" who took Angela's Italian dictation and translated her autohagiography into Latin was remarkably frank about his deficiencies as a writer. He acknowledges that he often failed to grasp Angela's meaning; omitted parts of her account that were of less interest to him; and inconsistently recorded her first-person narrative, sometimes using the third person and sometimes her own voice. Most candidly, he admits that Angela herself often rejected his transcript as obscure and distorted:

In truth, I wrote [her words], but I had so little grasp of their meaning that I thought of myself as a sieve or sifter which does not retain the precious and refined flour but only the most coarse. . . . And this will give an idea of how very rough was my understanding of the divine words I was hearing from her: One day after I had written as best I could what I had been able to grasp of her discourse, I read to her what I had written in order to have her dictate more to me, and she told me with amazement that she did not recognize it. On another occasion when I was re-reading to her what I had written . . . , she answered that my words were dry and without any savor, and this also amazed her. And another time she remarked to me: "Your words recall to me what I told you, but they are very obscure. The words you read to me do not convey the meaning I intended. . . ." And another time she said: "You have written what is bland, inferior, and amounts to nothing."[61]

In her important study of Angela's *Memorial*, Catherine Mooney shows how deeply the scribe's questions, omissions, and emphases shaped their jointly authored text. He did not hesitate, for example, to include a revelation that Angela had expressly told him to "destroy" because it had been so "incompetently and badly written."[62] It is significant that the scribe made no attempt to conceal his incomprehension or even Angela's deep dissatisfaction with his work. For, like Theoderic, he could present his own intellectual failings as a proof of his subject's sublimity. As Mooney observes, clerics like Theoderic, Beatrice's hagiographer, and Angela's "Brother A." took "delight in contrasting unlearned women's ineffable visionary knowledge with mere human knowledge."[63] Such scribes and biographers did not necessarily share a set of common interests over against those of their female subjects. The author of the *Vita Beatricis*, for example, downplayed speculation on the Trinity (which could have attracted unwelcome clerical attention) while emphasizing Beatrice's illness and asceticism, favorite themes of Netherlandish hagiography. The more speculative "Brother A.," in contrast, notes that he omitted much of what Angela said about Christ's passion and her own sufferings, while questioning her eagerly about the Trinity. But both writers share with Theoderic an emphasis on the difficulty and obscurity of the women's discourse, seen as a sign of their intimacy with God and hence their authority. Taken together, these examples of the gulf between autohagiography and its clerical mediation suggest that, in the many cases where a *vita* is our only source for a woman's piety, more than a measure of skepticism is due.

The Historical Destiny of the *Vita*

The *Vita S. Hildegardis* not only records an extraordinary life; it is an extraordinary text, composed at a pivotal moment in hagiographic history. But it is worth asking, in conclusion, whether the historical influence of this *vita* warrants the significance I have claimed for it.

Commissioning the *Vita* was only one of many steps taken by Hildegard's daughters, friends, and patrons to secure her canonization.[64] Related actions included Volmar's redaction of her correspondence as an official *Liber epistolarum* (*Book of Letters*); production of the deluxe illuminated *Scivias* and *Liber divinorum operum* manuscripts, as well as the massive *Riesenkodex* or "giant book" containing her collected works; composition of a hymn, liturgical lessons, and eventually a rhymed office for her feast day;[65] encouragement of pilgrimage to her shrine, where the nuns maintained a record of miracles;[66] preparation of an altar cloth depicting the abbess as a saint with nimbus;[67] and of course the requisite petition to Rome. Clearly no effort or expense was spared. Pope Gregory IX, who initiated the canonization proceedings in 1227, was personally well disposed to the cause, proclaiming that he looked forward to "exalting upon earth her whom the Lord had honored in heaven, i.e., canonizing her and inscribing her name in the catalogue of saints."[68] Indeed, as I have argued, the more radical step had already been taken by Eugene III in 1147/48. Canonizing an aristocratic abbess would not have been unusual, whereas authorizing a female visionary to write was unheard of.

Nevertheless, the canonization failed, despite the encouragement of both Gregory IX and his successor, Innocent IV. It may seem tempting to posit a political motive for the aborted process, especially in view of Hildegard's sensational preaching, her intervention in the papal schism, and the role her prophecies would play in the later antimendicant controversy.[69] Yet this thesis loses its plausibility if we look beyond the particulars of Hildegard's case to the broader politics of canonization in the later Middle Ages. As André Vauchez has shown in his comprehensive study of causes between 1198 and 1431, papal canonization was a comparatively rare event. Of 72 processes conducted during that period, only 36 or 50 percent were successful; and of 46 processes in the thirteenth century, only 23 (again 50 percent) resulted in papal canonization.[70] If we examine causes on behalf of women or of monastics, the figures are still less favorable. Of 26 religious proposed for canonization between 1200 and 1400, only 12 or 46 percent were successful, and only one of these (Clare of Assisi) was female. Similarly, of thirteen women whose causes were examined between 1198 and 1461, only six or again 46 percent (five of them laywomen) were canonized.[71] Not a single Benedictine nun was raised to the altar during this period of more than two and a half centuries. In fact, Hildegard was the only one whose cause was even reviewed by the papacy. It appears in retrospect that, far from jeopardizing her canonization, the visionary-prophetic spirituality highlighted by the *Vita* was responsible for its near-success.

If we seek a specific explanation for the failure, it appears that Hildegard was not canonized because a committee of ecclesiastical bureaucrats turned in sloppy paperwork, and the committee appointed to replace them never finished its job. The newly formalized curia took its task of overseeing causes seriously. Even the petition for Bernard's canonization, which had never stood in doubt, was initially rejected by Alexander III and passed muster only after his *vita* had been revised by its principal author.[72] In Hildegard's case the sticking point was the authentication of miracles: Gregory IX rejected the commissioners' report because of insufficient detail in recording dates, places, and names of the witnesses and beneficiaries.[73] By 1233, when the papal inquisitors conducted their hearings, most of the original witnesses were dead and the saint's posthumous cures had ceased. To explain this embarrassment, the nuns borrowed a leaf from

Bernard's book. According to the *Exordium Magnum Cisterciense* (*Foundation of the Cistercian Order*), the abbot who succeeded Bernard at Clairvaux ordered the saint under holy obedience to stop working miracles because the crowds would disturb the brothers' peace. Hildegard's nuns said they had asked the archbishop of Mainz for a similar injunction because their prayers had been troubled by the steady influx of pilgrims.[74] But Rome was not impressed.

Not only did the *Vita S. Hildegardis* fail in its immediate political objective, it also circulated less widely than its authors might have hoped. Klaes records only eight complete manuscripts, ranging in date from the 1180s to circa 1490, along with two abridgments and three lost manuscripts.[75] By comparison, Jacques de Vitry's life of Marie of Oignies survives in twenty-six Latin manuscripts plus a French and an English version; Thomas of Cantimpré's life of Christina the Astonishing is extant in twelve Latin, one English, and three Dutch exemplars—even though neither Marie's nor Christina's cause was ever heard in Rome. Their *vitae* did not travel in the same circles as Hildegard's, with the exception of a single late-medieval legendary.[76] Despite its limited diffusion, however, the *Vita S. Hildegardis* enjoyed considerable influence through two indirect channels.

Guibert of Gembloux, who learned of Theoderic's completed *Vita* and retouched it toward the end of his long life, maintained close relations with the monks of Villers, a house where Hildegard was held in deep reverence. Three of its monks considered themselves her spiritual sons, and after 1176, her *Liber vite meritorum* (*Book of Life's Merits*) and *Liber divinorum operum* were both being read at the abbey. Hildegard had also made the monks a gift of her *Symphonia*, which may have been used liturgically at Villers, and after her death the brothers composed a festal hymn for her. It would be surprising, then, if they had not possessed a copy of her *Vita*, probably in Guibert's recension, which today survives in two manuscripts from Gembloux. In the thirteenth century Villers became a center for both hagiography and the pastoral care of nuns, supervising at various times the Cistercian nunneries of La Cambre, Aywières, Salzinnes, La Ramée, and Florival among others. While the links binding Hildegard to Villers and the thirteenth-century religious women have often been noted,[77] it is possible that not only her memory and liturgical cult, but also her *Vita* influenced the new wave of mystical hagiography from the Low Countries. In this respect it is interesting that an abridgment of the *Vita S. Hildegardis*, composed by Guibert or someone close to him in the early thirteenth century,[78] reveals a marked preference for Hildegard's autohagiography over the efforts of Gottfried and Theoderic. In a terse introduction, the redactor casts their work aside with the claim that "no one else's pen has recorded, or rather commended, her life more reliably than she has written of herself."[79] The abridgment consists almost solely of first person passages, with an appendix on miracles, and encourages readers to seek out still more of Hildegard's "visionary words," said to be well known in the vicinity of Mainz. This reverence for the holy woman's *ipsissima verba* testifies to the same insistence on authenticity that would characterize the scribes and biographers of Gertrude the Great, Mechthild of Hackeborn, Angela of Foligno, and Beatrice of Nazareth.

Far better known than the *Vita* was Gebeno's *Pentachronon*, addressed to a mixed audience with more broadly historical and political concerns. Gebeno, as we have seen, sharpened and gave lasting credibility to Gottfried's claim that Hildegard's works had received papal authorization at Trier, as well as underlining Theoderic's insistence on their obscurity.[80] The *Pentachronon* served mainly to perpetuate her fame as a prophet and kept an important, if thematically limited, selection of her writings in wide circulation. But near the end of his anthology, the monk of Eberbach outdid the *Vita* itself by inscribing the abbess in a roster of the greatest twelfth-century saints, among them Bernard, Aelred of Rievaulx, Hugh and Richard of St. Victor, Thomas Becket, and Joachim of Fiore.[81]

In the divergent aims and audiences of Guibert and Gebeno, we see the beginning of two contrasting trajectories for the late-medieval reception of Hildegard. Guibert's sphere of pastoral influence extended, through Villers, to the Cistercian nunneries and Netherlandish beguinages of the thirteenth century. In this milieu Hildegard became the Mother of Mystics—the formidable "first woman" in a long series of female visionaries whose lives mirrored hers in significant respects. Hadewijch, for example, knew of the Rhenish seer and cited her in her *List of the Perfect* as "Hildegard, who saw all the visions."[82] The *vitae* of these Netherlandish mystics, like Hildegard's, stressed revelations, patient suffering of illness, prophetic gifts, and heroic struggle with demons. Yet their subjects lived out the pattern on a reduced scale, as it were: few were writers, none were preachers, and most achieved only local fame and fell short of canonization. Unlike Hildegard's, their lives remained largely circumscribed by a religious version of the "private sphere" to which women of all stations were increasingly confined. If their words come down to us at all, refracted through hagiographic lenses, it is chiefly of their own souls and inner experience that they speak. Gebeno, on the other hand, kept the public

Hildegard alive. Eschewing female comparisons, he ranked her beside the great canonical authors and ecclesiastical statesmen of her time, all necessarily male. In the texts he chose to anthologize, she spoke not of herself but of the great public issues—clerical reform, heresy, the future of the Church, the coming Antichrist—that fired the passions of the age. It was chiefly through Gebeno that Hildegard had a readership at all in the late Middle Ages, and because of Gebeno's polemical interests, that readership was primarily male.[83]

Radically different as these two Hildegards are, both are firmly grounded in the *Vita*, a hagiographic crossroads where older and newer paradigms meet and part. Not until the fourteenth century, with the towering figures of Catherine of Siena and Birgitta of Sweden, would the realms of mystical piety, authorship, and high-profile political action again be united in a woman. And not until the twentieth would the many Hildegards—public and private, historical and legendary—be reunited in a composite image of this still-uncanonized, neo-canonical saint.

3

Holy Woman or
Unworthy Vessel?

The Representations of Elisabeth
of Schönau

Anne L. Clark

IN 1152, in a rather obscure Benedictine community of women and men in the Rhineland, a twenty-three-year-old nun declared that she saw visions. Almost immediately, word spread of this claim. Hildelin, abbot of the monastery, undertook a public preaching tour in 1154–55 to announce some of the apocalyptic warnings she revealed.[1] A monk from the diocese of Metz heard of her revelations and came to Schönau to investigate for himself.[2] Within a decade, the controversial nature of some of her revelations was commented on by a theologian in Paris.[3] Within twenty-five years, there is evidence for the popularity of her visions in Cistercian monastic circles in France.[4] Within a century, a chronicler could testify to the many monastic libraries that owned copies of her works.[5] By the end of the Middle Ages, her visions had been translated into Provençal, German, and Icelandic. At least 145 medieval manuscripts are known to have transmitted her works, and her visions enjoyed their first printing in 1513.[6]

Although the earliest interest in Elisabeth of Schönau (d. 1164/65) seems to have been stimulated by oral dissemination of her visions, her more substantial reputation was based on the codification and dissemination of her visions in literary texts. This codification of Elisabeth's visions resulted in the creation of several different kinds of texts. The earliest records of her visions were gathered into a brief, chronologically ordered text called *Liber eiusdem de temptationibus inimici, quas primo sustinit et de revelationibus divinis quas post modum vidit* (*Book of the Enemy's Temptations which she first endured and the Divine Revelations which she then saw*). This text describes Elisabeth's experiences from May 18 until August 29, 1152. It was later expanded to include records describing events until August 15, 1154. This text is retrospectively known as the first book of visions or first visionary diary. A second visionary diary circulated in an original form chronicling events from May 14 until August 11, 1155, and in an expanded form with records of events apparently later but without sufficient internal evidence to date them. A third book was created by collecting miscellaneous records of visionary experience, usually not dated, as well as several letters. Three thematic texts were also produced. *Liber Viarum Dei*, a series of sermons about the various paths to heavenly reward, records visions received from June 3, 1156 until August 22, 1157. A very brief text about the bodily assumption of the Virgin Mary, *Visio de resurrectione beate virginis Marie*, includes visions from August 22, 1156 until August 15, 1159. In *Revelatio de sacro exercitu virginum Coloniensium*, visions from the autumn and early winter of 1156 about St. Ursula and the Eleven Thousand Virgins are recorded. Elisabeth's visionary utterances are also transmitted in twenty-two extant letters. Yet Elisabeth was not "the author" of these texts. Rather, the visionary texts were the product of a relationship between herself and her brother Ekbert.

At the time in which Elisabeth began to assert her visionary claims, Ekbert was a cleric at Saint Cassius in Bonn. Unlike his sister Elisabeth, who from about the age of twelve had spent her life within the walls of monastic enclosure, Ekbert had traveled to France to study philosophy in Paris, making important political connections there as well, and had returned to Germany with expectations of ecclesiastical advancement. But his career path took a different route. His frequent trips to Schönau to visit Elisabeth culminated in his decision to convert to the monastic life. Three years after the onset of Elisabeth's visionary experiences, Ekbert made his profession and joined the men's community at Schönau.[7]

Ekbert's decision to move to Schönau not only marked a decisive turn in his own life but also had profound implications for Elisabeth's career. Before this point, Elisabeth had begun to confide her visions to her fellow nuns, who wrote them down.[8] She also told them to Ekbert when he visited her, and he too began to make written records, although originally they agreed not to publish them during Elisabeth's lifetime.[9] Despite their decision, the visions were being disseminated in other, less discreet ways: Abbot Hildelin preached her most apocalyptic visions in a series of public sermons in the region and some of the brothers of Schönau sent letters to unnamed parties in Cologne announcing aspects of her revelations. These forms of publication provoked mixed reactions; skepticism as well as sincere belief was generated by the news of her visions.[10] Ekbert's move to Schönau may have been at least partially precipitated by his desire to manage the publication of Elisabeth's visions more effectively.

Ekbert's "management" of the publication of Elisabeth's visions was a task sanctioned by their monastic environment: Abbot Hildelin ordered Elisabeth to reveal her visions to Ekbert so that he could record them for posterity.[11] Thus Elisabeth's position as a monastic, her much less extensive education than that of Ekbert, and the general expectation of women's intellectual and religious subjection to male authority structured her relationship to her brother.[12] She portrays herself as relieved to have his cooperation,[13] yet she also describes herself as not fully complying with the terms of their relationship, as when, for example, she describes herself as withholding some of her visions.[14]

Ekbert describes his own activities as transcribing some of Elisabeth's utterances and translating into Latin any divine revelations that Elisabeth received in German.[15] His incomplete recording of her visions he attributes to practical reasons (the expense of parchment and the requirements of his other obligations) and to his weariness at the criticism Elisabeth's visions sometimes elicited.[16] Ekbert's biographer gives a more pointed picture of his selective recording: "Diligently investigating all the marvels which our Lord worked with her, he put into writing those things that he saw to be appropriate for the use of the faithful, but those things that he knew would not profit the readers, he totally concealed."[17] Ekbert's suppression of potentially controversial material can be seen in comparing the various redactions of the visionary collection that he produced in his continuing preoccupation with enlarging and refining the collection. Yet even here, there is no evidence of a wholesale suppression of Elisabeth's visions, although it is impossible to know how much material may never have been included in any redaction.[18]

More striking is his biographer's reference to his other role, his diligent investigation of the marvels surrounding his sister. But not only did Ekbert inquire about what Elisabeth learned, he asked questions to prompt her learning. He instructed her to carry questions of interest to him into her ecstatic trances and there seek information that was otherwise out of his reach. This activity can be seen particularly in the visionary texts that record events that transpired after his permanent move to Schönau: some of these texts, most notably the visions about the bodily assumption of the

Virgin Mary and the revelations about St. Ursula and the Eleven Thousand
Virgins of Cologne, were produced in response to questions Elisabeth was
directed to explore through her visionary experience.

But Elisabeth was not simply a passive respondent to Ekbert's interventions as investigator. Some of his directions she resisted by announcing
that no visions would be forthcoming about his queries. Other directions,
those more in alignment with her own religious interests, she dedicated
herself to pursuing, but sometimes with results that Ekbert probably did
not expect. For example, Elisabeth announced an unprecedented revision
of the church calendar to celebrate what she believed to be the correct
anniversary of the Assumption of the Virgin Mary.[19] Interestingly, even
though Ekbert's biographer praised him for suppressing unedifying material, Ekbert did in fact allow controversial visions to remain in the texts.
When Elisabeth saw a vision of a woman in the heavens and identified
the figure as a symbol of the humanity of Christ, Ekbert "investigated" by
interrogating the purpose of such an unusually gendered expression. Elisabeth responded that the humanity of Christ was symbolized by a female
figure so that the symbol could also refer to the Virgin Mary.[20]

This incident reflects many aspects of the relationship between Elisabeth and Ekbert: Ekbert's authority to question Elisabeth about the meaning of her visions; his sensitivity to maintaining conventional gender
boundaries; Elisabeth's acknowledgment of his authority by fully engaging his question, yet her response that in no way rejects her earlier statement; her visionary utterance in which conventional gender boundaries
are blurred; her further elaboration of her visionary utterance in response
to his misunderstanding; Ekbert's recording of his own intervention and
of material that diverged from his own expectations. In the end, Ekbert
controlled the textualization of this incident as well as that of all Elisabeth's utterances. But, as many of the visionary records attest, Ekbert was
involved in producing these records because he believed in Elisabeth's
visionary experience, and he believed in its reality in such a way that he did
not see his own interventions as in any way compromising it. It was his
questions and his commitment to enshrining her utterances for posterity
that became for Elisabeth the arena in which she could further elaborate
the message of her visionary experience. And his questions became part
of the story she told about herself, part of the story that enabled her to
have the freedom to express and the means to communicate her religious
vision to a broader audience than the members of her immediate community, who could listen to her oral accounts.[21] But it was Ekbert finally who

determined the shape of the texts that would be published: none of them were published until after his permanent move to Schönau, he incorporated the records made by the other Schönau nuns according to his own discretion, he suppressed what he felt necessary, he continued to publish new material even after Elisabeth's death, and he wrote introductions to some of the texts that directed readers' attention to what he considered significant about her visions.[22]

This sketch of the relationship between Elisabeth and Ekbert and their collaboration in producing the visionary texts leaves a central question as yet unanswered. Is it possible to distinguish Elisabeth's self-presentation from the images of her created by Ekbert and compare the two? This question takes us squarely into the dynamics of their relationship, for the conceptualization of Elisabeth's identity was clearly an issue that sister and brother developed in conversation with and observation of each other. Elisabeth's shift from understanding her visions as primarily relevant to her own inner life, to understanding herself as a medium of divine revelation for the entire Church, is explicitly grounded in discussion with others. Ekbert came to change his mind about the need to publish her visions during her lifetime in response to Elisabeth's new claims about divine mandates to shout to the world a message of repentance. A mutually reinforcing dynamic can be seen here: her sense of her experience as having more universal and compelling significance was supported by conversation with others; her sense of its heightened significance encouraged Ekbert's involvement in creating the visionary texts; his involvement made her more confident about publishing the visions; her confidence in publishing the visions enabled her greater ease in articulating their significance.

Although these dynamics are discernible in the records of the visions, describing them in this way raises the question of chronology or influence. Was it Elisabeth or Ekbert who was responsible for the first move toward the representation of Elisabeth as prophet or medium of divine revelation, the image that is the predominant characterization of Elisabeth in the visionary texts? That this question cannot be satisfactorily resolved is not simply the result of the lack of adequate documentation of the earliest days of Elisabeth's visionary career. Rather, the question itself, with its suggestion of an absolute dichotomy between self and the culture in which self is produced, is misleading. Instead, the ways Elisabeth and Ekbert interacted with each other, as well as the ways Elisabeth interacted with the larger world of potential critics and sympathizers, constituted the activity that enabled the development of her understanding of herself as a prophet.

Rejecting the chicken-or-egg question of the origins of her self-under-standing does not, however, mean that we lose the possibility of tracing distinctive voices in the texts. Although both Elisabeth and Ekbert came to see her as a source of divine revelation, their representations of this pro-phetic role diverged significantly. Let us turn to consider the contours of these representations.

The most obvious way that Ekbert shaped the representation of Elisa-beth was by making his own additions to the visionary records. For ex-ample, in a prayer that he originally appended to the conclusion of the first visionary diary in its expanded form, Ekbert meditated on the paradox of human unworthiness and yet God's willingness to "place [his] spirit upon" such delinquent creatures of dust and ash. "Neither age, nor sex, nor rank, nor anything external" is disdained by this "lover of the human race."[23] Although he does not refer to Elisabeth by name in this medita-tion on divine favor bestowed on an "unworthy receptacle," he anticipates themes that he will later elaborate in his introduction to the second vision-ary diary, his most extensive reflection on Elisabeth's identity.[24]

In his introduction to the second diary, Ekbert responds to the dispar-agement of Elisabeth's earlier visions. The devaluation was based, it seems, not on an assessment of the content of her revelations but rather on the expectation that genuine visions would not be vouchsafed to a woman, an unworthy vessel of divine revelation:

Indeed, our God is not inhibited by the murmuring of those who, thinking them-selves great and disdaining what appears weaker, do not fear to mock the riches of his goodness in her [Elisabeth]. . . . It scandalizes them that in these days the Lord deigns to magnify his mercy chiefly in the weak sex. But why doesn't it occur to them that it happened like this in the days of our fathers: when the men were given over to negligence, holy women were filled with the spirit of God so that they prophesied, vigorously ruled the people of God or even triumphed gloriously over the enemies of Israel, as in the case of Hulda, Deborah, Judith, Jael, and others like them?[25]

Ekbert defends Elisabeth's claims of divine inspiration by resorting to bib-lical precedent. Most significantly, since the criticism was based on gender, that is, the mockery of the "weak sex," gender is foregrounded in this de-fense. First, he tries to make Elisabeth's experience conform to tradition by comparing her to a series of biblical women filled with the spirit of God. Second, he also declares that such female leadership is due to the sinful failure of men to discharge their responsibilities. Thus his defense of Elisabeth also functions as a criticism of those men whose disdain for

Elisabeth is part of a larger picture of male pastoral failure.[26] In this passage, Ekbert moves beyond the general paradox expressed in his prayer that God chooses any unworthy receptacle to the more pointed paradox that the folly of men leads to the divine empowerment of women.

In the visionary records that can with most confidence be attributed to her own views, Elisabeth's representation of herself as divinely inspired also works within the context of authoritative, biblical precedent, and awareness of gender categories. In words that evoke biblical models of direct contact with God or the prophetic experience of divine revelation, she fashions an image of herself standing in that tradition of messengers of divine will. In a crucial chapter in the first visionary diary, Elisabeth describes an experience that transpired on March 27, 1154, and marks a major development in her description of her mission:

I was standing alone in the oratory, concentrating on my prayers. And behold, a ray of abundant light from heaven suddenly poured over me, warming me like the sun when it shines in its strength [cf. Rev. 1: 16]. And I fell flat on the ground with a violent force and went into a trance. . . . After a little while, the angel of the Lord came and quickly raised me up and stood me on my feet saying: "O human, rise and stand on your feet and I will speak with you, and do not be afraid, because I am with you all the days of your life [cf. Ez. 2: 1–2; Is. 43: 5]. Act manfully and let your heart be comforted and wait for the Lord [Ps. 26: 14]. And say to the apostates of the earth, 'Just as once the people crucified me, so I am crucified daily among those who sin against me in their hearts.'"[27]

The chapters immediately following this account in the first visionary diary describe similar experiences, some of which also include Elisabeth's description of her response to the new angelic mandate: "The angel of the Lord said to me, 'And you, son of humanity, tell those who inhabit the earth—listen people! The God of gods has said, "Repent, for the kingdom of God is at hand"' [cf. Mt. 4: 17]. . . . And I said, 'Lord, I do not know how to speak and am slow of speech' [cf. Jer. 1: 6; Ex. 4: 10]. And he said, 'Open your mouth and I will speak, and the one who hears you, also hears me' [cf. Lk. 10: 16]."[28]

Elisabeth portrays herself as having bodily experienced a power that overwhelmed her, as having been restored to bodily capacity by an angel who then charged her with the mission of preaching an ominous message of warning to sinners. The words she attributes to the angel and to herself are heavy with biblical resonances of prophetic commission. The striking down of the apostle Paul on the road to Damascus, the resistance and claims of verbal inability of Moses and Jeremiah, the assurance that those who listen to the Lord's disciples are in fact hearing the Lord's words, are all evoked in these scenes. Thus Elisabeth, like Ekbert, represents her experience in terms that highlight the continuity between her and authoritative convention. But the differences between their representations are also striking. Most obviously, Elisabeth speaks the language of experience rather than the language of comparison, which is Ekbert's mode of expression. Ekbert compares her to biblical models and highlights the points of similarity. Elisabeth's language does not stray into the realm of logical comparison. Instead, she proclaims her embodiment of the experience of inspiration: the experience of ecstasy or trance, of overwhelming heat and an incapacity to remain standing, of being forcibly raised up, or of opening her mouth and having somebody else's words come out. The biblical echoes enable her experience to be interpreted as part of the tradition of prophetic teaching, but she herself does not pause in her pronouncements to clarify the point.

Like Ekbert, Elisabeth also deals with issues of gender in her representation of her prophetic identity, but here the contrast with Ekbert's view is even more striking. Both Elisabeth and Ekbert are aware of the fact that their contemporaries did not generally expect to learn the will of God from the women in their midst. Ekbert's response is to emphasize the biblical precedents for women's active role in religious matters, and to account for both the past and present disruptions of expectations about gender by pointing to the failure of male religious leaders. There was a clear sense of the continuity of history and the stability of gender categories for Ekbert. For him, Elisabeth's activity is best understood in light of the roles of other women, and women could play these roles when the historical circumstances were appropriate. But Elisabeth herself does not cite or evoke any biblical model of a woman inspired to do the will of God. In fact, she uses prophetic language that is specifically gendered as male. She describes the angel addressing her as "son of humanity" and telling her to "act manfully." These passages do not suggest that Elisabeth saw herself as male. But they do attest to her acute sense that she understood herself to be called upon to engage in a male activity. Her protestation of verbal inadequacy underlines this sense that speaking out in the Lord's name is not within her ability or training. Thus her sense of her own activity is not domesticated within a proper sphere of women's activity in the appropriate circumstances. These passages suggest Elisabeth's view of prophetic proclamation as something "other" to her even as she embraces this vocation.

Several years later, Elisabeth describes a scene in which she explicitly names another woman in the context of defining her own role as medium of divine revelation. She relates that the year before the onset of the *Liber Viarum Dei* visions, she had the following experience:

On a certain day while I was in a trance, [the angel] had led me as if to a meadow in which a tent was pitched and we went into it. And he showed me a great pile of books kept there and said, "Do you see those books? All of these are still to be dictated before the judgment day." Then, raising one from the pile he said, "This is the *Book of the Ways of God* which is to be revealed through you after you have visited sister Hildegard and listened to her." And indeed it began to be fulfilled in this way immediately after I returned from her.[29]

But Elisabeth's testimony to the relevance of Hildegard of Bingen to her own development is fundamentally different from Ekbert's comparison of Elisabeth to women prophets in the Bible. Elisabeth's words here do not share the apologetic function of Ekbert's comparison by rendering the surprising gender dynamics familiar. In fact, no apologetic function is obvious, since there is nothing in Elisabeth's expression that suggests that what she is doing needs justification. Gone are her protestations of inadequacy to the task of divine revelation, and gone are her uses of male language, both of which are seen in the passages from the first visionary diary quoted above. In their place is an affirmation of an event in her mundane (i.e., nonvisionary) life—a visit to a nearby fellow Benedictine nun who is not even noted by Elisabeth as a visionary or recipient of revelation—and an acknowledgment of having listened to her.

Her acknowledgment of Hildegard is not the only way in which this self-presentation differs from Elisabeth's earlier attempts at describing herself. Unlike the passages from the first visionary diary in which Elisabeth articulates her mission as a verbal one—she describes herself as commanded to speak or to shout—this passage from the *Liber Viarum Dei* shows an explicit consciousness of herself as involved in the creation of a book. The first visionary diary certainly includes Elisabeth's references to the creation of textual records of her visionary proclamations, but there her self-portrait consistently focused on the image of oral proclaimer, of one whose mission is to open her mouth and speak. But here Elisabeth sees herself as the channel for producing a book of revelations, and it is in this role that she not only acknowledges the relevance of Hildegard of Bingen but also sees her own activity as one example in a long and continuing tradition; she sees her book as one from a huge pile still to be produced before the end of the world. Thus her self-understanding is cast not primarily in terms of authoritative precedents but in terms of a vision of future successors. And her sense of herself as producer of a book is found in a context where there is no hint of anxieties about verbal proclamation. Elisabeth's interest in the constitution of her visions as a book can also be seen in a final warning added to the *Liber Viarum Dei*, in which all future scribes are adjured by God and his angel to diligently correct their transcriptions of this book and to append the adjuration itself.[30] A letter that she composed during the final months in which the *Liber Viarum Dei* was being completed likewise suggests this new image. Addressing the bishops of Trier, Cologne, and Mainz, Elisabeth asserted that the angel told her to command them to read this book and announce its warnings to the universal Church. Confident in her own role in producing a book of revelations, Elisabeth now delegates the mission of verbal proclamation to those who have the authority to preach.[31]

This apparent decline in Elisabeth's anxiety and the emergence of her sense of identity as revealer of a book may both be due, in part, to Ekbert's influence. The creation of the *Liber Viarum Dei* took place in the period after Ekbert had moved to Schönau and undertaken the systematic production of the visionary texts. Elisabeth seems to have become comfortable with the idea of the codification of her visions and this was probably due to her general confidence in Ekbert's management of the publication of her visions. Although there is no reason to attribute her shifting self-image to Ekbert's ideas about who she was, this is a concrete example of how Elisabeth's self-understanding was shaped by the dynamics of their interaction. His service as secretary and editor provided the context in which Elisabeth could conceptualize herself in a new way. With the anxiety of being a "proclaimer" diminished, she could affirm the influence of another woman and see herself as part of a process that stretched forward in history. Her place in the unfolding of history was also established by her representation of her visions as a book, with all the connotations of permanence and authority associated with books.

Elisabeth's representation of herself was also deeply marked by other issues that seem not to have seriously interested Ekbert. These are the closely related issues of Elisabeth's personal piety and her life within the community. For all of Ekbert's efforts to assert the truth of Elisabeth's visions or the legitimacy of her voice in articulating them, he did not cite piety or righteousness as part of his apologia or even as a way of providing context for interpreting the career of Elisabeth. In his introduction to the first visionary diary, he offers a bare description of the setting of her visionary experience ("when she had been living with religious women in the monastery for eleven years"), a clause that could have been so easily and even formulaically elaborated to include a simple adverb (piously, humbly, obediently). In the passage from the introduction to the second visionary diary cited above he goes so far as to compare Elisabeth to holy women in the biblical past, but without asserting a comparable holiness on Elisabeth's part. In a letter he wrote to Abbot Reinhard of Reinhausen, which accompanied a fiery letter of admonition to Reinhard from Elisabeth, Ekbert makes his fullest defense of the veracity of Elisabeth's visions and the legitimacy of his own role in preparing the texts. He repeatedly emphasizes the divine origin of Elisabeth's words and the error of seeing the texts as womanish fictions. Yet he broaches the subject of piety only when he defends himself from the potential accusation of involving himself in false sanctity by propagating lies in creating these texts.[32] Whether or not Ekbert was aware of the intellectual traditions that affirmed that prophecy or divine inspiration could be granted to unworthy ones,[33] his representation of Elisabeth did not link her revelations to her holiness or virtue.

Ekbert's lack of interest in portraying Elisabeth's piety may have been due to several factors. This silence parallels his repeated attempts to deny any intellectual abilities on Elisabeth's part. His denial of her skills in Latin and his references to her lack of education, both belied by other evidence in the visionary texts, serve primarily to emphasize the divine origin of her visions. Perhaps he avoids any representation of Elisabeth's holiness lest her proclamations be interpreted as having their source in her own sanctity, in her dedication to God, in her commitment to righteousness and her indignation at the waywardness of God's people. Even if this suggestion about his silence cannot be proven, we can at least observe that what Ekbert does attend to and in fact emphasize at great length is the content of her revelations. It is exclusively the message and not the messenger that stirs his effort and is featured in his representation.

Ekbert's lack of attention to Elisabeth's piety could also have been influenced by a reticence to praise the holiness of a living person. The typically complex community dynamics through which sanctity comes to be attributed to a living individual would have been even further interwoven with issues of family politics in the case of Elisabeth and Ekbert.[34] That Ekbert may have been hesitant to attribute holiness to a living person is supported by the fact that in his description of her death, Ekbert does for the first time offer a portrayal of Elisabeth as holy woman and exemplary member of her community. "Behold our Elisabeth, that elect lamp of heavenly light, outstanding virgin honored by the abundant grace of God, splendid gem of our monastery, leader of our virginal company, alas how she has been withdrawn from this light before her elder years."[35] In none of his introductions to the visionary texts or letters to others about Elisabeth does he even note that she became the mistress (*magistra*) of the nuns at Schönau, let alone characterize that role of spiritual leadership within her community, which he does in detail in this text.

This hesitance to praise Elisabeth as a holy woman during her lifetime is also confirmed by the evidence that as more time elapsed after her death Ekbert further elaborated this new image of his holy sister. Comparing the two extant versions of *De Obitu Elisabeth* reveals his increasing efforts to enhance his portrayal of Elisabeth.[36] Both versions of the text portray Elisabeth as an exemplary monastic, humble, devout, faithful, energetic in penance, miraculously sustained in her final days, and, most importantly, source of divine revelation. But in the later version these characteristics are more fully developed. For example, originally content to state the fact of her self-mortification ("beyond the pain of the wounds which the Lord's hand inflicted upon you, you always added the sacrifice of willing affliction"[37]), in the later version of the text he catalogues her rivers of tears, innumerable prayers and genuflections, the rending of her tender flesh by coarse cloth, the incisions in her sides from a binding belt, and her meager diet. Although Ekbert never shifts into a wholly hagiographic mode—both versions include his prayers that Elisabeth may be granted a heavenly reward for her virtues[38]—he has nevertheless created an image of Elisabeth that roots her visionary experience in a pious life of extraordinary Christian devotion.

It is too simple, however, to suggest that Ekbert's new interest in portraying Elisabeth as a pious woman was made possible simply by her death. Ekbert's expanded introduction to the first diary, his introduction to the second diary, and his prologue to the complete collection were all published only after Elisabeth died. Yet in none of these texts does he refer to her death or begin to refashion his image of her. This fact suggests that there is something else to consider in understanding his new representation of Elisabeth in *De Obitu*. This other factor is Elisabeth's own representation of herself in the visionary records, a representation in which the issues of her personal piety and righteousness are foregrounded in a way that differs sharply from his own early silence.

The records of her earliest experience are replete with Elisabeth's references to her own experience of religious engagement. The self-image she presents is of a nun devoted to her vocation and engaged wholeheartedly in the life of her community. This is not, however, an image of self-aggrandizement, for she represents herself doubting the very foundations of her faith and unsuccessful in many of her attempts to banish the demonic source of her torments. Moreover, she repeatedly emphasizes that she receives these visions because of God's grace and not due to her own merit. But while such an affirmation in Ekbert's writing suggests his conspicuous lack of interest in her piety or virtue, for Elisabeth the visions are comprehensible only as *her* religious experience, as part of *her* life of prayer and devotion.

Furthermore, despite Elisabeth's emphasis that divine favor and not her merit is the cause of her visions, there is an interesting ambiguity about merit that recurs in the visionary records. At several points, Elisabeth asserts that the typical pattern of her visions was disrupted by an unusual delay which she interpreted as due to her own fault. This ambiguity about merit and divine favor can be seen in an example from the *Liber Viarum Dei*:

Having concluded the preceding sermon, the angel of the Lord delayed longer than usual in visiting me. I attributed this to my failings and began to worry to myself. I struggled diligently with tears and prayers, and the members of our convent helped me by our communal prayer. And when seventeen days had passed from when he had finished the previous lesson, I was standing alone in the oratory around the third hour, pouring out my heart to the Lord and saying, "In all the things you have done for me up until now, Lord, you have not regarded my merits. Rather, in your mercy you have done all these things. For this reason I beg you not to hold back because of my failings or those of anyone else, without leading to a good conclusion what you in your goodness have deigned to begin in me." [39]

Elisabeth then asserts that the angel suddenly appeared to her and began the sermon she was praying for.

This pattern of a perceived cessation in visionary experience followed by Elisabeth's anxiety about her own failings as cause emerges at several points in the visionary records. [40] Usually this pattern ends with the resumption of visionary experience, but in one extended example in the second visionary diary, Elisabeth portrays herself learning of the "iniquity" (*iniquitas*) that rendered her unworthy of her accustomed visitations from the Virgin Mary. She declares that St. Peter told her, "Behold, you have become tepid in her service; and you do not devote yourself to the ministry owed to her like you used to." [41] Elisabeth then portrays herself attempting to atone for her negligence, a negligence shared by her sisters, [42] in the process of which her customary visionary powers are still withheld and she is told by the angel that she must make confession of her sin.

Elisabeth offers this self-portrayal in the context of a series of visions in which her own piety—her personal prayer life, her participation in the communal prayer of the Schönau nuns, and her visionary experience—is contrasted with the priestly powers of the abbot to celebrate Mass and hear confessions. It is striking that Elisabeth's sense of sin emerges in a context in which she suggests a strong awareness of the difference between the possibilities her piety offers and the sacerdotally mediated channels of grace that she can have access to only as a laywoman in relation to a priest.[43] At least a muted awareness of the implications of her gender seems to mark her self-presentation here. Elisabeth does go on to represent this failing as having been successfully addressed, but only with the aid of the abbot and other members of the community collaborating in sacramental acts of atonement.

This scene adds nuances to the image of Elisabeth as visionary that have no correlate in Ekbert's portrayal. First, Elisabeth's self-portrayal in this scene shows her sense of visionary life as deeply rooted—even if in troubling ways—in the ongoing life of her monastic community. Ekbert quite openly acknowledges that Elisabeth's visions often occurred in the immediate context of the liturgical offices.[44] But for Ekbert, this is just background. For Elisabeth, the life of her community, whether it be the psalm chanting of the nuns or the eucharistic services celebrated by the abbot and brothers, could actually affect the course of her visionary life. This can be seen not just in this incident but also in the passage from the *Liber Viarum Dei* cited above, where Elisabeth prays to God to not withhold his revelations "because of my failings or those of anyone else."[45] Elisabeth thus portrays her visionary experience as taking place within a complicated world with many agencies, in contrast to the perspective of Ekbert, for whom the only agency is that of God.

Most significant among these agencies is, of course, her own. Her portrayal of her agency is most startling in her declaration of her sin. This is not a humility topos. Nor is it a meditation on the paradox of God's inscrutable choice of an unworthy vessel, a theme Ekbert developed in his prayer *Tua sunt*. Rather, it is Elisabeth's declaration of the relevance of her devotional life. She offers a picture of her visionary life in which her piety matters, her righteousness affects the course of what she is enabled to see. The relatively few cases where Elisabeth declares a suspension of her regular visionary experiences allow us to read with new eyes the many more testimonies where she portrays herself receiving visions while in the midst of devout prayer.

The significance of Elisabeth's self-portrayal as a devout Christian is a subtle dynamic of one particular text whose subject is ostensibly the portrayal of other holy women. The stated purpose of *Revelatio de sacro exercitu virginum Coloniensium* was to enhance the cult of St. Ursula and the Eleven Thousand Virgins. Elisabeth begins this text by asserting her willingness to publish her revelations despite potential criticism because she expects to be rewarded "if this martyrdom shall receive some increased honor from those things which the Lord has deigned to reveal through my labors."[46] Likewise she ends the text with Saint Ursula herself praying for God to reward anyone who retells or, literally, refreshes (*renovabit*) their passion. If the goal of the text is the increased devotion to these saints, then the model of virtue here is Elisabeth herself. The representation of female holiness is thus broadened beyond the ideal of Ursula and her companions to the ideal of devotion to Ursula and her companions. And for Elisabeth that model of devotion is not simply one of patronage between powerful saints and petitioning humans. Rather, Elisabeth's relationship with these saints is created in a world in which she has power to help them and in which she wields her visionary power to negotiate her relationship with other human beings.[47] Thus as Elisabeth represents female holiness in traditional terms as martyrdom and virginity in her portrayal of Ursula and her companions, she simultaneously constructs a new image of female holiness in her self-portrayal as a woman whose piety is attested to in her own narrations of visionary experience and as a member of a community encompassing saints in heaven as well as her sisters and brothers at Schönau.

Ekbert seems to have understood the claims Elisabeth made in this text, for in *De Obitu Elisabeth* his praise includes the exclamation, "O how many souls of the elect obtained their desired consolations through your negotiation!"[48] And in a vision narrated in the third visionary diary, a text that bears heavy traces of Ekbert's influence on style and content,[49] the angel is described as comparing Elisabeth to St. Paul and other holy people whose spirit turns radically inward to focus on spiritual matters.[50] Thus it seems clear that Ekbert's own understanding of Elisabeth was becoming more complicated as he became willing to associate holiness with her experience of divine inspiration.

The dynamics of this interaction between Elisabeth and Ekbert were crystallized not only in the words captured in writing, but in the overall shape of the collection of visionary texts. His introductions to these texts alert the readers to the miracle of God's activity and thereby an ostensibly unlikely female medium of divine revelation is rendered believable in the larger scheme of divine intervention in history. But these introductions, with their gaze directed toward the work of God, are followed by texts that proclaim, "I saw," "I felt," "I learned," "I said." The difference is not simply first person narration. It is the affirmation that her experience is the source of her revelations. Elisabeth's attempt to convey the power of that experience and its impact on her life resulted in an image of her prophetic role that is less easily contained than Ekbert's image of her. Whereas for Ekbert the visionary experience was simply the work of God, Elisabeth portrayed herself as participating in a complex web of relationships among herself, her community, her angelic guide, the saints, and God, all of whom acted on the course of her visionary life. Whereas for Ekbert her life was largely irrelevant to the import of her revelations, Elisabeth portrayed her own religious state as intimately tied—as both cause and effect—to her experience of divine inspiration. Whereas for Ekbert the unlikeliness of a woman receiving divine revelation could be rationalized by attention to biblical precedent, Elisabeth initially portrayed a sense of her experience as alien to her identity as a woman. And her later reference to her visit to Hildegard of Bingen points again to her affirmation of her personal experience of human relationships as relevant to the course of her visionary life.

Despite these differences, Ekbert was not oblivious to the impact of Elisabeth's self-presentation. The full fruit of this impact comes in *De Obitu*, a text which he composed as a letter to his kinswomen at Andernach, but which only circulated as an epilogue to the collection of visionary texts.[51] That Ekbert could produce *De Obitu* as an epilogue to the visionary texts was enabled, not by his own words which tended to divert attention away from Elisabeth, but by the image that Elisabeth created of herself. In effect, Ekbert wrote the final chapter—an account of her holy death—in a *vita* comprised of the records of Elisabeth's visionary experience, the records in which Elisabeth portrayed herself as deeply engaged in the messy process of struggling to be a holy woman. That he could append such an epilogue to the collection is evidence of two fundamental aspects of their relationship: his control over the shape of the visionary texts and his openness to being influenced by Elisabeth's claims about her experience. That a collection of Elisabeth's visions and *De Obitu* could be incorporated as *Vita et Visiones beate Elyzabet* in a *legendarium* constituted solely of saints' lives, in which Elisabeth is repeatedly referred to as blessed (*beata*) and which concludes with a final notice describing Elisabeth as "a virgin of most holy way of life" suggests that the Schönau visionary corpus could be and was read not only as a record of divine revelations but as the portrayal of the life of a holy woman.[52]

Peter Dinzelbacher has discussed the appearance of new styles of religious literature in the thirteenth century, pointing to the growing emphasis on interior life in hagiographic texts, the addition of biographical information in revelation literature, and thus the creation of hybrid texts that draw on both these previously distinct traditions. He rightly emphasizes that it is difficult to draw clear genre boundaries in this literature. Dinzelbacher also attributes the appearance of this new kind of literature to the appearance of new kinds of experience: mystical union and the experience of divine grace seem to have become more frequent and normative in the twelfth century, and much of this literature is about women's extraordinary experiences.[53]

The corpus of texts attesting to the visions and life of Elisabeth of Schönau is one of the earliest examples of this new style of literature. These texts certainly provide support for this characterization of a new literary genre about women's extraordinary experience. Yet there is another crucial factor in the corpus of visionary texts about Elisabeth that is not covered by Dinzelbacher's characterization. The texts are not simply *about* Elisabeth. Elisabeth's role in producing the visionary records—her self-representation and her influence on Ekbert's representation of her and on his commitment to textualizing her visions—must be seen as contributing to the reshaping of conventional genres. Thus the development of this hybrid genre needs to be reexamined in light not just of women as the subject matter of these texts but of women as agents in producing these texts. The contours of the relationship between Elisabeth and Ekbert, the ways in which their differences shaped each other, can be traced in the images they delineated and in the organization of the texts that contain those images. The challenge in reading these texts today is to see that interplay between Ekbert's authoritative voice introducing the messages vouchsafed to an unworthy vessel and Elisabeth's passionate insistence on the relevance of her own experience as a religious woman.

4

Imitatio Christi or
Imitatio Mariae?

Clare of Assisi and Her Interpreters

Catherine M. Mooney

UNTIL RECENTLY, little scholarly attention has been paid to the life and writings of Clare of Assisi. For example, while scholars have searched assiduously for over a century for early manuscripts of the texts by and about Francis of Assisi, the same has not been true for texts by and about Clare. The thirteenth-century Process of Canonization, considered one of the key sources for her life, was located and published only in 1920.[1] The Latin text of the Testament attributed to her, of utmost importance for the biographical details of her life, long depended on a seventeenth-century edition[2] until curiosity finally stirred scholars to locate, between 1954 and the late 1980s, five earlier manuscripts.[3] While the numerous documents by and about Francis of Assisi have been repeatedly—one is tempted to say "endlessly"—published, edited, interpreted, and debated, Clare's brief corpus did not even appear together in the original Latin until 1970.[4]

Since then new editions of texts by and about Clare have steadily appeared.[5] Although Franciscan scholars were slower than others to respond to the new interest in the field of women's history and, more important, to draw on the groundbreaking studies that have marked particularly the field of medieval religious women, studies about Clare have at long last begun to flourish, especially since the celebration in 1993/94 of the 800th anniversary of her birth.[6]

A striking aspect of a number of these studies is the extent to which scholars of Clare see her not just as an influential figure for her contemporaries and subsequent history, not just as a woman able to achieve and gain fame in a world and Church dominated by men, but as a woman whose life, writings, personality, spirituality, and theology are integrally connected to her gender. Marianne Schlosser, who discusses Clare's use of the terms mother, sister, and bride to describe herself or her sisters, calls Clare "uniquely feminine."[7] We know that the same would not be said of Francis, although he too referred to himself as a mother,[8] spoke of his friars as mothers to each other,[9] and exhorted men and women in general to be mothers and spouses of Christ.[10] His friars spoke of Francis as a mother as well,[11] referred to him as the spouse of Christ,[12] and followed his example and advice that they be mothers to one another.[13] While relatively little is made of this feminine imagery so strikingly applied to Francis and other men in writings by and about Francis,[14] Clare's sex and her quite conventional use of female imagery are regularly underscored in scholarly and nonscholarly commentaries regarding her. In 1993 Pope John Paul II, speaking of Clare's writings, commented on the difficulty of expressing "what only a woman's heart could experience."[15] Chiara Lainati, one of the more prolific modern scholars of Clare, states that "Clare, as a woman, sums up in herself all the symbols that humanity past and present includes in the feminine, the 'eternal woman,'" and "that no other woman has been so 'Woman,' so 'Madonna.'"[16] Clare, according to another writer, is "womanspirit."[17] The noted Clare scholar, Jean-François Godet, refers to her feminine style of writing and argues that her "woman's way of seeing" and "speaking" are evident especially in the "feminine" themes and symbols of her writing.[18] In 1990 the Franciscan journal *Laurentianum* devoted a volume to articles united by the theme "Clare: Feminine Franciscanism" and in 1991 a week-long gathering sponsored by the Tuscan Province of the Friars Minor took up the theme "Clare and the Charism of Women."[19] While a few scholars have begun to delineate how social constructions of femaleness and femininity function within texts by and about Clare,[20] many others continue to identify Clare as specifically feminine without nuanced discussion of the medieval or modern meanings attached to such a claim.

In the remainder of this essay, I will discuss one of the ways in which medieval and modern commentators have tended to see Clare in a specifically female category by exploring the theme of imitation, both *imitatio Christi* or imitation of Christ, one of the central spiritual themes of the high and late medieval period,[21] and *imitatio Mariae*, the imitation of Mary, the Mother of God.[22] The fact that we have authentic writings from Clare affords a critical control unavailable to us in the study of so many other medieval holy women who did not leave texts of their own. Through comparison of her texts with those written about her by her male contemporaries we can begin to examine the extent to which medieval assumptions about women influenced or even skewed Clare's representation by these interpreters. Clare proves to be a particularly rich subject for analysis also due to her association with Francis of Assisi, an association so close in life and in the minds of many of their admirers that they might aptly be considered a couple. The proximity of these two saints, one female, one male, chronologically, geographically, in their religious ideals, and in friendship, provides yet another important control. Thus, while focusing on the theme of *imitatio* in texts by and about Clare, I will also digress occasionally to compare and contrast the same theme as it appears in the numerous texts by and about Francis. In this way, I shall highlight how hagiographers employed the pivotally important religious theme of *imitatio* in their interpretation of both saints, yet, by applying it diversely in their discussions of the two, used it also to distinguish the sanctity of Francis from that of Clare.

Clare, Francis, and the Theme of *Imitatio*

Clare of Assisi was born about 1194 and survived to about age sixty, dying in 1253. A relatively well-known saint, she is familiar to most people as the female and lesser counterpart of Francis of Assisi. Francis had embarked upon his religious career as a simple layman, one of thousands of lay people at that time exploring new articulations of religious life, both formal and informal. Such men and women were searching to devote their lives to God, not in the monastic milieu which had predominated until then, but among people, in towns and cities, free of the vast lands, riches, and feudal obligations which they viewed as encumbrances to an authentic following of Christ and his apostles, the *vita apostolica* as it was then termed.

Clare and Francis have traditionally been juxtaposed in a sort of partnership in this search for the *vita apostolica*, a partnership at once parallel and astonishingly asymmetrical. The parallels between the two are too abundant to enumerate exhaustively: it will suffice to point simply to a few of the most prominent parallels connecting the corpus of writings each has bequeathed to us and to several salient parallels in compositions by their contemporaries describing the two.

In their own writings, for example, Francis and Clare each left written Testaments, final Blessings, and rules for their respective followers. Both

Clare's rule and Francis's are introduced by papal bulls approving them, entitled *Solet annuere*.

There are other parallels in writings about these two saints. It is entirely to be expected, of course, that elaborate legends be composed about each of these prominent saints shortly after their deaths. Two years after Francis died in 1226, the Franciscan Thomas of Celano, following a commission, wrote the first life of Francis.[23] Similarly, a commissioned *vita* of Clare appeared about two years after she died in 1253. It is notable that many scholars, indeed, most in the English-speaking world, have long attributed Clare's legend to Thomas of Celano. If they are correct, then Celano's authorship constitutes yet another significant resemblance joining the two. If, on the other hand, their supposition proves wrong, it suggests the degree to which observers of Clare and Francis have been conditioned to expect and predisposed to accept parallels between the two.[24] Within a few years of the composition of both of these *vitae*, a versified text closely related to the earliest prose *vita* of each saint also appeared.[25]

Given the central importance within Franciscan tradition of the motif of *imitatio*, such parallels are hardly surprising. Nor is it coincidental that Clare's Testament, Blessing, and Form of Life (sometimes known as her rule)[26]—precisely the documents that would enhance her likeness to and imitation of Francis, who wrote similar texts—are the most dubious documents in her corpus. The Testament, which differs stylistically and linguistically from the other works attributed to Clare, is noteworthy for the explicit and intimate ties it establishes joining Clare and her sisters to Francis, a relationship many friars were already trying to ignore by the time of Clare's death but which her sisters and other friars, conversely, were anxious to emphasize.[27] The earliest Latin manuscript of the Testament can be dated, perhaps, to the late fourteenth century. The Blessing, which shares the weak manuscript tradition of the Testament,[28] conspicuously incorporates most of the Blessing which Francis, drawing from the Book of Numbers, gave to his follower, Brother Leo.[29] Although most scholars this century attribute the Form of Life largely to Clare's own authorship, only a few passages are written in her own first person voice. Many passages repeat or adapt sections of earlier rules given to Clare and her sisters or derive from the papally approved rule that Francis left his friars.[30] Moreover, any contributions by Clare to the Form of Life plausibly involved significant collaboration by others, such as Rainaldo di Segni, the sisters' Cardinal Protector who later would become Pope Alexander IV. That others saw this rule as likening Clare to Francis is clear from the fact that an ancient tradition soon imposed upon it a division into twelve chapters, thereby enhancing its similarity to Francis's papally approved rule.[31] Modern scholars who accept the authenticity of these texts point to them as evidence that Clare consciously took Francis as a model to be imitated.[32] One sort of circular reasoning sometimes infused into the authenticity question of texts attributed to Clare are arguments that a particular text is "essentially a feminine" document.[33] Whatever the truth regarding the authenticity of these documents, it is clear that *somebody*, be it Clare or another, sought to model her after Francis.

Clare's corpus, with or without these debated texts, is exceptionally brief. Virtually all scholars who study Clare, the majority of whom are Franciscans, accept as authentic Clare's composition of four letters to Agnes of Prague (totaling about fourteen pages in modern English editions) and the twelve-page Form of Life. The presence in the Form of Life of many passages taken from earlier rules does not diminish Clare's authorship in their eyes since they think Clare, as author, consciously incorporated these sections.[34] Many scholars also accept as Clare's the five-page Testament and one-page Blessing despite periodic and vociferous objections to the contrary. Finally, few scholars accept in its current form a letter to Ermentrude of Bruges, although some believe it to be a conflation of two no longer extant letters to Ermentrude. For the purposes of this essay, I will rely above all on the letters to Agnes and secondarily on the Form of Life, Testament, and Blessing whose relationship to Clare is more open to question.

Imitatio Christi is one of the most prominent spiritual themes associated with Francis of Assisi. In his own life and even more in the early literature and iconography about him, Francis is repeatedly represented as another Christ, an *alter Christus*, a term first applied to him in the early fourteenth century.[35] Poor, suffering, and preaching to the masses, Francis was so like Christ that he received the stigmata, the five wounds of Christ, physically, in his own body. In similar fashion, Clare's life as depicted in early writings about her appears to be patterned after that of Francis. Francis met with familial opposition to his conversion, and so did Clare. Each initially spent several days in a Benedictine monastery before embarking on their individual religious journeys. One of Francis's first religious acts after vowing to follow Christ was to rebuild the church of San Damiano; one of Clare's first religious acts after making vows before Francis was to take up residence within the church Francis had rebuilt. Francis founded the order of male Franciscans; Clare founded the corresponding order for women. Just as a reluctant Francis was forced to become leader of the friars, so did he in his turn compel Clare, diffident and resisting, to take charge over her sisters. In 1224, the same year that Francis received the stigmata, Clare, significantly, contracted a debilitating illness which she bore until her death and which those around her similarly interpreted as a sign of her sanctity and union with the suffering Christ. After their respective deaths, the body of each saint rested for a short time in the church of Saint George until, in each case, the body was given final rest in a large basilica built in the saint's honor. Each saint, renowned already during life and beloved by the papacy, was canonized two years after death. It seems only logical then that two early texts call Clare *emulatrix sancti Francisci*, emulator of St. Francis.[36] One modern scholar has even called her an *alter Franciscus*, although the term never appears in medieval sources.[37] One might point to other parallels, particularly Clare's faithful and oft-noted following of Francis regarding the all-important issue of poverty, but the salient point is this: in most of these incidents, Francis is depicted by hagiographers as following, copying, or imitating Christ, while Clare is pictured as following Francis.

In other words, Clare's imitation of Christ, which most of her medieval and modern admirers acknowledge, is often one remove from Francis's imitation of Christ. The two are unequal partners, alike and yet not alike, corresponding, yet asymmetrical. Clare, for example, has been characterized—one might even say caricatured—by her contemporaries, later commentators, and, until recently, many scholars as the dedicated devotee and helper, docilely heeding Francis's directives.[38] The order of men Francis founded was identified as the First Order; the "Poor Ladies," the order which Clare established shortly after Francis's foundation, was eventually—and tellingly—designated as the Second Order. Despite notable differences, some scholars see Clare's order as a conscious copy of his.[39] In contradistinction to Francis and his city-dwelling, street-preaching friars, the women who coalesced around Clare resided outside the town walls, confined within a small cloister, their voices silent in accord with the religious rules granted them—some would say imposed—by their ecclesiastical superiors. The cleric who composed the papal bull approving Clare's canonization clearly delighted in his characterization of her: "Clare was concealed, yet her life was revealed; Clare kept silence, yet her reputation cried aloud; she was hidden in a cell, but known throughout the towns."[40] It is precisely these attributes which are underscored repeatedly in subsequent hagiographic depictions of Clare. In contrast, while these qualities are not absent from Clare's own writings, they by no means constitute the central themes in any of her own texts.

It may surprise some readers to learn that, although Francis did indeed speak of "following Christ," to be discussed below, he never explicitly used the vocabulary of *imitatio Christi*, the term so many people today identify with his Christlike life. Early hagiographical texts only sporadically refer to Francis as imitating or being an imitator of Christ. The anonymous allegorical work, *Sacrum commercium* (ca. 1227), Thomas of Celano's *Vita prima* (1228–29), and *Vita secunda* (1244–47) each include single references to Francis as imitator of Christ.[41] Only with later hagiographical works do the term and notion gradually become more common. The term appears twice in the brief Testament attributed to Clare (ca. 1253), three times in Bonaventure's *Legenda maior* (1261–63), and five times in the *Speculum perfectionis* (1318).[42] The work most known for the parallelism it establishes between the life of Christ and the life of Francis, Bartholomew of Pisa's *De conformitate vitae Beati Francisci ad vitam Domini Iesu*, was composed only toward the end of the fourteenth century, well over 150 years after Francis's death.

Imitatio Mariae

Such differences between a saint's own writings and those about him or her are evident in Clare's case as well. The subtle shaping of Clare's character by her medieval interpreters, virtually all of whom were men, and by some modern scholars as well, continues the theme of *imitatio* and centers on Clare's relationship to Christ and to the Virgin Mary. The earliest (albeit very indirect) suggestion that Clare resembled Mary may come from Francis himself, who once applied the epithet "spouse of the Holy Spirit" to Mary and who, in a quotation attributed to him and inserted into the 1253 Form of Life, spoke of Clare and her sisters as having "betrothed themselves to the Holy Spirit."[43] The unusual formulation, whether or not it was intended to establish an analogy between the sisters and Mary, is striking and occurs nowhere else in Francis's writings. A few months after her death, Clare is compared explicitly to other women and to Mary by witnesses testifying in the Process of her canonization. Three sisters each testify in almost identical terms that Clare's holiness was beyond description and that no other woman was greater than Clare, except for the Virgin Mary.[44] After fifteen sisters had testified, the ecclesiastics managing the inquest assembled the entire convent of sisters who, led by their abbess Benedecta, "said with one accord . . . that all that was found in the holiness of any other holy woman, except the Virgin Mary, could be truly said of and witnessed in Lady Clare."[45] Although it would hardly be surprising to hear that Clare's sisters placed her above other women (and below Mary), plentiful evidence shows also that much of their testimony was elicited from them as they responded to specific questions repeatedly put to them by their ecclesiastical interrogators.[46] The comparison of Clare and Mary, whatever its origin, is memorable because medieval interpreters writing after the Process continue to juxtapose Clare and Mary, but instead of alluding to Clare's inferiority (however slight) to the Virgin, they begin to describe the two in more mutual terms, describing Mary as Clare's model, and Clare as Mary's imitator.[47]

The first explicit suggestion that Clare modeled herself after the Virgin Mary is made by the anonymous author of the influential *Legend*, the account of Clare's life composed just a year or two after her death and based, in part, on the Process. He portrays Clare not only as a follower of Christ or as Christlike,[48] but also as a follower of Mary, the Mother of God. He calls Clare the "footprint (*vestigium*) of the Mother of God," and indirectly intimates that men pattern themselves after men, and women after women: "Let the men follow the new male disciples of the Incarnate Word; let the women imitate Clare, the footprint of the Mother of God, the new leader of women."[49] Later, he writes of Clare that she, by her own manner of living, showed "her footprints to her followers."[50] The Minister General Bonaventure probably had such passages in mind when six years after Clare's death, in 1259, he urged the abbess and sisters of San Damiano to follow the "virtuous footprints of your most blessed mother [Clare]."[51]

The author of the *Legend* more subtly likens Clare to Mary. He glories in the fact that both Clare's and Francis's orders originated in a church named after Mary. Once again we encounter both analogy and asymmetry between the two saints. The hagiographer, who invokes both Mary's virginity and her maternity, is employing the most common language for Mary at this time. He remarks that the significance of this church of Saint Mary for the birth of the order of women is the fact that Mary is the preeminent Mother and Virgin, a model for Clare and her followers whose virginity and spiritual fecundity he underlines. The significance of the church for Francis and his followers, however, is that there the "Mother of mercies" brought them forth (*parturire*). Mary is birthing mother of both orders, but model for the women alone.[52]

Another early interpreter, Clare's friend, Bishop Rainaldo, in his introductory remarks to the 1253 Form of Life, declares that Clare and her sisters followed in "the footprints of Christ himself and his most holy Mother."[53] Later, this same man, now Pope Alexander IV, appears as the probable author of a hymn in which he acclaimed Clare as "the footprint of the Mother of Christ," this time dropping altogether the allusion to Christ's footprints.[54]

An arresting detail here is that in their discussions of Clare both of these men use the metaphor of "footprint," a common image in an age in which the notion of following Christ was gaining in popularity. Clare too revealingly employs the metaphor in her own writings, but in every case the footprints she is following are Jesus' not Mary's. In her second letter to Agnes of Prague (ca. 1235), Clare praises Agnes, who, emulating holy poverty, with a spirit of humility and charity, has clung "to the footprints of him to whom you have merited to be joined as a spouse."[55] In her third letter (ca. 1238) she states that Agnes wonderfully supplies what is lacking in Clare and in the other sisters in their imitation "of the footprints of the poor and humble Jesus Christ."[56] In the Testament, Clare exhorts her sisters to persevere always in holy poverty, according to the form of life Francis had given them and as he had encouraged them in his words, examples, and many writings. His example was as a follower of Christ: "And our most blessed father Francis, having imitated [the Son of God's] footprints, did not while he lived ever turn away in his example or teaching from this holy poverty that he had chosen for himself and for his brothers."[57] Clare appears also to speak indirectly in two papal documents, both known as the Privilege of Poverty.[58] Each document grants to Clare and her sisters the right to live without property and in each, the words of the pope in question seem to recall and recapitulate Clare's own words from her petition to the pope. Addressing Clare and her sisters, each pope writes: "you propose to have no possessions whatsoever, clinging in all things to the footprints of him who for us was made poor, the way, the truth, and the life."[59]

Translation of the Third Letter to Agnes

It is important to note that in the foregoing passages from the Testament and her petition to the pope Clare associates following the footprints of Jesus specifically with poverty. In her letters to Agnes, she associates following Jesus' footprints specifically with poverty and humility. Attention to her own language in this regard provides the key, I think, to the meaning behind one final instance of her use of the term footprints. The passage appears in her third letter to Agnes. Its intepretation in one important translation, I want to suggest, has overlooked Clare's own use of the term footprints to describe a following of Christ in favor of later hagiographic depictions of Clare as a follower of Mary.

In 1988 the Franciscan scholar Regis Armstrong, in his introduction to his translation of works by and about Clare, alluded to the *Vita prima* of St. Francis composed by Thomas of Celano. Armstrong wondered whether Thomas perceived the role of Clare

as similar to that of Mary, the Mother of the Church, to whom the apostles looked for embodied guidance and knowledge of Jesus after His Ascension? Certainly their positions bear resemblances. For at this very time the friars were beginning to see strong likenesses in the lives of Christ and Francis and to take seriously the theme of the "conformities" between the two. But Thomas makes no reference to the similarity between Mary, the Mother of Jesus, and Clare.[60]

Although Armstrong thus acknowledges that there is no explicit evidence revealing Thomas of Celano's thoughts on the matter, he then proceeds to bolster the Clare/Mary analogy by citing the anonymous author of Clare's *Legend* who referred, as I noted above, to Clare as "the footprint of the Mother of God."

Armstrong's desire to see Mary as model for Clare and his cognizance of occasional hagiographic remarks likening Clare to Mary clearly influence his reading and subsequent translation of an important passage in her third letter to Agnes. In 1982, six years before he suggested the aptness of the Clare/Mary analogy, his co-translation with Ignatius Brady of this passage rendered her words thus:

Therefore, as the glorious Virgin of virgins carried [Christ] materially in her body, you, too, by *following in His footprints* [cf. 1 Pet 2: 21], especially [those] of poverty and humility, can, without any doubt, always carry Him spiritually in your chaste and virginal body.[61]

In Armstrong's subsequent 1988 translation, where he speculated in his introduction regarding the resemblance of Clare to Mary, he translated the same passage thus:

As the glorious Virgin of virgins carried [Him] materially, so you, too, *by following in* her *footprints* [cf. 1 Pet 2: 21], especially [those] of poverty and humility, can, without any doubt, always carry Him spiritually in your chaste and virginal body.[62]

In some intriguing footwork of his own, Armstrong has reinterpreted Clare's advice to Agnes, in the process re-routing Agnes's direction from following Christ's footsteps to following Mary's. It is important to note that in both translations the phrases which have parallels in Scripture have been italicized. The partial italicization in the latter translation of the phrase "so you, too, *by following in* her *footprints*" (cf. 1 Pet 2: 21) indicates, of course, that Armstrong is aware of his substitution of the feminine pronoun "her" for the masculine pronoun "his" present in 1 Peter 2:21, which clearly refers to following Christ's footprints.[63]

What's going on here? In Armstrong's defense, it should be pointed out that the Latin text being translated, *sequens eius vestigia*, could be rendered as either "following his" or "following her footprints" since *eius* is both the feminine and masculine singular possessive pronoun. Translators, whose work rendering texts accessible to a wider audience is too little esteemed, perforce open themselves to criticism since the very nature of their task demands that they interpret the texts they translate. Nor is Armstrong the only translator to interpret Agnes as following Mary in this passage.[64] However, it is clear from all of the above passages of Clare's writings that when she speaks of following the footprints of poverty, or poverty and humility, she is always referring to a following of Christ, just as the pope does when he repeats back to her her request to live without property.[65] This is consistent with Francis of Assisi's own use of the footprints metaphor, which he employs in five different passages in his own writings. On every occasion, Francis is speaking of following Christ's footsteps, and he twice associates this following explicitly with poverty.[66]

Clare's dense use of imagery in the third letter to Agnes as elsewhere in her writings is profound and subtle, but also clear upon careful examination. That the "footprints, especially [those] of poverty and humility" which Clare advises Agnes to follow are those of Jesus is made plain by the fact that earlier in this same letter Clare includes one of her explicit references (discussed above) to "the footprints of the poor and humble Jesus Christ."[67] A few verses later, she states that Agnes, with *humility*, the virtue of faith, and *poverty*, embraces the treasure hidden in the field.[68] Clare further signals Agnes's likeness to God when she calls Agnes God's coworker or assistant (*adiutricem*)[69] and exhorts her to "transform yourself entirely through contemplation into the image of divinity itself."[70]

Elsewhere in her writings, but without using the metaphor of footprints, Clare speaks clearly of "following" (*sequor*) Christ as does Francis in his own writings.[71] She counsels Agnes to "look upon him made contemptible for you and follow him, making yourself contemptible in the world for him."[72] In another letter she expresses her hope that Agnes (*Agna*), "together with the other holy virgins, sing a new song before the throne of God and the Lamb [*Agni*] and follow the Lamb [*Agnum*] wherever he may go."[73]

Moreover, in contrast to Francis's single use of the term *imitatio*, which appears in a variant reading and which Francis employs to refer to the saints,[74] Clare employs the term eight times, a fact made more graphic when one considers that Francis's corpus is at least three times longer than hers, even if we accept all the works attributed to her as authentic.[75] In her second letter to Agnes, Clare calls Agnes an *imitatrix* of God the Father;[76] she advises her friend to copy or imitate the counsel (*consilium imitare*) of the then Minister General Brother Elias,[77] not to imitate any contrary counsel;[78] and finally, to gaze upon, consider, and contemplate Christ, while desiring to imitate him.[79] In her third letter, she refers to Agnes's and the sisters' imitation of Jesus.[80] In the Testament, she refers to Francis as imitator and lover of Christ,[81] who imitates Christ's footprints,[82] and she exhorts her sisters to imitate the simplicity, humility, and poverty taught them by Christ and Francis.[83] Thus, with the exception of the two instances in which she alludes to imitating or copying the human counsel of Elias or others, when Clare speaks of imitation, she always is speaking of the imitation of Christ or, in one case, God the Father. Moreover, she speaks primarily of women carrying out this imitation. In no case does she mention imitation of Mary, female saints, or any other women. And the virtues with which she explicitly associates this imitation are, in descending order of their importance, poverty,[84] humility,[85] and, less prominently, simplicity,[86] charity,[87] and, a concept central to Francis's following of Christ, the passion of Christ.[88]

Finally, elsewhere, using neither the explicit language nor the imagery of *imitatio*, *vestigia*, or "following" alone, Clare communicates that it is Christ after whom she and her sisters are to pattern themselves. For example, in one of the few passages of the Form of Life written in the first person and thus more likely to be her own composition, Clare says to her sisters: "And for love of the most holy and beloved [Christ] child wrapped in poor little swaddling clothes, laid in a manger, and of his most holy mother, I admonish, beg, and exhort my sisters always to wear poor garments."[89] Later, commenting on the fact that the sisters should own nothing, "serving the Lord in poverty and humility," she adds that they are not "to be ashamed, because the Lord made himself poor for us."[90] Numerous examples such as these can be drawn from her writings to highlight Clare's vision that she and her sisters, even while devoted to Mary, should each make herself an *alter Christi*.

There are just two instances in Clare's writings in which Mary is mentioned along with Christ as a model to be followed, both, it should be noted, from texts with a more tenuous connection to Clare. The first appears in the 1253 Form of Life, in another of the few passages written in the first person:

And so that we, and indeed those who will come after us, would never turn away from the most holy poverty with which we had begun, a little before [Francis's] death he again wrote to us his last will, saying: "I little brother Francis wish to follow the life and poverty of our most high Lord Jesus Christ and of his most holy mother, and to persevere therein until the end." And I entreat you, my ladies, and I counsel you to live always in this most holy life and poverty.[91]

In this passage, then, the admonition to follow not only Christ, but also Mary, belongs first to Francis and only secondarily to Clare. The second passage in which both Jesus and Mary are presented as models appears in the more contested Testament. Clare is exhorting her sisters to be faithful to the poverty which she and they have promised to the Lord and to Francis and for which they had received privileges from Pope Innocent III and his successors.

For this reason, with bended knees and deferential spirit, I commend all my present and future sisters . . . to the Lord Cardinal Protector . . . so that, for love for God who lay poor in a manger, lived poor in the world, and remained naked upon the cross, [the Lord Cardinal] always ensure that his little flock observe holy poverty, which the Lord Father begat in the Church by the word and example of our most blessed father Francis who followed the poverty and humility of his beloved Son and his most glorious virgin Mother, and which we promised to the Lord and to our most blessed father Francis.[92]

In this allusion, Mary is an example of poverty and humility along with Christ, but it is Francis who is said to be following the example of Christ and his Mother. For their part, Clare and her sisters are to "observe" (*observari*) the poverty that they promised to the Lord and Francis. And if, even without more explicit reference to following or *imitatio*, it were to be argued that Clare in this passage is dynamically following anyone, it would be Francis. Thus, in keeping with hagiographic depictions of her mentioned earlier in this essay, it is only subsequent to Clare's following of Francis and by virtue of his own imitation that she could be said to be following, at one remove, Christ and his Mother. A structural analysis of this text shows that the example of Mary is at the furthest remove from Clare, separated from her by both Christ and Francis as exemplars to be emulated.[93]

In passages in Clare's writings where Mary does appear, her role is overwhelmingly that of mother, Christ-carrier, and God-birther. This throws important light on Mary's role in the debatable translation from her third letter. In this passage, it is Agnes's following of Christ's footsteps, in his poverty and humility, which secondarily likens her also to Mary, but only insofar as Agnes's virginal body is spiritually analogous to Mary's material body as a receptacle for Christ. Clare makes her meaning clear by setting up various analogies apparent in the letter's structure, language, and imagery. Structurally, Clare first describes Mary's material role; then, speaking generally, she describes the faithful soul's analogous spiritual role; and finally, speaking more particularly, she remarks upon the expression of this spiritual role in the person of Agnes herself. In her language and imagery, note the analogies Clare establishes between Mary's physical "womb" and "lap," which enclose and hold the "Son whom the heavens could not contain," on the one hand, and the "dwelling place" and "throne" for Christ within the faithful soul, on the other hand, which, spiritually speaking, similarly contain the Creator whom "the heavens and the rest of [his] creatures cannot hold." It is Agnes's conformity to Christ's poverty and humility, mentioned earlier in the letter, which then liken her, spiritually, to Mary's material roles as virgin mother, Christ-carrier, and God-birther.

I speak of him, the Most High Son, whom the Virgin bore and after whose birth remained virgin. May you cling to this most sweet mother, who gave birth to a Son whom the heavens could not contain, but whom she nevertheless carried within the small enclosure of her holy womb and held on her girlish lap.

For who would not shudder at the snares of the enemy of humanity, who, by means of the arrogance of transitory things and deceptive glories tries to reduce to nothing that which is greater than heaven? For surely, by the grace of God, it is clear that the soul of the faithful person, the most worthy of [his] creatures, is greater than heaven, since the heavens and the rest of [his] creatures cannot hold the Creator, and the faithful soul alone can be his dwelling place and throne, and this solely because of the charity which the impious lack. [He who is] the truth said, "Whoever loves me is loved by my Father, and I will love him, and unto him we shall come and we shall make our dwelling within him."

Therefore, just as the glorious Virgin of virgins [carried Christ] materially, thus you, following his footprints, especially [those] of humility and poverty, can, without any doubt, always carry [him] spiritually in your chaste and virginal body, containing him in whom you and all things are contained.[94]

Consistent with all her other writings, Clare here advises Agnes to follow Christ's footsteps, a following which will then liken her to Mary in terms of spiritual motherhood.[95]

A collective examination of all the passages in which Clare alludes to Mary powerfully corroborates that for Clare, Mary is first and foremost identified with the related notions of mother, God-birther, and Christ-carrier,[96] then virgin,[97] and finally intercessor.[98] The subordination of Mary's role to Jesus' is also consistent throughout Clare's writings. In her letters, the Form of Life, and the Blessing, Clare never mentions Mary independently of Jesus and always makes her secondary to him.[99] The Form of Life refers to the Marian feast of the Assumption within a list of seven feasts upon which the sisters are to receive communion.[100] Mary is mentioned in the Testament always in conjunction with other holy persons or things, for example, Jesus, St. Francis, the saints, the Church Triumphant and the Church Militant.[101] Mary appears in Clare's writings, but never as a major focus of concern or devotion.

Francis also refers to Mary in numerous passages. Like Clare, he most often describes Mary as mother, God-birther, and Christ-carrier.[102] Along these same lines and serving as important corroborative evidence for understanding Clare's imitation of Mary as limited to her virginal body being a receptacle for Christ, Francis repeatedly alludes to Mary as receptacle of Christ. She is, for Francis, Christ's palace, his tabernacle, his home, his garment.[103] In the words of Thomas of Celano and Bonaventure, Francis "embraced the Mother of Jesus with an inexpressible love because she had made the Lord of Majesty our brother."[104] Alongside this overwhelming emphasis on the related notions of Mary as mother, God-birther, and Christ-carrier, is the equally important epithet "Virgin" which Francis applies to Mary on a dozen occasions.[105] All of these descriptions position Mary in relationship to Christ and secondary to him.[106] In a revealing passage, Francis states that men and women can be the mother of Christ by "carrying him in our heart and our body" and "give birth to him through holy deeds."[107] For Francis, then, as well as Clare, one is like Mary insofar as one carries Christ within oneself.

Thus the evidence within Clare's own writings, which significantly parallels the meanings conveyed in Francis's texts, shows overwhelmingly that Clare understood herself and her sisters to be following Christ's footsteps, conforming their lives to his, in a word, becoming Christlike. Clare gives far less attention to Mary as model, limiting its meaning strictly to carrying Christ spiritually within herself. Although it is beyond the purview of this essay to discuss this point fully, it should also be noted that while Clare speaks of an active *following* of Christ's footprints, the anonymous author of her *Legend* and Pope Alexander both referred to her as *being* the "footprint of the Mother of God," a phrase insinuating imitation, but placing Clare in a passive rather than active role.[108]

Why then do those who write about Clare gradually introduce the notion of Clare as imitator (or imitation) of Mary when everything we know of her own views has her following Christ? Here I propose three likely possibilities regarding the medieval theological context which newly interpreted Mary's role as *mediatrix* between heaven and earth; the difficulty medieval men had in thinking of women, even an extraordinary woman such as Clare, as their spiritual equals in *imitatio Christi* and the ease with which they elided their views of Mary with notions regarding women; and the particular circumstances of the Franciscan order during and after Clare's life.

Theological Context

The pressure to move Clare in line behind Mary receives unambiguous support from the theological context of the high Middle Ages. While Mary held a prominent position in the theology of many fourth- and fifth-century Greek Fathers who stressed her role as the mother of God in their attempts to explain the union of humanity and divinity in Christ, her role remained relatively minor in the western Christian tradition. Although the Council of Ephesus in 431 defined her divine motherhood and solemnly declared her to be *Theotokos*, God-birther, western theologians at the time seldom employed the equivalent Latin term, *Genitrix Dei*, in their discussions of Mary, nor did the western Church witness the proliferation of Marian feasts so evident in the east.[109] Mary's prominence grew gradually in the western Christian tradition: early theologians such as Ambrose (d. 397) and Jerome (d. 419/20) commented on her virginity, for example, and later theologians such as Paschasius Radbertus (d. 865) began to highlight her role as a medium for the communication of grace.[110]

Nevertheless, it was only in the eleventh and twelfth centuries that Mary engaged the passion of western theologians and faithful alike, as attested by the many cathedrals erected in her honor and her prominent place in Christian iconography, literature, drama, homilies, prayers, such as the popular Ave Maria, and theological speculation.[111] Lives of our Lady, accounts of Marian visions, and collections of her miracles conspicuously multiply in both Latin and vernacular versions beginning in about the twelfth century. Devotions to Mary's relics proliferated, ranging from her "sacred tunic" to the very milk from her breasts, sold in the marketplaces of many cities. In both eastern and western Christianity, fashioning new titles for Mary and employing old ones became a kind of growth industry. Titles such as queen of virgins, enclosed garden, silent and humble maid seemed peculiarly suited to the virtues Clare's contemporaries wished to accentuate in their portrayals of her.

Peter Damian (d. 1072), Bernard of Clairvaux (d. 1153), and Richard of St. Victor (d. 1173) are among myriad theologians who reinvigorated the ancient theological parallel drawn between the adversaries Eve and Mary, the Second Eve. In their eyes, it was appropriate that a woman reverse the victory the devil won over the first sinner, the woman, Eve.[112] Whether these theologians helped shape the assumption evident in works about Clare that women are appropriately patterned after women and men after men, or whether they merely reflect the commonly held assumptions of their worlds, we can see how easy it would be for learned churchmen who came after them, the men who wrote about Clare, to mirror the same assumption.

Marian devotion and doctrine at this time are redolent with the theme of *imitatio*. A storm of debates swirled around the question of Mary's immaculate conception: was she, like her son Jesus, conceived in a sinless state by her own parents? She was also considered to be cosufferer and coredemptrix with her son. Her lamentations at Christ's death were celebrated in a new liturgical genre, the *planctus Mariae*; biblical exegetes and devotional writers included dialogues between Mary and her son in which she beseeched him to let her die with him.[113] It was commonly believed that Mary, paralleling Christ's own Ascension, had been bodily assumed into heaven. In popular piety, people even speculated that Mary, like her son, had been resurrected shortly after her death.[114] Yet the question arises: if theologians could devote endless treatises to discussions of Mary's likeness to Christ, then why might some of them tamper, albeit unconsciously, with Clare's own self-presentation as a follower of Christ?

Central to understanding this issue is a characteristic of Mary brought distinctively into relief in this period—her role as *mediatrix*, a title that achieved prominence in the west in the eleventh and twelfth centuries when Mary became commonly identified as well as *Genitrix Dei*. As Bernard of Clairvaux put it, Mary, the *mediatrix*, was "the way through which the Saviour came" to us and also the one "through [whom] we ascend to him who descended to us through [her]." [115] In a famous formulation, he called Mary the "aqueduct" through whom the waters of eternal life flow to us and through whom we can draw close to Christ and the Father. [116] Because the mediator Christ's divinity might intimidate us, Bernard regarded the wholly human Mary to be the mediator par excellence: through her we could communicate with Christ. [117]

This theological formulation of Mary as *mediatrix* is echoed strongly in both learned and popular accounts of the saints' lives in which women, much more than men, are viewed as mediators, channels, or bridges connecting this world with the supernatural world. A review of Italian male and female saints from the period immediately preceding Clare and especially the period following her indicates that holy women were customarily portrayed as conduits. [118] On the physical plane, it is obviously women who bring human life into the world through their own bodies. But spiritually too, holy women were depicted as conduits through whom divine knowledge flowed to humanity. They are called "vessels" far more often than men. Their interior bodies were so intriguing to men both physically and spiritually that in the cases of Clare of Montefalco and Margaret of Città di Castello, the clerics and physicians peering inside the women during embalming found startling physical evidence in the form of the instruments of the crucifixion and stone etchings of the Holy Family of the women's interior connection to the spiritual realm. [119] While the sanctity of men tended to be based more on their "this-worldly" offices and achievements, such as preacher, priest, or learned theologian, holy women's sanctity derived more from their relatively easy access to the other world through visions, locutions, and divinely infused forms of knowledge. It is worth noting that among these same saints Mary, biological mothers, and other women often played pivotal roles in men's conversions. By contrast, female saints tended to accord much less importance to Mary, their biological mothers, or the mediating role of other women. As women themselves, gifted with intuitive visions or other paramystical powers, they had their own access to the other world. This provides one explanation for the more minor role which Clare accords to Mary in her own writings, and the tendency of some of her male interpreters, who viewed Mary and women as *mediatrices* of the divine, to discover parallels between Clare and Mary, despite Clare's assertion that she followed Christ.[120]

Another important facet of the theological context regards the long-standing association of men with spirit, rationality, and even divinity, on the one hand, and women with body, physicality, and humanity, on the other. These associations assume new relevance in the high medieval period, when devotion to Christ began to focus above all on his humanity and suffering physicality. As Caroline Bynum remarks,

Whereas male writers used the traditional dichotomy of male and female to criticize particular women and to differentiate sharply between male and female roles, male and female characteristics, women used the dichotomy differently. To women, the notion of the female as flesh became an argument for women's *imitatio Christi* through physicality. Subsuming the male/female dichotomy into the more cosmic dichotomy divine/human, women saw themselves as the symbol for all humanity.[121]

Bynum's point is consonant with the translation I rendered above regarding Clare's advice to Agnes to follow Christ and become, secondarily, like Mary insofar as Mary's material body was a receptacle for Christ. Bynum notes that "Women's devotion was less to Mary's social or religious role as woman than to her physical role as bearer of humanity." [122]

Christ, Model for Men; Mary, Model for Women

The tendency of some medieval authors to model Clare after Mary rather than Jesus is a subtle and perhaps unconscious effort to reserve Jesus, who is after all God, as the model par excellence for men, leaving women in their appropriately subordinate position. Ecclesiastics and hagiographers devoted to Clare subtly distanced her from Christ and enhanced the spiritual stature of Francis by depicting Clare, more than her own words or life justified, as a follower of Francis who himself was a follower of Jesus. Clare's proximity to Christ is further diminished when, evidence to the contrary from her own writings notwithstanding, she is portrayed as a follower of Mary. While such a description places her in a decidedly exalted position vis-à-vis most women and men, it is still secondary to a following of Christ. Although both Francis and Clare spoke repeatedly of following Christ, hagiographic and iconographic depictions of Francis increasingly emphasized his *imitatio Christi*, while those of Clare diminished her own claims in this regard and enhanced instead the role of Mary as her model. In a telling extension of this same logic, Clare is increasingly proffered as the model par excellence for other women. By the time the well-known Italian treatise *The Considerations on the Holy Stigmata* was composed, sometime between 1370 and 1390, Clare's transformation is plainly apparent. The anonymous author reasons that just as Christ had renewed his life and passion in a man (*uomo*), Francis, through whom many (*molti*) in the world would be drawn to the path of truth and penance, so had "the Mother of Christ promised to renew her virginal purity and humility in a woman (*femmina*), sister Clare, in such fashion that through her example she would snatch many thousands of women (*femmine*) from our hands."[123]

While it is reasonable to assume that Clare would be presented as (and indeed was) a leader and model for her sisters just as Francis was for his friars, there is no reason why her followers should be less encouraged than the friars to pursue the Christian life by imitating Christ, who was God, or even Francis, who was thought by the friars and many others to be the closest copy of God. The assumption that women more aptly follow women than men meant that Clare and her sisters were encouraged, far more than men, to imitate the female and thus subordinate side of the asymmetrical pair, Mary/Jesus, and Clare's sisters and other women were encouraged to follow the lesser side of the asymmetrical pair, Clare/Francis. Such female identification and self-replication, while not surprising, has the logical effect of ensuring that female/male asymmetries continue. It is also by no means peculiar to representations of Clare. Barbara Newman's essay in this book on Hildegard of Bingen and Anne Clark's on Elisabeth of Schönau each point out that, although these women tended to compare themselves to prominent biblical men, their hagiographers stressed their likeness to biblical women.

The Franciscan Context

The tendency to portray Clare as a follower of Mary and women as followers of Clare (and Mary) is probably related to the friars' growing desire, evident even within Clare's own lifetime, to renounce all responsibility and relationship with the female branch of their order.[124] One need only examine the shift in attitudes toward the Poor Ladies apparent in the first two official *vitae* of Francis by Thomas of Celano. Celano composed his first *vita* about 1228–29 around the time of Francis's canonization on July 16,

1228.[125] He drew upon things he himself had heard Francis say in addition to reports from "faithful and trustworthy witnesses."[126] Sometime between 1244 and 1247, Celano composed a second *vita*, this time drawing on information elicited by the General Chapter of 1244, which had invited all the brothers to report anything they knew to be true "concerning the life, signs, and wonders of blessed Francis."[127] While Celano's *Vita prima* may be viewed as a simple and relatively spontaneous attempt by Francis's followers to record his deeds soon after his death and honor him on the occasion of his canonization, the *Vita secunda* represents a more anxious effort to scour the order for those pieces of information about him which were "true" and "reliable" as opposed to so many other views being propagated about Francis in numerous texts circulating within and without what had by then become a deeply divided order.

Clare and her sisters are mentioned but incidentally or not at all in most of these accounts of Francis, a powerful reminder of women's secondary status. Celano refers to them in both his *vitae*, yet there is an unmistakable shift in tone between his *Vita prima* and his *Vita secunda*. In the first *vita*, after narrating how Francis had rebuilt the church of San Damiano, Celano warmly relates how this church later became "the blessed and holy place where" Francis founded "that glorious and most excellent order of poor Ladies and holy virgins" just six years after his conversion. Clare, says Celano, was the "strongest and most precious stone" in the foundation of this structure. He grandiloquently enumerates her many qualities and heaps further extravagant praise upon the order itself, "a noble structure of the most precious pearls" beyond our capacity for understanding and certainly beyond the meager limits of human expression, outstanding in charity, humility, virginity, poverty, silence, patience, and prayer.[128] Later in the *vita*, Celano returns to the subject of Clare and her sisters when he recounts Francis's death and the moving scene in which the saint's coffin was solemnly carried to the church of San Damiano to allow the women to see their beloved father one final time. Poignantly and at length, Celano describes their lamentation and pitiable cries, their struggle to let him go, and the grief this aroused in those observing their leavetaking.[129]

Less than twenty years later, with Clare still alive, Celano composed his second *vita* of Francis. By this time, there was already significant controversy among the friars regarding their obligations to serve as chaplains for and otherwise assist the Poor Ladies, some being strongly committed to Clare, whom they saw as faithful to Francis's ideal, and others strongly opposed. Signs of the struggle are plentiful. A few years before Celano began the *Vita secunda*, the Franciscan Minister General Haymo of Faversham (1240–44) succeeded in convincing Pope Gregory IX to release the friars from any duty to serve the sisters as spiritual directors. Clare vehemently objected. She immediately sent away those friars who assisted her and her sisters in obtaining food. If they had to live without their spiritual "food," then they could certainly forgo material food. Her pointed action convinced the pope to reimpose upon the friars their duty to serve the women spiritually. Events such as these are further elucidated by information regarding specific friars, such as a certain Stephen, who is known to have adamantly opposed any association between the friars and the Poor Ladies and who is thought to have influenced Celano along these same lines.[130]

In this context, it is hardly surprising that Celano's *Vita secunda* simply leaves out the touching scene of Francis's funeral procession pausing at San Damiano to allow Clare and her sisters a final farewell. In fact, Clare is not mentioned a single time by name. Celano gingerly walks a fine line, at one moment acknowledging the intimate ties joining the "poor ladies" with Francis and the friars, and in the next defining strict boundaries between them. He astutely tries to have it both ways. After praising the women's order, he adds that "though their father [Francis] gradually withdrew his bodily presence from them, he nevertheless gave them his affection in the Holy Spirit by caring for them." His care for them, which at first seems to be a crystal-clear offer of service to the women is, once stated, immediately qualified. Francis

firmly promised them and others who would profess poverty in a similar way of life that he would always give them his help and counsel and the help and counsel of his brothers. This he always carried out as long as he lived, and when he was close to death, he emphatically commanded that it should be always so, saying that one and the same spirit had led the brothers and the poor ladies out of the world.

At times the brothers wondered that Francis did not visit the holy servants of Christ with his corporal presence more often, and he would say: "Do not believe, dearest brothers, that I do not love them perfectly. For if it were a fault to cherish them in Christ, would it not have been a greater fault to have united them to Christ? Indeed, not to have called them would not have been a wrong; not to care for them once they have been called would be the greatest unkindness. But I give you an example, that as I have done to you, so you also should do. I do not want anyone to offer himself of his own accord to visit them, but I command that unwilling and most reluctant brothers be appointed to take care of them."[131]

The import of this studied ambiguity is clinched in Celano's next two passages. The first recounts several incidents illustrating Francis's objections to friars visiting female monasteries.[132] It is possible that the strictures Celano here places in Francis's mouth reflect certain indiscretions committed by some of the friars in the years since their founder's death. But it is notable that no distinction is made between the strictly cloistered women of San Damiano, for whom no evidence of any indiscretions survives, and any of the (in any case) few other nuns who might possibly have had irregular contacts with any friars. The second passage relates the well-known story in which Francis, forced against his will by his vicar to preach to the Poor Ladies, goes and instead sprinkles himself with ashes to teach them

that they should regard themselves as ashes and that there was nothing in his heart concerning them but what was fitting this consideration. This was the way he acted toward these holy women; his visits to them were very useful, but they were forced upon him and rare. And this was his will for all his brothers: he wanted them to serve these women in such a way for Christ, whom they serve, that like them that have wings they would always guard against the snare laid out for them.[133]

At the most obvious level of interpretation, Francis is simply preaching penance by doing penance. The stern ending of the episode, however, and especially its location at the conclusion of a series of passages warning of women's dangers, subtly suggests a darker interpretation, an inextricable association between women and the need for penance—penance for men so easily ensnared when they attend to women and penance for women who are, by virtue of their sex, part and parcel of that very snare.

This characterization of the Poor Ladies as potential temptresses is consistent with other comments in the *Vita secunda* regarding Francis and women, passages which betray a harsh misogynism absent in the *Vita prima*. Celano's newly misogynistic Francis, for example, considered "familiarities with women" "a honeyed poison . . . which lead astray even holy men." He told the friars that "avoiding contagion from association with [women] . . . was as easy as walking in a fire without having the soles of one's feet burned." Women were so unwelcome to Francis that, says Celano, "you would think that his caution was not a warning or an example but rather a dread or a horror."[134]

The shift in attitude toward Clare and her sisters so patently evident in comparing these two *vitae* by the same author appears in later Franciscan history and writing as well. In 1260, just a few years after her canonization, Pope Alexander IV rebuked a friar for publicly preaching against Clare's cult.[135] Venerated by the papacy and the citizens of Assisi, Clare received scant recognition in Franciscan sources after the generalate of Bonaventure

(1257–74).[136] Given the desire of so many friars to minimize their obligations to the Poor Ladies, Franciscan writers had good reason to characterize them as temptresses and to downplay Clare's importance. Wittingly or
not, they minimized her role by depicting her less as a follower of Christ
(which following put her on a par with their founder Francis) or even as his
follower, and more as an imitator of Mary and an apt model for imitation
by other women. Such distinctions maintained the men and the women in
fully discrete categories, the way most friars seemed to want it.

Iconography

Early iconographic depictions of Clare confirm both the growing tendency among her interpreters to identify her with Mary and also the friars'
increasing reluctance to be associated with the Poor Ladies. The only surviving thirteenth-century narrative depiction of her life, the famous Santa
Chiara Dossal of 1283, depicts Clare and Francis together and also includes
a scene depicting the miracle where she multiplies bread, a scene likening
her to Christ.[137] The nuns of Clare's community likely wanted the two
saints to appear together on the dossal to affirm the connection of Clare's
order to Francis and the friars. As Jeryldene Wood notes, it served as a
visual rebuke to the friars who wished to repudiate the women.[138] By the
early fourteenth century, various depictions of Clare were associating her
clearly with Mary. In the painting by Pietro Lorenzetti (d. 1348), Clare
stands beneath Mary at the foot of the cross, with Francis positioned beneath John the Evangelist who, according to Franciscan tradition, prophesied Francis's stigmata.[139] In the vault above the high altar of the church
of Santa Chiara in Assisi, Clare is depicted alongside Mary in one of four
quadrants of eight female saints.[140] In yet another early fourteenth-century
work, this one commissioned, significantly, for a house of her own followers, Clare's death is likened to Christ's, Mary's, and Francis's.[141]

Indeed, it is notable that the thirteenth-century images which do survive of Clare, including those which depict her together with Francis,
appear to have been commissioned largely by houses of her own followers.[142] The friars' churches, in contrast, are virtually bereft of images of
Clare. Clare does not appear once in any of the scenes in the ten histori-
ated panels dedicated to Saint Francis. In the few images where she does
appear, her importance derives not from any suggestion that she herself
was a great follower of Francis or saint of the Franciscan order, but from

5

Inside Out

Beatrice of Nazareth and
Her Hagiographer

Amy Hollywood

IN A DISCUSSION of ritual, the anthropologist Talal Asad argues that *The Rule of Benedict* and other medieval texts offer evidence that within medieval European Christian culture, rituals were not expressive or symbolic of some other reality, but rather were the "apt performance of what is prescribed, something that depends on intellectual and practical disciplines but does not itself require decoding."[1] According to Asad, it is a mistake of modern western intellectualist traditions to assume that belief precedes practice; rather, following Marcel Mauss and Pierre Bourdieu, Asad argues that bodily practices inculcate belief. The body, according to this view, is the material site of enculturation. Mauss introduces the term *habitus* to designate the embodied set of dispositions, learned and internalized through bodily practices and constitutive of the subject.[2] The *habitus*, according to Bourdieu, is "history turned into nature,"[3] the site on and in which ideologies constitute subjects.[4] The result of this theoretical insight is the claim, made by Mauss and Asad, that a crisis of belief may be best understood as "a function of untaught bodies."[5]

Sarah Beckwith demonstrates the importance of the *habitus* and theories of bodily practice for materialist feminist analysis. In an important essay on the *Ancrene Wisse* and its prescriptions for female bodies and subjects, she expands the theoretical claims made by Mauss, Bourdieu, and Asad and at the same time takes issue with some contemporary feminists' idealized association of women with "the body":

although women have historically borne the burden of representing immanence for others, that does not give them privileged access to the body as a "woman's symbol," for women do not have particular forms of representation that are exclusively their own, but only particular relations to cultural representations and discourse.[6]

In the essay, Beckwith analyzes the anchorite's relationship to her own body, through enclosure and penitential practice, and to the suffering body of Christ, through discursive and imaginary meditations. She argues that the anchorite's rule creates a particular form of interiority through the prescription and enactment of a precise set of bodily and discursive practices. Her reading offers a convincing account of the ways in which the *Ancrene Wisse* prescribes practices formative of the subjectivity of those whose lives are governed by it. She expands on the work of anthropologists and sociologists like Mauss and Asad by making use of psychoanalysis to articulate the process through which an imaginary bodily ego, experienced in a fantasmatic identification with the suffering Christ, is the interior result of bodily practices and meditations.[7]

Beckwith's work offers an important corrective to easy assimilations of women and bodiliness within medieval texts and contemporary theory, for she demonstrates the complex workings of culture and power structures in the formation of women's subjectivities and their experiences of themselves as suffering bodies.[8] I will return to this analysis below, demonstrating its usefulness in thinking about medieval women's texts. Yet an immediate problem presents itself: Beckwith's primary source for her analysis is a rule written for women by a male cleric. Although she distinguishes between "the life imagined" and that "lived in the anchorite cell," Beckwith assumes the compliance of the text's female audience.[9] I will argue here that we cannot take male-authored texts as our primary source of information for women's "relations to cultural representations and discourse," particularly when writings by women are available to us.[10] Moreover, some of these women-authored texts suggest studied resistance to the forms of female religiosity and subjectivity prescribed for them within male-authored texts. This resistance centers around the suffering body and the interplay of interiority and exteriority within religious life.

Here I will briefly follow out the logic of these theoretical arguments as they can be seen in one medieval hagiography, *The Life of Beatrice of Nazareth*. It offers a particularly apt place in which to study the relationship between exteriority and interiority in women's religious life and practice because these are the governing metaphors of the text. In addition, *The Life of Beatrice* offers an excellent opening to the question of the relationship between men's prescriptions for women and women's self-understanding, for we possess not only the *vita*, but also at least a portion of Beatrice's own vernacular writing on which the hagiographer claims to base his account. What emerges is a surprising picture of the differences between the way one medieval woman describes the life of a loving soul and the way her life and texts are read by one of her male contemporaries, a picture that calls into question many twentieth-century assumptions about medieval women's religious belief and practice.[11] Genre and gender both shape these differences. Beatrice's hagiographer describes her life in ways easily assimilated to twentieth-century theories of bodily practice and dispositions. Beatrice's text, however, challenges not only the picture of her life presented in *The Life of Beatrice*, but also contemporary theoretical accounts of the relationship between interiority and exteriority, soul and body, belief and practice.

*   *   *

Beatrice of Nazareth (1200–1268) spent most of her life in one or another of the three Cistercian monasteries founded by her father; within these houses she assiduously followed *The Rule of Benedict*, copied book manuscripts, prayed, meditated, studied, and later served as prioress. She also wrote religious works in the vernacular, although only a short treatise, "Seven Manners of Loving God," survives.[12] The external events of Beatrice's life, then, were unexceptional. Yet the treatise suggests that her inner life boiled and teemed with waves of violent love and insane desire. Within the religious world of thirteenth-century Northern Europe, at least some people revered the ecstatic experiences described by Beatrice in her treatise and understood them as marks of extreme sanctity.[13] We can speculate that such a reputation for sanctity led the abbess of the monastery at Nazareth, or someone else close to Beatrice, shortly after her death, to commission a book about her life. The hagiographer had at his disposal Beatrice's own "book"; in fact he claims that *The Life of Beatrice* is merely a translation of Beatrice's work into Latin.[14] Only for the account of Beatrice's death does he acknowledge that he must turn to the evidence of other "reliable people," including Beatrice's sister Catherine.[15] Yet despite the excellence of his primary sources, Beatrice's hagiographer found his task challenging. The problem posed by Beatrice's life (and presumably her book) was how to write a hagiographical narrative about a woman whose life and writing present little evidence of those practices marked as holy within medieval hagiographical literature—heroic or radical asceticism, extraordinary acts of charity, miracles or healings—and only scant evidence of the visions and otherworldly journeys central to thirteenth-century "mystical" hagiographies.[16]

Beatrice's hagiographer never acknowledges this problem in the blunt terms in which I have posed it here. It can be deduced, however, from an examination of the *The Life of Beatrice* itself, from a comparison of the *vita* with Beatrice's own writing, and from certain suggestions made by the hagiographer about the ways in which his text may pose difficulties for the reader accustomed to more traditional hagiographical works. So, simply looking at the *vita*, the reader is immediately struck that there are only sparse details about Beatrice's asceticism, no corporal miracle accounts, and little evidence of visionary experience. The problem faced by Beatrice's hagiographer and his solution to that problem are made even more apparent, however, when we compare Book III, Chapter 14 with its source text, "Seven Manners of Loving God." As I will show, whereas the hagiographer's summary of Beatrice's life is filled with bodily illness, paramystical phenomena, and ecstatic experience, "Seven Manners of Loving God" is intent on the mad love of the soul and her ecstatic union with love, who is God.

Before examining these two texts in more detail, however, we should note that Beatrice's hagiographer does come close to an explicit statement of his problem late in the book:

Others may perhaps wonder at the miracles worked by signs and acts of power so copiously and superabundantly by the saints of old. They may wonder at the demons chased out of those possessed, the corpses raised to life, and many other things like these or greater than these. The Lord said of these in the Gospel: "He that believes in me shall also do the works that I do, and greater than these shall he do." Yet, with all due reverence to the saints, I prefer Beatrice's love to many miracles and signs, of which it is said elsewhere: "Signs are given not to believers, but to unbelievers," especially since many arrive at the kingdom of heaven without signs.[17]

And, he continues, no one will come to the kingdom of heaven without love. Although Beatrice's life may be lacking in corporal miracles such as healings, exorcisms, and resuscitations, it abounds with spiritual miracles comparable to those of the biblical prophets.[18] Under pressure from expectations for remarkable signs of Beatrice's holiness, her biographer consistently translates her internally felt experience into external, visible markings on the body of the saint. Yet Beatrice describes the spiritual life, as we will see, as occurring interiorly and with no mention of visible manifestations.

The Prologue introduces the central metaphorical structure governing the *vita* as a whole and that through which the hagiographer solves his dilemma. Beatrice's life will be seen as a complex and often ambiguous interplay of exteriority and interiority, hiddenness and manifestation, darkness and light. The hagiographer uses the topos of humility to explain the seemingly hidden nature of her virtues and sanctity, while at the same time exposing them to the light for the edification of his readers. Moreover, he ascribes this double movement to Beatrice herself:

The Lord says in the Gospel: "Take heed that you do not do your justice before men, to be seen by them," and again elsewhere: "So let your light shine before men, that they may see your good works, and glorify your Father who is in heaven." Beatrice so combined in one obedience the seeming discrepancies of these two precepts of the Lord that she foiled the strategies of the ancient enemy by first hiding her secret carefully within herself, and then bequeathing it for her neighbors' needs by bringing it forth openly in due time.[19]

Here the biographer refers to Beatrice's decision, toward the end of her life, to make known the book in which she describes the seven manners of the loving soul and, presumably, other teachings since lost. Yet he also suggests a way of understanding his externalization of the soul's experience, a movement that governs the *vita* as a whole. Throughout, he will bring forth that which Beatrice harbors and hides within. He will do this by describing Beatrice's body as bearing the marks of her interior life.

The Life of Beatrice is divided into three parts, describing Beatrice's initiation into the religious life, her progress in the virtues, and her life in perfection. The early sections of the book lend themselves well to the kind of analysis of bodily practices and their role in the formation of the subject made by Asad and Beckwith. The hagiographer's account of Beatrice's external penitential practices is stereotypical and comprises only three of the *vita*'s fifty-four chapters. Moreover, much of the description of Beatrice's ascetic practice is almost identical to that found in the life of the male Cistercian, Arnulph.[20] This becomes particularly interesting given the tendency in contemporary scholarship on medieval women to associate them with intense ascetic activity, for the hagiographer's borrowing from another text for this element of the *vita* suggests Beatrice herself did not write about ascetic practice.[21] In fact, medieval women's writing before the fourteenth century tends not to include accounts of ascetic practice.[22] As I have argued elsewhere, contemporary accounts of medieval women's ascetic practice may tell us more about how medieval men understood women's sanctity than about medieval women themselves.[23]

Much more crucial for an understanding of the way in which the *vita* depicts bodily practices as formative of the self are its detailed descriptions of Beatrice's spiritual exercises, particularly her use of devotional images and meditational practices. These exercises center on the cross, unlike Beatrice's treatise in which Christ is named explicitly on only one occasion and the cross appears only obliquely. The *vita* insists that it is the ordering of her spiritual life through meditational practice that leads Beatrice to experience the presence of God. This is apparent in the ordering of the narrative; the hagiographer first discusses the external life, then spends three chapters on the ordering and exercise of meditations, her profession into the religious life with its monastic regulation, and her friendship with Ida of Nivelles. Ida prays that Beatrice might receive special grace and has visions promising this grace to Beatrice. Only after this textual preparation, implying Beatrice's preparation through corporal and spiritual exercises, does the hagiographer describe her first rapture. That rapture, moreover, occurs during compline; Beatrice first "quieted herself" and "with a great effort . . . raised her heart to the Lord," meditating on the text of the antiphon. She raised herself up, through meditation, to the Father's presence and only then did "she immediately leap up there, seized in an ecstasy of mind."[24] Without preparation through spiritual exercise, the hagiographer clearly implies, Beatrice would never come to experience the presence of God and absorption into divine love.

After describing this first rapture, the hagiographer returns to Beatrice's spiritual exercises, emphasizing their importance for her continued pursuit of union with God. Late in Book I, the hagiographer describes methods Beatrice uses against forgetfulness.

Day and night she wore on her breast a wooden cross, about a palm in length, tightly tied with a knotted string. On it was written the Lord's passion, the horror of the last judgment, the severity of the judge and other things she wanted always to keep in mind. Besides this she also carried tied to her arm another image of the Lord's cross painted on a piece of parchment. She had a third, painted on a piece of wood, set before her when she was writing, so that wherever she went, or whatever exterior work she did, all forgetfulness would be banished, and by means of the image of the cross she would keep [firmly] impressed on her heart and memory whatever she feared to lose.[25]

The subsequent chapter describes Beatrice's habit of prostrating herself before "the feet of the crucified Lord, before his image"[26] whenever troubled inwardly by harmful thoughts or misfortunes. Eventually the presence of external reminders becomes unnecessary:

Thereafter for about five unbroken years she had the mental image of the Lord's passion so firmly impressed in her memory that she scarcely ever quit this sweet meditation, but clung from the bottom of her heart with wonderful devotion to everything he deigned to suffer for the salvation of the human race.[27]

The external practice of prostration before images and meditation on them leads to their internal appropriation and the transformation of the self. By the end of the *vita*, Beatrice no longer carries images of Christ, or even sees them continually in her mind's eye, but has herself become the image of Christ on earth for others.[28]

Not only does the hagiographer demonstrate the ways in which exterior practices elicit internal experience, he also consistently portrays these interior experiences as marking themselves externally on Beatrice's body and in her behavior.

Therefore it frequently happened that, whether she willed it or not, her interior jubilation of mind would break out in some manifestation, and the mind's inner jubilation would betray itself outwardly either in laughing or dancing a gesture or some other sign.[29]

Throughout the text tears, fainting spells, trancelike states, laughing, and dancing are the external manifestations of Beatrice's internal state.[30] She is frequently depicted as attempting to hide these external signs from her companions,[31] or feigning illness as a mask for her inner jubilation.[32] At other times, illness is itself described as a sign of her interior state.[33]

Throughout the text, the hagiographer simultaneously marks and blurs the distinction between interior and exterior introduced in the preface. He seems both to require the language of interiority and its subversion through the externalizing of Beatrice's spiritual state. It is as if he cannot adequately express the nature of her interiority without reference to her body. Once again, the hagiographer ascribes this problem to Beatrice herself:

Even if she could not explain in words what and how much spiritual delight she received, or what she sensed and tasted in this melting, it was to some extent apparent outwardly by the fainting of her bodily senses.[34]

The claim seems plausible and yet attention to the divergences between Beatrice's treatise and the *vita*'s translation of that text raise questions about whether the hagiographer is here describing a dilemma faced by Beatrice herself, or rather one that challenged him in his attempt to fit her life and work into prevailing hagiographical and theological patterns.

The interplay between interiority and exteriority also runs through the imagery of the *vita*, particularly when describing Beatrice's meditational practice. Here the hagiographer stresses her use of traditional images of enclosure and the maintaining of boundaries between inner and outer.[35] Beatrice compares the soul to a monastery and to an enclosed garden, emphasizing the virtues that keep guard over the boundaries between the monastery or garden and the world.[36] Just as the religious woman must guard against bad thoughts and desires entering into the soul, so the monastery is an enclosed space whose boundaries are carefully guarded. In both instances, boundaries must be maintained for holiness to be achieved.[37] Yet the language of enclosure also appears negatively, for life in the body is described as a prison (in the one metaphor also found in Beatrice's treatise), suggesting the desire for escape from the rigid enclosures in which she lives.[38] This desire—the desire for death and the complete absorption of the soul into Love—is crucial to the seventh manner of loving and the point on which the hagiographer most starkly diverges from Beatrice's text.

The externalizing and somatizing movement evident throughout *The Life of Beatrice* reaches its greatest intensity in Book III, in which the hagiographer describes Beatrice's life of perfection. After describing the founding of Nazareth, the hagiographer's attempt to find a narrative pattern in Beatrice's life breaks down and he devotes some miscellaneous chapters to her spiritual teachings. Although only the source for Chapter 14 remains, I suspect that treatises similar to "Seven Manners of Loving God" lie behind these other chapters. In each, we find suggestions of complex spiritual teachings combined with somatic and visionary phenomena. As with the *vita* as a whole, I think these passages must be read through what we learn in reading Book III, Chapter 14 against its vernacular source text.

Beatrice's hagiographer, coming to the close of the book, ends with an account of the love she had for God and the love she had for her neighbor. He uses "Seven Manners of Loving God" as a way of discussing Beatrice's love for God and at the same time as a way of recapitulating the narrative of her life that he has just provided for the reader. His translation, then, bears the marks of the emphases and themes that he has made central to that life—the interplay of interiority and exteriority, Beatrice's desire for a shortcut to perfection in her attempt to return to that state in which she was before she was created, the tension between the enormity of what she owes to God and her bodily ability to repay him, her desire for self-knowledge (understood as humility), and her desire for death. Comparing the *vita* and the treatise makes clear, however, the way these themes and the particular readings of them given by Beatrice's hagiographer diverge from Beatrice's own theological and mystical views.

The hagiographer immediately alters the treatise in that he assumes the soul about whom Beatrice speaks is her own.

Treatise: There are seven manners of loving, which come down from the heights and go back again far above.[39]

Vita: These then are the seven degrees or stages of love, seven in number, through which she deserved to come to her beloved, not at an even pace, but now as if walking on foot, now running swiftly, and sometimes even flying nimbly on agile wings.[40]

Beatrice writes in an impersonal third person voice. Her text, while impassioned, is impersonal, distanced, and generalized in its narrative structures. The movement described is that of the soul and of the divine; at times it becomes impossible to distinguish between the soul's love for God and God as love, marking the absorption of the soul into the divine. The hagiographer personalizes and particularizes Beatrice's general description of the relationship between the divine and the loving soul.

Despite the hagiographer's translation, Beatrice's vernacular treatise does not recount degrees or stages so much as different manners of loving, manners with often scarcely apprehensible differences.[41] At issue for Beatrice is the continual movement of presence and absence between the soul and God, a movement that parallels that between the Lover and the Beloved in the Song of Songs. In learning to acquiese to this oscillation, the soul comes to experience a deepening sense of the divine love and presence. The soul is no longer the bride or beloved, but rather the housewife of God,[42] one whose life is marked, not by a dialectic of ecstasy and despair, but by a steady sense of the underlying presence of God in reality.[43] Yet this moment of quiet, which is the apparent apex of the spiritual life on earth, is only the sixth manner of loving. It too is followed by a return of mad love and the soul's desire to be fully absorbed into God, a desire that can only be fulfilled with death. In personalizing and somatizing the seven stages of loving, the hagiographer subtly alters this mystical path. Moreover, in making the madness of love a bodily experience, the desire for death becomes a movement toward death, one whose extremity causes difficulties for the hagiographer and leads to his most obvious abridgements of Beatrice's text.

The first manner of loving is an active longing, in which the soul, according to Beatrice, desires "to keep the purity and the nobility and the freedom in which it was made by its Creator, in His image and likeness."[44] The hagiographer interprets this in terms of ascetic practices, describing how through "corporal exercises" (*corporalibus exercitiis*) she sought "to obtain that liberty of spirit we mentioned."[45] For Beatrice the soul's desire is too great to be fulfilled by any creature. Again the hagiographer reads this in terms of the weakness of the flesh, hence clarifying the need for corporal exercises. Yet all of this is absent from Beatrice's text. A similar corporalizing movement occurs when the hagiographer describes Beatrice's desire for self-knowledge. For the loving soul, this entails a recognition of its essential nature as one with divine love. For the hagiographer, on the other hand, the intense self-scrutiny demanded by love leads Beatrice to "bodily languors" (perhaps better, illnesses) by which she was "so weighed down . . . that she thought death was near."[46]

The humility of the second manner of loving, which desires to serve all most faithfully, is portrayed by the hagiographer in terms of Beatrice's life of service and humility in the convent.[47] As in the first manner, then, the hagiographer attempts to read Beatrice's life itself as an enactment of the mystical journey described in her treatise. He also makes subtle shifts in Beatrice's theological arguments. According to Beatrice the soul desires to serve God for nothing, asking for no answer, no grace, and no glory. The hagiographer keeps the metaphors of Beatrice's text and yet includes a long section, not in the treatise, describing the rewards God gives her for her service. Moreover, he goes on to describe the third manner of loving as a desire to "repay, through loving service, the love which God is,"[48] whereas Beatrice's language speaks of the soul's desire to satisfy love. Fear plays a crucial role in Beatrice's actions within the *vita*; Beatrice herself insists that the loving soul knows nothing of fear and acts only out of love for love.

As in other sections of the *vita*, the personalization of Beatrice's text involves an externalization of the mystical. This becomes further apparent in the fourth manner of loving. Beatrice describes a passing away of the body, making use of a mystical commonplace to express the overwhelming nature of love's presence to the soul. The hagiographer takes this mystical commonplace and transforms it into a bodily expression.

Treatise: When the soul feels itself to be thus filled full of riches and in such fullness of heart, the spirit sinks away down into love, the body passes away, the heart melts, every faculty fails; and the soul is so utterly conquered by love that often it cannot support itself, often the limbs and the senses lose their powers. And just as a vessel filled up to the brim will run over and spill if it is touched, so at times the soul is so touched and overpowered by this great fullness of the heart that in spite of itself it spills and overflows.[49]

Vita: In this stage the holy woman's affection was so tender that she was often soaked with the flood of tears from her melted heart, and sometimes because of the excessive abundance of spiritual delight, she lay languishing and sick in bed, deprived of all her strength. . . . Just as a vessel filled with liquid spills what it contains when it is only slightly pushed, so it happened frequently that Beatrice, pushed as it were, would let spill out by many signs of holy love what she felt inside; or else she would undergo a kind of paralyzed trembling, or would be burdened with some other discomfort of languor [illness].[50]

What Beatrice describes from the inside is transposed by the hagiographer into external and visible form, making use of the commonplaces and topoi of hagiography to facilitate his translation. Beatrice describes the passing away of the body's faculties in the soul's ecstasy; the hagiographer underlines the *signs* on the body that such an experience is occurring. The state of the soul is made manifest in the body, in its tears, weaknesses, and illnesses in the face of intense spiritual experience.

A similar externalization of the bodily aspects of Beatrice's text can be seen in descriptions of the fifth stage, in which her writing achieves an intensity and fervor meant to evoke the madness and violence of love. The strength of divine love is felt in both body and soul, the lines between the two becoming increasingly difficult to decipher.

Treatise: And at times love becomes so boundless and so overflowing in the soul, when it itself is so mightily and violently moved in the heart, that it seems (*dunct*) to the soul that the heart is wounded again and again, and that these wounds increase every day in bitter pain and in fresh intensity. It seems (*dunct*) to the soul that the veins are bursting, the blood spilling, the marrow withering, the bones softening, the bosom burning, the throat parching, so that her visage and her body in its every part feels this inward (*van binnen*) heat, and this is the fever of love.[51]

While Beatrice uses bodily metaphors to express the intensity of her experience, its significance, and its divine referent, the hagiographer focuses on the sensibly marked body.[52]

Vita: Indeed her heart, deprived of strength by this invasion, often gave off a sound like that of a shattering vessel, while she both felt the same and heard it exteriorly. Also the blood diffused through her bodily members boiled over through her open veins. Her bones contracted and the marrow disappeared; the dryness of her chest produced hoarseness of throat. And to make a long story short, the very fervor of her holy longing and love blazed up as a fire in all her bodily members, making her perceptibly (*sensibiliter*) hot in a wondrous way.[53]

In the hagiographer's account, Beatrice possesses a divinely marked body, uncommonly like those found in the hagiographies of other medieval women. Beatrice's enlarged heart and open veins, moreover, are found elsewhere in the *vita*, suggesting the influence of the treatise's metaphors on the text as a whole.[54]

For the hagiographer, Beatrice's body is the visible site of her sanctity—it suffers, weeps, groans, grows hot and glows, in its progression from the first aspirations toward divine love and the final achievement of union with that God who is love. Just as external practices shape the self, these internal transformations must manifest themselves externally. Throughout the *vita* the body and the soul are portrayed as mirroring each other; yet the violence of Beatrice's spiritual exercises and the manifestations of her soul's ecstasy make this reciprocity between body and soul also appear as a conflict. A struggle exists in Beatrice's own text, but in a different place and with different repercussions. The struggle of or with the body does not provide the content or enactment (perhaps more graphically, the picture) of the ascent to God. For Beatrice in the treatise, the interplay of God's presence and absence is internally experienced and described, thus providing a depiction of the soul's movement toward God. Only in the seventh manner of loving, when the soul desires death, does the body become a force with which the soul must contend, for the body now is named as a constraining prison that keeps the soul from immersion in the divine. In the earlier manners, Beatrice uses bodily language to convey her suffering; yet the hagiographer needs a more graphic, objectively apprehensible means of conveying her sanctity to the reader. He focuses attention on the *visible* body and its markings, for only through Beatrice's wounded body can the divine presence be seen.[55]

According to Beatrice, when the soul has passed through the six manners of loving, having become love itself and returned to her own nature, which is love, she laments her misery on this earth and desires to be freed from the body. Yet this very sorrow, and the internally experienced fissuring of the body that her desire brings about, becomes a part of the union between the soul and God. The hagiographer, although emphasizing the suffering body in his rendition of Beatrice's text, feels called on to soften her expressions of desire and their vehemence. He both literalizes and fears the audacity of Beatrice's desire to be with God.

Vita: The vehemence of this desire was so excessive that she sometimes thought she would lose her mind for its grievousness, or would shorten the days of her life because of her anguish of heart and great damage to her vital bodily organs.[56]

Fearing for her health, the hagiographer tells us, Beatrice avoided thinking about heaven and her future bliss when such thoughts affected her body in this way. Again, Chapter 14's recapitulation of the *vita* clarifies central issues in the text, for the hagiographer has struggled with Beatrice's desire for death since Book II, Chapter 16, when the theme is first introduced. For the hagiographer, this desire is an affliction that he wishes to depict Beatrice as overcoming. Yet despite his claims to resolution the desire continually recurs.[57]

For Beatrice, the desire for death and its attendant *internally* experienced suffering are central to the movement of ascent to the divine.

Treatise: So the soul refuses every consolation, often from God himself and from his creatures, for every consolation which could come to it only strengthens its love and draws it up towards a higher life; and this renews the soul's longing to live in love and to delight in love, its determination to live uncomforted in this present misery. And so there is no gift which can appease or comfort it, for the soul's one need is to be in the presence of its love.[58]

This portion of the text is not included in the *vita*, the hagiographer having lost the meaning of the treatise at this point; he writes that Beatrice's experiences "can be conceived only by [mental] experience, not by a flood of words."[59] His literalizing tendencies make it impossible, theologically and narratively, to follow Beatrice in the soul's mad desire for death. As for her contemporaries Hadewijch, Mechthild of Magdeburg, and Marguerite Porete, for Beatrice the will is the locus of the conflict that leads to the experience of union and exile. The body is not the focus of battle, nor is it said to be externally marked by this struggle (either through ascetic practices, tears, illnesses, fevers, or paramystical phenomena), but the internal disposition of the will and affections. Thus the desire for death does not threaten death directly, as it does within the hagiography, in which internal dispositions threaten literally to tear Beatrice's body apart.

Hagiography tends to represent the internal disposition of the soul through external narrative devices. This becomes most pronounced in texts describing women's lives.[60] Various factors might contribute to the greater emphasis on the mystically marked body in hagiographies of holy women. In the Middle Ages women are identified with the body, and this identification seems to demand that their sanctification occur in and through that body.[61] Furthermore, women's access to religious authority was, in the thirteenth century, primarily (if not solely) through visionary/auditory/sensory spiritual and mystical experience.[62] Linked to embodiment through its ties to the imagination and often described using bodily images and metaphors, such visionary and auditory experience was also at times described in terms of its interiorly apprehended effects on the bodily experience of the holy woman. Yet the medieval hagiographer wanted externally sensible *signs* of such experience in order to verify the claims to sanctity of the woman saint. This is provided by a transposition of her accounts of internal experience to the externally visible body. The visionary woman becomes a vision, a divinely marked body, a spectacle for the viewing pleasure of her contemporaries.[63] For this reason, the internal mystical life of Beatrice is transformed into a series of bodily practices and struggles, of battles represented and enacted on the body of the holy woman.

Caroline Walker Bynum suggests a slightly different explanation for the fluidity of interiority and exteriority within medieval texts, arguing that hagiography's externalization of mystical experience is both understandable and unexceptional.

It is exactly because mystics experienced God with more than intellect, and felt comfortable using sensual language to express the experience, that they and their hagiographers sometimes differed over whether a vision was seen with the eyes of the body or the eyes of the mind. An inner, glorious, wordless moment, described in highly affective language to a sister or a confessor, easily became a vision or an apparition or a miracle as it was retold by one excited hearer after another.[64]

This argument fits well with the theoretical claims made by Mauss, Bourdieu, Asad, and Beckwith about the relationship between bodily practices and interior dispositions. For these theorists the fluidity between internal and external experience marks an implicit recognition of the role bodily practices play in the development of interiority and a refusal—on the basis of this relationship—to give priority to one over the other. Yet if distinctions between external and internal are so fluid in the medieval period, why are certain forms of exteriority so persistently highlighted within medieval texts about women? And why does Beatrice insist on the interiority of that which she sees, hears, and tastes and on the spiritual nature of her absorption into the divine? What is at stake for Beatrice in insisting on this interiority against the externalizing tendencies of hagiography, with which she was no doubt familiar?

These questions become even more pressing when we recall what is absent from Beatrice's text. Her hagiographer stresses the role of external practices in the formation of a sanctified subjectivity. Beatrice does not mention ascetic practices or spiritual exercises, such as the use of texts, images, and meditational practices so crucial to the picture of her development given in the *vita*. Her work is similar to that of other medieval women's texts, particularly her beguine contemporaries. Mechthild of Madgeburg, for example, describes her first "greeting from God" as coming unbidden and without any special preparation.[65] In part sparked by a desire to emphasize the freedom of God's gift to the soul, the refusal to discuss the "works" of the body and the soul also highlights human freedom.

Yet according to modern theories—and it would seem some medieval texts—through bodily practices dispositions are literally incorporated; in the process, bodies in practice and in contact with the world construct interiority. Contemporary psychoanalytic accounts of the construction of interiority through bodily practices and intersubjective relations may help explain the emphasis on interiority—and in particular on suffering interiority—found within Beatrice's treatise. Freud argues that the ego itself is primarily a bodily ego, an imaginary construct in which the limits and boundaries of the body are defined through its experiences of pleasure and—most crucially for Freud—pain: "pain seems to play a part in the process, and the way in which we gain new knowledge of our organs during painful illness is perhaps a model of the way by which in general we arrive at the idea of our own body."[66] Our subjectivities are constructed by bodily practices and by the body's experience when it encounters the world, with pain taking a preeminent role in the formation of the bodily ego and hence of subjectivity. Phenomenologists also argue that we become most conscious of ourselves as embodied beings through those experiences in which corporeality intrudes itself on our attention—experiences predominantly of limitation and suffering.[67] The tendency toward the formation of subjectivity out of suffering bodily experience is heightened within medieval Christianity with its emphasis on the suffering body of Christ, often culturally associated with femaleness.[68]

Our bodily egos are formed not only through bodily practice but also through other processes of identification. For the psychoanalyst Jacques Lacan, the mirror stage describes that moment when the subject is formed through its recognition of itself in an external image (the image of a unified body in the mirror, for example, or the recognition of the child's subjectivity seen reflected in the face of the mother).[69] Lacan's theory of the mirror stage enables him to show that we always come to know ourselves as split and other than ourselves, for we always come to know ourselves through another. Because of this split in subjectivity and because of the subject's dependence on another, the subject is constituted and its existence threatened in the same moment. This can help make sense of the relationship between bodily practices and spiritual exercises centered on imagery, for the contemplation of images of divine suffering become internalized and then enacted in and on the bodies of those represented within these texts. In internalizing the cross of Christ, for example, her hagiographer depicts Beatrice as attempting to overcome the gap between her own subjectivity and that of the divine other through which it is constituted. Beckwith similarly argues that

just as in Lacan's mirror stage, the anchoress encounters the crucified Christ as the Other, who is at the same time the internal condition of her identity; she meets him, in Lacan's terms, in *affairement jubilatoire* and *connaissance paranoiaque*, or, in theological terms, in a perpetual oscillation between presumption and despair.[70]

Beckwith thus shows how the subjectivity formed through the practice of the *Ancrene Wisse* involves the formation of an imaginary bodily ego experienced in and as a fantasmatic identification with the suffering body of Christ. It is, moreover, a subjectivity always at odds with itself, for Christ "is at once the guarantor of . . . identity and the annihilator of it."[71]

A crucial passage in "Seven Manners of Loving God" suggests that Beatrice has so internalized her identification with the divine as to experience internally what was first learned in relationship to images of the cross. Throughout the treatise she has spoken of the divine as love, lord, and God; only in the seventh manner of loving does she name Christ.

Therefore the soul is filled with great longing to be set free from this misery, to be loosed from this body; and sometimes it says with sorrowing heart, as the apostle said: *Cupio dissolvi et esse cum christo*, that is "I long to be set free and to be with Christ." So it longs greatly and with a tormenting impatience for death to this world and for life with Christ.[72]

The soul's desire for life with Christ makes this life one of unbearable torture, "a blessed martyrdom, a cruel suffering, a long torment, a murderous death and an expiring life."[73] The textual citation suggests meditational practice. Moreover, the image of Christ has been so thoroughly internalized that the soul itself is formed and constituted in the image of Christ, although it is important that Beatrice identifies this suffering only obliquely with Christ, reserving the name "life in Christ" for future bliss rather than present suffering. In following her invocation of Christ with a statement of the soul's spiritual martyrdom, however, the reader quickly identifies the soul as living the passion of Christ on earth. Through its practice, the soul so internalizes Christ as to share in an imaginary identification with his suffering exile. On the one hand, the bodily practices have been so successful that the soul created through them feels trapped within the body and desires to burst the limits of the body itself.[74] On the other, the fissure in the self described by Lacan remains, experienced now as the alterity of the body.

Reading Beatrice's text against her hagiography suggests an important supplement to this reading, one that acknowledges Beatrice's agency and resistance to prevalent cultural norms. As I have shown, the hagiographer insists on externalizing Beatrice's experience. Whereas she becomes absorbed in love through love, for the hagiographer Beatrice's suffering flesh—its expanding heart and bursting veins—itself becomes a sign of Christ's presence on earth. This externalization is demanded by the hagiographical genre and by cultural prescriptions about women, sanctity, and the body. Presumably, Beatrice herself was familiar with these same presuppositions; hagiographical texts were routinely read within convents and many of the thirteenth-century examples appear to have been written for this purpose.[75] In rejecting the externalizing movements of hagiography, both in relation to the road to the divine and in the account of the nature of one's identification with Christ, Beatrice implicitly rejects precisely the association of women with the body, and hence with bodily suffering, so crucial to the hagiographer. Her desire for freedom, then, can be understood as a desire to free suffering women's bodies from their literalistic identification with the suffering body of Christ. She crucially displaces typical understandings of the "life in Christ," arguing that it is not the present life of suffering imprisonment, but rather life in internal and eternal rapturous identification with divine love. For Beatrice the formation of the free soul still occurs through suffering, suggesting that her displacement of identification with Christ from suffering to ecstasy is only partial—rather than identifying with the suffering flesh, she emphasizes the interiority of her passion. It is the soul, not the body, who suffers in an internal suffering that is itself one with the ascent as long as one is on this earth. The further movement toward freedom, and the claim that the soul can be uncreated, free, and without suffering in this life, will occur in the work of Marguerite Porete and Meister Eckhart.

As Beckwith shows in her reading of the *Ancrene Wisse*, the body is not only a key site for the reproduction of material conditions and social relations, but also the site in which the social order can be reformed, re-invented, and reimagined. In her reading, the *Ancrene Wisse* represents just such a reformist moment, one in which the penitential and Christo-logical changes of the later Middle Ages are prescribed and then, Beck-with assumes, enacted in the bodies of late medieval anchorite women. But oddly, given her feminist and materialist concerns, Beckwith conflates male-authored textual prescriptions for women's bodily practice with that practice itself. In the example I have focused on here, Beatrice's treatise shows some evidence of an imaginary bodily ego formed out of ascetic practice and identification with the suffering Christ, yet Beatrice refuses to externalize her imaginary suffering body and only obliquely acknowledges its source in images of the suffering Christ. Her reticence about bodily as-ceticism and meditational practices centered on the suffering of Christ sug-gests that she challenges even the prescriptions for the suffering self found in texts like the *Ancrene Wisse*.[76] For Beatrice, sparing the body demands breaking the fluidity between internal and external, thereby marking off interiority as the site of suffering and ecstasy.

In closing her essay, Beckwith suggests that ascesis creates an imagi-nary ego that incarnates the ambiguities of embodiment. Following Judith Butler, she argues that the imaginary ego generated within the *Ancrene Wisse* is an object "neither interior nor exterior to the subject, but the per-manently unstable site where that spatialized distinction is permanently negotiated."[77] The imaginary ego is the very oscillation between interior and exterior, bodily and spiritual, material and imaginary. We therefore have a new way to understand the ambiguity of Beatrice's language, which uses sensual imagery to describe the movements of the soul. Yet we cannot lose sight of the fact that the hagiographer refuses ambiguity by exter-nalizing Beatrice's experiences, whereas Beatrice refuses this ambiguity by insisting on the interiority of the soul's experience.

Beckwith argues that the aim of asceticism is to transcend ambiguity; it is, she writes, "indeed an impossible, defiant, and hopelessly blighted attempt to move beyond the subject's permeability to history and to tran-science; it ends up producing the spectacle of that historically marked transcience."[78] Asceticism is the attempt to attain a redeemed and redeeming body through overcoming corporal limitations, to attain the always already lost unity of the mirror image through a denial of the split within subjectivity. According to Beckwith, this attempt is always doomed and leaves behind it a record of its failure in depictions of suffering women's bodies. Yet again, Beckwith's account rests on a conflation of women's practices and male-authored texts, for it is male clerics' descriptions of and prescriptions for female asceticism that result in depictions of fissured, bleeding, and suffering women's bodies in and through which others see the divine. Through the suffering of women's bodies, the transcience, historicity, and ambiguity of the reader's subjectivity is, perhaps, provisionally overcome. Beatrice, however, does not describe bodily asceticism but, to use her language, a spiritual one. We might also think of it as a linguistic asceticism, in which Beatrice desires to regulate the ambivalence of language, firmly locating her experience within. She implicitly attempts to avoid the fate described by Beckwith; her text suggests a desire to avoid becoming a spectacle of ambiguity, transcience, and bodiliness through which her contemporaries can find their wholeness (either through healing miracles, intercessory prayers, or simply the experience of reading). Beatrice hopes to transcend not only history but also the bodily asceticism others demand precede that movement into the self. Although she may not be successful in her attempts to write the free self, it is important to acknowledge the subtle shift in her understanding of asceticism and her defiance of predominant prescriptions and norms.

All of this is, I think, related in complex ways with modern attempts to write the histories of mysticism and of the modern subject, and the curious refusal to take account of sexual difference within these histories.[79] Denys Turner argues in a recent book on the Christian apophatic tradition that the central metaphors of interiority, ascent, lightness, and darkness signify radically different things within the early Christian and medieval contexts and nineteenth- and twentieth-century discussions of mysticism:

Put very bluntly, the difference seems to be this: that whereas our employment of the metaphors of "inwardness" and "ascent" appears to be tied in with the achievement and cultivation of a certain kind of experience—such as those recommended within the practice of what is called, nowadays, "centring" or "contemplative" prayer—the medieval employment of them was tied in with a "critique" of such religious experience and practices.[80]

Turner suggests that the hypostasization of a particular kind of experience as mystical may be the product of nineteenth-century studies of mysticism rather than being drawn from apt readings of medieval texts.[81] Yet he describes the apophatic mystic as reacting against "religious experience," understood as extraordinary experience of some kind. Turner tries to explain this contradiction by arguing for a twofold use of metaphors of interiority within medieval texts. Yet the tension or conflict between apophatic mysticism and the pursuit of extraordinary experiences remains.

What Turner misses is the place of medieval women mystics and their religious experience—visionary, auditory, and sensory in response to the demands of their contemporaries for some authorizing, divine agency, yet also increasingly interiorized in an attempt to escape from the externalizing demands of male-defined female sanctity. Women's writings from the thirteenth century are both visionary and apophatic; often there is an unproblematic movement between the two, the visionary moment serving as the material that is subsequently negated in a union without distinction between the soul and the divine. Other texts, like Beatrice's "Seven Manners of Loving God" and Marguerite Porete's *Mirror of Simple Souls*, eschew the visionary mode and suggest a tension between it and ecstatic and apophatic movements. Not only are external works and signs sublated, but so also is the visionary as the soul moves further inward in its experience of the divine. After the condemnations of Marguerite Porete, Eckhart, and the so-called heresy of the Free Spirit at the beginning of the fourteenth century, and with the increased persecution of the beguines following these events, this alternative movement inward is complicated by an emphasis on autohagiographical gestures within women-authored texts.[82] Yet a revised genealogy of mysticism suggests that women's mystical texts are one of the places in which the interiority of the modern subject constitutes itself.

Mauss, Bourdieu, Asad, and Beckwith want to undermine modern conceptions of the self and of belief, arguing for the bodily nature of both and thereby demonstrating the complex interaction of nature, culture, and power in the formation of human subjects. Beckwith argues that this is a necessary theoretical move if we are to understand the complexity of women's subjectivities and their relationship to structures of power. She suggests a necessary alliance between feminist politics and history and materialist analysis. The fruitfulness of her readings suggests she is right and yet her reliance on male-authored texts needs to be supplemented and revised in light of medieval women's works, like Beatrice of Nazareth's "Seven Manners of Loving God," in which the soul becomes increasingly interiorized in a desire to become increasingly free. In forging this interiority, medieval women's texts are an important source for modern conceptions of the internalized self now under attack from materialist theories like those of Bourdieu, Asad, and Beckwith. Beatrice claims the autonomy of the internal self in order to free herself from cultural demands for a visibly suffering female body. Marguerite Porete will go further, attempting to free the soul from all suffering, internal and external.[83] The female imaginary in late medieval Christian culture, then, was not always and entirely governed by male prescriptions; some women rejected prescriptions for bodily and spiritual exercises centered on identification with the suffering body of Christ. Their resistance, paradoxically, generated an early version of that interiorized, disembodied subject often identified today with masculinity. This subjectivity may well be untenable—the instability of a soul who seeks death in order to be free suggests as much—yet its existence within medieval women's texts must be acknowledged in the process of rewriting and reevaluating the history of medieval and modern subjectivities.

6

A Marriage and
Its Observer

Christine of Stommeln, the Heavenly
Bridegroom, and Friar Peter of Dacia

John Coakley

THE CONTENTS OF the late thirteenth- or early fourteenth-century *Codex Iuliacensis*, now published, provide a remarkably rich depiction of the lives of a reputed female saint and her closest clerical admirer. The woman in question was a beguine, Christine of Stommeln (1242–1312), the man a Scandinavian Dominican friar, Peter of Dacia (1230/40–1289). Peter met Christine and visited her repeatedly in her home town of Stommeln while he was a student in nearby Cologne at the important Dominican school (*studium generale*) there, in 1267–69. Afterward he kept up a correspondence with her, first from Paris (1269–70) and later from various Dominican houses in Sweden where he spent the rest of his life except for two trips abroad, which included visits to her in Stommeln.[1] The *Codex Iuliacensis* contains a collection of much, if not all, of the correspondence, comprising sixty-three letters—thirty-two of which he himself edited as a self-contained collection, with occasional interpolated comments—including overall twenty-two by himself, fourteen by Christine (written down for her by various collaborators), and seventeen by others in their circle.[2] The manuscript also includes a poem by Peter in praise of her, his own theological commentary on that poem, his accounts of some nineteen visits he made to her in Stommeln, an autobiographical narrative called the *quaternus* or notebook, ostensibly dictated by Christine to the parish priest John of Stommeln, and a series of narratives about her sufferings, the substance of which she ostensibly conveyed to another John, probably the local schoolmaster.[3] Both the priest and the schoolmaster wrote these things down at Peter's behest; without Peter we would probably not know anything of Christine, and indeed after his death nothing more was recorded of her.[4]

In this essay I shall compare what Peter says about Christine in these texts with what she says about herself. A caveat is necessary first about the kind of conclusion that can be expected from such a comparison. This comparison is not the enterprise it would be if these were, say, the letters or journals of two independent modern authors bent on self-disclosure. As Christine Ruhrberg has compellingly argued, these texts in the form in which we have them are fundamentally hagiographical, in the sense of being aimed at demonstrating the sanctity of Christine rather than presenting, in anything like a modern sense, a coherent picture of an individual's spirituality.[5] Consequently what we are comparing here are two demonstrations or depictions of sanctity—that is, of what extraordinary virtues and experiences set her apart and justify calling her a saint. One of the demonstrations is, as it were, "*auto*hagiographical," but no less hagiographical for that. Furthermore in the case of that "autohagiography" it is clear that others besides Christine herself—namely, the parish priest, the schoolmaster, briefly a Dominican named Lawrence (who wrote some of her letters for her after the death of the parish priest in 1377) and also (as ultimate editor) Peter—had some hand in producing her letters and narratives, and so the voice that speaks in these writings (sometimes in the first person, sometimes in the third) cannot be heard simply as hers; rather, it represents a collaborative effort.[6] The real historical Christine is, as I shall suggest, surely *in* that voice, but she cannot be discretely extracted from it.

On the basis of the texts thus understood, I shall argue that although there is a great contrast in tone and emphasis between what Peter says about Christine and what she says about herself, nonetheless the two voices are in fundamental harmony; indeed, within the composite witness of the *Codex Iuliacensis*, they function as two coordinated elements in a single overall strategy to present Christine as a saint. The contrast between them is, to be sure, striking. Christine's letters and narratives, on the one hand, focus upon the trials both external (in the form of corporeal violence) and internal (in the form of religious doubts) that demons inflicted upon her. Peter's letters and narratives, on the other hand, make much of Christine as a bride of Christ—a woman in privileged mystical contact with the divine, as evidenced in observable episodes of rapture—and explain the significance of such contact in theologically elaborated detail. But in spite of this contrast, a close look shows that mystical experience also has a central, if unelaborated, place in Christine's writing, and conversely that Peter considers Christine's subjection to demonic trials to be part and parcel of her status as bride of Christ. And although one might at first imagine that the two voices present two contrasting (though even so, perhaps not contradictory) modes of access to the divine—access mediated by theological understanding in Peter's case and direct, unmediated access through experience in Christine's case—only one mode of such access is the proper subject of these texts. For Peter, even as he theologizes, still longs only for the mystical experience he attributes to Christine and from which he claims to benefit vicariously through the devotion she elicits in him. Thus the voices are harmonious and complementary; Christine's tells us of the circumstances and conditions of her sanctity, and Peter's tells us of his own appropriation of that sanctity. Together they give expression, not to two ideals of sanctity, but to one.

Peter's View of Christine

Peter develops his understanding of Christine in two sometimes overlapping ways: by applying analytical categories so as to give her life a theological interpretation, and by making personal revelations that demonstrate the place he considers her to occupy in his own life. Either way, Peter pictures her (I shall suggest) as completing something otherwise incomplete; and accordingly the concern that brings him to her, and that forms the necessary though often implicit background for his portrait, is precisely his own sense of incompleteness, a perceived lack of fulfillment, in both an abstractly theological and a more concretely personal sense.

It is in the poem about Christine and the accompanying commentary, which comprise the first part of the *Codex Iuliacensis*, that Peter gives his most explicit theological interpretation of Christine, so let us begin there. Here, and particularly in the commentary, Peter develops the theme of the relation between grace and nature. The poem, forty-three lines in length, which takes Christine as its subject without actually naming her (so as not to provoke detractors, he implies),[7] is obscurely worded at points and difficult to summarize, but in general celebrates her virtues with particular emphasis on her stigmata and the pains she sustained at the hands of demons. Four lines in the middle of the poem give a summarizing interpretation of Christine's activity in terms that call attention to her surpassing of nature:

Mos, os, cor, cultus, cibus et gradus, actio, vultus!
Ieiunat, vigilat, patitur, pugnatque triumphat!
Ornat naturam virtus naturaque curam
istis ostendit propriam, quas gloria pendit.

Her way of life, speech, feeling, demeanor, her food and gait, her activity, her
countenance!
She fasts, vigils, suffers, fights and triumphs!
Virtue adorns nature and nature shows its proper care
For those things worthy of glory.[8]

Although of all the verses in the poem it is only these and the quatrain
following them that specifically address the notion of the surpassing of
nature, nonetheless that notion dominates the long accompanying commentary—indeed it almost monopolizes the part of the commentary that
survives—in such a way as to suggest that Peter intended it as an interpretative key to the poem.[9] Thus Monika Asztalos has shown that of the
thirteen chapters that comprise the commentary in her edition, fully nine
(chaps. 3–11) are devoted to vv. 27–28 alone, and specifically to "the dog-
matic system compressed into these two verses."[10] In a nutshell, that "system" describes the interrelation between nature and grace, whereby grace
adds itself to nature (*ornat naturam virtus*) and nature in turn cooperates with grace (*naturaque curam . . . ostendit propriam*) in order to receive
the reward of eternal beatitude. In essence, this "system" closely follows
the thought of Thomas Aquinas, under whom Peter must have studied in
1269–70, and whose commentary on the *Sentences* of Lombard appears to
be Peter's major (and acknowledged) source here; and the axiom "grace
enriches nature" (*gracia naturam ditat*), which Peter employs repeatedly
as he discusses various categories of grace, has the same thrust as the Tho-
mistic axiom "grace perfects nature" (*gratia perficit naturam*).[11]

Within that explicit interpretative context, the poem and commentary
present Christine as one who remarkably displays grace and its reciprocal
relation with nature. The verses following the ones quoted above make
the point:

Raptus, amor, placor, ardor, odor, livor et cruor, angor!
Eructat, iubilat, subridet, deficit, orat!
Istis natura gaudens superat sua iura,
hoc ultra votum prebet quia gracia totum.

Her rapture, love, contentment, ardor, fragrance, her bruises and blood, her anguish!

She gushes, shouts for joy, smiles, withdraws, entreats!
Rejoicing in these things, nature surpasses its laws,
And grants what is beyond its promise because all is by grace.[12]

Therefore, she displays grace and its proper relation to nature both in the sense that by her ascetic virtues her natural self heroically cooperates with grace, and also in the sense that she displays the rare *gracia privilegiata* by which she tastes future beatitude.[13] Such grace appears in dreams, prophecies, and visions, but preeminently in the experience of rapture (*raptus* or *excessus mentis*) wherein a person leaves behind all bodily senses, passions, and thoughts; and in his writing about Christine it is this rapture that interests Peter particularly.[14]

One of Peter's letters to Christine sums up this theological train of thought:

God created the rational spirit in his image and likeness, and joined it to the mud of the earth with a bond of such friendship that he did not wish it to be separated from him whatever its misery; and now, as though forgetting all his other works, he draws that same spirit to him with such sweetness, influencing it and enticing it toward himself, that it forgets both the mud and itself, and considers all to be dung, that it might win Christ [cf. Phil. 3:8]. O sweetest Jesus! O most violent love and lover! Do you wish to dissolve the agreement that was made with good Reason? "No," he says, "but I wish in this way through the spirit to convert and attract to me the body whose senses have been prone to evil since adolescence, so that, once my Spirit has been tasted, all flesh would become but a trifle. And I will establish this clearly whenever I convey to someone in the present life the exuberance of my beatitude and sweetness, in such a way that the mind of that person goes beyond proper nature, and the person wishes to be with me more than with self, and desires to be loosed both from itself and in itself, so as to enjoy me. In this way I will draw the spirit to me, marked by my image, and through it I will convert the mud that is composed of all things, so that, just as corporeal and spiritual things are created by me, so both according to the means possible for them are beatified in me and alienated in a certain way from themselves, so as to be transformed in me."[15]

If Peter thus makes a "conceptual" or theological point of Christine's surpassing of nature, his treatment of her raptures in his accounts of his visits gives empirical narrative support for that point.[16] He first describes a rapture in his account of his second visit, when, after a meal at the house of the parish priest, someone sang the hymn *Jesu dulcis memoria*, interspersing German words. He himself was moved to tears, and Christine entered a rapture:

And this girl was taken (*rapta*) by such a departure of mind (*excessum mentis*) that all her senses ceased their working and her whole body hardened and she gave no sign of sensible life, and—to add to the astonishment—what it was that had drawn her spirit could not be discerned. While these things were happening I wept for joy, as I admit, and was astounded by the marvel and I gave thanks to the Giver for the gift of such divine outpouring; for I attributed none of this to nature or to human activity, but recognized with reverence the divine presence in this event. . . . And seeing therefore that no mortal human could have arranged this, I judged it to be what I have read about in the Apostle: "if we depart from our mind [it is of God]," [2 Cor. 5: 13] for it seemed to me that I had not seen anything else like it, and I began all the more excitedly to consider what was happening, and pay attention to her words, and ponder her movements and actions, and commit them to the depths of my memory, because I attributed all these things to the prerogative of extraordinary grace.[17]

Thus he specifically identifies her *raptus* or trance with the actions of grace —presumably the same *gracia privilegiata* of the poem-commentary—as distinct from nature. He elaborates the theme in accounts of subsequent visits. In the account of the fifth visit, when he once again observes her enter such a trance while he himself is giving an impromptu lecture to a small assembly of persons at Stommeln, he makes a point of the fact that it was only then that he learned, "from clerics who were present," that this trance was called a *raptus*.[18] In the account of the seventh visit, he tells of a learned friar from Tuscany, Albrandino, who, having heard about Christine, accompanied Peter to Stommeln and attended her while she went into rapture after receiving communion. Since her body did not harden immediately, Albrandino at first voiced his doubt about the supposed marvel, but when he returned later he not only found her then quite hardened but also, when she awoke, observed a cross-shaped wound in her hand and berated himself for his prior unbelief; and when, as he then held her hand, she suddenly went into another rapture and her arm stiffened so as to trap his hand against the wall in hers, he decided (as Peter reports him saying) that the pressure from her hand was "not natural" but rather "supernatural," since it lacked movement or tension.[19]

Peter thus both employs a theological vocabulary to explain Christine's significance and uses his narratives to show what he meant. He also does something more: in some ostensibly self-revealing passages, he speaks of Christine's significance for his own psyche.

One way in which Peter sounds this personal note is by construing his encounter with Christine as the fulfillment of a desire he had first formulated in childhood. In the account of his first visit Peter says that as far as he can remember, he delighted as a child to hear of the "life and character, passions and deaths" of the saints, Christ, and the Virgin and had thoughts of renouncing the world. Among these thoughts a desire emerged that God might grant the grace

to show me some one of his servants, in whom I might learn the ways of his saints not just through words but through deeds and examples sure and clear; to whom I might be joined and united in heartfelt love; whose actions might instruct me; whose devotion might kindle me and rouse me from the torpor that had oppressed me since childhood; whose conversation might enlighten me; whose friendship might console me; whose examples might clear up all my doubts, especially about the ways of the saints.[20]

Over the course of the subsequent twenty years, he continues, he had met many affecting persons, male and female, but the desire had continued to be unfulfilled; but then at the end of the account of the visit, after having described with careful attention the violence a demon was apparently inflicting on her body, the strange elation he felt as he observed her patient travail, and the hot nails the demon had used to wound her, which she obligingly produced and gave to him and his companion, he implies that his prayer was finally answered. That night at Stommeln, he says, was no night at all but a time of illumination (cf. Ps. 138: 11–12 Vlg.) for him, for it was then that he first tasted "how sweet the Lord is" (Ps. 33: 8 Vlg.) and it was then that (and here he first introduces the nuptial imagery that he will cultivate) he "first merited to see a bride of my Lord."[21] Later, in his third visit, when she happened to open her hand so that he could see a wound on her palm in the image of a cross, so beautiful and intricate that no human could have painted it, he connected this first sight of her stigmata with the childhood wish, calling that sight a "thing I had desired since infancy."[22]

Peter's interest in discussing Christine's place in his own life, an interest visible already in that opening self-disclosure about his childhood, finds its most nuanced expression in two extended passages in which he pictures her as Christ's bride and himself as a third party to the marriage. Here we see Christine as something more to him than the answer to a prayer to be consoled or instructed by a saintly person, as in the first visit narrative; he now considers her—or more precisely, his observation of her—to be his very salvation, or at least the only means by which he can supply a certain profound spiritual deficiency in himself. In his attempt to supply it, he presents himself therefore as something of a voyeur. What precisely his deficiency is, I shall consider in a moment; but first let us examine the passages in question.

In the first of these passages, in one of the letters Peter sent from Paris

(Letter 5), he imagines himself as a wedding guest at the nuptials between Christine and Christ. Here his avowed purpose is to deflect her attention away from himself: she had written him (Letter 4) that she missed his attentions and that it was not the same for her when she was with anyone else, and Peter tells her to direct her affection to Christ instead.[23] More precisely, he tells her that if she does direct her affection to Christ, then he, Peter, will be a beneficiary. For her joy will then affect him too—"for how shall I not rejoice in the good of the one whom I have loved as I love myself?"[24] He then introduces the marriage metaphor:

Someone says that the friend of the bridegroom "rejoices with joy on account of the voice of the bridegroom" [John 3: 29]. And what, I ask, would he do, if he also sometimes heard the voice of the bride, of whom it is said, "your voice is sweet and your face beautiful" [Cant. 2: 14], for the bridegroom and the bride say, "come" [cf. Rev. 22: 17]. Who, I say, hearing this, would not rejoice? I dare to say: he would not only rejoice but also would cry out and bring forth a good word; so let the one who hears also say, "come," and most especially if in the meantime, being forearmed with love, steeped in devotion and clothed in knowledge, it is given to him to be present at such nuptials, to enter the bridal chamber with duty and reverence, and to listen intently and devoutly to the wedding song.[25]

Here he is evidently thinking of his observation of Christine during his visits. It is interesting to note that he makes use of the phrase "friend of the bridegroom" who hears the bridegroom's voice (John the Evangelist's epithet for John the Baptist, John 3: 29–30), but instead of applying it precisely to himself—as for instance an earlier Dominican writer, Jordan of Saxony, had done in identifying himself as the one who brought his saintly female correspondent Diana of Andalò to "marriage" with Christ—Peter alters the image to depict himself rather as a guest of both bride and bridegroom.[26]

    In fact, as the letter progresses it is more on the mark to call him a friend of the *bride*, given access to the "marriage" by *her*. For it is in her raptures that Peter discerns Christ's presence, aided by the evidence of her stigmata, which he considers her evident bridal garment.[27] That image carries an echo of the parable of the man without the wedding garment who is cast out of the wedding (Matt. 22: 11), whom he, lacking stigmata, identifies with himself. Accordingly he adjusts the marriage image once more to suggest that he himself is not present at all, in fact is not worthy to be present, until he comes (as he hopes) to the afterlife.[28] In the meantime he has heard from Christine what he has not "merited" to hear from

Christ directly: "from the words or answers of the bride of which I have heard many, I have inferred his sayings or promises."[29]

The other image of himself as third party to Christine's marriage, in Letter 10 (also from Paris), makes an even more vivid point of his own inadequacy to attain direct access to Christ. Here, after an extended discussion of Christine's surpassing of the natural (some of which I have quoted above), he tells her, as in the earlier letter, that he longs to be witnessing her marriage to Christ, presumably as he did in Stommeln. "With what affection," he exclaims, "would I take pleasure in the joining and intimacy, the conjunction and the combined rejoicing of you and your beloved, the two whom I so love and desire, and who are even dearer to each other, when from you I would hear your vows of devotion, words of delight, sounds of obedience, prayers of expectation, the joy of acceptance, of exultation, of enjoyment, the desire of continuation, the sigh of separation and the tears of desolation!"[30] But here he proceeds to invoke, not the parable of the wedding guest or the image of the friend of the bridegroom, but rather the biblical story of Rachel and Leah after their marriages to Jacob (Gen. 30). For imagining himself present at the marriage, he suddenly construes himself as the bridegroom's rejected wife. Thus he asks rhetorically whether he should not be "indignant and spiteful at that person, however formerly beloved, who snatched from me my husband"; and—here recalling the strategy of Leah, who lured Jacob temporarily from Rachel's bed to her own with a bribe of mandrakes—he asks whether he should dare to say to Christ, "come in to me, because I have bought you with a price [Gen. 30:16]?"[31] But the answer is of course no; he lacks the substance of the figurative bribe—namely "purity and love, devotion and honest conduct, continual and fervent conversation, sublime and affective contemplation"—and at any rate his "sister" Christine is more acceptable to the bridegroom, being beautiful in virtue and fecund in good works. If he cannot rightly complain, therefore, what can he do?

What therefore remains for me, older in years and already unsuccessful in marriage—because I am cold in heart, wrinkled in face, poor in income, sterile in childbearing and, overshadowed by my younger sister, an object of disdain—except to avoid displeasing the one whom I have not deserved to please? I know what I will do: I will show myself familiar with my sister and devoted and obedient to her husband, so that she might at least tell me something about her flood of joys and her secrets, and that he might come the more freely, frequently, festively and familiarly, when in one of the sisters he finds the marriage bed prepared and in the other a ready obedience of the the body, and in both the desire of devoted expectation. I will therefore please the bridegroom with prayers, please him with gifts, please him with dutiful works; and I will say to him, so that I might more easily allure him, please him better and draw him more strongly, "I have a more beautiful younger sister; go in to her, join with her, embrace her," so that the memory of me will not be removed from his affections.[32]

In his picturing here of the triangle between himself, Christine, and Christ, at least two different movements are evident. On the one hand he seems to be saying, in an almost pandering way, that he will find merit with Christ by presenting Christine to him, and on the other hand that he will learn of Christ by associating himself with Christine. In either case Christine serves him as a means to bring himself closer, in some sense, to Christ, and this is consistent with the argument of the earlier letter; nonetheless the conceit of sisterhood introduces a new element. For in casting himself as her sister and thus identifying himself much more closely with her he is able to make himself out as her losing competitor, and thus to highlight his own inadequacy as all the more striking because he is without the excuse of a generic difference. To put the matter another way: he is not a favored outside observer, brought in to see the wedding, but rather himself a humbled insider, a failed bride, living with the conviction that in theory he could, and perhaps should, have been as acceptable to Christ as Christine—a conviction that then tends to emphasize his difference from her the more strongly, and to add a touch of shame.

By way of bringing all this together, let us ask: what exactly was Peter's supposed failure? What was the inner lack that he considered Christine to supply? Was it his sinfulness itself—in which case he would have been looking to Christine to aid in his salvation, to supply her merits for his sake, to intercede for him, and thus to serve classically as a *saint* for him? Although there is one passage in the letters in which he describes her in terms that might suggest such a role for her—asking her to remove him from the gates of hell—still on the whole it is not intercession or even specifically salvation that he looks for from her.[33] No; what he wants from her is some awakening impetus for his own devotion. For it is precisely devotion that he considers himself to lack. He wants to feel pious emotions that otherwise he has not felt, and even though he claims at best to experience Christ only vicariously as he observes Christine, nonetheless he credits her with being able to elicit in him the feelings that were wanting.[34]

So far I have spoken of the *young* Peter's view of Christine. But it would appear that changes came over time. It was when he was a student at Paris in 1269–70 that Peter wrote the passages I have just been discussing, in which he sees himself as third-party observer of Christine's marriage with Christ and ascribes to her the power to bring him to devotion. In letters that he would write ten years later, after returning to Sweden from his 1279 visit to Stommeln, he is still thinking of triads involving himself, Christine, and Christ, but their terms have perceptibly changed so as to allow him to focus upon his *mutual* relationship with her as he had not done at the time of Letter 5 (see above).[35] Peter can speak now of a kind of bigamy, whereby Christine is married not only to Christ but also to himself: in one letter he writes that of his "many solaces in this life, one that gladdens me especially, is that it is given to me to understand why it is said 'for I have betrothed you to one man, to exhibit you to Christ as a chaste virgin' [2 Cor. 11: 2]. . . . You who are dearest to me and are through divine love betrothed both to God and to my soul, pray the Lord that we keep the chaste faith of this betrothal and that we might know the pledge of our love to be undiminished."[36] Now he is calling *himself*, in a certain sense, her bridegroom—as he would clearly not have done in the Paris letters. It is true that he goes on to say to her that he loves her only because she is the "vessel of divine habitation," and that in another letter written shortly afterward he once again invokes her status as a bride of Christ, dallying with him in a paradise from which Peter has been excluded.[37] Even so, Peter is no longer merely Christine's vicarious observer. Accordingly, he is willing on one occasion to downplay completely his difference from her, as he in one passage declares that if he considers himself for a moment as though he were "perfect" (i.e., puts aside—as he has not done before—his awareness of his inferiority to her) he discerns "a certain similarity in us—a similarity to the eternal fellowship and intimate love of the saints," in the sense that the love between them, which begins and ends in God, is not bound by time or place.[38] Elsewhere he speaks of the overcoming of their difference when he says that God, having joined the human body and soul together at the time of creation, similarly "has united us, though far apart and dissimilar in daily activity, in one bond of friendship."[39] And he shows himself willing to call attention to what he has done for her as well as what she has done for him, as when he says that it was for her consolation that he had hoped not to die on his recent journey, because he knew that she dreaded outliving him.[40] And when he explains at great length that it is for the sake of Christ—and not ultimately for herself—that he loves Christine, he is clearly doing so to justify (whether against real or merely rhetorical detractors) his new willingness to say outright that he loves her: "let the world cry out, jeer, disparage, rage, and argue; I will nonetheless love the bride of my Lord from the bottom of my heart for the sake of the bridegroom."[41]

The Consolations of Christine

Let us turn now to the putative writings of Christine herself—her fourteen letters to Peter, the autobiographical notebook or *quaternus* that she ostensibly dictated to the parish priest John of Stommeln, and the narrative of her sufferings that she ostensibly conveyed to the schoolmaster—and compare the Christine of those writings with the Christine of Peter's fascinated narratives and twenty-two letters. First, a caveat: it is indeed a "putative" Christine that we are hearing in these texts since, as I have suggested at the outset of this essay, her collaborators, namely Peter, the parish priest, and the schoolmaster, all had some hand in their production; and so we have here a collaborative literary persona, not just the self-perceived historical Christine. On the other hand, the historical Christine surely had a role in creating this literary persona; and at the end of this section, after examining that persona, I shall tentatively consider the question of how she might be reflected in it.

As I have argued, what fascinated Peter about Christine, especially in his youth, was the mystical experience he attributed to her, and of which he wrote using the scholastic concepts of nature and grace as well as a repertory of nuptial imagery. When we come to these writings of Christine herself, though, it is remarkable how little they say about the substance of the bride's encounter with the bridegroom, which Peter would have so liked to hear about. Instead, these texts mainly concern her persistent vexations by demons, which are described in considerable, often sensational, detail. The tone of these vexation stories is a far cry from the sublime themes of Peter's letters: the demons torture her physically by threatening her, wounding her, abducting her, and exposing her naked to the elements, and they tempt her to despair and disbelief by a wide array of sinister illusions and seductive thoughts. But it would be a mistake to conclude from the prominence of these vexation stories, and the relative paucity and lack of specificity about mystical encounters with Christ, that those encounters were of secondary importance to her.[42] For a close look at the vexation stories and their place in the texts shows that her mysticism, though certainly not explained or elaborated in the way that Peter explained and elaborated it, is nonetheless clearly acknowledged, and that its absences are so important as to suggest precisely its centrality for her. Moreover, certain of the texts (as I shall point out) include accounts of visions and revelations given to her, which, though not properly mystical in the sense of describing an extraordinary state of consciousness of God, such as Peter wanted to hear from her, yet do assume and underline the notion of her chosenness and favor in the sight of God and on occasion allude to her mystical encounters. Furthermore the placement of these accounts within the texts calls attention to triumphant themes in her spirituality, especially in regard to issues of belief and continence. Accordingly, these texts present a picture of Christine that does not conflict with the picture we receive from Peter, but rather complements it; in either case we have a portrait of a mystic, but in one the mysticism itself is the focus, whereas in the other we are shown a spiritual life that revolves—however turbulently—around that mysticism.

In her letters and narratives, many of Christine's descriptions of the demons' vexations show them obstructing her from partaking of communion, and in some cases they also call attention to her consequent exclusion from the special graces which—for her—arose from communion, namely the raptures that she typically underwent afterward.[43] Such obstruction occurs as a result of the demons' violence. In one of her earliest letters, for instance, she describes a demon menacing her for several weeks in the summer of 1269 (and eventually injuring her) with a piece of white-hot iron, terrifying her to such an extent that "I did not delight in hearing Mass, or the word of God, nor could I talk of God or pray in any way, without terror of the fiery iron"; and when, after she had taken communion at Mass, she went to her habitual place east of the altar where she would often experience her raptures, nothing happened.[44] Or, more commonly, she might be kept from communion by more seductive or discursive temptations rather than by threat of violence. Thus in another early letter she describes a temptation in the form of an obsessional thought that whatever she prayed was in the name of the demon who was trying her, and says that at Mass when the host was elevated the demon appeared substituting himself for it and claiming to be her God. Later, she says, she had doubts about the incarnation and consequent reservations about the worthiness of her bridegroom, and felt tempted to blaspheme, and experienced communion as a source of bitterness in contrast to previous experience.[45] Although it is certainly true that the allusion in such passages to her raptures, let alone her putative mystical experience within those raptures, is indirect, nonetheless the stories make it clear that it is to keep her from the occasion of such experiences that the demons do their worst.

In the late letters that she ostensibly dictated to John the schoolmaster (Letters 25, 26, and 29), and also in the narratives that she ostensibly conveyed to him, the obstructive function of the demons' vexations is much the same. The references to the mystical experience in such contexts are now much more direct but are not any more genuinely informative of their substance.[46] For example, after a period of extraordinarily violent treatment at the hands of demons during Advent—including an episode in which they stripped her, tortured her with sticks, and threw her into an icy marsh to be rescued by angels—Christine is described going to her accustomed place in the church on Christmas day and receiving a visit from the bridegroom, "in which nuptials she abounded in such wonderful joys and delights, that until the third day she had no awareness of anything."[47] Later in Lent after the demons had hung her body by hooks and cut pieces from it, she underwent an ecstasy in which "she was taken up in the embrace of her bridegroom and was ineffably consoled there."[48] Or again, after an Advent of exhausting tortures from the demons, on the Friday before Christmas, "that sweetest bridegroom, taking up her blessed soul, transported it to the secret marriage bed of his most beloved heart, where divine consolations gladdened her in the same measure as the multitude of her preceding afflictions."[49] Here, to be sure, the vexations are wilder than in the early correspondence and the nuptial language is stereotypical; the vexation-story, in the schoolmaster's hands, is becoming a well-developed genre. Nonetheless the importance of the vexations' obstructive function, and consequently the importance of what was being obstructed, remain constant.

In the *quaternus*, which she ostensibly dictated to the parish priest in the spring and summer of 1270, the demonic vexations also loom large, though with visions added alongside them.[50] That narrative consists of a brief narrative of Christine's early life until the onset of her demonic vexations, followed by a long series of accounts of those vexations (in the midst of which is reported a three-year peaceful hiatus) and concluded by an episode that begins with a vision of hell and proceeds to her penitential invitation to a serpent to enter and ravage her body; and in all of this, visions serve to punctuate the narrative and organize it in such a way as to call attention to her sanctity.[51]

The brief narrative of her early life which opens the *quaternus* begins and ends with visions, which in good hagiographical fashion establish her as favored by God. The vision at the outset presages the events that follow. In that vision, which Christine received at age ten, Christ appeared to her as a "most beautiful youth," saying, " 'dearest daughter, behold, I am Jesus

Christ; promise me your allegiance, such that you will always serve me. If anyone else asks some other allegiance of you, say that you have promised it to Jesus Christ in his hands'—which therefore she promised—'[and] you will stay with the beguines.'"[52] She then recalls this vision when she pictures herself learning to say the psalter at the age of eleven as though she were speaking to Christ, "to whom she had promised allegiance"; and the prophetic conclusion of the vision was fulfilled when she left home at age thirteen, against her parents' wishes, to live in Cologne with the beguines, pursuing an extreme asceticism of fasting, solitary prayer, and corporeal self-discipline.[53] Then at the end of this narrative of her early life, just prior to the accounts of her vexations—which, as we shall see, will include doubts about the Passion of Christ—she describes a vision of Christ's Passion which gave her great pleasure; and she desired (in anticipation of the later appearance of stigmata on her body) something by which to be reminded of it.[54] Thus the narrative establishes her devout and holy credentials before anything is said about her demonic trials.

When the *quaternus* then proceeds to describe those trials, which began two years into her sojourn at Cologne, the demons' obstruction of her contact with God looms large just as in the early letters, but now mystical experiences are introduced to sprinkle some happy endings among the stories. Although there are some instances of external violence in the *quaternus*, the demons' vexations of preference here are inward temptations, and especially religious doubts, which in several cases the mystical experiences serve to dispel. For instance, following close upon a temptation to kill herself on the demon's promise of immediate transit to heaven (a temptation which itself had no supernatural resolution), the narrative reports a series of doubts about the power of the Eucharist, the divine creation of the world, and the care of God and the saints for herself—which were dispelled when, on asking for a sign of the reality of the body of Christ in the Eucharist, she saw, in the priest's hands at the moment of the elevation of the host, a child who identified himself as Jesus.[55] Another such obstruction took the form of a roaring sound that she heard over a four-week period whenever she would hear Mass or hear anyone sing or talk about God, or when she herself prayed until finally she asked to have the sound taken away, and then "immediately she heard a very excellent voice singing about God, and joy came into her heart as she had never had from a song."[56] Perhaps the most striking paramystical resolution occurs in response to doubts she experienced about Christ's Passion, when the demon had planted the idea in her mind that it was the invention of priests, and as a result she could not discern a good taste in communion as was her wont, "nor could she sense her beloved at all when she prayed."[57] It was in response to her prayer to be free of this temptation, and to receive something to signify the Passion to her, she says, that a crown of thorns came down upon her head, and the blood flowed over her head and neck, and she passed out, and the "unbelief" (*infidelitas*) had vanished when she came back to herself; then on the Maundy Thursday following she first received the stigmata, and ever afterward thoughts of the Passion caused her to pass out, that is, presumably to go into the raptures that had already fascinated Peter.[58]

Such paramystical resolutions also occur in the *quaternus* to conclude episodes in which she has been tempted by the appeal of a secular life, or of sexuality. One particularly long series of temptations has the demon trying to draw her away from her continence, by promising her wealth, and then (once again planting doubts of clerical authority) suggesting that "religious and clerics and all continent persons are deceived, because it is a heresy to live that way, since from the beginning God ordained that everyone live in matrimony"[59] (cf. Mark 10: 6–8); by appearing to her, along with other demons, in the form of a woman enjoying her husband sexually and displaying motherly affection to her child; and finally by threatening to spread a rumor that she had borne a child.[60] At the end of this series of trials she had a dream in which Christ exhorted her to patience, called himself her bridegroom, and promised her heavenly reward for her perseverance — after which the temptation departed.[61] Another, spectacular, temptation occurred when the demon came to her house in the form of a certain robber to whom she had been frankly attracted, trying at first to seduce her, then attempting to rape her, then producing an illusion in which he killed her father after her refusal to save him by submitting. Finally she wounded herself with a knife to preoccupy herself with pain in the event of rape; and when afterward she worried that she would die of her wound, Christ appeared to her as a "beautiful youth" (*pulcherrimus iuuenis*) and recalled her inaugural vision to her, assuring her that she would not die this time, commending her for her faithfulness and assuring her that when she did die, her death would be precious to him like that of the martyr Catherine (presumably of Alexandria). Afterward the pain of the wound disappeared.[62] Finally in the closing episode of the *quaternus*, after a snake is described entering her body and consuming her interior parts as a purgatorial punishment, the resolution comes when the Virgin is described giving Christine a sweet drink that took away her pain. Thus does the *quaternus* end.[63]

The Christine of the *quaternus* is thus willing to speak directly about her supernatural experience. Not every demonic trial in the *quaternus* is resolved by such supernatural visions; some of the trials appear to subside by themselves, others upon her simple denunciation of the demon.[64] Nonetheless the visions are very conspicuous, standing at the beginning and end of the text, punctuating it at several points in between. Clearly they tend to be attached to stories of inner religious conflicts, wherein she sees herself questioning tenets of the Christian faith or else obstructed from exercising devout intentions. The visions turn these inner conflicts into demonstrations of her sanctity or more specifically of God's extraordinary favor toward her because of her perseverance.

But even though the *quaternus* thus attributes supernatural experiences to Christine, nonetheless her own involvement in those experiences is not described, and in this it is similar to all her other putative writings. Indeed what she relates is only the objective content of certain visions. For example, in her description of her inaugural vision at the beginning of the *quaternus* Christine registered no joy or sweetness in this encounter with Christ; on the contrary, it made her anxious, as she wondered by what means she would go to the beguines. We hear nothing of the bride's delight in the bridegroom. Indeed, even though the recollection of this vision at the end of the *quaternus* appears to refer to it as a betrothal, actually there is no marriage language in it; Christ's quoted demand contains only the language of feudal obligation.[65] To be sure, an interpolated comment from Peter in the *Codex Iuliacensis* declares that when he visited her almost a decade later in 1279, she said Christ's presence had been so glorious in the vision that she had been rapt for three days and nights afterward—but (whether she really said so later or not) such an experience does not belong to the *quaternus*, at this or any other point.[66] Similarly, in the description of her sojourn at Cologne, another interpolation from Peter informs us that in conversation she had told him that she experienced raptures there, for which reason the beguines thought her either epileptic or insane, but once again this is Peter's interest showing; the *quaternus* itself describes no raptures.[67]

We can conclude that the picture of Christine in her own putative writings—showing a young woman repeatedly struggling against demonic influences that would keep her from faithfulness to Christ and repeatedly winning the struggle—is finally compatible with, even complementary to, Peter's imaginings of the mystical bride, though it certainly has a different focus.

But finally, as promised, I ask: what are we to make of this conclu-

sion in terms of the *real* rather than "putative" Christine? The picture of
Christine in these texts is thoroughly hagiographical, that is to say it is so
pervaded by the purpose of demonstrating her sanctity, that one cannot
hope to filter out hagiographical motives in order to reveal a true historical picture of Christine's character and experience apart from them. That
is not to deny that these texts reveal reliable historical information about
her; there can be little doubt, for instance, of the fact that both she and
others considered her to be vexed by demons, or of the chronology of her
life and its various circumstances as the texts reveal them.[68] But the conveyed meaning or understanding of those vexations and indeed of the rest
of her life are not facts of the same order; they belong to that literary
and hagiographical entity of the text itself, where no sure filter separates
Christine from her collaborators. Still, if this means that we finally cannot
isolate Christine's view of herself from others' view of her here, neither
can we finally isolate others' view from her own. And thus it would seem
very possible—and given the lack of any clues to the contrary, I believe
likely—that Christine participated more or less fully in this hagiographical conceptualizing of her life. In that case she would have assimilated in
some measure, or at least accepted, vocabulary and concepts, such as the
language of bridal mysticism, that may not have been hers originally or to
which others gave clearer articulation—so that if the persona here is not
of her own invention, nonetheless it is likely that the real Christine resides
somewhere within, rather than apart from, that persona.

Observer and Bride

There is, of course, no mistaking the differences between the figures of
Christine and Peter as they appear in the *Codex Iuliacensis*. One might even
call them opposites, each possessing or displaying something missing in
the other. Thus Christine lacks Peter's learning, thus Peter lacks Christine's
intimacy with God, thus her spectacular suffering makes him appear quite
complaisant by comparison. And thus, as we have seen in detail, each
shows interest in what the other does not: whereas Peter reverently observes her mysticism, or at least its external concomitants, Christine occu-
pies herself with all the trials, doubts, temptation, and other adversity that
have obstructed that experience.

But their very oppositeness hints precisely at their complementarity,
within the world of the texts of the *Codex Iuliacensis*. For it is rooted in that

complementary oppositeness that always exists between saints and venerators—that, in fact, *creates* saints, in the sense that venerators begin to recognize saints as such precisely when they discern in them the extraordinary virtue they consider themselves to lack. Just so, the venerator has every reason to celebrate the saint's favored position with Christ, whereas the saint herself is reticent, and accordingly often skirts around that subject, humbly exposing her shame and degradation rather than her mystical exaltation, of which her very humility becomes paradoxically a sign and seal. Peter's is an "outside" depiction of sanctity, Christine's an "inside" one. Consequently, appearing as they do together in this collection of texts assembled mostly at Peter's initiative, a comparison between them cannot be understood fundamentally as a comparison of "spiritualities"—that is, a comparison of their respective ways of encountering the divine within their experience of the world. No doubt in some sense their spiritualities were different. But such a comparison, on the basis of the texts we have, would imply some base line of similarity between these two figures—and, within the world of these texts, they are *not* similar, but, by definition, opposites, standing on either side of that fixed boundary between saint and venerator which also defines each in terms of the other and so makes them inseparable.

7

Henry Suso and Elsbeth Stagel

Was the *Vita* a Cooperative Effort?

Frank Tobin

AMONG THE COOPERATIVE ventures between men and women in the production of religious writings in the Middle Ages, the relationship between Henry Suso and Elsbeth Stagel offers a paradigm for examining the problems that can arise when one attempts to determine with any degree of accuracy and probability the role played by each in such an endeavor. To illustrate this and to provide a basis for remarks to follow, we shall begin, after recalling some information about them, by examining the difficulties, doubts, and opinions which scholars have put forward over time.

Henry Suso (1295/97–1366) entered the Dominican order at the age of thirteen in his home town of Constance. Chosen to become *lector* at the Dominican house there, an office which made him responsible for the training of the young Dominicans and for the intellectual life of the community, his years of study were extended beyond the usual and he was sent to his order's *studium generale* in Cologne. Here, in an institution founded by Albert the Great, who had brought Thomas Aquinas as his student there with him, Suso came into direct contact with another famous Dominican, Meister Eckhart. After his return to Constance in 1326/27, Suso served as *lector* (though for a time he was relieved of his duties because of suspicion of heresy) and also briefly as prior of the community, whose exile from Constance (1338–46/49) he shared during the struggle between pope and emperor. Aside from his duties inside the priory, Suso devoted much time to the *cura monialium*, the spiritual direction of Dominican sisters, and was especially active at the twenty-five-mile-distant convent at Töss.

Here Suso made the acquaintance of Elsbeth Stagel (ca. 1300–ca. 1360), daughter of a respected Zurich family, who had entered the convent as a young woman and remained there until her death. As told in Suso's writings, a close spiritual bond developed between them. We learn of her spiritual progress under his guidance and of the help she provides him in his writings, especially with his autobiography or *Vita*. Besides mentioning her collaboration with Suso on his life's story, the *Vita* tells us that she is also the author of the extant sister-book *The Lives of the Sisters at Töss*.[1] She is also said to have collected Suso's letters to her and to other sisters.

About 1348 Suso was transferred to Ulm where he remained until his death in 1366. We know little of his priestly duties there, but he spent time (probably 1362–63, after Stagel's death) preparing an authoritative edition of his German works which he called the *Exemplar*.[2] It contains:

1. *The Little Book of Truth*. Originally written about 1328, it treats in dialogue form the nature of detachment and discernment by examining who God is, what creatures are, and what their relationship can and should be.

2. *The Little Book of Eternal Wisdom*. Written 1328–30, this is a manual of devotion, again in dialogue form, offering material for meditation on Christ's suffering and death.

3. *The Little Book of Letters*. This contains eleven heavily revised letters taken from the twenty-eight letters contained in *The Great Book of Letters* (not part of the *Exemplar*) said to have been collected by Stagel, as mentioned above. Didactic in purpose, they are so arranged as to chart the path of personal spiritual development from its beginning to its final goal.

4. *The Life of the Servant* or *Vita*. This is Suso's autobiography, which, he tells us, draws on material his spiritual daughter Elsbeth Stagel had written down. Besides works included in the *Exemplar* and *The Great Book of Letters*, Suso wrote the *Horologium Sapientiae*, a revised and expanded Latin version of his *Little Book of Eternal Wisdom*. His authorship of a *Little Book of Love (Minnebüchlein)* is a matter of dispute, and at least two of the four extant sermons attributed to him are probably not authentic. After this brief review of information basic to our inquiry, we can now proceed to examine Suso's and Stagel's possible literary collaboration.

Although we are principally concerned with opinions on the extent to which Elsbeth Stagel contributed to the composition of Suso's *Vita*, calling to mind an earlier dispute among scholars can help provide the proper context. At the beginning of the twentieth century, Suso's own part in determining the final form of the *Vita* was called into doubt—not because

Stagel was thought to have been its main author, but rather because its completion, as well as the final work on the *Exemplar*, was thought to have occurred after Suso's death. Only one of the reasons offered for doubting Suso's authorship need concern us here. One of the doubters, Henri Lichtenberger, noted that, in addition to the fact that miracles, visions, and the like were found in the *Vita* and nowhere else in Suso's works, the presence of many episodes redounding to Suso's credit were irreconcilable with this holy man's humility. Lichtenberger relegated the *Vita* to the genre of legend whose characteristics, he argued, were not compatible with autobiography.³

It was the Germanist Julius Schwietering who, if one judges by the course subsequent scholarship has taken, silenced the doubters once and for all.⁴ He saw no reason to find legend and autobiography mutually exclusive genres and theorized that the passages showing Suso in a good light (which are balanced by several episodes demeaning and embarrassing to Suso) had Stagel's notes as their origin. He argued that because of the edification such passages would engender in readers, Suso let them stand in his final editing.⁵ This point, however, is not Schwietering's chief argument for making Suso the *Vita*'s author rather than some posthumous editor or editors. Rather, it is the quality of the work. Schwietering's main strategy is to overwhelm all objections and misgivings by demonstrating that the *Vita*, in its structure, style, and totality, is a work of literary excellence and belongs among the works deserving the attention of literary historians.⁶ In passing we should take note of the slight lapse in logic in Schwietering's way of arguing. If successful, his argument proves that the author of the *Vita* possessed a great talent for and understanding of literature. It does not prove that Suso was this person. For the rest, Schwietering takes Stagel's collaboration very seriously, assigning to her a substantial role in the evolution of the *Vita*, and he declares that the next important scholarly task is to distinguish her contribution from Suso's.

In addressing this question now ourselves, we can do no better than to begin with the commonsense approach taken by the editor of the critical edition of Suso's German works, Karl Bihlmeyer.⁷ He follows in the main what Suso tells us in the pertinent passages in the *Exemplar*. Suso, he relates, wishing to correct the mistakes copyists have made in his writings and fearing that his works might be lost to posterity if they fell into the hands of the spiritually lax, decided to create an authorized edition of his most important writings. He is engaged in this pursuit, everyone agrees, in 1362–63. Concerning the *Vita* itself, Bihlmeyer notes that it received its definitive form at this time with Suso as the sole revisor and editor, since Stagel is mentioned as deceased in the prologue (8, 3).

Suso divides the *Vita* into two parts. Chapters 1–32 relate events in Suso's own life, mostly events occurring before his acquaintanceship with Stagel. Bihlmeyer assumes that this part relies heavily on Stagel's notes for its content. The second part falls into two sections. Chapters 33–45 center on Stagel—how Suso became acquainted with her and her spiritual progress under his guidance. Chapters 46–53, which Suso says he added after Stagel's death, contain instruction on the mystical life in the form of a dialogue between the servant (Suso) and his daughter (Stagel). Parts of Chapters 33–53, Bihlmeyer says, very likely existed previously as letters sent by Suso to Stagel after his transfer to Ulm. Although Bihlmeyer assigned Stagel a substantial role in the genesis of the *Vita*, he considered it very probable that Suso heavily revised the material he received from her; and he supports this view by comparing the *Vita* with the *Lives of the Sisters at Töss*, a sister-book which, at the time, everyone assumed had been written by Stagel. The refined style of the *Vita*, its aesthetic sense, and its theological sophistication, he stated, find no counterpart in the sister-book.[8]

Most investigations into Stagel's literary activity since the contributions of Bihlmeyer and Schwietering have either played down her impact on the *Vita* or questioned whether there was any real collaboration at all. Before looking at the arguments in these studies, it will be helpful to examine in detail those passages in the *Exemplar* which speak of Stagel directly, of her relationship to Suso, of how the *Vita* came to be, and of how it is intended to function. Aside from mention of Stagel as the recipient of Letters 3 and 8 in the *Little Book of Letters*, four passages require our attention: the prologue to the *Exemplar*, the prologue to the *Vita*, and Chapters 33 and 35 in the second part of the *Vita*.

In Chapter 33, which Bihlmeyer thinks Suso wrote after Stagel's death (probably when appending the final chapters [46–53] as part of his final editing[9]), Suso has left us an endearing portrait of his spiritual daughter. He praises her as a model of all virtue and describes how intensely she desired to embark upon the path of spiritual perfection. Much of Suso's encomium is so general that it could be applied to any holy sister. Two things he mentions, however, individualize her. First and less important, she suffered from failing health. Second, she was in the habit of *writing down* things she discovered that might benefit her or others spiritually. In fact, Suso continues, she "completed a very good book" which describes the virtues of some of the convent's deceased sisters.[10] Indeed, "drawn by

God to his [Suso's] life and teachings with great devotion," she "unobtrusively drew out of him the story of his breakthrough to God and wrote it down, as it is written above and as follows." [11]

In the rest of the chapter Suso gives us an intimate description of their early contacts: she, an overly eager neophyte who has been introduced by someone to some of the heady phrases of speculative mysticism [12] and who wishes to ascend immediately to the heights; and he, the experienced guide, cautioning her of the need for patience, discernment, and an examination of her own motives. She would do well, he advises, to concentrate on ascetical practices and good actions, as exemplified in the lives of holy persons. Taking this gentle remonstrance with good humor, she writes back that her wish is not for "clever phrases but rather for a holy life." Humbly but with spirit she reaffirms her determination to persevere, come what may; and she urges him that, if the examples of holy lives are to be her spiritual fare, then just as the pelican nurtures its young with its own blood, he should nourish her with his own personal experiences rather than with the lives of others. With charm and self-effacement he replies that she can hardly be thirsty for his "swill" (*grobem trank*, 99, 15) after imbibing the noble teachings of Meister Eckhart; but he then instructs her as to what her first questions should be as she begins her spiritual quest. Besides capturing well the personality of the young nun and the spirit of their relationship, Suso, through the example of the pelican, strategically coming from Stagel's pen, provides the justification for narrating his personal life.

Toward the end of Chapter 35, writing to console Stagel, who was then suffering from an illness that had afflicted her for some time, Suso makes direct mention of her part in his writing, telling her that "God has struck not only you with this. By striking you he has struck me as well. I have no one else who has been as helpful with such industry and devotion to God, as you were while still in good health, in bringing my books to completion." [13]

While these two passages from the body of the *Vita* seem to urge the reader to take them at face value, comments in the two prologues have raised serious questions about Stagel's collaboration on the *Vita* and have provided a point of departure for those doubting or diminishing the Dominican sister's role. Indeed, one must admit that what the prologues tell us about how the *Vita* came to be and how we are to understand it add as much to our puzzlement as to our enlightenment.

In the prologue to the *Exemplar*, Suso gives a brief explanation of the four books it contains and says of the *Vita* that it describes someone be-

ginning the spiritual life *mit bildgebender wise* (literally "in an image-giving
manner"; 3, 3) and shows *togenlich* (3, 4) how a beginner should order
one's inner and outer self. Given the use of *bildgebend* elsewhere in the
Vita,[14] we would do well to understand the first phrase to mean something
like "by concrete examples" or "by providing a model." However, with
the adverb *togenlich*, which ranges in meaning from "darkly," "secretly," or
"hiddenly" to, less commonly, "without a fuss" or "simply," Suso's statement takes on a certain ambivalence. *Bildgebend*, literally "image-giving,"
could, especially when combined with *togenlich*, also imply a certain lack
of factuality in the *Vita* in favor of image-creating—that is, metaphorical
or analogous manners of expression.

Suso then continues, saying that the *Vita* narrates "*mit glichnusgebender wise* many holy works, which in truth happened thus."[15] The untrans-
lated phrase can mean "in a manner similar to," "equal to," or "the same as"
(what is being described). However, since *glichnus*, in addition to meaning
"sameness," is also the word for "parable" or "allegory," Suso might again
be taking back with one hand what he has given with the other.

Although I favor a simple reading of these lines (that Suso intends the
Vita to give readers models to live by and to narrate events as they actually
happened), two factors (besides the fact that some events narrated strain
our good-faith effort to believe) deserve mention that vitiate such an interpretation. First, in younger years, Suso had been accused of heresy and
had to answer charges before a chapter meeting of his order in Maastricht
in 1330.[16] The ordeal left him shaken and probably influenced the direction of his writing away from theology and toward devotional literature.
One can well imagine his wish, late in life, not to have every word of
the *Exemplar* weighed theologically on the exact scales of strict orthodoxy.
Thus he may well be seeking to give his utterances in the *Exemplar*'s prologue a certain ambivalence. Second, in the prologue to the *Horologium
Sapientiae*, written earlier, the ambivalences on the same subject are hard
to miss, and it is difficult not to consider them intentional.[17] Commenting
on *visiones*, a word that may have wider application than the word *vision*,
Suso states that those contained in the *Horologium* should not all be taken
literally (*secundum litteram*), even though many of them literally happened
(*ad litteram*). Rather, he is using figurative speech (*figurata locutio*), just
as Nathan spoke in parable when confronting David with his sin,[18] and as
the woman of Tekoa did before David.[19] Then Suso refers to the story of
Tobias and the angel,[20] in which the angel actually lies about who he is, if
his words are taken literally, and can be absolved of such a charge only if

his words are taken according to how he meant them (*secundum sua signifi-cata*). Suso concludes by saying that the attentive reader will easily be able to perceive the hidden mysteries of this figurative way of speaking if that reader employs cleverness and diligence (*sollertem curam*).[21] Through such remarks, directed as they are to the works as a whole and not to specific passages or incidents, Suso both gives the reader free rein in interpreting and covers himself against possible attacks.

Suso engages in mystification not only when explaining how one should take his words. His account of Stagel's and his own participation in the genesis of the *Vita* also leave the reader, especially the clever and diligent reader, puzzled as to what really happened.[22] He got to know a holy person, he tells us, who asked him to tell her of his own sufferings, so that she might draw strength from them. On his visits she would ask the person questions to which he responded "in spiritual confidence" (*in goet-licher heimlich*). She wrote his personal accounts down but did so "surrep-titiously" (*verstoln*), so that he would not know. Later, finding out about this spiritual theft (*geislichen dúpstal*), he demanded she hand it over. He burned what he got hold of at the time. Having gotten the rest, as he is about to burn that, too, "a heavenly message from God" (*himelscher bot-schaft von got*) stops him. What comes next[23] remained unburned, "as she wrote the larger part with her own hand" (*als si den meren teil mit ir selbes handen hate geschriben*).

This account hides as much as it reveals. The modern reader reacts with disbelief. How could Suso not suspect through all their conversations that she was recording what he told her? If he burned some of it, what was lost? Does not his burning what he immediately gets hold of smack of topos? What exactly was the "heavenly message from God"? The image of the angel staying Abraham's hand as he is about to sacrifice Isaac comes to mind. If something very dramatic happened, why does he not relate it? He is quite willing to describe dramatic incidents elsewhere, as his portrayal of many incidents in the *Vita* attests. Are we really getting the unburned portion just as she wrote it? One is left with the feeling that Suso's account does not "add up."

If one considers it to be Suso's intention to provide the reader with information here, one must admit that his efforts fall far short of the goal. Given the quality of his writing otherwise, it seems unlikely that the per-ceived shortcomings of this passage can be attributed to lack of ability. The obfuscation would seem to be intentional.

In light of all this, it is not surprising that various doubts began to arise in secondary literature about the nature and even the existence of any real collaboration on the *Vita* by Elsbeth Stagel. The first voice raised was that of Kurt Ruh in 1957. Focusing on Suso's account of Stagel's "spiritual theft" in the prologue to the *Vita*, Ruh characterized the story as a *Fiktion* or *Roman*, whereby it should be noted that the German words *Fiktion* and *Roman* emphasize reliance on imagination and distance from reality or historical events more than do their English counterparts *fiction* and *novel*.[24] The decades since he made this remark have not softened Ruh's view. Suso, he still affirms, can legitimately be called the sole author of the *Vita*; and he repeats his remark about the prologue's being a *Fiktion*, referring to its *romanhafte Diktion* (romance-like diction) and to a similar *Fiktion* of the times in which the author of the courtly-knightly novel *The Younger Titurel*, who is known to history as Albrecht, maintains throughout most of the story that his famed predecessor Wolfram von Eschenbach is the actual author. Ruh relegates Stagel's role to the early stages of the *Vita*'s origin. Whatever part her notes might have had, Suso's revised edition is what we now have. Besides, he adds wearily, this is a minor problem that deserves no more attention.[25]

Stagel's reputation as an author has also been undermined from another direction. In a study exemplary for its careful and balanced use of evidence, Klaus Grubmüller convincingly impugns the assumption that Stagel was the principal author of the *Lives of the Sisters at Töss*.[26] He presents strong arguments for restricting her authorship to the book's prologue, the life of Elsbeth von Bechlin, and a few additions in the lives of other sisters.[27] In spite of making a good case for Stagel's authorship of at least these parts, Grubmüller is reluctant to assert even so much, because, as he says, one cannot exclude the possibility that Stagel's fame as reputed co-author of Suso's *Vita* caused her name to become later associated with the writing of the Töss sister-book in order to enhance its value.[28]

Ursula Peters also expresses doubts about what we really know about Stagel as an author, but she argues by using the Töss sister-book, not Suso's *Vita*, as her point of departure.[29] She notes that Stagel is only mentioned by name once in the entire book—in the life of Elsbeth von Cellikon as the sister who looked after Elsbeth von Cellikon during her sickness and "wrote all this about her."[30] Peters, like Grubmüller, assumes that someone other than Stagel wrote this life but used Stagel's written material. Peters notes further that Stagel appears by name in the *Vita* only in Chapter 33, where she is referred to as the author of the Töss sister-book.[31] Therefore, Peters concludes, the Stagel mentioned once in Suso's *Vita* has no other secure existence aside from being the sister in the sister-book whose notes supplied material for Elsbeth von Cellikon's life.[32]

At this point it would seem that Stagel, except in name, is in imminent danger of disappearing completely into an impenetrable academic fog. Rescue from her fate at the hands of these Germanists, if rescue it is, comes from a historian, Peter Dinzelbacher. In a debate with the Germanist Siegfried Ringler, carried out in a series of articles, published lectures, and book reviews in which others soon became involved, Dinzelbacher championed the view that, by and large, the information and stories narrated in medieval religious literature are based on historical fact. More specifically, the debate had to do with visions and whether one can draw conclusions about an actual visionary experience and its characteristics from how it is told in a medieval spiritual text. Soon, however, the question was enlarged to include whether one can assume a historical reality at the base of any incident related in such literature. Stagel and Suso were peripheral to the debate, which centered on holy lives (*Gnadenviten*) and revelatory literature more stereotypical in content and less literary than Suso's *Vita*. Since the debate has implications for our inquiry, however, a summary of the chief arguments of each side is in order.[33]

Dinzelbacher's view was that one is able to assume that holy practices, anecdotes, visions, and the like described in religious literature were reports of things that actually occurred, that they were based on real experiences. Ringler and many other Germanists emphasized the distance of such texts from actual experiences and the necessity of knowing how the texts are to be read, or what they are and are not really telling us. The key to knowing how to read a text, they maintained, is to recognize to what genre it belongs, what the conventions of that genre are, and to what end that genre and consequently the specific text were written. In other words, the Ringler camp is saying that what determines what is narrated about a holy person is not whether it actually occurred, but rather whether it is part of the genre to which the text belongs and whether it helps the text achieve the purpose for which it was written. Since, they say, the purpose of these texts narrating holy lives is not to impart information about the holy person but rather to teach holiness and to edify, the content will be determined accordingly. Visions, miraculous interventions, extreme ascetical practices, and the like will be described quite apart from whether they actually occurred. They are part of the genre "holy life" and for this reason occur in such texts. Thus attempts to draw conclusions from them about what actually happened are misguided and fruitless. In a discussion on the revelations of Elsbeth von Oye, Walter Haug put forward this position succinctly: one can only talk about the text and not about the kind of experience upon which it is based.[34] Texts, then, are the object to be studied. Conclusions about the kind of culture and society that produced them are possible: here, for example, that people believed in visions, miracles, and saints, and that religious writers tried to provide models of holiness for their readers. But one cannot naively suppose that they relate real events.

Dinzelbacher, along with others who agree with him at least in part, insists that these writings are a reflection, if not always an accurate one, of actual experiences and events. Does the genre "holy life," they ask, in itself exclude all connections to actuality? Does the use of conventions in relating an incident drain it of all "real" content? Does the wish to edify and to provide a model for holiness require that the holy persons be described in such stereotypical fashion that nothing from their actual lives remains? Given the interest in the thirteenth and fourteenth centuries in canonizations and the canonization process, how can it be assumed that the people of the times were unaware of or unconcerned with the difference between truth and fiction? Certainly, as Richard Kieckhefer states, testimony as to someone's holiness could be expected to be influenced by the positive predisposition in those attesting to the holiness of the person being investigated. However, we should not consider that witnesses and by extension hagiographers are "insincere or dishonest—only that their reverence for the saints conditioned what they saw as relevant testimony and that in subtle or less subtle ways their devotion could color their perceptions and recollections."[35] That fiction and legend crept into the narration of holy lives is virtually certain. Deviation from a norm, however, presupposes the existence of the norm, and it is evident that, at least among the educated, there was the wish that persons should be the object of veneration only if there was evidence of actual holiness in their lives.

A full reconciliation of these two opposing views would seem to be impossible. Yet neither position can be ignored with impunity. It must be conceded to the literary scholars that historical readings of medieval religious texts often reveal a naivete about how one extracts meaning from them and has occasionally led to absurdities. One must also concede that one can only attain varying levels of probability when drawing upon these documents for information; but then most historians have resigned themselves to this fact, as is evidenced by the rich variety of their interpretations of historical persons and events. To the assertion that one cannot get beyond such texts and is only justified in drawing conclusions about the texts themselves, one might respond, first, that it is indeed true that conclusions drawn from the text about the text carry much greater weight than those reaching beyond the text. Second, however, to state categorically that one can draw no conclusions from the text about a connection to historical events is a violation of one's own principle, for, in saying this, one is drawing a conclusion that goes beyond the text.

One is advised, therefore, to approach these texts cautiously, aware that different kinds of writings may yield results differently. Because of their differing characteristics, for example, assuming a connection between some of the information given in Mechthild von Magdeburg's *Flowing Light of the Godhead* and historical fact seems more reasonable than in the case of the sister-books with their overwhelmingly more stereotypical contents.

Applying this way of proceeding to the Suso-Stagel relationship, we shall try to take the best from both approaches. First, we shall examine additional indications for and against an actual literary partnership between them. Then, focusing on the texts and abstracting from any possible relationship to fact, we shall ask what the consequences of Stagel's presence were for the *Vita*.

The Suso-Stagel Collaboration Considered as Fact

Paradoxically, in denying to Stagel the role of chief author of the Töss sister-book, Grubmüller offers evidence that strengthens the conception of Stagel as Suso's collaborator. As we have seen, Bihlmeyer played down Stagel's role in the genesis of the *Vita* in part because the *Vita* exhibits a more refined style and aesthetic sense than does the sister-book.[36] While we would do well to respect the view of more recent scholars on the dangers of using the generally ill-defined word *style* in determining authorship, the sections of the sister-book Grubmüller thinks may have been composed by Stagel do have characteristics that set them off from the rest of the book, as he points out. Grubmüller notes the obvious literary consciousness of the author; the use of the first person singular in place of the otherwise pervasive *we*; the description of how (like the Stagel of the *Exemplar*) she pumps the holy person for information and does so "with carefully weighed words";[37] that she writes for the sake of edification and to reveal God's grace. All these factors point up similarities to the figure of

Stagel and the role assigned her in the *Exemplar*.[38] One might cautiously add that these sections of the sister-book strike one as being less stereotypical in content, more lively and literary, and with a larger concentration of Suso-esque vocabulary than the book as a whole.[39]

The strongest arguments for viewing the Stagel of the *Vita* as a fiction come from considerations of genre, that is, from the similarity of the *Vita* to the courtly romance. Schwietering first drew attention to this similarity; his purpose in doing so, however, was not to denigrate Stagel but to establish the high literary quality of the work. In response to earlier critics who characterized Suso as a spiritual minnesinger in prose, he compared the hero of the *Vita* to a courageous knight ready to do battle and points to two chapters (20 and 44) where Suso explicitly compares his spiritual combat and quest to knightly endeavor. He shows how the allegory of spiritual knighthood runs through the entire text and points to structural similarities: the episodic plots of both, the crucial turning points, and the struggles in overcoming suffering.[40] Grubmüller, in turn, in support of Ruh's view of Stagel as collaborator being a fiction, remarks that it is a fiction forced upon the *Vita* by the genre model of the courtly romance.[41] Alois Haas makes another structural similarity explicit in referring to the "double course" (*doppelter Kursus*) both employ.[42] Finally, Ruh refers to the "romance-like diction" (*romanhafte Diktion*) in the prologue of the *Vita* as evidence of the fictional presentation of Stagel and her role.[43]

One may object to these arguments arising from the nature of genre both on general-theoretical grounds as well as for reasons specific to this case. The general objection is that, in arguing for the prescriptive nature of genre in the Middle Ages, one is making a very bold assertion on limited evidence. First of all, there is the problem of the lack of any binding treatment of poetics. This requires scholars to base their claims about genre on what the poets actually did. Indications of a pervasive appreciation for traditional rhetoric abound. This is much less the case with poetics. Undoubtedly there was at least an unconscious and seldom articulated idea of genre at work in the case of most poets, but one can legitimately ask how dominant such an idea was and to what extent or in what sense it was prescriptive. Evidence for the prescriptive nature of genre is most convincing in Ringler's study of fourteenth-century holy lives with their extremely stereotypical story elements, their lack of literary ambition, and their narrowly focused intent. Literary genius, on the other hand, has often revealed itself in the violation of genre prescriptions, as the case of the medieval lyricist Walther von der Vogelweide's love poetry attests. And Suso's *Vita* certainly demonstrates literary ambition and talent, despite the presence of stereotypical elements.

Perhaps more telling is the objection to attributing the *Vita* to the genre of courtly romance. Should it really be considered, first and foremost, in the context of courtly romance? It would be foolish to deny the presence of important elements, in both content and form, that it borrows from this popular and influential medieval genre—just as it would be to overlook the elements of holy legend present in it. But one can find a more suitable category for the *Vita* closer at hand: the autobiography.[44] Certainly the *Vita* at its core has much more in common with Augustine's *Confessions* than with courtly romances. It, too, follows the search of a restless soul for peace in God, and, as in the *Confessions*, the trials and gropings of the hero ultimately work to proclaim God's goodness and his readiness to extend his grace.

Schwietering calls attention to the different orientation of the *Vita*. It is *confessio*, he says, in the service of pastoral care and only indirectly bears witness to God's glory, while this latter is the immediate goal of the *Confessions*. He emphasizes that the courtly romance, like the *Vita*, also describes the path of the hero's purification and focuses on a crucial turning point or conversion in his life.[45] One can readily admit all this and still comfortably maintain that the *Vita* is basically an autobiography, albeit with frames of reference added from the courtly romance and the legend. As autobiography it records the path of the soul from within the soul, despite the use of the third person throughout to refer to the hero. In contrast to the knightly hero, whose conversion is more often than not a secular and not a religious affair which the reader, with no access to the interior of the hero, can only interpret from his actions and occasionally from his words, the servant's interior life, in true autobiographical fashion, lies open before us. There is no need for us to interpret. We are privy to every thought, desire, hope, and fear that moves him. The struggles he endures are those of the human soul and not of the knight. Despite the addition of a courtly-knightly context, the *Vita* finds its most essential roots in the traditions of Christian spirituality and asceticism extending back to the desert fathers. In its dramatic and open portrayal of the dangers to life and reputation its hero faces, it resembles another autobiography popular at the time: Abelard's *Historia Calamitatum*.

If the *Vita* has to be viewed chiefly as an autobiography and cannot simply be relegated to the genre of courtly romance, it follows that there is no compelling reason stemming from considerations of genre that Stagel be viewed as a fiction. True, Suso must confront the uncomfortable task of explaining what induced him to publish his life's story, whose hero resembles in so many ways the heroes of hagiographies. This might well have induced him to play up Stagel's participation in the writing as part of his justification. Genre, however, did not compel him to create Stagel and her role.

If we ask whether Stagel as an author or writer ever becomes visible in the text of the *Vita*, one must admit that any vestiges are well hidden. Since everyone agrees that Suso edited the *Vita* after Stagel's death, the question can perhaps be given a partial answer by asking what sort of editor Suso was. It is generally recognized that editing in medieval times was often carried out with few inhibitions about preserving the integrity of a · text. Besides the preservation of orthodoxy, which was a concern of Suso's in editing the *Exemplar* for publication, revisions were usually determined as to their nature and extent by the purpose to which the text was to be put. Fortunately, however, we do not have to rely on such generalities regarding Suso, since he has left us two examples of his editing practices. First, Chapters 3 and 4 of the *Vita* are in large part a reworking of passages from the *Horologium Sapientiae* (373, 6–383, 18 and 596, 7–23).[46] Second, of the twenty-eight letters of the *Great Book of Letters*, Suso selected and revised eleven to be included in the *Exemplar* as a structured unit called the *Little Book of Letters*. We have detailed analyses of both of these examples of Suso's editing.[47]

Summarizing the main conclusions of these studies, one can say that Suso was in the habit of making numerous and extensive revisions in the material intended for inclusion in the *Exemplar*. From these changes one can conclude that he is adapting the material for a broader, spiritually and literarily less sophisticated audience to which he wishes to impart fundamental spirituality at the cost of refinement and complexity. He consistently clarifies and simplifies. He omits less familiar biblical quotations and references. He decreases the emotional intensity of his writings, omits much imagery, and eliminates rhetorical devices in favor of directness. In the interest of objectivity, flights of mysticism are also excised. In short, conscious literary stylist though he obviously was, Suso sacrifices poetry as well as the complexity of advanced spirituality to what he foresees to be the needs of a more anonymous and spiritually less sensitive audience.

It seems probable, therefore, that Suso took great liberties with any material he might have received from Stagel. What evidence we have points in that direction, and there can be little doubt that in overall conception and structure the *Vita* is of Suso's making. It also seems unlikely that anyone might devise a method of determining more specifically the relationship of Stagel's hypothetical notes to the state of the *Vita* as it left Suso's hand. One might add that, since the *Vita* was written for the same purpose as the other parts of the *Exemplar*, namely, to teach and to edify, one would expect Suso to go about editing it as he did the parts whose sources are available to us.

In response to such assumptions and conclusions, two minimally unsettling objections come to mind. First, if one agrees with Pleuser's plausible view that, in contrast to some other parts of the *Exemplar*, the *Vita*'s primary audience was to be nuns,[48] one could conclude that Suso might have been less heavy-handed in revising because he could expect more from this audience and would feel less constrained by didactic purpose. One must admit, however, that there is little in the text of the *Vita* to warrant this conclusion. While the private religious practices which he describes are eminently suitable for imitation by nuns, they generally remain on the level of basic asceticism. And while the inclusion of several stories embarrassing to the hero points to greater openness and trust in the intended audience, this is hardly something upon which to build a case for Stagel's collaboration.

Second, one could argue that much of the *Vita* is so different from the passages revised from the *Horologium* or the letters that conclusions reached about them have little to tell us about how Suso may have used material from Stagel in other sections of the *Vita*. Because such an objection remains vague and hypothetical, however, one seems obliged to base opinion on the evidence available and conclude that it was Suso who was responsible for composing the *Vita* as we have it, though one cannot rule out his dependence on Stagel for material, and this may have left its mark on some formulations as well.

It must be admitted that our search for convincing evidence for Stagel's collaboration in the *Vita* has been disappointing. The cases both for and against it grow apace. On the one hand, the parts of the Töss sister-book she may well have written show literary talents unusual in sister-book writing, and there is no compelling reason to assume Suso created her out of whole cloth. On the other, Suso's manner of editing makes it unlikely that actual writing done by Stagel can be discerned in the text we have, and there are indications that what Suso tells us about her collaboration was not written with historical accuracy as his primary concern. Despite this lack of demonstrable historicity, a sensible and sensitive reading of the *Vita* indicates that extreme skepticism is uncalled for. Fiction in the *Vita* is not the opposite of fact but has, rather, a symbiotic relation to it, and this would seem to apply to the Stagel presented there as well.

One can first note that incidental information presented as fact has gone uncontested by scholars. Suso tells us, for example, that he went to the Netherlands to a meeting of his order and was accused there of heresy (chap. 26), that he often went to Strasbourg (chap. 27), that he was studying in Cologne when his mother died (chap. 42), and that he once served as prior during a time of austerity (chap. 43). If this information goes unchallenged, why should one find it more difficult to believe that he had a spiritual daughter at the Töss convent who suffered from ill health and was in the habit of writing down what could further virtue (chap. 33)?

When one goes beyond incidental information, one must admit that the wish to edify and to achieve dramatic effect has often codetermined the content of narrative sections. To cite but one example, Chapter 38 narrates how Suso is falsely accused of fathering a child. As one reads the story, one cannot help but be overwhelmed by the conviction that things could not have happened as described. There are simply too many improbabilities.[49] More likely than not, however, as with most stories in the *Vita*, there is a factual core at its base which Suso then heavily doctored.

We should read what Suso writes about Stagel in the same manner as we properly do the rest of the *Vita*. In so doing we must admit she is a fiction in the sense explained above. One can reasonably suppose that a close bond formed between Suso and his idealistic and virtuous spiritual daughter through both conversations and letters. Quite plausibly she helped him with his writings, in part through notes she had made of his pious stories and instruction given in private or to the whole community.[50] Her health declined and she died. Having said this, prudence requires that one assert little more. One can only move on to the fictional Stagel, that combination of fact and ideal found in the text, and measure that Stagel's impact on the *Vita*.

Stagel's Role in the *Vita*

If the designation *author* in the traditional sense can be safely conferred on Suso alone, it is equally important to emphasize in how many ways Stagel left her imprint on the *Vita*. Her influence on form and content and her presence in the book are so strong that, while not its coauthor, she can rightfully be called Suso's partner in its genesis. Suso's years of pastoral work among women, and especially in convents, is so clearly reflected in his writings that he has been linked to the feminization of spirituality in the fourteenth century.[51] In the *Vita* one can point to the importance of a personal, affective relationship with God and the frequent occurrence of visions, especially what Augustine called spiritual visions—visions by means of images—as opposed to intellectual or imageless visions, as being characteristics usually thought of as elements of feminine spirituality. It was his idealization of Elsbeth Stagel, however, both as a spiritual daughter and as a restless seeker of high spiritual aptitude, to which the *Vita*, especially the second part, is so heavily indebted.

Even in historical biographies authors cannot escape the charge that, in choosing to emphasize this or that about their subject at the expense of other factors, they are fictionalizing. Nor can the portrait painter or photographer be said to be a purveyor of objectivity. In this sense, Suso's alleged fictionalization of Stagel is at most a matter of degree, and he creates a figure that serves as a model not only for his readers but for himself as well. As Pleuser recognized, it is Elsbeth to whom he speaks in the second part, not just by involving her in the rhetorical device of dialogue, but as to one really present.[52] She functions as a kind of ever-present literary and spiritual super-ego to whom he must answer. She is also his audience, as she was for some of his most beautifully written letters. It is often the case in the realms of literary and artistic endeavor that the capacity of the audience to appreciate quality greatly heightens the artist's success in achieving it. Analogously Stagel's presence spurs Suso on as he writes and edits the *Vita*.

When we examine the structure and focus of the second part of the *Vita*, we see that in it Suso has created a memorial to his spiritual daughter.[53] Though in parts of the narrative section (chaps. 33–45) Stagel functions as a peripheral figure, as a whole the section functions as a replica of the first part with Stagel at its center instead of Suso. In the first part Suso describes his own spiritual progress from its beginnings through those stages attainable through concrete models (*bilde*). Paradoxically and as his spiritual daughter had requested, he also serves as the principal model for imitation. In the narrative section of the second part it is Stagel who is both instructed by models and serves as a model for imitation. The instruction and themes of these chapters are determined by her specific needs and experiences. Suso narrates how at her beginning she makes a general confession of her past life and how in a vision he sees spiritual father and daughter united in the presence of angels amid signs of future divine favors to be showered upon her (chap. 34). He instructs her through the sayings of the "old fathers" but, given her delicate health, insists that she not punish her body severely (chap. 35). Indeed, suffering and how to respond to it appropriately appears in several chapters as a leitmotif in their exchanges. Through stories he warns her of the dangers of flirtations (chap. 41) and the value of spiritual friendship (chap. 42). The occasion of encountering a knight offers him the opportunity to take up the themes of courage and perseverance in spiritual combat (chap. 44). Finally, at the end of a chapter praising one of Suso's favorite devotions—to the holy name of Jesus— in which one is assured that God treats kindly those on their final journey who hold that name in special veneration, the narrative sections ends, the beginning made by the "holy daughter" is declared complete, and the daughter's spiritual journey enters a new stage, one beyond models or images.

In the final chapters of the *Vita*, Suso returns to the realm of speculative mysticism that he had cautiously avoided since writing the *Little Book of Truth* and the accusations of heresy which followed. He takes up again the mystical teachings that Stagel had so enthusiastically wished to hear about at the beginning of their acquaintanceship, when he had tactfully but firmly advised her to begin on a less elevated path. That he chose to cast this section in the form of a dialogue with her is a special tribute showing the deep respect he had for her spiritual achievement and intellectual capacity. Finally, the spiritual father, seeing that she has advanced to an understanding of "the most perfect and bare truth,"[54] realizes that she no longer has any need of his guidance. In a final letter he can only urge her to listen for God's voice within her.

It is significant that Suso ends his life's story with Stagel's saintly death. He, the spiritual guide, has no further function when his daughter surpasses him in death and in perfection. Hence it is fitting that, in the final paragraph, she appears to him apotheosized, "having entered into the naked Godhead."[55] From this final vantage point, one the author has chosen for us, the question of literary collaboration loses much of its significance. Following its author's lead, we might wish to consider, rather, her centrality in so many ways to the whole undertaking of the *Vita*.

Mystical Death,
Bodily Death

Catherine of Siena and Raymond
of Capua on the Mystic's
Encounter with God

Karen Scott

IN STUDYING THE SPIRITUAL writings dictated by Catherine of Siena (1347–80), an artisan's daughter and an illiterate lay mystic and activist in fourteenth-century Italy, and the writings about Catherine by Raymond of Capua, her highly educated Dominican confessor and later her main hagiographer, one might expect to find the laywoman absorbed in popular piety, private affective devotion, and visions, and the male cleric interested in more abstract scholastic theology and public action. Significant differences do exist between the thinking of these two authors, but the contrast that is usually drawn between educated and illiterate, male and female, clerical and lay, and learned and popular does not apply here in any simple and clear manner, at least insofar as their treatment of holy women is concerned. Raymond was fascinated by the tangible effects of God's grace on this unusual female mystic's body. He did tell several stories about Catherine's apostolates and he did discuss some of her doctrinal contributions, but his focus was her paranormal bodily experiences and visions, which he used as the subtle theologian he was to prove her holiness and establish her cult as a saint. In contrast, though Catherine described several of her own mystical experiences, in particular shortly before her death, she usually preferred to write a more sober theology of the ordinary soul's encounter with God. Rather than manifest miraculous divine gifts, in her view the body was the necessary means of practicing the love of God and neighbor. While Raymond relied on special supernatural authority to portray her as an extraordinary holy woman and, somewhat more discreetly, to give legitimacy to her singular female apostolate, Catherine did not write about herself as a woman endowed by God with unusual spiritual power. Instead, she defended her action as a peacemaker and reformer by speaking in an urgent and practical tone of the obligation for all, including herself, to hear God's call and respond vigorously to the needs of souls, cities, and Church. Thus, it was the male observer who was most interested in the extraordinary effects of mysticism on his female subject's body, and not the woman herself.

The different portrayals of Catherine by herself and her confessor make a study of her mysticism and encounters with God both more problematic and interesting than one might first have expected. To some extent these rich and differing images of her result from the fact that Catherine and Raymond were writing at times, in genres and languages, and for purposes that were quite different. Catherine dictated in her native Sienese dialect a voluminous correspondence, of which some 380 letters have survived, mostly over a period of six years between 1374 and her death in 1380.[1] Dictation was her mode of composition because she was uneducated and unable to write in her own hand, and she selected as secretaries several female and male disciples, mostly lay people. Catherine's missives give her correspondents doctrinal and practical instructions on a variety of subjects, including virtue, prayer, and the significance of Christ crucified. She also wrote often to city governments, kings, prelates, and popes to suggest a course of action in political and ecclesiastical affairs. As her letters were a form of preaching that seems not to have been controversial, unlike her traveling and direct speech, they became a major component of her apostolate to bring peace to Italy, to reform the Church, and to help save souls. In particular, the correspondence gives testimony to Catherine's work as a peacemaker between Florence and Pope Gregory XI between 1375 and 1378, to her contribution to Gregory's decision to move the papacy from Avignon to Rome in 1376, and to her attempts between late 1378 and her death in April 1380 to help end the Schism dividing the Church after the election of Pope Urban VI. She wrote the political and ecclesiastical leaders of her day with assertive gusto and evident pleasure, convinced that it was God's will for her to do so. Only rarely, however, did Catherine narrate external events, confide personal feelings, or discuss her mystical experiences in her letters.

While Catherine's correspondence highlights her activities, two other kinds of writings by her reveal more of her inner life. There is a collection of twenty-five short prayers, the *Orazioni*, which her disciples heard her uttering between 1376 and 1380 and wrote down.[2] Her long treatise, which she simply called "my book" and which later publishers entitled *Il Dialogo della Divina Provvidenza*, was a 1378 work in which she enlarged and made more general a letter of spiritual and doctrinal instruction addressed to her confessor Raymond of Capua in the autumn of 1377.[3] The *Dialogo* is a comprehensive summation of her spirituality and doctrinal views at that time, presented in a dialogue form that she used occasionally also in her letters to convey her experiences of prayer. Catherine's book records a conversation between God the Father and "a soul." While God explained theological issues and described the sorry state of souls, society, and Church, the "soul" asked God questions, expressed thanks for the answers she received, grieved over the sorry state of the world, and prayed vehemently for the salvation of all. The *Orazioni* are similar to the *Dialogo* in structure and content, but these prayers contain only Catherine's side of her conversation with God, and the intercessions she uttered there reflect the more specific issues that concerned her at different times rather than the more general ones of her longer treatise.

As expressions of Catherine's own spiritual experience, the *Orazioni* and the *Dialogo* show that she believed she enjoyed an ongoing, intimate, and passionate relationship with God. However, the kind of mysticism portrayed in her letters, book, and prayers is unlike the various approaches to the divine adopted by other fourteenth-century mystics, such as Julian of Norwich, Henry Suso, Birgitta of Sweden, Meister Eckhart, or the author of the *Cloud of Unknowing*. For the most part the encounters with God described by Catherine are neither visionary, nor marked by spectacular somatic manifestations of the Spirit, nor prophetic or apocalyptic, nor purely contemplative, nor apophatic. Instead, Catherine sought an ever deeper rooting of Christian doctrine within her soul—memory, intellect, and will—through an exchange of words with God. Her mysticism is expressed in speech about divine love, not in visions or silence, and it is unusually sober and theological in nature. Finally, the exceptionally social dimension of Catherine's mysticism is evident in the intercessory focus of her recorded prayers, in her emphasis on the importance of social action based on prayer, and in her insistence that her model of prayer should be taught to all, and not just to a spiritual elite.

While Catherine's letters, prayers, and *Dialogo* were dictated orally in Sienese dialect, were didactic and theological in tone, and were composed in the various circumstances of her apostolate, Raymond of Capua wrote his very long and literate Latin biography of Catherine, called the *Legenda Major*, by combining supernatural narratives with learned commentary on her sanctity and calls for her canonization.[4] Raymond was a prominent Dominican theologian who was also the Master General of his order at the time he completed this work, some fifteen years after Catherine's death. He sought Catherine's canonization to give spiritual legitimacy to several pressing causes of the 1380s and 1390s: the observant reform of the Dominicans and the reunification of his order and Church separated by the Schism. He also became one of Catherine's greatest advocates after her death because he genuinely admired her sanctity. Many of the *Legenda* stories are based on Raymond's memories of Catherine, for he had been her disciple, friend, and confessor during the last five years of her life. He also relied on his interviews with witnesses, on his knowledge of some of Catherine's writings, and on some documents collected by her other confessors—notebooks that unfortunately have now disappeared. A skillful raconteur, Raymond relished recounting episodes of Catherine's youth not mentioned in her own letters or treatises: her pious childhood, early visions, vow of virginity, adolescent rebellion against her parents' wish for her to marry, and ascetic life as a Dominican Sister of Penance, or *Mantellata*, at home. It was also her hagiographer and not Catherine herself who told the most memorable stories about her adult life: her fasts, her prophecies, her miraculous conversions of sinners, her wondrous healings of sick people, and above all her many visions, the most famous ones being her mystical marriage with Christ, her drinking from the wound of Christ's side, her exchange of hearts with Christ, her reception of Christ's stigmata, and her mystical death.

Enjoying at the time of writing the advantages (and disadvantages) of hindsight and distance from those events, Raymond organized them into a hagiographical narrative meant to strengthen his case for Catherine's canonization. He saw her as the humble receptacle of God's power and strength, so filled with the Holy Spirit that she could become the divine mouthpiece. The *Legenda* is also an account of her body's progressive death, first by privations and fasts, and later by supernatural experiences so strong that her weak female body could survive only by receiving more and more extraordinary graces. Although Raymond did mention Catherine's charitable work in Siena, her peacemaking in Florence and Avignon, and her attempts to end the Schism at the end of her life, he classified her apostolate as prophecy and miracle, not ordinary activity. For him the mature

Catherine was really a dead woman whose body was maintained in life by God in a supernatural manner so that he could save souls through her prayer and preaching.

Though these two views of Catherine overlap, the "dead" female recipient of supernatural power Raymond described is quite different from the lively and assertive apostle and the socially-oriented mystic Catherine presented herself to be. The variety in the portrayals of her reflects the differences between Catherine's perspective on herself as a laywoman, activist, and mystic who was dictating letters and treatises as her life was unfolding, and Raymond's perspective on her as her ecclesiastical superior, confessor, disciple, and hagiographer who was writing after her death to argue for her canonization. These two sets of texts are marked by so dissimilar a focus and mentality that scholars working on her life and thought need to take a position, explicitly or implicitly, on how best to approach the available sources. There are several strategies for dealing with this textual situation, each with its own consequences for an evaluation of Catherine's historical identity and significance. After assessing a number of these strategies, this essay will examine in some detail a rare, but important instance in which the two authors were writing about the same mystical incidents. Though each writer told the story from her or his particular perspective, there are also several interesting convergences. The analysis of this episode will enable us to speculate further about what Catherine's mystical experience might have been like, about how Raymond's portrayal of her mystical life might have taken shape, and about how scholars can approach the textual challenges involved in the study of medieval women mystics.

*   *   *

A first conclusion one could draw from realizing the extent of variation among the Catherinian sources is the inability of any text to convey meaning, and consequently the decentering of scholarly study from Catherine herself to something else. Postmodernist positions of this sort assume that all identity is unstable and fluid, that discourses do not refer reliably to realities outside of themselves, and that what is left unsaid in a text is most likely more significant than what is written; therefore, one simply cannot know "who" any person was from the documents that have survived, and one should not try to do so. Like a flat, fractured, and fragmented object in a Cubist painting, the available representations of Catherine appear unrelated, images sometimes blurred and unfocused but always fashioned, constructed, and in flux, and they cannot be superimposed and made to harmonize with one another. Scholars can study the creation of one or several images of her, the reception of these images by varied audiences, the power relations reflected in these images, and the spectrum of options in late medieval Italian society and culture which these images might represent; but Catherine the historical figure of the fourteenth century is lost entirely and forever, subsumed into textual and social constructions by Raymond and herself which bear no known relation to "her."[5]

The postmodernists' critique offers a welcome corrective to the optimistic positivism of earlier generations of scholars who believed that the various kinds of information contained in Catherine's and Raymond's portrayals of her could be amalgamated, that apparent differences between the two kinds of texts could be reconciled, and consequently that the Catherine of history could be easily and reliably resurrected.[6] Biographers read Raymond to obtain facts about her childhood and adolescence, her miracles and prophecies, her visions and ecstasies; and they read Catherine to learn about her apostolic travels and her spiritual and theological thought. When the two authors happened to discuss a common topic, such as her practice of fasting, her sojourns in Avignon and Rome, her relations with her disciples, or her teaching on self-knowledge, such scholars simply stitched their stories and information together into one great narrative. Their assumption was that both kinds of documents were equally true because both authors were well informed about their subjects and were persons of integrity. Each source supplied what the other omitted, and there were no serious contradictions between them. In all fairness, there may be instances when relying on both kinds of sources in an additive way is warranted. Besides the evident differences, there are also interesting overlaps between the writings of the two authors. Still, when earlier Catherinian scholars wove stories together from both sources, they seemed unaware of the variety of perspectives and ideas present in the various texts, and thus perhaps lost sight of some of the complexity of Catherine's life and experience. If a postmodern critique implies a closer reading of the two kinds of texts and a greater sensitivity to the impact of gender, class, and ecclesiastical status on each author's perspective, then it is clearly beneficial.

Postmodernist thinkers, however, go too far when they deny that anything can be known about a person from the past, or when they fail to look for anything but the differences among sources or the "silences" and "margins" of texts. The question of "what actually happened" may be impossible to answer with yesterday's degree of certainty, but there are several other worthwhile ways of investigating the issue of Catherine's historical identity that lie somewhere between the positivistic and postmodernist extremes. Rather than declaring Catherine totally unknowable or viewing her uncritically as the amalgam of what the different documents say about her, one can approach the variety of sources by giving privileged status to one author over the other and by deeming one author's perspective more reliable or historically significant than the other. In particular, I will argue here that Catherine's writings are the sources that should be considered "normative." As for those topics about which she was reticent to speak, such as her experiences of extraordinary mysticism, one should evaluate what little she offers carefully and not confuse her perspective with Raymond's.

If one asks which sources a study of Catherine's place in the history of medieval spirituality should be based upon, it appears obvious that her own writings should be given priority over Raymond's. The pioneering work of Robert Fawtier early in this century argued convincingly that the manuscript tradition for Catherine's correspondence and *Dialogo* was strong and for the most part historically reliable. Fawtier went on to critique much of Raymond's *Legenda* as an unprovable account of miracles and prophecies.[7] Though current scholarship is less skeptical a priori about medieval supernaturalism, and the old question, "Could this have happened?" has been replaced with a more historically sensitive and less anachronistic one, "What did medieval people believe happened?" there are still good reasons today to prefer Catherine's presentation of her own mysticism over Raymond's miraculous narratives. Her writings show her to have been considerably less interested and immersed in exceptional and supernatural occurrences than he believed her to have been. The *Legenda* tells many stories of publicly witnessed ecstasies, miraculous cures, and other awesome manifestations of the Spirit in her body, but her *Dialogo* conveys a mysticism that is more private and interior, more accessible and imitable by all, and more theological.

It seems likely that Raymond presented an improved and magnified version of his subject's spirituality to impress his various audiences, when in reality Catherine's experience of God was humble and ordinary. He did this, first, because as a master of narrative who wanted to make his *Legenda* entertaining, he needed to include stories with dramatic happenings; an inward-focused account of her life would have been much less exciting. Second, his biography is based on what he and others witnessed of her life, on what could be seen of her from the outside, as it were, for it is

clear that he was not a mystic himself, but had only Catherine's own gestures and explanations to give him a clue about what was happening to
her. Raymond may have read more into her gestures and words than she
did herself. Third, aspects of the *Legenda* may be a pious fabrication determined by the late medieval ecclesiastical models of female sanctity and
elaborated in view of her canonization. Raymond's repeated depiction of
Catherine as a "dead" body and an empty vessel filled entirely with divine
grace was meant to convince his audience that she was indeed a saint. To
that end it was more important for him to show her in moments worthy of
"admiration" than of "imitation."[8] If his text is governed by such external
standards, then it tells us a great deal about Raymond and his milieu, and
very little about Catherine herself. Indeed, she sought neither to entertain,
nor to develop her own cult as a saint, nor to impress ecclesiastical canonization experts. Her goal as a writer was always didactic, to share with
others the fruits of her own spiritual experience and theological insight.
While Raymond's "Catherine" tells us much about the history of how live
saints were perceived and dead saints were revered, and that is important,
Catherine's own portrayal of herself tells us much more reliably what a live
mystic actually experienced and valued.

Another argument for privileging Catherine's voice over Raymond's
is to focus on her gender. Considering how rare it is for a medieval Italian
woman mystic's own words to have survived, as opposed to hagiographic
accounts or writings heavily controlled by male confessors, feminist scholars would give more weight to Catherine's voice to circumvent the necessity of studying women of the past through the eyes of men and to seek
better answers, for example, to questions about medieval women's developing self-image, consciousness, and mode of thought.[9] Since compared
to the *Legenda* Catherine's letters contain much more information about
the political and ecclesiastical affairs that she was involved in, she clearly
knew better than her confessor did what she was doing at various times.
Raymond's relative lack of data on Catherine's apostolates is explained by
his frequent absences from her. He probably did not receive all of the letters she sent him. With the passing of fifteen years or more, his memory
was less reliable than were Catherine's own words uttered about herself as
events were occurring. Finally, in his desire to foster her canonization, he
downplayed or omitted information that would have made her appear too
strong a woman to be considered a saint.

The consequences of paying attention predominantly to what Catherine wrote about herself are quite significant, for then her life appears to

have been immersed in politics, church affairs, spiritual direction, and the elaboration of doctrine. This confident and assertive "Catherine" calls into question the generalization that late medieval holy women were silenced by their society and Church and had to retreat into visions and contemplation, or into heresy, as their only opportunities for self-expression. Privileging Catherine's writings and emphasizing her active identity undermines the view that *all* late medieval women suffered under the impact of the classical typology that identified men with reason, soul, theology, speech, and action, and women with emotion, body, devotion, silence, and contemplation: this typology is inadequate to explain Catherine's self-image and confident career as a female apostle. If a fourteenth-century Italian woman like Catherine could combine in original ways many of the qualities traditionally ascribed to male and female, and do so without incurring the excessive wrath of Church or state, then the limits on female creativity imposed by late medieval misogyny might not have been quite so narrow as has been thought. In addition, Catherine is usually viewed as one of the most important religious figures of her time. The active bent of her spirituality and her relative lack of emphasis on extraordinary supernatural phenomena such as visions and prophecies might lead historians to wonder whether the female mystics known to us only through hagiographical accounts would appear less otherworldly or conventionally holy if we had access to their writings as we do in Catherine's case.

*   *   *

So much for giving privileged status to Catherine's voice: there are convincing reasons to do so, and if one follows this path the consequences for a scholarly understanding of her historical significance are important. Her example shows that late medieval Italian women's spirituality may have been less centered on the supernatural and more actively concerned with the world than has often been supposed. However, the question of how historians should deal with the variety in Catherinian sources cannot be resolved quite so simply, because there are also several very good arguments for giving weight to Raymond's voice, and in some cases for considering his testimony as reliable as Catherine's. Keeping in mind his particular hagiographical perspective may serve less to discredit him as a source for Catherine's life than to lead to more complex, perhaps more interesting speculation both about the possible nature of her mystical experiences and about the sources of her fame as a holy woman.

There are several good reasons for paying attention to the voice of Catherine's hagiographer. First, the *Legenda* offers, more or less in chronological order, certain kinds of basic biographical information that do not appear in any of the other sources about her. The saint's life can be especially useful for the twenty-some years of Catherine's life that preceded the beginning of her own writing career. Any speculation about the impact of her familial and urban milieu on her early psychological, spiritual, and social development must rely on the critical assessment of certain *Legenda* passages, because for many aspects of her childhood, adolescence, and young adulthood no other documents exist on which to base such a study. Raymond presented vivid portraits of Catherine's relatives, discussed the family workshop she grew up in, and told engaging stories about her adolescent struggles to live an ascetic life at home and to be accepted by the Dominicans in Siena. He named in passing so many people and places that it is possible to map out the particular urban spaces of Catherine's youthful charitable activities in Siena and to gain an idea of who her earliest friends, disciples, and detractors were.[10] Though Raymond was writing to secure Catherine's canonization and surely skewed his narratives to fit his view of her as a holy woman, and though his information about her early days is all second-hand, for he did not know her in person at that time, his facts about her family and the Sienese topography are consistent with what can be known from other sorts of historical evidence.

If Raymond's accounts of Catherine's early years may be reliable, one can argue that his view of her adult activities in Siena, Florence, Avignon, and Rome deserves a hearing too. He was her confessor and best friend for the last five years of her life, he personally knew her entourage, and he interviewed her friends while she was alive and after she died, including long lists of his informants at the end of every *Legenda* chapter. As a churchman versed in ecclesiastical and secular diplomacy, and as someone who was present at Catherine's side during some of her most important peacemaking trips, Raymond was well placed to explain and interpret the significance of her politically oriented apostolates. In addition, one can test his version of the latter part of her life by comparing his work to her letters. Though Raymond usually presented Catherine's external activities discreetly, by keeping his passages about them short and by obscuring them, as it were, within sentences and sections focused on her prophetic and mystical gifts, his accounts are consistent with the more abundant information contained in her correspondence.

On occasion the *Legenda* even adds to our understanding of how

Catherine's active work took place, as when Raymond mentioned that he served as her interpreter during her meeting with Gregory XI in Avignon.[11] Since Italian was her only language, while the pope spoke only French and Latin, it is quite plausible indeed that she needed a translator to communicate the Florentines' message of peace and her own desire to see the papacy return to Rome and begin serious church reform. Raymond's role in the event is the kind of detail that he can add, however self-servingly, to our knowledge of Catherine's activism, for she did not think to mention it in her correspondence. Insofar as the general outline and some of the details of Catherine's active life are concerned, then, there is good reason to argue that Raymond actually gains in credibility when his saint's life is compared to her writings.

The use scholars should make of Raymond's stories about Catherine the mystic is more difficult to ascertain, however. Though she wrote a great deal about her apostolic work while she was engaged in it, she had relatively little to say about personal visions and extraordinary experiences. For the most part we cannot use her words to evaluate Raymond's much more frequent narratives about her divine ecstasies. One conclusion that could be drawn from this silence is that Catherine did not care about or receive exceptional bodily manifestations of the Spirit, and that Raymond's portrayal of her mysticism was entirely the product of his hagiographic imagination. However, there is a very good argument to the contrary: the importance of humility in medieval Christian spirituality. People like Catherine who were consciously seeking a life of holiness were unlikely to make public through their words anything about themselves that would set them apart as more graced or moral than their contemporaries. Her writings show that she saw herself as an ordinary sinner in need of divine mercy and as a pilgrim on the path to God, and not as a person who had reached a high degree of perfection and lived constantly aware of God's presence. While Raymond had good reasons to insert any supernatural event he knew of into the *Legenda*, it was consistent with Catherine's humble presentation of herself to omit references to such exceptional experiences.

We have shown above how and why Raymond's *Legenda* is lacking, especially in relation to Catherine's active life. Likewise, Catherine's writings need to be evaluated critically, especially in relation to what she may have censored about the supernatural dimensions of her spiritual experience, and why. A variety of sources indicate that people frequently accused her of pride or singularity because of her excessive fasting, mysticism, and apostolates, that she struggled with self-doubt and guilt over these accusations, and that she had to defend herself often.[12] She may have decided not to publish her exceptional experiences in order to impress the people she dealt with every day by appearing more humble and holy, to avoid criticism or misunderstanding, to be freer in her prayer, or to protect her apostolic activities on behalf of peace or church reform. She wanted the focus of her public writing to be away from herself as an individual, and firmly on God and on her correspondent, or on the human condition in general. She believed that discussing what made her different from her audiences would have lessened her effectiveness as a teacher and preacher, drawing more attention to herself than to their relationship with God and neighbor.

We can also find less manipulative kinds of motives for Catherine's relative silence about her mysticism. For her, divine union was an interior and intimate happening within the soul, and so stories about exceptional moments affecting her body could not convey the essence of her experience. Union was best expressed in theological language and symbolic imagery of universal import and applicability. She may also have omitted such stories out of a sense that loving her neighbor, bringing peace, and reforming the Church were actually more important priorities to her than mystical ecstasy. Moreover, the relatively few letters by Catherine that do tell stories about her visions, dreams, and mystical union are addressed to her confessors, mostly to Raymond of Capua when she and he were engaged in apostolates in different places.[13] Catherine's discretion about personal matters in her letters and her tendency to reserve such sensitive confidences to Raymond point to his role as her religious superior and confessor. Raymond may have asked her to reveal to him her most personal affairs and to be silent about them with other people orally and in writing.

Catherine's habit of confiding personal matters to her confessor in her letters reinforces the possibility that Raymond's *Legenda* contains important information about her spirituality. If she wrote him about her unusual experiences when they were physically separated, she very well may have spoken to him about them regularly when they were together. Raymond stressed that when he and Catherine were not separated by circumstance, they talked often, she confided in him, and she confessed her sins to him. He was very careful to delineate which informant gave him every bit of information about her life, and more often than not he said that Catherine herself was his source. Moreover, some of her letters to him say that she missed his company and imply that they usually talked about important personal matters when they were together.[14] Thus, the *Legenda* may very well contain traces of that intimate, mystical, extraordinary "self" that

Catherine believed it was inappropriate or unnecessary to communicate to the general public, but which she felt obliged to tell her confessor about.

There is no way to verify Raymond's assertion that Catherine's oral exchanges with him became the foundation for his account of her supernatural experiences, but we can examine the extent to which his treatment of her in his saint's life was influenced by the information we know he must have received from her letters. Oddly, one discovers that there is very little overlap between the mystical narratives of the *Legenda* and the ones contained in Catherine's letters to Raymond. This makes it difficult to evaluate Raymond's version of her spirituality in the light of her writings and to distinguish any patterns in his hagiographic refashioning of what she confided to him. However, a look at the texts may help at least in part to elucidate why the two authors omitted each other's mystical narratives; and the one significant instance in which Raymond and Catherine both discussed the same incident does allow us to study something of each author's approach to writing about such experiences.

Most of the stories about visions that figure so prominently in the *Legenda* are absent from Catherine's own writings. For example, although there are many instances where she used heart and wound imagery to convey her understanding of union with God, nowhere in her correspondence, *Dialogo*, or *Orazioni* did she describe, as Raymond did, visionary experiences of drinking from the wound in Christ's side, or exchanging her heart with Christ, or receiving his stigmata.[15] Perhaps there are circumstances that explain her silence on these subjects. Raymond explained that he obtained the first two of these stories (and a series of other similar ones) from a notebook kept by Tommaso della Fonte, one of the Dominican friars that preceded him in his role as confessor, and he also specified that these experiences took place in 1370.[16] Since this was several years before Catherine began to send her extant letters, it makes sense that there are no accounts of these events. By 1375 when she received the stigmata Catherine was writing many letters, and so one can wonder why she did not include a narrative of that event in her correspondence. However, Raymond emphasized that he was present at her side when she had that famous mystical experience. Because he witnessed the stigmata and had ample opportunity to question her about what had happened afterwards, one can surmise that she would not have felt the obligation or need to write to him about this incident. Thus, Catherine's silence about some of her mystical experiences in her letters to Raymond can be explained by the fact that she was not yet writing or that her confessor was with her at the time they occurred. We shall see below the important function of these stories in the *Legenda*.

If Catherine's silence about some of the most famous visions attributed to her may seem odd, even more surprising is the fact that most of the (rare) accounts of mystical prayer in Catherine's letters to Raymond are absent from the *Legenda*. Putting these accounts in approximate chronological order, the first one is in Letter 273, from the summer of 1375. Catherine recounted to Raymond the recent execution of a young man whom she had assisted in his last days; after he was beheaded she had a vision of his soul entering into the wound in Christ's side and going to heaven, as a bride goes to her groom. She wrote at the end of the letter that she envied her friend, wishing she had been the one to die and now enjoy eternal life.[17] Raymond did not include this story in his saint's life, though her later hagiographers did: Tommaso Caffarini identified the young man as Niccolò di Toldo, a Perugian envoy and spy, and he told with relish the story of Niccolò's conversion by Catherine and his execution.[18]

Second, Letter 219 told Raymond about a dream Catherine had on April 1, 1376, a few days before she was to travel to Florence and then to Avignon to visit Pope Gregory XI as a peacemaker for the Florentines. She wrote that she entered into the wound in Christ's side with her disciples, and there God gave her a mission to carry the olive branch and the cross to the Christian people and the Infidels and God told her "to announce to them a great joy," that is, to travel and to preach. Then she was "drowned in the divine essence," together with the saints. God also told her that much good would come from the tribulations the Church was currently experiencing.[19] When this letter was written, Raymond was in Avignon on a mission to convince Gregory XI to end the war with Florence and reform the Church. Catherine wanted to encourage him in this apostolate by telling him that God was on their side and to indicate that she too had a special and active role to play in the divine plan for peace and reform.

The *Legenda* does not include this important account of Catherine's apostolic call, nor does it describe a fairly similar series of experiences found in Letter 226, which she wrote in response to a letter from her confessor. These mystical events occurred, she said, "the day after I left your side": Raymond's absence had saddened her, but God consoled her by giving her "a great joy," and her body felt as if it were "dissolving and being undone, like wax in the fire." She described next how God responded to her strong desire for confession, in Raymond's absence, by directly giving her absolution for her sins. God then "overshadowed" her with a great fire of love and granted her certainty and purity of mind. She shifted to prayer for the pope and the Church, and God responded with news of future exultation and peace. The result of this mystical encounter, like the one described in

Letter 219, was a confirmation of Catherine's call to preach peace: God told her to be comforted, to announce the truth with courage, and to remember he would always be with her in her apostolate. She then had a "taste of eternal life" with the saints.[20]

Fourth, Raymond did not seem to know about Letter 272, which Catherine sent him in the autumn of 1377.[21] This text is important because it describes the vision of Christ as bridge and a long conversation with God that Catherine used later as the foundation for the *Dialogo*. However, she sent the letter originally to instruct Raymond about his own spiritual path, in response to letters she had received from him and from Pope Gregory XI. She had asked "a servant of God" to present to God "four petitions, holding herself and her [spiritual] Father before the spouse of Truth [before God]."[22] God's response to "the third petition, which was hunger for your [Raymond's] salvation," was a message about her confessor's need to take heart and cultivate patience by resting in and walking on Christ the bridge.[23] There followed a long theological and spiritual discourse based on this central image of the bridge. During the dialogue, God also told Catherine to ask him to grant mercy to sinners and to the entire world.

After recounting her experience, Catherine confided to Raymond: "Oh dearest and sweetest Father, then, in seeing and hearing so much from first sweet Truth [God], it seemed that my heart was half leaving me. I die and cannot die. Have compassion on your wretched daughter."[24] She went on to explain that God helped her come down from the heights of her mystical experience by miraculously giving her "the aptitude to write," through the teaching of John the Evangelist and Thomas Aquinas. The lesson was successful, for Catherine stated that she wrote Letter 272, as well as another letter also sent to Raymond, "in my own hand." She confided that this writing was an important outlet that kept her heart from breaking under the emotional and spiritual strain of her intense encounter with God.[25] Raymond's silence about these episodes is surprising: we know that he was quite familiar with the *Dialogo*, for he inserted a Latin translation of its last chapters toward the end of the *Legenda*, and in those concluding chapters Catherine recapitulated the main points of her book, including the image of Christ as bridge with some of its doctrinal implications for her.[26] However, the *Legenda* makes no reference to the original context of Catherine's vision of the bridge or to the message it held for Raymond in the letter she sent him, nor does it mention the writing miracle and its comforting effect on her.

Raymond's silence about these four letters that recount Catherine's most significant mystical experiences between 1375 and 1377 has puzzled scholars because one would assume a hagiographer so hungry for the visionary and miraculous side of his saint's life would have been eager to include and embellish them. Robert Fawtier concluded that much of Letter 273 and the end section of Letter 272 containing the writing miracle story were suspect, perhaps added to the correspondence by later editors like Tommaso Caffarini to strengthen the case for her mystical gifts and expedite her canonization.[27] This explanation is a possibility, but it cannot be proved. If we assume that the letters are genuine, Raymond may have failed to mention these letters or their content simply because the letters never reached him, or because he did not keep copies of them or have access to copies made by her secretaries, or because after more than fifteen years he had forgotten about these particular episodes.

If Raymond did receive these letters and remember their contents, though, it is likely that he omitted these episodes from the *Legenda* because they made too strong a statement about Catherine's charitable, ecclesiastical, and spiritual apostolates for him to be able to present her as a conventional holy woman. Moreover, these letters conveyed her continued experiences, between summer 1375 and autumn 1377, of a blissful and deeply satisfying kind of union with God resembling bodily death, and of repeated calls from God to develop her apostolates of charity and preaching in new ways. As we shall see below, for theological and spiritual reasons it did not fit Raymond's chronology of Catherine's mystical development to portray her experiencing new instances of mystical death and receiving new divine calls to the apostolate after 1370. So the *Legenda* concentrated these kinds of supernatural events in the early phase of her life, and omitted the stories about her mature experiences. Both Raymond's words and his silences involved a significant reshaping of the information she had sent or told him about.

*   *   *

Though in most instances there is no overlap between the two authors' stories about mystical experiences, there are two letters by Catherine about her visionary activity that do parallel important passages from Raymond's *Legenda*. Moreover, he stated several times that he was basing his account on letters she had sent him. These texts offer the rare opportunity to study to what extent his work as a hagiographer was influenced by

Catherine's own mystical confidences and to examine how he fashioned his narrative to suit his own agenda. Composed in early 1380, these are the last letters Catherine sent Raymond, when she was in Rome trying to help end the Western Schism several months before she died, and he was in northern Italy working to the same end. In Letter 371 she spoke of God's pressing her heart onto the Church to help reform and unite it.[28] In Letter 373 she described her soul being separated from her body. This was unlike Catherine's earlier accounts of mystical union (set forth in Letters 273, 219, 226, and 272) in which she had used language of her body's "dying," "drowning," and "dissolving like wax," and of her heart's "half leaving her" to convey an experience of her soul's being delighted, comforted, and strengthened in God. In contrast, the later mystical death described in Letter 373 was so horrifying that it left her unsure whether she would recover enough strength to stay alive.[29] Letters 371 and 373 concern the last months of Catherine's life, a time when illness and exhaustion were indeed bringing her nearer to bodily death. As we shall see, Raymond used the information he received from her in his own creative ways.

In these letters Catherine recounted in passing several unusual experiences that predated the winter of 1380, ones that resemble Raymond's accounts of her mystical marriage and mystical death. In Letter 371 she said that during a recent and very intense prayer experience, she had remembered "all the graces received during my life, past ones and present ones, and the day my soul was espoused in Him [in God]."[30] In Letter 371 she recalled also a previous experience of prayer resembling death: she wrote that she had been "feeling a disposition coming, like the one she had felt at the time of death."[31] She went on to explain that her current experience resembled that earlier "death," but that it was also "new." She now felt the more alienating sensation of her soul being separated from her body as if they had nothing to do with each other: "God put me before Himself. Even though I am always present to Him, for He contains every thing within Himself, this was in a new way, as if the memory, intellect, and will had nothing to do with my body."[32] In Letter 373 Catherine described that earlier "death" in a little more detail and analyzed what made it different from the more frightening experience she had just gone through. She wrote, "I was immediately thrown down. And as I was thrown down, it seemed to me as if the soul had left the body. This was not like that other time, when the soul left the body, for then my soul tasted the good of the Immortals [the saints], receiving that greatest good together with them. This time it seemed like an unusual thing, for I did not seem to be in the body, but I saw my body as if I were someone else."[33]

Catherine's cryptic allusions to these earlier experiences of mystical marriage and mystical death imply that she and Raymond had previously discussed them in greater detail. He would understand what she meant by such expressions as "tasting the good of the Immortals," and he would appreciate the fine distinctions she was making among the various kinds of encounters with God involving "death." Catherine's shorthand style implies a history of familiar conversations with Raymond. Moreover, her struggle to find language to describe the different types of separation between body and soul, to pinpoint what exactly was new and frightening about her most recent experience, as opposed to what had been "good" and pleasant about her previous ones, reveals her expectation of continuing discussions with her confessor about these matters. One concludes that Raymond did not simply make up his stories about Catherine's mystical marriage and death, and that indeed he must have received some of his information from her. Catherine was quite reticent about narrating the details of these mystical events in these letters, however. These are the only instances in which she referred to these famous experiences, and she said so little about them that it is difficult to evaluate Raymond's much more elaborate narratives in relation to hers.

While Letters 371 and 373 make only quick references to earlier experiences, they both describe much more fully the mystical events of January and early February 1380 that had just occurred. Letter 371 is structured as a prayerful conversation with God about the sorry state of ecclesiastical affairs Catherine was witnessing in Rome. The circumstance that occasioned the intense encounter with God was her growing concern about the division of the Church, Christ's bride, between two warring popes, Urban VI and Clement VII, each of them supported by his own group of prelates and secular leaders. Called by Urban VI in late 1378 to work in Rome for church unity by supporting the legitimacy of his papacy, Catherine had been sending letter after letter to rulers and ecclesiastics on both sides of the conflict, seeking to induce them to bring peace and reunite the Church.[34] For her there was more at stake even than finding solutions to these problems of war and church disunity, however, because in her view love of neighbor and unity with the Church were necessary expressions of one's love of God and salvation, and ultimate separation from God was a serious risk for everyone, for popes and bishops, rulers and subjects on both sides of the conflict.

Catherine vowed to devote all her energy to ending the Schism. Yet when she sent Letter 371 in early 1380, over a year after her arrival in Rome, the Schism was still far from being resolved, and she attributed this to a lack of personal holiness on all sides, including her own. Urban VI had not turned into the Christlike pastor, conciliator, and church reformer she had hoped for; the "Antipope" Clement VII was settling in Avignon; ecclesiastical reform seemed more distant than ever; and secular rulers were not more inclined to peace. Catherine could see that her letters, entreaties, and ordinary prayers would not be sufficient to induce the necessary conversions. The encounter with God described in Letter 371 concerned the more radical change of heart and the all-encompassing action that Catherine believed she would personally need to undertake in order to obtain real results.

After a short introduction on the God-given dignity of the human person, the dialogue between God and Catherine began with his painting in vivid (Catherinian) imagery a grim picture of the state of the Church in her day: "Look with grief and bitterness, and you will see that no one comes to this bride [the Church] except with an outward garment on, that is for temporal gain. She lacks those who would truly seek her marrow, who would seek the fruit of the blood [of Christ]. . . . I grieve that no real ministers can be found. Indeed it seems that she is totally abandoned."[35] In a process that Catherine described frequently in the *Dialogo* and that was typical of her prayer, she was brought by God's words to a deeper and more urgent concern about the ills of the world, in this case with churchmen's corrupt emphasis on personal profit rather than the "fruit of the blood" of Christ. In her view, ecclesiastical politics, which she called the Church's "external garments," were far less important than the Church's "marrow," or true spiritual purpose, which was the ministry of salvation, the transmission to all people of that eternal reconciliation for which Christ shed his blood and gave his life on the cross. If the Church was "abandoned" by all of her clergy, as God told her, if the ministers no longer preached the truth or administered the sacraments in union with the Church but cared only for personal profit, then the salvation of all was in jeopardy, and this was indeed a matter for God's—and Catherine's—bitter grieving.

From an attitude of receptive listening to, and grieving over, God's complaints about the clergy, Catherine shifted next to a more active approach. She asked God, "What can I do?" In response God told her to surrender her life to him as a prayer for the Church: "Offer again your life, and never allow yourself to rest."[36] To encourage her to take this radical step of self-surrender one more time, God went on to speak about what was needed more broadly to enhance church unity. All Christians should develop their desire for church reform and should offer constant prayers, while government leaders should offer temporal support for the same ends. Pope Urban VI was "sweeping" the Church clean through the fear he was inspiring in his subjects, and that was good, but he should seek peace above all, both within himself and in his relations with others. The "pillars" and "columns" of the Church, that is, the cardinals and bishops, should "cover the defects" of Pope Urban VI by working harder themselves for ecclesiastical reform, and thereby enhance their ministry of communicating Christ's blood. It seemed that these proud prelates would not truly convert from their corrupt ways without a major spiritual push from God, however, and Catherine expressed her willingness to serve as God's indefatigable instrument in this essential task.[37] After recounting this conversation, Catherine specified that it had occupied the greater part of a day. In the evening she returned to prayer, felt a deathlike disposition coming upon her, and remembered all the graces of her past life, including the day she was "married" to God. "I attended only to what could be done," she wrote Raymond, "that I could make a sacrifice of myself to God, and this for the holy Church, and in order to take away the ignorance and negligence of those people whom God had put in my hands."[38]

Therefore, after hearing God's version of fourteenth-century conciliar theory, in which everyone is responsible to help reform the Church but the bishops are especially important, Catherine finally accepted to offer her life to God "again." She must have offered her life many times before, and she wrote about it in these terms in the *Dialogo* and in her *Orazioni*, but this time she did so more specifically as a prayer for the "pillars" and the "columns," that they might reunite the Church. She noted further that demons were trying to distract her from this offering of self by screaming and beating her body, but she did not pay attention to them. Catherine's next words speak again of "sacrifice," of Christlike annihilation expressing her desire to be emptied of herself, and thus to die, so that the Church temple or body might be filled with grace and built up again: "Oh eternal God, receive the sacrifice of my life into the mystical body of the Church [for the clergy]." Finally, she narrated the mystical culmination of her encounter with God, conveying with more complex language her understanding of what this total self-surrender might entail. She said to God: "I have nothing [to offer] but what you have given me. Take my heart and press it onto the face of this bride."[39] When God acquiesced to her request and pressed her heart onto the face of the Church, she added, "He drew my heart to Him with such force that unless He had encircled and reinforced it with His strength my life would have gone away, but He did not will the vessel of my body to be broken."[40]

Catherine ended her account of her mystical encounter with God on a positive note by referring to the preservation of her life. She went on to celebrate the victory of her humble faith over the demons' desire to frighten her. She then explained that she had heard words and promises from the divine Majesty that were so attractive and delightful that no human tongue would be able to speak about them adequately.[41] Finally, at the very end of the letter she seemed to take great joy in repeating an insight that already figured prominently in her *Dialogo* and that her recent experience had just confirmed for her: "It is not through the suffering of our bodies that the devil is or will be defeated, but by the power of the fire of God's most ardent and inestimable love."[42]

Catherine's varied references to her heart in Letter 371 convey her particular approach to mysticism.[43] When early on in the dialogue she shifted from offering her "life" to offering her "heart" to God, she was implying the simplifying of her complex identity. She integrated the active and lively self involved in "restless" travels and preaching into one metaphor, the "heart." Moving further along the path toward self-annihilation and union with God, Catherine said next that this heart, her one central reality, did not belong to her but to God, and that she could give God only what he had already given her. Here she shifted from a focus on self in dialogue with God and on self cooperating actively with God, to a surrender of self to God and grace alone. Catherine was *not* saying here that God had literally given her his own physical heart during a special supernatural event and that she was now returning that heart to God in another moment of mystical ecstasy, as Raymond of Capua would later interpret this kind of language.[44] Rather, her statement is connected to a general theological insight about the human condition that is found often in her writings: that one's entire being is a gift from God, that God is "the one who is," while she, as creature, sinner, and contingent being, is "the one who is not." Catherine was saying that her being, here summed up in the one image of her heart, is entirely God's gift and is owed back to God. In surrendering all to God she was simply fulfilling her debt as a creature to her Creator and recognizing the ontological reality that human beings live entirely "in God." As God's use of the word "again" implied, this was a kind of self-surrender that Catherine could repeat and wanted to repeat many times, not a once-in-a-lifetime special mystical event.

Catherine's selection of the "heart" to represent the self she was surrendering to God takes on special meaning in a second context, as well: Christ's heart. In her writings and thought this is a fundamental image of the divine nature and represents the central mystery of God the Father's merciful love for humanity and generous desire to redeem sinners. Catherine and all human beings exist not only because as creatures they owe their being to God, but also because as sinners they are redeemed by Christ and live only through divine love and mercy. The gesture of returning God's heart to God meant that Catherine recognized and trusted that all the love within her heart was God's very love, with all God's goodness, force, and effectiveness, and that she deserved no credit for her love and its achievements. Moreover, in Catherine's writings Christ's heart is particularly associated also with the crucifixion and with images of wounds and blood. Through the open wound in Christ's side one can see his pierced heart. The wound, the heart, and the saving blood pouring out of it are the tangible exterior manifestations of God's invisible being as self-emptying, sacrificial love for humanity. In Catherine's imagery, Christ's wound is a large cavern or womb where all people can bathe in the cleansing blood, and therefore be safe from evil and fully love each other. The wound is also a tavern where abundant wine, Christ's blood, flows freely for all to get drunk on. As a place of cleansing and drinking, the wound becomes an image for the Church, with her sacraments of baptism and communion, as well as an image of the eternal banquet in heaven.

When Catherine offered God her heart in prayer, she meant not only to say that she was surrendering her ego, her being, and her love back to God, but also to state her desire to imitate Christ and be intimately united to him in loving and helping to redeem sinners. Her heart was only pressed or squeezed, while Christ's was pierced, but the results of her sacrifice would be similar to his: Catherine wanted her life blood to flow too (though certainly to a lesser degree than Christ's), her inner love for others to be made manifest, and people needing God's mercy to be saved. Catherine believed that united with Christ's abundant blood, her own drops of blood would purify the corrupt Church and wipe clean the face of his bride soiled by the Schism. In a somewhat similar passage from the *Dialogo* Catherine had heard God promise that he would wash his bride's face —and reform the Church—not through war or punishment, but through Catherine's own love, tears, and sweat.[45] Now, nearly two years later, Catherine offered the divided Church a "bloodier" and more effective bath.

Finally, in this story there is a physical aspect to Catherine's heart without which the near-death experience at the end does not make sense. Almost imperceptibly Catherine shifted from describing her inner world to relating events occurring in a realm both more concrete and more visionary, one where God acts with great power upon both her mind and her body. What allowed her to bridge this divide between her soul and her body was a concentration on her heart as the summation of "her life," which included this time, in a way that was most unusual in her writing, her physical identity as well as her emotional and spiritual being. Catherine's body imagery allowed her to introduce an element of personal physicality and external factualness to a narrative which up to this point had functioned on a more abstract or interior level. Her near-death experience was the only hint that her dialogue with God had been anything more than a conversation taking place within her imagination, or that her self-sacrificing surrender to God might have tangible consequences for her bodily survival. In Christ's case, the shedding of blood had both expressed God's desire for world salvation and caused physical pain, weakening strength, and death. By saying she was surrendering her heart to God for the Church, Catherine was accepting her own physical death as a possible consequence.

The shift from heart as metaphor to heart as internal organ making physical human life possible held certain advantages for Catherine. Bodily death entailed a greater sacrifice, and in the context of her attempts to help end the Schism the most radical and complete offering of self seemed necessary. Moreover, in stating that physical death was a possible consequence of "God's drawing of her heart to Him," she was showing a parallel between mystical union and death that emphasized the completeness of her surrender to God. Because it brought the final and eternal union with God, bodily death for Catherine was far more desirable than a mere spiritual experience. How close her body had come to total disintegration (and how radical her offering of self for the Church had been) was reflected in her statement that only a supernatural action on God's part had allowed her to live, as a vessel or wine cask stays together only if strong metal bands surround it. Finally, Catherine's shift from using heart imagery to discussing her failing physical heart reflected the fact that she was indeed deathly ill during the winter of 1380, and this circumstance made Letter 371 unlike anything she had written earlier.

Letter 373 is the second letter Catherine sent Raymond during the winter of 1380, and it contains unusually detailed accounts of her personal experiences. She told about her developing prayer and illness between the feasts of the Circumcision of Jesus (January 1) and the Purification of Mary (February 2), and beyond. She placed herself in specific rooms of her house in Rome, such as the chapel, the study, and her own cell, and she mentioned activities in specific places outside her house, such as her prayer for the Church at St. Peter's every day between Terce and Vespers. The events that she set in these times and places resemble the ones she narrated in Letter 371: a deep experience of prayer involving also frightening encounters with demons and a kind of mystical death.[46] However, by mid-February 1380 when she sent this letter, Catherine's tone was less optimistic than in Letter 371, conveying to Raymond her increasing uncertainty about whether she would be able to survive her illness: "Oh sweetest Father, I will not be silent about the great mysteries of God, but I will narrate them to you as briefly as possible, as my fragile tongue will express them. . . . I do not know what the divine goodness will do with me, whether God will make me stay on or will call me to Himself."[47]

At the center of Letter 373 there is a short dialogue between God and Catherine herself that took place during an experience of mystical death. She was thrown down on the ground, unable to move her body, with her soul fixed on the Trinity and on her prayer for the Church, for her friends, and for her own salvation: "It was like this for a very long time, so long that the *famiglia* [her disciples] cried over me as if I had died. In this, all of the demons' terror had gone away. Then there came the presence of the humble Lamb before my soul, and He said: 'Do not doubt, for I will fulfil your desires and those of my other servants. I want you to see that I am a good Master, like a vessel maker who unmakes and remakes his vessels as he pleases. I know how to unmake and remake these vessels of mine. And so I take the vessel of your body and I remake it in the garden of the holy Church, in a way that is other than [what I have done] in the past.'"[48]

Though the divine message Catherine heard, that the vessel of her body might yet be put together again for further service of God and neighbor, was quite positive, the narrative that followed turned darker. Catherine lamented that after her soul returned to its vessel and she came back to bodily life, the demons tormented her again; she felt a great pain in her heart, one that was still with her at the time of writing; and she began to doubt whether her body was possessed by an unclean spirit. Then she received a divine call to pray for the city of Rome, which was about to revolt against the pope. She prayed, and received some assurance that peace would be restored. She went on to explain to Raymond how she was currently obeying God's call: "When it is the hour of Terce, I rise from the Mass, and then you would see [what looks like] a dead woman going to St. Peter's. And I enter once again to work in the ship of the holy Church."[49] Catherine called this life of prayer, pain, and uncertainty about her fate a kind of martyrdom of desire for peace and church unity: "It seems to me that I am supposed to confirm this time with a new martyrdom for what is the sweetness of my soul, that is, for holy Church. Then, perhaps [God] will make me rise again with him, and will put an end both to my miseries and to my painful desires. Or he will hold to His usual methods, and will encircle my body again."[50] Catherine concluded Letter 373 with a series of messages for Raymond and her other friends, in a kind of spiritual testament that pointed to her awareness that bodily death was now very near.

*   *   *

Raymond's narrative of Catherine's struggles in Rome during the winter of 1380 was based on Letters 371 and 373, and perhaps also on other letters of hers that have not survived. This account is placed in a chapter following his explanation of how Catherine was called to Rome by Pope Urban VI.[51] Next, Raymond put his translation of the end of the *Dialogo* and a chapter on Catherine's bodily death. During most of her sojourn in Rome and at the time of her death, Raymond had been in northern Italy, and thus he was not a witness to these events. As a result, his account relies heavily on Catherine's writings and manifests also his own narrative skill, spiritual perspective, and hagiographical agenda.

Letters 371 and 373 gave Raymond the general framework for his treatment of Catherine's last months, but unlike her focus on surrender to a God of mercy, he emphasized her struggles with demons and saw her accepting death from a God of justice in reparation for the sins against the Church. Raymond's account is also full of concrete details that are missing from Catherine's extant letters. Angered by her successes in prayer for the Urbanist papacy, he said, the devil decided to sow discord between Urban and the people of Rome, and Catherine responded by praying assiduously. "As she wrote to me herself, she saw in spirit the entire city full of demons, who everywhere were inciting the people to the crime of parricide and were uttering horrible shouts against the virgin while she prayed."[52] A debate ensued between Catherine and God, in which she tried to calm the divine desire for justice and vengeance. Using imagery reminiscent of Letter 371, but without describing any kind of mystical death, Raymond explained that the stress of this struggle with God was so terrible that only God's power kept Catherine's "little body" together. "In this disputation, if I do not remember this wrong, she occupied several days and nights, with great affliction and labor for her little body. She was still praying, the Lord was arguing for justice, and the demons were calling out against her, as I wrote above. Such was the fervor of her prayer, as she herself wrote to me, that, and I speak in her words, if the Lord in his ordinary way had not encircled her body with his strength, as wine casks are usually strengthened and held together with circular bands, without a doubt her little body would have totally collapsed and fallen apart."[53]

Raymond went on to say that Catherine won her "war" with God, but that she did so by agreeing to die a martyr's death at the hands of the demons. She prayed, like Jesus: "Let whatever penalty that is owed [out of justice] by this people be done to my body. I will willingly drink from this chalice of passion and death for the honor of your name and for your holy Church." Raymond commented that "from that hour the murmurs of that people [the Romans] ceased, first a little and then totally, and the virgin, filled with virtues, bore the entire passion. Indeed, since by divine permission those infernal serpents had obtained full power over her little virginal body, they showed their furor with great cruelty."[54] The narrative proceeds with statements that Raymond attributed to Catherine's letters about her tangibly receiving terrible blows, lashes, and death threats from the devils. He then told about her going to St. Peter's every day to pray, until she finally died on April 29, 1380.

Raymond's repeated references to Catherine's letters show that he believed he was conveying faithfully what she said had happened to her during the last months of her life, and indeed there are similarities between the two authors' accounts. Both mentioned Catherine's successful prayer asking God to solve problems in Rome at the beginning of the Schism, as well as her daily prayer at St. Peter's. Both envisioned the mystic's encounter with God as analogous to death or hastening of death, and both recounted frightening episodes with demons. However, although Raymond's story does depend on Catherine's and there is some basis, then, for concluding that his writing of the *Legenda* was grounded in her confidences over the years, the two narratives are so different in the details, tone, and theological assumptions that one must posit also a significant reshaping of it by the hagiographer.

The *Legenda* story includes no account of Catherine's pressing her heart on the face of the Church, as in Letter 371, or of anything resembling the terrible mystical death experience recounted in Letter 373. While it is Catherine's loving passion for the Church and unflagging hope in the future that makes her letters memorable, Raymond's story stressed her war with cruel demons, a feature of Catherine's letters that was present, but not so central. Whereas she reiterated that she remained uncertain about whether or not God would keep her alive in the usual way after powerful encounters with him, he implied that she had agreed to die in order to save Rome and thus that her fate was determined. Finally, while Raymond explained Catherine's bodily death as a punishment for the Romans' sins due to God's justice, her letters make it clear that apostolic prayer could save souls not because it involved vicarious physical suffering and atonement, but because it brought the mystic into a deeper participation in God's mercy and love symbolized by Christ's heart. Thus, the two authors' different treatments of the same story reflect their particular theologies. Raymond significantly altered Catherine's account because of his own perspective.

Furthermore, to explain why Raymond omitted the 1380 stories about Catherine's heart and mystical death found in Letters 371 and 373, as well as the 1376 stories about her divine calls found in Letters 219 and 226, it is necessary to examine the central argument for her canonization that he wished to present in the *Legenda*. Raymond assumed that his audience was unsympathetic to the idea of active women saints: he stated that during her life Catherine had been maligned for being an itinerant preacher and public kind of mystic instead of the usual kind of holy woman who prayed in her cell, and the apologetic tone of the *Legenda* shows that in his view her reputation as an active mystic was well known and still a problem fifteen years after her death. The canonization of this unusual kind of woman would be hard to orchestrate. Raymond's solution was to place the episodes of Catherine's mystical marriage, mystical death, and divine call to the apostolate at early stages of her life, and to concentrate there any information he might have had about her subsequent experiences. He especially wanted to present Catherine's mystical death as a definitive, once in a lifetime turning point in her early spiritual development in order to defend the holiness of her subsequent activism as that of a mystic already entirely possessed by God and dead to herself.[55] If she had received a variety of calls from God and several death experiences after that major turning point, as her letters make it plain that she actually did, then his argument for her canonization would have been weakened.

Raymond's strategy was to place the main events of Catherine's active life as a mature adult between two sets of holy and supernatural experiences that he felt would justify to a critical audience the dignity of the active life and Catherine's unique saintliness: her mystical death, and her bodily death. The ordering of the chapters is key: first, her early good works in Siena and her unusual ability to fast; next, her most famous ecstatic experiences, leading up to and including her mystical death; next, her miraculous conversions of souls and physical healings; and finally, her actual death and entrance into the court of heaven. Raymond portrayed the early Catherine as growing in grace and in union with God, as allowing more and more her selfish self to die and her soul to be filled with God, and as letting the female weakness of her "little body" be taken over by God. As a consequence of this, an overflowing or superabundance of divine love made it possible for her to avoid human food, to be "rapt out of her senses," and to become a living miracle effecting supernatural conversions and healings.

There is a loosely chronological ordering of the events. Raymond said that many of the early mystical experiences he described occurred in 1370, when Catherine was twenty-three years old and before she had really begun her public apostolate. More significantly, however, he shaped Catherine's life according to a theological scheme of general spiritual stages, in which the soul's progressively greater openness to God brings her closer and closer to death; then she experiences a mystical death manifesting conclusively her death to self and her life in Christ. Next, because in this death she has been so entirely surrendered to God, the soul can mediate divine grace completely to others, as a kind of live saint, and she can receive a definitive divine call to the apostolate; finally, when God ceases to need her services, He stops keeping her supernaturally alive, and she experiences actual death.

Raymond's narrative of his saint's progress toward mystical death in 1370 incorporates some of the features of Catherine's letters from ten years later, especially imagery of heart, vessel, and death. He began with a statement of the usual effects of Catherine's mystical raptures on her body: "Such a plenitude of grace superabounded in her that she was occupied almost constantly in actual contemplation. Her spirit adhered so fixedly to the Creator of all things that most of the time her inferior and sensitive part [her body] was left without sensitive acts. . . . When she was engaged in this actual contemplation, her eyes were totally closed, her ears could not hear any sound, however loud, and all the senses of her body were deprived of their own function for this time."[56] Next Raymond told a series of stories in which Catherine's ecstatic experiences began to threaten more and more seriously the life of her body, symbolized and literally represented by her heart. Christ appeared to her, opened her left side, took her heart out and left her living several days literally without a heart. Then he appeared to her again in a bright light and put his own heart, which Raymond said was red and shining, into Catherine, leaving a visible scar, the first of several stigmata in her flesh.[57] After this event, Catherine told her confessor (Tommaso della Fonte, one of Raymond's predecessors, who had left notes Raymond was using) how close to death she had come: "Do you not see, Father, that I am not the woman that I was, but am changed into another person? . . . Such joy and such jubilation possess my mind that I greatly wonder how my soul can stay in my body."[58]

Using further information from Tommaso's notebooks, Raymond compared Catherine's ecstasies to Mary Magdalene's raptures, and he told stories about Catherine's seeing God's secrets, about her heart entering Christ's heart, and about her heart being wounded. On another occasion she drank the drink of life from the wound of Christ's side, and felt such sweetness that she thought her bodily life was ending due to the pure love she was experiencing.[59] After a particularly powerful ecstasy following communion she asked God to allow her to suffer and to unite her will with His. She now entered into the wound of Christ's side and she found such knowledge and such sweetness there that she wondered again why her heart was not shattered by the magnitude of this love.[60] After another exhilarating communion experience she lay exhausted on her bed at home, levitated, prayed for her confessor's and her other friends' salvation, and in a second stigmata experience, received as a pledge of God's acceptance of her prayer an invisible but painful wound in her hand, as if a nail had pierced her flesh.[61]

At this point Raymond digressed to tell a related story that occurred in 1375, some five years later, and that he said he had witnessed personally: Catherine's reception of Christ's stigmata in her hands, feet, and side. Adapting to Catherine's case an iconographic tradition probably derived from representations of St. Francis's stigmata, Raymond created a masterful narrative about a mystical experience that was visible to others, but was essentially interior and spiritual for Catherine. Raymond said that Christ crucified appeared to her, that red lines came from his wounds into her, and that these red lines changed into light when she asked that the wounds not be visible in her body.[62] Initially the stigmata experience was so painful that Catherine fainted, and all expected her to die. Her disciples prayed for her recovery, and she awakened from the swoon, invigorated, and the pain gone.[63] At this point Catherine had threatened to die several times in Raymond's narrative and she had experienced a few near misses, reflecting her growing death to self and developing supernatural life, but she had not actually died yet.

Finally, after some other digressions and accounts of Catherine's visions regarding St. Paul and St. Dominic, Raymond came to the high point of this section of the *Legenda*: Catherine's mystical death and the complete annihilation of her bodily life for four hours. This event had taken place in 1370, years before the stigmata, but Raymond placed it here after the stigmata to mark the culmination of her spiritual progress. Catherine had reached the point of being so completely filled with divine love that she had actually asked God to free her from the prison of her bodily life.[64] God allowed her for a time to suffer more and more of Christ's passion, especially a pain in the heart which Raymond accounted for in entirely physical terms.[65] Finally, the magnitude of the divine love within her caused her heart to break in two: "She experienced with her senses how much the Savior had loved her together with the entire human race, in enduring so very bitter a passion. From this there was created in her heart such a violence of charity and love that her heart was not capable of remaining whole without being entirely broken in two. The same thing happens when a vessel contains a liquor of great power or virtual vigor. The container is broken because of the power of the content. And then, when the restraint is gone, the power that had been confined is poured out in all directions; for there was a disproportion between the container and what it contained. . . . Such was the power of this love that the heart of the virgin was rent in two from top to bottom."[66]

This death was so real that all the women of the neighborhood witnessed Catherine's passing, and then after four hours they all saw her miraculously return to life. Raymond added that several years after this event he personally interrogated Catherine about what had happened. She revealed to him that indeed her soul had actually been separated from her body, that she could still feel physically the pain of her broken heart, and that during her mystical death she was taken on a tour of hell and purgatory, after which God told her to return to earth to begin a special mission.[67] The "power" held previously within the "vessel" of her body was now ready to be "poured out in all directions." Therefore, after narrating multiple near-death experiences, stigmata, ecstasies, and a "real" death that turned out not to be a final death but that demonstrated the very high degree of Catherine's holiness, Raymond introduced the theme of her apostolate.

The *Legenda* had included several earlier stories about Catherine's receiving a divine call to the active life, in particular one right after her mystical marriage with Christ. However, for Raymond the mystical death marked the beginning of Catherine's apostolic travels outside of Siena and of her more important and controversial career as a peacemaker and church reformer in Italy and southern France. God said to Catherine: "The salvation of many souls requires that you return, that you no longer live as you have until now, that you no longer live in your cell. It is necessary that you leave your own city for the salvation of souls, but I will always be with you, and I will guide you. You will carry the honor of my name . . . , and I will give you a mouth and a wisdom that no one will be able to resist. I will lead you before popes and the rectors of churches and of the Christian people, and in my customary way, with the weak I will confound the pride of the strong." [68]

By placing God's call for Catherine to begin her political and ecclesiastical mission immediately *after* her experience of complete mystical death in 1370, Raymond was taking a courageous stand in favor of the holiness of female activism. Following in this matter St. Bernard's (and not Catherine's) spiritual theology, he said that first the weak soul needs to be filled thoroughly with contemplation, to the point of bursting, annihilation, and union with God, and only then might she go out to save souls and reform the Church. [69] In Raymond's scheme of holiness, both the mystical and the apostolic lives are present as separate and successive steps in the journey to God, and the active life represents a more advanced stage. With this ordering of the narrative Raymond provided Catherine's political and ecclesiastical action with the surest justification to possible detractors. Anyone thoroughly filled with the fire of divine love must normally die, he argued, for no body can stand such power, and the heart is destroyed. So if Catherine went on living after her mystical death, it was because God's grace kept her heart and the vessel of her body from breaking again. Raymond could conclude that since the only reason God preserved her life was for her service of neighbor and Church, clearly her apostolate was exceedingly good.

By concentrating his stories about Catherine's mystical death and her calls to the apostolate in her early adulthood, Raymond succeeded in his intent to justify the holiness of her mature life. Given what is known from her correspondence about her travels and public work between 1370 and 1380, it is clear that Raymond was seeking to uphold a dimension of her life that had truly been important to her. However, his defense strategy also altered in other significant ways the image of her life and thought that he had received from her letters and confidences. He omitted important episodes in Catherine's spiritual life that occurred during the last five years of her life because they implied that his subject was still developing at that late date in her relation with God and her understanding of her call. He placed what information he had about her mysticism in earlier sections of the *Legenda*. While Catherine's accounts of her special experiences of prayer always put her apostolate at the center of her concerns, Raymond set his most dramatic stories at a time in her life before she had received the call to go out into the world. Thus, he made her mysticism appear more exclusively focused on union with God than she did. Moreover, Raymond's depiction of Catherine's mysticism may have been colored by his recollection of what she had experienced during her last illness when her little female body was weak, empty, passive, and in pain. Thus, unlike Catherine, he focused on the numerous visible and physical manifestations of her special encounters with God, such as her scars, pain, bodily swoons, apparent deaths, and mystical death that were witnessed by many people.

Though the *Legenda* was based in part on Catherine's letters and oral confidences, it was shaped quite significantly by Raymond's own hagiographic agenda and spiritual theology. It tells us much about Raymond's concerns and is instructive about Catherine's fame as a holy woman after her death, but its perspective on her differs in important ways from her own. Consequently, Catherine's own writings must remain the major document for her spiritual life, her apostolic actions, and her thought. These texts, which highlight her lively, energetic, and assertive personality, the importance of her apostolates, and her reticence about discussing supernatural happenings in her body, convey the historical Catherine's public persona. Her rare letters to her confessor about her more intimate mystical experiences combine passionate statements of concern for her Church and world, with expressions of delight over her soul's repeated and ever new experiences of union with God. Even when she was about to die and her body was failing, Catherine's tone was marked by love for others and unflagging hope in the future. This image is as close as we can get to the live Catherine of the late 1370s.

9

Authorizing a Life

The Collaboration of Dorothea of
Montau and John Marienwerder

Dyan Elliott

"I also want you and your Confessor to speak about the operation of my goodness as long as you live, and if you were to wish to stop speaking, I would not permit it out of zeal for my glory. And for [this reason] I would impell you to speak, and him, moreover, to hear. And because I united (*coniunxi*) the two of you, bestowing the grace of speaking of my goodness, give thanks to me magnificently. Indeed you yourself have no will. Let both of you have one will—one which he ought to possess, not you! In his presence, humble yourself to the lowest depths! Do not hide, but open, the secrets of your heart to him!"[1]

These words were spoken by Christ to the mystic Dorothea of Montau (d. 1394), as characterized by her confessor John Marienwerder (d. 1417). The divine command is the eleventh in a succession of twenty-four "proofs" which John advanced in order to establish the authenticity of Dorothea's visions. Christ's remarks pertain to the collaboration of John and Dorothea in the redaction of her revelations—a union imbued with nuptial overtones, as the use of the verb *coniungere* would suggest. And in fact, as we will see, throughout the corpus on Dorothea, John and Dorothea's union is metaphorically infused with matrimonial imagery. It was in many ways an unlikely match. The groom was a learned theologian and the bride an illiterate laywoman.[2] And yet, in the context of other mystical collaborations of the later Middle Ages—where the woman provided the dowry of mystical grace and the groom the home of literacy—this kind of ostensible disparity was becoming something of a spiritual commonplace.[3]

The personal histories of both Dorothea and John, moreover, rendered this union not only possible but highly advantageous. In her hometown in Danzig, Dorothea had met with ridicule and rebuff for her mystical spirituality. In desperate need of a spiritual director with whom she could share her mystical experiences, she sought out John. He, in turn, an able theologian with a once promising career at the University of Prague, had ended up in something of a dead end job as a canon at the cathedral of Marienwerder.[4] So John was waiting for new material on which to exercise his theological mastery.[5] When the two lovers met, they were instantly united by common interest, although their goals were probably not identical. Dorothea sought validation of her invisible spiritual life, whereas John sought to become the recognized interpreter of her spiritual experience — a goal that coincided with his ambitions to have Dorothea canonized.

In the interest of these divergent, but closely related, goals, a process of double authorization ensued. In mystical discourse, proof of its authenticity must, necessarily, reside outside the text, through what the text alludes to, but cannot contain or express. Both participants in this mystical collaboration must, in other words, define themselves in relationship to this divine excess.[6] If the divine "reserve" constitutes the place of authorization, it must first be demonstrated that Dorothea has been to this place — even though the place itself must elude coherent symbolization. The legitimacy of Dorothea's spiritual life and mystical revelations was thus addressed via a rigorous examination by John Marienwerder and his friend, John Reyman — a canon lawyer.[7] Their positive prognosis was most likely put before the bishop of Pomerania, John Mönch.[8] The second and arguably more challenging step in this double authorization was for John Marienwerder to establish himself in some relationship to this divine excess through Dorothea. If successful (and only if), John would have convincingly distinguished himself as the spokesperson for and ultimate authority on Dorothea. Not only was such an authorization essential for his hopes to have Dorothea canonized, but canonization itself would ratify John's initial assessment of Dorothea's authenticity. It is this second form of authorization, the authorization of John, that is the focus of my inquiry. I intend to explore some of the ways that the clerical quest for self-authorization in the writing of a mystic's *vita* and revelations virtually obscures the independent contours of a mystic's spirituality, and ultimately of her (or his) life. I also hope to suggest some of the ways in which the very process of redaction possibly alters the lineaments of an individual's spirituality.

Dorothea's Spiritual Odyssey to John

John's unrivaled expertise on Dorothea must first be established beyond all doubt. This was most obviously achieved by the sheer volume of writings he produced on Dorothea in the decade following her death in 1394. If we consider only the major works, there were four *vitae* and two collections of revelations. The short *Vita prima* and the more prolix *Vita Lindana* were both completed in 1396. These *vitae* were followed by a book of revelations known as the *Liber de festis* (1397), which arranged Dorothea's visions around important liturgical feasts. The most ambitious *vita* from the point of view of length and theological sophistication, now referred to as the *Vita latina*, was completed in 1398. The *Septililium*, a second collection of revelations named for the seven graces Dorothea received in the course of her communications with Christ, was produced ca. 1400. The present study will only be considering these Latin writings. But a final work referred to by modern scholars as the *Vita germanica*, written in the German vernacular and consisting mostly of extracts from the *Vita Lindana* and the *Septililium*, was finished in 1405.[9] All of these works were written with a view to Dorothea's canonization—a lengthy procedure begun the year after Dorothea's death only to be abandoned in 1525. Although John's ambitions for Dorothea were long deferred, she was eventually canonized in 1976.

I have been deliberately foregrounding John's productive capacities over the events of Dorothea's life out of deference to the fact that the latter are, for us at any rate, almost exclusively derivative of John's *vitae* and renderings of Dorothea's revelations—works which understandably focus on the mystic's inner at the expense of her outer life. But the bare events of the external life are soon told. Dorothea was born in Montau in 1347 into the well-to-do artisan class. In 1363 at the age of seventeen, she was married to a weaponsmith in Danzig named Adalbert to whom she bore nine children, although only one survived infancy. Beginning in 1382, Dorothea embarked on a series of pilgrimages accompanied by Adalbert. Impeded by ill health, however, Adalbert did not accompany his wife to Rome for the Jubilee year of 1390. He died in 1391 during Dorothea's absence. Only at this point did the widowed Dorothea, following the advice of her confessor Nicholas of Hohenstein, travel to Marienwerder in order to consult John Marienwerder about her tumultuous inner life.[10] With the help of canonist John Reyman, John Marienwerder undertook Dorothea's spiritual direction. After their careful examination of Dorothea's faith, the two Johns supported Dorothea's desire to become an anchoress, and she was officially enclosed in a cell (*reclusorium*) attached to the cathedral of Marienwerder on May 2, 1393, where she remained until her death on June 25, 1394.[11]

Dorothea's outer life presented undoubted challenges to even the most able of hagiographers. For instance, the difficulties of molding a very married woman into a plausible saint when the subject had been married for twenty-seven years and widowed only four, were palpable—palpable but not insurmountable. The example of the recently deceased Birgitta of Sweden (d. 1373), who was presented as central in Dorothea's spiritual development, testified to the relaxation of pristine prejudices against a sexually active past.[12] Like Dorothea, Birgitta had experienced a long marriage, lasting some twenty-eight years and producing eight children. Although Birgitta's widowhood of twenty-nine years had the merit of being of much greater duration than Dorothea's, both had achieved their spiritual eminence in widowhood. Moreover, both women had made a transition to chastity late in marriage. In this last respect, Dorothea had outstripped her pious prototype: Birgitta and her husband Ulf had lived in a spiritual marriage for approximately two years, compared to Dorothea's impressive ten-year period of sexual abstinence.[13]

But the real challenge to John's mastery of his subject came not from Dorothea's outer life, but from her inner life.[14] At the time of her death, John had known Dorothea for slightly less than three years. The pall that so short a relationship might cast over John's claims to expertise becomes especially apparent if one considers that her earlier confessor, Nicholas, had known Dorothea for twenty-four years and had acted as her spiritual director for twelve years.[15]

The potential charge of too cursory an acquaintance with Dorothea was resolved by the radical telos which John imparted to his description of Dorothea's spiritual development—one which required a foreshortening of her past and a dramatic telescoping to her relationship with himself—the final and most intimate of her spiritual directors. This was, of course, delicate work since John could not afford to efface all the precious early signs of Dorothea's eventual spiritual prestige. Thus Dorothea, like most female saints, had an early spiritual awakening that coincided with a severe scalding by hot water at the age of seven.[16] She experienced raptures throughout her marriage, but ones that were curiously contentless compared to what came later. Even so, such experiences were crucial in signaling celestial favor and an auspicious dissociation from worldly pleasures. The raptures were also depicted as provoking Adalbert's verbal and physical abuse, so that Dorothea emerged as a martyr within marriage by virtue of her indefatigible patience.[17]

But most of Dorothea's spiritual graces were crowded into the last seven years of her life. In 1385 at the age of thirty-nine, Dorothea experienced a mystical extraction of her heart—a crucial event in her spiritual development that led, as we shall see, to a new and more comprehensive mode of confession as well as more frequent and more lucid ecstasies.[18] In 1389, Dorothea's confessor advised her to seek counsel from John Marienwerder. Upon hearing about John, she experienced a vision in which her future spiritual father appeared to her.[19] Two years later, after the death of Adalbert, Dorothea sought out John in the cathedral of Marienwerder. The romantic undertones implicit in her prescient vision of John are brought to fruition when on their first interview she confesses to and receives communion from John:

Immediately her soul was glued to her own most recent Confessor through so immense a friendship (*amiciciam*) as quickly as she had ever had for any person, loving him with all her heart and trusting him so much that she [opened] the secrets of her heart to him.[20]

Such expressions automatically have the effect of effacing the hold of husband and previous confessor alike. Yet most important for our purposes is that it is only in the last twenty weeks of Dorothea's life, during her enclosure in the *reclusorium*, that she was authorized by God to reveal her revelations to John, who accordingly began to record them.[21] A number of these revelations turned upon the mysterious wounds of love that Christ had impressed on Dorothea's body and that she had hitherto concealed from the world.[22] God's timely mandate placed John in singular possession of his penitent's past.

Confessor and Penitent

As Dorothea's confessor, John was naturally privy to the secrets of her heart in a way comparable only to God's privileged access. This was in keeping with the medieval understanding of the priest as judge of the penitential forum, an aspect of the private realm of conscience over which he presided as God's representative.[23] Most devout Christians would be expected to be aware of the chains of spiritual clientage which bound them to their confessors. But the level of dependency was all the greater for a female mystic, in proportion to her greater vulnerability to allegations of heresy. John's hold over Dorothea may have been greater still. If Dorothea's first meeting with John approximated love at first sight, their spontaneous affection was soon ratified by her twofold vow to John, taken at Christ's behest. In order "to stabilize" (*stabilire*) Dorothea, Christ first required that she vow never to leave John—creating a bond that Dorothea felt (and Christ confirmed) to be a kind of marriage.[24] Four days later, Dorothea vowed obedience to John, whereupon "no longer knowing any will of her own, she did and omitted whatsoever [John] enjoined and ordered without any exception."[25]

A vow of obedience to the confessor is hardly unique to Dorothea. In the high and later Middle Ages, many other female mystics, Birgitta of Sweden included, were reputed to have taken such vows. In fact, Birgitta allegedly did nothing without her confessor's permission.[26] But John's representation places a still higher premium on Dorothea's obedience, particularly with regard to speech acts. Only this level of control could establish him as the uncontested purveyor of Dorothea's visions and words. Thus the visionary Christ frequently reiterated the exacting level of obedience required: "'I totally commit you to your Confessor: if he were to order you to speak, speak; and as long as he were to order you to be quiet, be quiet!'"[27] The obligation of obedience is seemingly redoubled upon her entrance into the *reclusorium*, on which occasion she was inspired to relinquish her entire soul and will to the judgment of God and the two Johns.[28] She was informed by Christ that she could not so much as reach a hand outside of the window of the *reclusorium*; nor could she speak with anyone unless she had her confessor's explicit permission.[29] Dorothea's last fourteen months were spent in the *reclusorium*. In other words, John's control is particularly ensured for the critical twenty weeks, Dorothea's final days, when she is at last authorized by God to reveal her visions and the process of redaction begins.

Dorothea's enclosure provided enhanced opportunities for supervision and enforcement of her vow of obedience. The impulse for surveillance is affirmed by Christ, who hinted to the two Johns, via Dorothea, that they should observe her more closely.[30] Of course the *reclusorium*, which would tend to make Dorothea's devotions something of a public commodity, could potentially be perceived as imperiling her verbal solitude by augmenting general access. Even so, Dorothea's compliance with John's level of control is upheld throughout the various *vitae*—even, or perhaps especially, in the breach. Thus on one occasion, Christ mystically reproved her for turning away from himself and his mother in order to speak to someone who was not approved by the two Johns.[31] The celestial mandate requiring that Dorothea share her revelations with the two Johns would assist in establishing a virtual monopoly over Dorothea's speech. The twelfth proof in John's list advancing the authenticity of Dorothea's visions is that she was supernaturally rewarded for communicating her visions to her confessors. This is explicitly contrasted with all other exchanges, for which she was often subjected to divine censure—whether because these discussions occurred on feast days, or that she spoke too much, or that little good came of them.[32] Conversation with the two Johns was in a special category of its own.

Confession and Memory

On a continuum with the relationship between confessor and penitent was the way confessional practice was depicted as informing Dorothea's entire life. The characterization of the mature Dorothea's confession closely incorporates some of the most esteemed confessional ideology of this period. "Her confession, moreover, was discrete, collected, speedy, voluntary, tearful, entire, undivided, individual, true, naked, and well circumstanced"— categories that correspond almost exactly to the stipulations of Raymond of Peñafort (d. 1275) for what constitutes a true confession.[33]

As a candidate for sainthood and an exemplar of the contemporary lay penitential movement, Dorothea's confessional habits would naturally exceed the mere letter of the law. For instance, although the fourth Lateran council (1215) had made annual confession mandatory for all Christians at Easter, Raymond of Peñafort notes that there was some discussion among authorities as to whether or not venial sins required sacramental confession—hastening to add that, in his opinion, it was safest to reveal all one's sins before the priest.[34] Adherence to the less exacting standard would have reduced Dorothea's confessional outpourings to a negligible flow since Dorothea was reputed never to have committed a mortal sin.[35] Of course, so low an incidence of confession was never a viable option for any plausible holy person. The mature Dorothea is, instead, described as confessing at least daily. So intense an interval need not arise from a need to confess in and of itself. It would also be theologically determined by Dorothea's fervent eucharistic devotion: daily communion required prior confession. Indeed, John is careful to delineate the interconnection between these two sacramental needs.[36]

But Dorothea is also represented as suffering from the kind of meritorious tenderness of conscience that had come to be closely associated with medieval holy women—at least since Jacques de Vitry's seminal portrait of his penitent Marie of Oignies.[37] Even the most minor sins were said to torment Dorothea.[38] In fact, John notes approvingly that she in no way differentiated between a mortal and a venial sin. Dorothea's scrupulosity infused new meaning into the confessor's traditional role of doctor (*medicus*).[39] As a dark analogue to the wounds of love that Christ inflicted on her body, Dorothea experienced wounds of sin in her soul—presumably invisible to the eye but purportedly more painful than their holy corporeal counterparts. Thus once, when she became too absorbed in gazing at the unusually appealing dinner that a certain scholar had brought her in the *reclusorium* for her daily meal:

Those wounds of her soul from the aforesaid sin of looking entered her, [and] aching exceedingly, she wept with great sobs. . . . Hence she was gravely wounded, afflicted by the severity of pains, and weakened by an abundant bitterness, unable to raise herself. . . . Weeping bitterly and wailing she called to the Lord that he should deem to send the doctor of her soul, namely her Confessor, so that she would show him her wounds.[40]

Even after John had arrived and administered the "salubrious unguent" of confession and penance, "she nevertheless remained sobbing and drawing deep gasps for a long time due to the vehemence of the painful affliction arising from the wounds [which had been] deeply impressed over a long duration."[41]

This urgent need to confess, a craving which was determined by multiple causes, would naturally strengthen Dorothea's dependence on her confessor. But this dependency was not necessarily exclusive to John: the rhythm of Dorothea's confessions were to some extent fixed long before he became her confessor. Dorothea was described as ardent to confess since she was seven years old, the age of her earliest spiritual awakening. The frequency of confession increased with marriage to once a day, and sometimes more.[42] Representations of these frequent and, perhaps, abundant confessions summon the specter of Dorothea's earlier confessor, with whom she had relations of greater duration and perhaps of equal intimacy. This presumption, necessarily undermining the authority of John's claims over Dorothea's life, is but another reminder of the way in which her past must necessarily raise an unruly contention against John's narrative control.

Again, these difficulties were conveniently allayed by the timely telos of Dorothea's inner development. The extraction of her heart in 1385 marked her initiation into a more intense spiritual life. Her visions became more lucid, she was inducted into heaven's mysteries, and the Lord spoke to her daily. The pace of her eucharistic devotion was also said to quicken.[43] Equally significant, however, was that the extraction of her heart also inaugurated a new manner of confessing which was divinely mandated. The Lord said to her:

"You have carried yourself behind your back, but put others ahead of you whom you considered to be more important than yourself up until now. Now you ought, looking, to stand in front of yourself and contemplate how you are inwardly disposed. Remember the distant period of your entire life by examining carefully how it was spent, what of good or of evil was done or omitted in that [time], so that then you can improve by the restorative polishing of penance to live and please me in a holy way." She, thus instructed by the Lord, placed herself before her own eyes, contemplating herself lucidly, [and] knew in herself what things were displeasing to God. . . . Therefore, from that time with the Lord God teaching her, she began to confess concerning the entire period of her life. Not indeed for the first time, because many times earlier she had confessed with a contrite heart and most abundant weeping the individual sins which occurred to her memory, but in a new way—renewed in the spirit of her mind—she thus confessed just as God informed her. For the Lord was assiduously supporting her through his presence and his grace, teaching her to recognize her sins, to weigh their gravity and number and to express them through open words to her confessor.[44]

In 1387, two years into this meticulous process, she appeared to herself as "transparent and accessible" (*transparens et pervia*), a condition which permitted Dorothea to see her past sins as if through a crystal. She retained this spiritual transparency until the end of her life.[45] But these intense confessions nevertheless continued for five years altogether. Finally in 1390, a year before her meeting with John Marienwerder, she received the assurance of the Holy Spirit that her past sins were forgiven.[46]

Thus, on the one hand, Dorothea's past was conveniently clarified and safely contained just in time for her to embark on the final and, arguably, the most spiritually intense chapter of her life under the direction of a new confessor. Dorothea's soul was something of a *tabula rasa*, rubbed clean for new divine inscriptions, which would be translated by John. On the other hand, Dorothea had done all of the difficult and important memory work which would also make her past accessible to herself. And John, as hagiographer, was also the beneficiary of these lucid rememberings since, just prior to her entrance into the *reclusorium*, she was once again ordered by God to make a life confession of all her past sins—even though they had already been forgiven by the Holy Spirit.[47]

God's confessional instruction is again subtly inscribed with the practice of contemporary confessional manuals. For instance, one understanding of frequent confession is that the same sins should be confessed repeatedly—a discipline that closely parallels Dorothea's process of clarification.[48] But what is especially striking is the way in which God's skillful manipulation of Dorothea's memory tracks the prescribed office of the confessor. John of Freiburg's *Summa confessorum* (ca. 1297) describes the circumstances under which a priest should subtly "lead back to the memory (*ad memoriam reducere*) of the person confessing the sins which [the confessor] heard or knew that [the penitent] committed."[49] God repeatedly performs this service for Dorothea, one which is described through the same idiom: "The Lord, shining around her with his light, led back to her memory (*ad memoriam . . . reduxit*) her little sins and oversights, and showed plainly that she had not lived in a pure and holy way."[50]

And so the confessor's role in the restoration of memory is fulfilled by God. Of course, this direct confessional link with God could also be interpreted as one of the many ways that holy women may be seen as bypassing clerical authority—especially since Dorothea received word from the Holy Spirit that all her past sins were forgiven.[51] And yet, the manner in which Dorothea's *vitae* are subtly suffused with confessional practice could also be construed as assimilating the confessor and God. I hasten to add that there would be nothing suspect or even particularly remarkable in such a conflation. On the contrary, it is not merely orthodox; the priest as a symbolic substitute for Christ is nothing less than the cornerstone of the entire sacramental system. Certainly, one of the aspects of Francis of Assisi's devotional profile that most recommended him to ecclesiastical authorities was his apprehension of priests, even sinful priests, in their christological function.[52] It was also alluded to earlier that, from a confessional standpoint, the priest's access to the internal forum was a privilege shared only with God. Thus John of Freiburg would argue that a priest, who was being pressured into breaking the seal of secrecy intrinsic to the confessional by his superior, was justified in swearing that he knew nothing "because he does not know as man but as God."[53] In this spirit of conflation, John Marienwerder and Christ are both referred to as doctors

of Dorothea's soul with an easy fluidity that occasionally fosters confusion.[54] Dorothea also, in response to Christ's instruction, who cautioned
never to delay confession lest she be caught unawares by death, often confessed to God first, and later to John—a practice, again, in keeping with
the best pastoral advice of the day.[55]

Even as the fusion of confessor and God augments the confessor's
symbolic role, it minimizes and conceals much of what one would assume
to be his practical role in the shaping of a saint's eventual *vita*: the framing
of proper questions. Raymond of Peñafort had spelled out a very explicit
and exacting pattern of interrogation for confessors, which he summarized
in a little ditty:

Who, what, where, through whom, how many times, why, how, and when,
Should be observed by all when applying the medicine.[56]

Indeed, confessional interrogation was standard practice in this period.
Raymond of Peñafort had argued against those authorities who were reluctant to employ it, contending that questions were not only an invalu-
able aid to a flagging memory but also in overcoming shame-faced reticence.[57] To Raymond's two reasons in favor of interrogation, we should
also amend a third: the proper question helps to elicit the appropriate (desired) answer.[58]

Throughout John's depiction of Dorothea's confessional practice,
however, he is careful never to mention the use of interrogation, or to
suggest its necessity. On the contrary, an episode from the *Septililium* depicts Dorothea as scorning one of John's female penitents for her lack of
preparation prior to confession, thus wasting John's precious time.[59] This
woman's lackadaisical habits throw Dorothea's confessional competence
into sharp relief. Dorothea, being scrupulously prepared, would presumably confess unprompted, thus not requiring some of the confessional as-
sists that Raymond had foreseen.[60] For instance, the overcoming of shame
as a motive for interrogation may not have pertained to Dorothea since
she was seemingly all too willing to accuse herself. But since John's acquaintance with Dorothea was so awkwardly belated, one can only imagine that the stimulation of memory was an important item on his agenda.
The careful solicitation of appropriate responses to a whole range of questions, moreover, was more crucial still. The rejection of an interrogatory
role would be tantamount to relinquishing control over crucial aspects
of Dorothea's past and how these were articulated—a sacrifice he could
scarcely afford to make. Nor did he. I would argue that John most cer-

tainly resorted to interrogation in confession (as elsewhere) since such private inquisitions leave their mark on his writings. And yet, his interrogatory role is deliberately covert. The various mnemonic aids practiced upon Dorothea were invariably depicted as resulting from divine illumination as opposed to clerical interrogation—a representation that provides John with a respectable and respectful distance from any active shaping of Dorothea's penitential life.

John's relative aloofness from any mechanism of recollection was, perhaps, all the more important since Dorothea's divinely illuminated memory was not restricted to confession alone. God also reminded her of the various marvels he had performed throughout her life, symptoms of merit rather than sin, in order to facilitate the writing of her revelations. Thus while John necessarily claimed that Dorothea could remember her revelations very clearly until they were written—an interval that was generally limited to a week but sometimes crept up to as much as four[61]— on one occasion she did forget. This occurred five days after the revelation had been received, while John was due for a writing session on the sixth day. God intervened, repeating the first word of the revelation, and the entire experience immediately returned to her memory.[62] Of the twenty-four signs that John cobbled together testifying to the authenticity of Dorothea's visions, one of the proofs turned on her divinely illuminated memory. Thus on the many occasions upon which Dorothea exhibited a becoming resistance to the writing process, a resistance premised on her humility:

Then God inflamed her with his charity, himself leading back to her memory many things forgotten, which he had mercifully conferred on her and done with her many years before the extraction of the heart. And he instructed her on how she should express those things to her confessor, as well as some other [things] that were hitherto inscribed in her memory and that she wished to keep hidden, so he would write them for the honor and glory of God.[63]

The initial authorization to reveal her visions carried with it a new infusion of memories from her past life. But even after this occurrence, during the last year of Dorothea's life, Christ appears to her as a beautiful man and tells her to run back in her memory and review her entire life and the various marvels he had performed in her—a process closely approximating the life confessions that were ordained in the five years following the extraction of Dorothea's heart.[64]

Only very rarely can something like the interrogatory process be reconstructed from John's writings. For instance, in the *Vita Lindana*, John records a set of twenty "sentiments" or "effects" visited on Dorothea, resulting from the reception of the Eucharist on different occasions. John then appends a chapter under the rubric, "Concerning the understanding of certain words set forth in [the description of] the aforesaid effects." He begins by pointing out that writing is a likeness (*similitudo*) of the thing represented—not the thing itself—then moves on to some of the difficulties inherent in the writing process:

Although this spouse of Christ, Dorothea, was a simple woman and completely illiterate, nevertheless through the light of wisdom infused in her from above by God—by which she was, as it were, vivified in spirit—with sufficiently candid words as she was capable [of articulating] in her stammering (*balbutiendo*), she expressed true and inestimably great mysteries, consonant with the similitudes of sacred Scripture. And for the purpose of writing more clearly on the experience of the spiritual effects with which she was marvellously visited by God, the person writing (who sometimes had difficulty with the material) would instruct, with God counselling and she being traversed completely by the supernatural light very clearly, that the grace of the visiting Lord should illuminate more in her and narrate the things that were supposed to be written in more appropriate terms.[65]

In plain speech, what seems to be occurring here is that John would express confusion, and doubtless ask questions, about certain aspects of Dorothea's revelations. Dorothea, accordingly, would solicit divine illumination in response to John's questioning. This conjecture is strengthened by the fact that a series of chapters, which are essentially glosses on key phrases in Dorothea's preceding "sentiments," follow the intervention of John cited above. Perhaps he later regretted even so occluded a characterization of their actual practice. The explanatory chapter and the glosses are, interestingly, dropped from the later and more prolix *Vita latina*. The glosses, in expanded form, reappear in the still later *Septililium*, but the explanatory chapter does not.[66]

The techniques of the confessor, admittedly filtered through God, are thus brought to bear on the writing process. Just as God, the spiritual master, comes more sharply into focus, John, the corporeal master, becomes something of an invisible man: invisible but palpable. The ubiquitous imprint of the confessional on Dorothea's spirituality also begs the question of where the confessional leaves off and the more informal disclosure of visions begins. Certain ecclesiastical authorities such as Jean Gerson (d. 1429) naturally assumed that the confessional would be the forum in which women revealed their revelations to their confessors.[67] This supposition might pertain to Dorothea as well, while the writing of the revelations would be postponed to a more propitious time. Although it is difficult to predict the precise mark of so sacramentally and hierarchically charged an environment, it is unimaginable that it would have no effect on the disclosures made. Would they be more restrained? more lugubrious? more abject? more lucid? In the collection of revelations known as the *Liber de festis*, at any rate, we are told that Dorothea wept throughout one particular confession due to the vision she had received concerning the soul of a former great leader now in hell.[68] Elsewhere in the same work, the Virgin Mary told Dorothea that she must accuse herself in confession because she had not formerly honored the feast of Mary's conception, although its import was only being revealed to Dorothea for the first time in this revelation.[69] Did the confessional occasion the disclosure of these revelations? Especially suggestive is the fact that at the end of the *Septililium*, John appends a series of Dorothea's confessions in German "for the edification of the simple"—an inclusion that blurs the boundaries between intra- and extra-sacramental entirely.[70]

Expression and Inexpression

The credibility of Dorothea's life (and John's integrity in the representation of that life) necessarily increases the more John distances himself from his holy penitent's memory work and the reconstruction of her past. Yet, it was impossible that he should effect such a distance in the recording of the revelations. Rather, the drama of redaction, and the role John assumed, is very much foregrounded in his various works. The command to write came directly from God, concomitant with the order that Dorothea disclose her revelations. Visions become the venue for divine comment on the writing process. Thus God describes the redaction of the revelations as a collaborative enterprise that he characterizes as improving over time. He expresses particular pleasure in John's work.[71] Various interventions suggest that God is something of a controlling and distinctly "hands-on" editor of the proceedings. Occasionally, he will signal topics of general interest for the eventual readers of the revelations: a treatment of the contemplative life or a discussion of the Eucharist are two such subjects.[72] But God's notice was also more particularized: thus he tells Dorothea to relate how she had discerned an unconsecrated host in place of the reserved host, insisting that she stress that this had occurred even before the extraction of her heart.[73] He also plays the censor, punishing Dorothea for doctrinal slips.[74]

In the course of such divine directives, John manages to accumulate considerable capital in what today might be perceived as distribution rights with regard to a warmly anticipated public. Several of these authorizations are deftly incorporated into the *Vita latina*'s twenty-four proofs concerning the authenticity of Dorothea's visions. In the seventeenth such proof, God ordered that Dorothea's various revelations on the Eucharist, described as hitherto sparsely written and somewhat scattered, be revised into "a new compilation—preaching the salvific fruit [to be] announced in the hearts of readers. . . . And the Lord added 'Those things written by you will be shown in the presence of superiors and greater prelates in the church.'" In the last of the twenty-four proofs, God urges the two Johns to take care that they arrange the various revelations appropriately and decorate the collections beautifully.[75]

But the authenticity of mystic discourse ultimately derives from its inexpressibility. In this regard, John emerges as the deftest expressor of the inexpressible. According to Certeau's analysis, "the wound" opened up by mystical speech gives rise to extensive written commentaries, by immediate interpreter and later historian alike, in vain attempts to suture the gap disclosed.[76] Demonstrating an uncanny awareness of this dilemma, John enlists the sheer volume of his literary production to point to its ultimate futility. God himself remarks that, even were the two Johns to write all day, they could only capture a modicum of the wonders worked in Dorothea.[77] John often seconds the Lord's designation of divine excess. Thus the *Vita latina* contains the following disclaimer: "Plainly the consolation of this Spouse was so spiritually rich and so various in manifold ways that to insert every detail recorded from her (I am quiet about those things which were omitted [i.e., never recorded]) into this work would be excessively prolix and difficult."[78] Likewise, in the discussion of Dorothea's "sentiments" on the Eucharist which occurs in the *Septililium*, already considerably expanded from its original form in the *Vita Lindana*, John again signals his necessarily very cursory treatment of the many mystical disclosures to which he was privy. Since Dorothea communicated daily, and he had recorded some three hundred of these sentiments, only a fraction of these was represented.[79]

The quantitative excess of Dorothea's visions is but a literal analogue to the mystical conundrum: the insufficiency of language for conveying spiritual truths. The divine mandates to write are riddled with the impossibility of communication. But what is especially interesting here is that the real impediment is not the scribe's inadequacy so much as the mystic's. This inadequacy was already mentioned earlier in the context of Dorothea's appeals to God for more appropriate terms of expression, prompted by John's queries. In a similar vein, God constantly suggests that even if Dorothea spoke with many tongues, or even an angelic tongue, her representations must fall far short of the reality.[80] Initially, God gave her the will and even the permission to express herself, but not the means. Eventually, however, she was told by God in a vision that she had but to ask, and he would provide her with the words necessary to communicate with the two Johns.[81] Elsewhere (presumably later) Dorothea claims that whenever she is dictating her revelations "'My most beloved Lord is near me directly putting words in my mouth (*directe ponens verba in os meum*).'"[82] Even so, Dorothea's efforts to articulate the meaning of her life and revelations are still described by God as the stammering of a child. But as her death drew near, God assured her that her soul would soon rise to heaven, where her deficiencies in speech would be amended: "'since you will have been stabilized (*fueris stabilita*) in that place, then you will know how to speak about this perfectly.'"[83]

Underlying the inexpressibility of Dorothea's visions, and her incapacity of expression, is the more fundamental problem of the hidden recesses of Dorothea's life.[84] Her spirituality was premised on a lifetime of secrecy. According to John Marienwerder's account, only three persons knew of the revelations before he preached her virtues at the funeral—clearly meaning himself, John Reyman, and the bishop of Pomerania, John Mönch.[85] Even after the divine authorization which permitted the disclosure of her inner life to this select circle, there were limits to what she could reveal. She could not speak about the things she experienced during rapture beyond what God wished her to say and in the mode he determined.[86] A similar secrecy shrouded the hour of her death, the time of which event had been disclosed to Dorothea but which she was not authorized to share with the two Johns—despite their efforts to countermand this prohibition.[87]

Indeed, the veil of secrecy which shrouded her life does not merely exclude the confessor/scribe or the eventual reading public, but even Dorothea herself. The experience of rapture, for example, was apprehended by her soul, not her memory—except for the few details that God deposited in the memory for eventual disclosure.[88] Christ told her that she should not even attempt to understand the various mystical consolations she enjoyed; occasionally he whispered to her soul in an incomprehensible language.[89] When attempting to assess the meaning of her life, Dorothea encountered a similar resistance. Thus even after she was authorized to reveal her hitherto concealed life, the limits of her disclosure were severely curtailed by her own ignorance:

With her entire life thus brought back to her memory, she was able to recognize it but to say nothing distinctly about it since the Lord closed it with an insoluble bolt to reason and understanding. Truly it was for her as if her entire life was a closed bolt shut fast between her two hands, but she was not able to open [her hands] to display her own life between them, so firmly was it shut in.[90]

God confirmed this impression of inaccessibility when he told Dorothea that her life was not only hidden from other people, but also to a certain extent from herself.[91] Only occasionally did these clouds briefly lift: once God fleetingly revealed Dorothea's entire life to her, and it appeared "purified, splendid, and well polished." But the moment she attempted to examine and understand it, this clarity receded.[92]

Any gradual process of elucidation that can be discerned occurs in response to the questions posed by the two Johns in their efforts to comprehend Dorothea's spirituality. The *Vita latina* contextualizes the divine mandate that occurred twenty weeks before her death by describing the way in which she was being pressured "many times by some people very familiar and beloved to her" to disclose her spiritual life, despite her disinclination. Dorothea, however, who "did not dare to contradict their suasions," appealed to God for counsel.[93] When permission for disclosure was then granted, but all coherent explanation still proved so recalcitrant, "the Lord ordered her to give this kind of general response to her confessors," which he proceeded to dictate.[94]

Despite rare pockets of illumination, however, the pervasive effect of Dorothea's *vitae* and revelations is one of fragmentation, occlusion, and mystification—an impression which is distinctly at odds with the imposition of a scholarly and explanatory superstructure on some of John's more sophisticated renderings.[95] The narrative strategy at work is clearly at one with the penultimate of the twenty-four signs aimed at authenticating Dorothea's visions, wherein God himself reasons that those reading the wonders worked through Dorothea would naturally be led to suppose that even greater things were experienced by her than were expressed.[96]

This legacy of a concealed past, hampered by the inadequacy of the informant, and most clearly expressed in allusions to its inexpressibility, becomes, in John's hands, something of a masterstroke of clerical self-authorization. In the prologue to the *Septililium*, he writes:

Concerning the degrees of charity and the displays of charity by the Lord God, who is charity, which were demonstrated in word and deed to his beloved spouse the lady Dorothea, I with reason am afraid to speak in as much as I am lacking in charity and full of the decay of the flesh. Furthermore I fear that, with iniquity abounding in me and charity cooling, that I was not well kindled to have understood the idiom of charity because no one truly knows it except one who has experienced it, but instead the language of this idiom was and is barbaric (*barbaricam*) to me. . . . I do not know by what judgment of God it was given to me, a pauper, rather than to any other living person to hear about these [revelations] one by one . . . and yet it was so enjoined on me from above by God that objection or excuse about my scruple had no place. No one should plead that I, knowing my insufficiency, introduce myself into this matter, since I was in a certain way compelled—for which I would nevertheless be rejoicing and willing, if such great inadequacy did not hinder.[97]

The above passage is interlaced with elements of the double-edged idiom of self-effacing self-aggrandizement so characteristic of mystic discourse. As such, it appropriately prefigures the mystical revelations which follow. John's expressed reluctance to write mirrors the almost invariable demurral of Dorothea, and female mystics generally, over revealing their visions in the first place—both sets of hesitations ultimately being resolved by divine pressure. The very substance of John's alleged incompetence—the impossibility of a nonmystic understanding mystical language—dimly reverberates with Dorothea's difficulties in translating her mystical experiences into mundane language. That the language of love is described as barbaric, that is, non-Latinate, is a not so subtle reminder that John's scribal role is twofold: the transcription of Dorothea's ineffable experience entails a simultaneous translation of Dorothea's (barbaric) vernacular into clerical Latin. So on the one hand, John exalts his role by drawing attention to the process of translating the lesser tongue of the illiterate into the language of the learned—thus invoking a hierarchy which affirms his superiority to Dorothea. On the other hand, his difficulties in comprehending the strange tongue also anticipate Dorothea's own incapacity to grasp the mystical words that the Lord uttered to her in the course of her raptures. In other words, by the very gesture of foregrounding himself and his scribal embarrassments in this way, John becomes a mundane *figura* for mystical discourse, generally, but Dorothea's experiences in particular.

Stabilization and Its Enemies: The Process of Canonization

John and Christ are represented as being of one mind in their aspirations for Dorothea, a program that can be summarized by the concept of stabilization. The first vow that Dorothea pledged to John at Christ's behest was intended to attach her irretrievably to this confessor, and thus to stabilize her (*stabilire*). Christ likewise promised that in heaven her stammering tongue would be stabilized (*stabilire*). John's parallel efforts are apparent in the very magnitude of the writings he produced in an effort to stabilize perceptions of Dorothea's life and, hence, his own life's work. Moreover, all of these works had been written with a view to the Church's acknowledgement of Dorothea's eventual stabilization in heaven through official canonization.[98]

The process of canonization, that supreme act of stabilization, would also be the ultimate test of John's mastery over Dorothea's past. There were considerable factors that conspired in his favor. Prussia, and especially the Teutonic Order (to which John belonged), was eager for a national saint.[99] The bishop of Pomerania, without whose cooperation the process would doubtless have ended in a *cul de sac*, was sympathetic to Dorothea's cause and presided at her funeral. As Christ had predicted via Dorothea, it was John who preached the sermon at her funeral.[100] Thus it was through her confessor and amanuensis that the aspirant saint's ascetic austerities, revelations, and dramatic wounds of love were first revealed to the general public. The effectiveness of John's preaching admits little doubt: many of the witnesses unabashedly attach their knowledge of and belief in Dorothea's sanctity to the preaching they heard. John also managed to complete and widely disseminate his works before the majority of the witnesses had testified at the inquest into the grounds for her canonization, as is evident from the ubiquitous references to the Dorothean corpus throughout the entire proceedings. At Dorothea's tomb in the cathedral of Marienwerder, a scribe was set up to record and publicize daily the miracles which were performed.[101] As a member of the cathedral chapter of Marienwerder who knew the various scribes, John was in an excellent position to oversee the burgeoning cult and to keep abreast of the various beneficiaries of the miracles and perhaps engage in some benign indoctrination regarding the saint's life and virtues—an important advantage since these individuals would constitute the majority of the witnesses in the canonization proceedings.[102]

John was not only present to testify at Dorothea's process, but also drew up the various articles for her canonization through which the witnesses would be interrogated.[103] In addition, he wrote a small treatise, known as the *Libellus de vita*, as an extra precaution, which was included in the official proceedings.[104] His friend, John Reyman, as well as the bishop, John Mönch, were also available as witnesses. But the speed with which the canonization proceedings were initiated, the very year of her death, although securing the presence of certain star witnesses, also carried with it liabilities. John had been able to supervise Dorothea's life to a truly remarkable degree during her three years in Marienwerder. But by far the greater part of her life had been spent in Danzig. Moreover, many of the people who had known Dorothea during her residency in Danzig were still alive at the time of these proceedings. Among these survivors was her previous confessor, Nicholas of Hohenstein.

Several awkward inconsistencies did emerge. For example, all of John's renderings of Dorothea's life stressed that the hour of her death was known to her, but that she was not permitted to reveal it, which was the substance of article III, 25. Two witnesses contradicted this contention. According to Katherina, a local widow of Marienwerder with whom Dorothea had boarded prior to her entrance into the *reclusorium*, Dorothea had divulged the precise date of her death to the witness. When John Marienwerder came to testify to the same article, he then acknowledged that he had heard that Dorothea had apprised Katherina of her approaching death—limited damage control which nevertheless indicates the extent of his surveillance over the entire proceedings.[105] But a testimony from Danzig managed to elude him. Katherina Seveldische, an old friend, claimed that Dorothea sent word of her impending death, and Katherina immediately set out to visit the *reclusorium* at Marienwerder. She was, however, turned back by a mysterious man, whom she retrospectively determined was the devil. The stranger inquired where she was going and, upon learning her destination, said that her quest was pointless since Dorothea's confessor was away and the recluse would not be able to speak to Katherina nor, indeed, to anyone else. But even here, all was not lost. Katherina's tale lent impressive, albeit unsolicited testimony, to Dorothea's obedience to her confessor during her time in the *reclusorium* (which was the import of article III, 19).[106]

One especially ominous fact did present itself. When addressing article III, 20 concerning the various adversities that Dorothea had endured, several witnesses deposed that Dorothea had formerly been charged with heresy—an occurrence that was widely known among the contingent from Danzig.[107] According to her confessor, Nicholas of Hohenstein, the bishop's official for the diocese of Włocławek along with certain other priests threatened "to burn her, because they heard from people certain unknown things (*incognita*) told about Dorothea, therefore they believed she erred."[108] Another witness, a certain Metza Hugische, provides still more information on the genesis of this accusation. Apparently when Nicholas was not available, Dorothea would occasionally confess to a certain priest named Ludike, who was well known and widely respected.[109] It was Ludike who seemingly denounced Dorothea on the basis of her excessive piety, but especially on account of the unusual things she said in confession.[110]

While this testimony seems to confirm the impression that Dorothea used confession as an opportunity to discuss her revelations,[111] it also shows us the reverse side of the confessional. The absolute seal of secrecy enjoined on the confessor recognized but two exceptions. It was clearly not only acceptable, but even commendable, for the confessor of a potential saint to reveal aspects of his or her holy penitent's confession posthumously for the greater glory of God. Similarly, a confessor was permitted to expose a heretic, at least according to some schools of thought—the rationale being that the heretic was no longer Christian and hence ineligible for the blanket protection that the confessional extended to other criminals.[112] Thus in different cities, Dorothea's confession had made her susceptible on both fronts. And here is the central dilemma of mysticism in a nutshell. If authorization for mystic discourse depends upon an inaccessible symbolic reserve, that reserve is, of course, subject to multiple construals. Indeed, it is impossible to allege the existence of such a reserve and simultaneously subject it to full control—try as John might.

Retrospectively, one can see that John was aware of the heresy charge and modestly prepared against its reemergence. Thus on more than one occasion in the course of his *vitae* he had pointed out that Adalbert thought it was no longer "safe" to live in Danzig (*non esse tutum, cum illis seu inter illos commorari*), and took his family on a pilgrimage.[113] John also observed how Dorothea, absorbed in divine sweetness, was incapable of living in the presence of others: "Whereupon certain men, not vivified but poisoned by the odor of her sanctity, turned the favor and glory of God into insanity."[114] This passage precipitates Dorothea's decision to seek counsel from Nicholas of Hohenstein, who, in turn, told her about John.

Yet also implicit in the accusation of heresy is the suggestion that Dorothea was already revealing her revelations when in Danzig, a possibility that wrecks havoc with the chronology articulated in John's *vitae* and restated in the articles of the process. Even though this possibility may have reared its ugly head, it quickly retreated. Most of the witnesses agreed that Dorothea never spoke about her spiritual practices. Occasionally she would drop tantalizing hints. For instance, Margaretha Creuczeburgische, a widow from Danzig, testified that Dorothea had said many times that "there were certain people upon whom God inflicted wounds of grace, divine and great," from which Margaretha concluded that Dorothea was not right in the head (*non fuit capax tunc tanti boni*).[115] But retrospectively, after hearing public opinion and rumor (*publica vox et fama*), she recognized Dorothea's sanctity.

Of course, the greatest threat to John's rendition of Dorothea's spiritual development would be expected to come from Dorothea's former confessor, Nicholas. John may have even purposefully attempted to diminish Nicholas's hold on Dorothea's legacy when he wrote in the *Libellus de vita* that Dorothea had only been Nicholas's penitent for eight years as opposed to a more accurate reckoning of twelve.[116] But the full measure of Nicholas's destabilizing potential was never realized. Just as Dorothea was supernaturally illuminated by divine memory, Nicholas seemed to have been visited by divine forgetfulness. With regard to the singular perogatives Christ visited on Dorothea (article III, 8), Nicholas claimed this was true because she had revealed certain revelations to him. When asked what they were, he answered that "he had not retained them in his memory, because then he did not care much about them." Likewise, concerning article III, 22—which advanced that Dorothea had received many gifts from God—Nicholas claimed it was true since Dorothea had repeatedly told him that she was the recipient of such gifts. But he could offer no further information because he had never asked what these gifts were, nor did Dorothea volunteer the information: "because, as the witness believed, the blessed Dorothea saw that the deponent was not disposed to grasp or understand such things."[117]

What is especially striking is the extent to which Nicholas depended on the testimony and writings of John Marienwerder for his account of Dorothea. Nicholas even cites John's rendition regarding events that occurred when Dorothea was still Nicholas's own penitent in Danzig, a deference which necessarily occasioned some difficulties. Thus John testified concerning the vision that Dorothea was said to have had about him before their climactic meeting on the basis of earlier accounts by Nicholas and Dorothea; Nicholas, however, only cited John.[118]

Even without such embarrassments, John's pronounced ascendancy is so marked in virtually all of the substantive testimonies that his very over-presence had the potential for destabilizing Dorothea's claims. The authority of John's preaching and writings invariably had the effect of reformulating earlier impressions of Dorothea in favor of his own sensational and skillfully articulated claims. One is perhaps most aware of the monovocality of the proceedings in the testimony of John Reyman, who, with John Marienwerder, shared the responsibility of supervising

Dorothea, occasionally hearing her confessions and even recording her visions. Both Johns had arrived together to testify at the canonization proceedings and both had prepared written statements in the event that something untoward prevented them from testifying. John Marienwerder asked that his written statement be included in the written process, regardless. It was accordingly appended to his testimony as the *Libellus de vita*, mentioned earlier. Reyman, on the other hand, asked that, should he be given the opportunity to testify, his written testimony not be included.[119] It is little wonder: Reyman's testimony is cribbed, often verbatim, from Marienwerder's *Libellus de vita*.[120]

Conclusion

Retrospectively, three potential threats to Dorothea's claims to sanctity seem to present themselves. First, there are the ways in which aspects of Dorothea's past contradict the narrative of her life articulated in the process of canonization. Additionally, the meaning of her mystical experiences is necessarily open to other constructions. Finally, John's efforts to provide against these two contingencies result in a kind of monovocality and an occasional over-correction that, at times, seem to subvert his carefully constructed claims. Yet the reasons behind the short term failure of Dorothea's canonization seem to have been political and external, and not owing to any intrinsic fault of the proceedings themselves.[121] There was, however, a growing faction that probably would have rejected Dorothea's claims to sanctity out of hand. Jean Gerson's *De probatione spirituum* (1415) not only challenged the canonization of Birgitta of Sweden, Dorothea's role model and perhaps her closest spiritual analogue, but also savaged the claims of female mystics, generally.[122] In a related work, Gerson attacks the extensive role that a confessor often played in the canonization proceedings of his holy penitent—a charge to which John Marienwerder was, of course, extremely vulnerable.[123] Without John's testimony, there would be no grounds for Dorothea's canonization whatsoever. This impression, implicit in John's writings on Dorothea and a kind of tribute to the extent of the control he exercised, is sustained to a potentially damaging degree by the process itself.

One unforgettable example from Gerson's arsenal of mystical abuses is of a married woman in Arras, illiterate and simple, who engaged in lengthy fasts, much to the annoyance of her husband but to the astonishment of the local community. In response to Gerson's questioning, however, she could offer no coherent reason for her spiritual practices. By her ashy color and her dazed expression, Gerson judged she was near death and attempted to warn her, but she would not listen.[124]

Gerson's contemptuous portrait of this nameless ascetic reads like a grim caricature of Dorothea's spirituality, particularly before her meeting with John. At this earlier stage in Dorothea's development, she is presented as experiencing mystical raptures with little understanding and fewer words—an impression that is rather strengthened than refuted by the process of canonization. Her spiritual life only seems to have acquired momentum and force during the course of her short but intense relationship with John. This impression may result from John's successful burial of her past, with the result that this door must forever remain shut. Or it may be that hitherto Dorothea had attached no fixed meaning to her life. She may only have slowly come to understand its meaning, with the assistance of divine illumination, in the course of her relationship with John— an interpretation that is deeply complicitous with John's representations. Another possibility also presents itself: that Dorothea's life only assumed meaning when John gave it meaning. Thus the inchoate perceptions of her past, present, and even future experiences were reformatted, much like the reconstructed memories of the witnesses who deposed at Dorothea's canonization. It is impossible to choose between these ideologically divergent but overlapping possibilities. Yet what does remain constant is John's word: that only in the last weeks of Dorothea's life, after having known John for a year and a half, did Christ finally put words in her mouth.

Notes

Foreword

1. André Vauchez, *La Sainteté en Occident aux derniers siècles du moyen âge d'après les procès de canonisation et les documents hagiographiques*, Bibliothèque des Etudes Françaises d'Athènes et de Rome 241 (Rome: Ecole Française de Rome, 1981), now translated as *Sainthood in the Later Middle Ages* (New York: Cambridge University Press, 1997); Michael Goodich, *Vita Perfecta: The Ideal of Sainthood in the Thirteenth Century* (Stuttgart: Hiersemann, 1982); and Donald Weinstein and Rudolph M. Bell, *Saints and Society: The Two Worlds of Western Christendom, 1000–1700* (Chicago: University of Chicago Press, 1982).

2. Aviad M. Kleinberg, *Prophets in Their Own Country: Living Saints and the Making of Sainthood in the Later Middle Ages* (Chicago: University of Chicago Press, 1992).

3. John E. Toews, "Intellectual History After the Linguistic Turn," *American Historical Review* 92 (October 1987): 879–907; Caroline Walker Bynum, "In Praise of Fragments: History in a Comic Mode," *Fragmentation and Redemption: Essays on Gender and the Human Body in Medieval Religion* (New York: Zone Books, 1991), pp. 11–26; Elizabeth A. Clark, "The Lady Vanishes: Dilemmas of a Feminist Historian After the 'Linguistic Turn'," *Church History* 67 (March 1998): 1–31; and see Frank Tobin, "Henry Suso and Elsbeth Stagel: Was the *Vita* a Cooperative Effort?" this volume, chap. 7.

4. Simone Roisin, *L'Hagiographie cistercienne dans le diocèse de Liège au XIIIe siècle* (Louvain: Bibliothèque de l'Université, 1947).

5. See Barbara Newman, "Hildegard and Her Hagiographers: The Remaking of Female Sainthood," this volume, chap. 2, p. 16.

Chapter 1. Voice, Gender, and the Portrayal of Sanctity

1. Caroline Walker Bynum's pathbreaking scholarship includes *Jesus as Mother: Studies in the Spirituality of the High Middle Ages* (Berkeley: University of California Press, 1982); *Holy Feast and Holy Fast: The Religious Significance of Food to Medieval Women* (Berkeley: University of California Press, 1987); and *Fragmentation and Redemption: Essays on Gender and the Human Body in Medieval Europe* (New York: Zone Books, 1991). So pervasive has been the influence of her work, apparent throughout this book, that I will not attempt to cite it every time it is relevant to a topic discussed in this introduction. Scholars are still indebted to Herbert Grundmann's *Religious Movements in the Middle Ages: The Historical Links Between*

Heresy, the Mendicant Orders, and the Women's Religious Movement in the Twelfth and Thirteenth Century, first published in German in 1935, trans. Steven Rowan (Notre Dame, Ind.: University of Notre Dame Press, 1995). Other influential scholarship includes Peter Dinzelbacher and Dieter R. Bauer, eds., *Frauenmystik im Mittelalter* (Ostfildern bei Stuttgart: Schwabenverlag, 1985); Elizabeth Alvilda Petroff, *Medieval Women's Visionary Literature* (New York: Oxford University Press, 1986); Ursula Peters, *Religiöse Erfahrung als literarisches Faktum: Zur Vorgeschichte und Genese frauenmystischer Texte des 13. und 14. Jahrhunderts* (Tübingen: Max Niemeyer, 1988); the fine essays in Renate Blumenfeld-Kosinski and Timea Szell, eds., *Images of Sainthood in Medieval Europe* (Ithaca, N.Y.: Cornell University Press, 1991); E. Ann Matter and John Coakley, eds., *Creative Women in Medieval and Early Modern Italy: A Religious and Artistic Renaissance* (Philadelphia: University of Pennsylvania Press, 1994); and Barbara Newman, *From Virile Woman to WomanChrist: Studies in Medieval Religion and Literature* (Philadelphia: University of Pennsylvania Press, 1995).

2. For example, Catherine M. Mooney, "The Authorial Role of Brother A. in the Composition of Angela of Foligno's Revelations," in *Creative Women in Medieval and Early Modern Italy*, pp. 34–63. On scribes, see also Lynn Staley Johnson, "The Trope of the Scribe and the Question of Literary Authority in the Works of Julian of Norwich and Margery Kempe," *Speculum* 66 (1991): 820–38; and Lynn Staley, *Margery Kempe's Dissenting Fictions* (University Park: Pennsylvania State University Press, 1994), pp. 1–38.

3. On the confessor's role, see also Janette Dillon, "Holy Women and Their Confessors or Confessors and Their Holy Women? Margery Kempe and Continental Tradition," in *Prophets Abroad: The Reception of Continental Holy Women in Late-Medieval England*, ed. Rosalynn Voaden (Cambridge: D. S. Brewer, 1996), pp. 115–40.

4. See also Anne L. Clark, "Repression or Collaboration? The Case of Elisabeth and Ekbert of Schönau," in *Christendom and Its Discontents: Exclusion, Persecution, and Rebellion, 1000–1500*, ed. Scott L. Waugh and Peter D. Diehl (Cambridge: Cambridge University Press, 1996), pp. 151–67.

5. John Coakley, "Gender and the Authority of Friars: The Significance of Holy Women for Thirteenth-Century Franciscans and Dominicans," *Church History* 60 (1991): 445–60; idem, "Friars as Confidants of Holy Women in Medieval Dominican Hagiography," in *Images of Sainthood*, pp. 222–46.

6. Scholarship regarding the body in the Middle Ages and its relevance for understanding religious women is vast. Various perspectives are represented by Caroline Walker Bynum, "The Female Body and Religious Practice in the Later Middle Ages," in *Fragmentation and Redemption*, pp. 181–238; eadem, *The Resurrection of the Body in Western Christianity, 200–1336* (New York: Columbia University Press, 1995); eadem, "Why All the Fuss About the Body? A Medievalist's Perspective," *Critical Inquiry* 22, 1 (1995): 1–33; Elizabeth Robertson, "The Corporeality of Female Sanctity in *The Life of Saint Margaret*," in *Images of Sainthood*, pp. 268–87; eadem, "Medieval Medical Views of Women and Female Spirituality in the *Ancrene Wisse* and Julian of Norwich's *Showings*," in *Feminist Approaches to the Body in Medieval Literature*, ed. Linda Lomperis and Sarah Stanbury (Philadelphia: Uni-

versity of Pennsylvania Press, 1993), pp. 142–67; Karma Lochrie, *Margery Kempe and Translations of the Flesh* (Philadelphia: University of Pennsylvania Press, 1991); Ulrike Wiethaus, "Sexuality, Gender, and the Body in Late Medieval Women's Spirituality: Cases from Germany and the Netherlands," *Journal of Feminist Studies in Religion* 7 (1991): 35–52; Dyan Elliott, "The Physiology of Rapture and Female Spirituality," in *Medieval Theology and the Natural Body*, ed. Peter Biller and A. J. Minnis (Woodbridge, Suffolk: York Medieval Press in association with Boydell and Brewer, 1997), pp. 141–73.

7. On the evolving depiction of holy women, see Caroline Walker Bynum, "Religious Women in the Later Middle Ages," in *Christian Spirituality: High Middle Ages and Reformation*, ed. Jill Raitt (New York: Crossroad, 1987), pp. 121–39; André Vauchez, *La Sainteté en Occident aux derniers siècles du moyen âge d'après les procès de canonisation et les documents hagiographiques*, Bibliothèque des Etudes Françaises d'Athènes et de Rome 241 (Rome: Ecole Française de Rome, 1988), esp. pp. 402–10, 427–48, 472–78; idem, *The Laity in the Middle Ages: Religious Beliefs and Devotional Practices*, ed. Daniel E. Bornstein, trans. Margery J. Schneider (Notre Dame, Ind.: University of Notre Dame Press, 1993), pp. 171–264; Donald Weinstein and Rudolph M. Bell, *Saints and Society: The Two Worlds of Western Christendom, 1000–1700* (Chicago: University of Chicago Press, 1982), pp. 220–38; and on later medieval depictions of holy women and men, see Richard Kieckhefer, *Unquiet Souls: Fourteenth-Century Saints and Their Religious Milieu* (Chicago: University of Chicago Press, 1984).

Chapter 2. Hildegard and Her Hagiographers: The Remaking of Female Sainthood

A German version of this essay has appeared under the title "Seherin — Prophetin — Mystikerin: Hildegard-Bilder in der hagiographischen Tradition," in *Hildegard von Bingen: Prophetin durch die Zeiten, Zum 900. Geburtstag*, ed. Edeltraud Forster (Freiburg: Herder, 1997), pp. 126–52. I would like to thank the many colleagues who invited me to present this paper as a plenary address at the International Medieval Congress at Leeds (July 13–16, 1998); at "The Greenest Branch" conference in Burlington, Vermont (November 5–8, 1998); and at the conference "Constructing Hildegard: Reception and Identity, 1098–1998" at Rice University in Houston (November 20–22, 1998). My gratitude is also due to Jennifer Carpenter, John Coakley, Peter Dronke, Thomas Head, Kathryn Kerby-Fulton, Robert Lerner, Constant Mews, and Catherine Mooney for their collegial suggestions.

1. *Vita Sanctae Hildegardis*, ed. Monika Klaes, *CCCM* 126 (Turnhout: Brepols, 1993). A good English translation is Hugh Feiss, *The Life of the Saintly Hildegard* (Toronto: Peregrina, 1996). The *Vita* and other texts concerning Hildegard's life are now available in Anna Silvas, ed. and trans., *Jutta and Hildegard: The Biographical Sources* (Turnhout: Brepols, 1998), which appeared after this volume went to press.

2. See Barbara Newman, "Three-Part Invention: The *Vita S. Hildegardis*

and Mystical Hagiography," in *Hildegard of Bingen: The Context of Her Thought and Art*, ed. Charles Burnett and Peter Dronke (London: Warburg Institute, 1998), pp. 189–210.

3. Important recent studies of hagiography and sainthood include André Vauchez, *La Sainteté en Occident aux derniers siècles du moyen âge d'après les procès de canonisation et les documents hagiographiques*, Bibliothèque des Etudes Françaises d'Athènes et de Rome 241 (Rome: Ecole Française de Rome, 1981), trans. Jean Birrell as *Sainthood in the Later Middle Ages* (Cambridge: Cambridge University Press, 1997); Donald Weinstein and Rudolph M. Bell, *Saints and Society: The Two Worlds of Western Christendom, 1000–1700* (Chicago: University of Chicago Press, 1982); Richard Kieckhefer, *Unquiet Souls: Fourteenth-Century Saints and Their Religious Milieu* (Chicago: University of Chicago Press, 1984); Renate Blumenfeld-Kosinski and Timea Szell, eds., *Images of Sainthood in Medieval Europe* (Ithaca, N.Y.: Cornell University Press, 1991); Aviad M. Kleinberg, *Prophets in Their Own Country: Living Saints and the Making of Sainthood in the Later Middle Ages* (Chicago: University of Chicago Press, 1992). To be used with caution are Michael Goodich, *Vita Perfecta: The Ideal of Sainthood in the Thirteenth Century* (Stuttgart: Hiersemann, 1982); and Thomas Heffernan, *Sacred Biography: Saints and Their Biographers in the Middle Ages* (New York: Oxford University Press, 1988). On female saints' lives see Caroline Walker Bynum, *Holy Feast and Holy Fast: The Religious Significance of Food to Medieval Women* (Berkeley: University of California Press, 1987); Brigitte Cazelles, *The Lady as Saint: A Collection of French Hagiographic Romances of the Thirteenth Century* (Philadelphia: University of Pennsylvania Press, 1991); Jo Ann McNamara, John Halborg, and E. Gordon Whatley, eds. and trans., *Sainted Women of the Dark Ages* (Durham, N.C.: Duke University Press, 1992).

4. For this epithet, derived from a letter of Henry of Langenstein (1383), see G. Sommerfeld, "Die Prophetien der hl. Hildegard in einem Schreiben des Meisters Heinrich von Langenstein," *Historisches Jahrbuch* 30 (1909): 43–61, 297–307; and Sylvain Gouguenheim, *La Sibylle du Rhin: Hildegarde de Bingen, abbesse et prophétesse rhénane* (Paris: Sorbonne, 1996), p. 182.

5. I use the term "abbess" loosely to translate Hildegard's title of *magistra*, which has no precise English equivalent. In fact she always remained juridically subject to the abbot of St. Disibod, though the dependence rankled; she is addressed as *abbatissa* only in a charter granted her by Frederick Barbarossa in 1163. Not until the thirteenth century did her successors at the Rupertsberg lay effective claim to the coveted title.

6. Guibert of Gembloux, Ep. 16, in *Guiberti Gemblacensis Epistolae*, ed. Albert Derolez, *CCCM* 66–66A (Turnhout: Brepols, 1988, 1989), 1: 216–20. For Hildegard's response see Ep. 103r in *Hildegardis Bingensis Epistolarium*, ed. Lieven Van Acker, *CCCM* 91–91A (Turnhout: Brepols, 1991, 1993), 2: 258–65.

7. This *vita* is printed as part of a letter to the monk Bovo, Ep. 38, in Guibert of Gembloux, *Epistolae*, 2: 369–79; for a translation see Silvas, *Jutta and Hildegard* (n. 1 above). Philip of Heinsberg, archbishop of Cologne and a correspondent and admirer of Hildegard, had asked Guibert to compose this *vita* sometime between Gottfried's death and the commissioning of Theoderic to complete Gottfried's unfinished task. See Ep. 15 (Guibert to Philip of Heinsberg) in *Epistolae*, 1: 210–15.

8. On Guibert's biography see Hippolyte Delehaye, "Guibert, Abbé de

Florennes et de Gembloux," *Revue des Questions Historiques* 46 (1889): 5–90, and Guibert, *Epistolae*, 1: vi–xi. Guibert's incomplete *vita* was apparently not among the texts he left at the Rupertsberg, as Theoderic, the final redactor of the *Vita S. Hildegardis*, shows no familiarity with it. For Guibert's role in collecting sources, see Klaes, *Vita*, pp. 39*–59*. Page numbers with asterisks in this volume refer to the editor's lengthy introduction.

9. Theoderic was commissioned by two abbots: Ludwig, abbot of St. Eucharius in Trier, a close friend of Hildegard, and his own abbot, Gottfried of Echternach, who also had ties with the Rupertsberg. Gottfried's accession in 1181 and Ludwig's death at the end of 1187 set the parameters for dating the *Vita*. See Klaes, *Vita*, pp. 77*–78*.

10. Klaes, *Vita*, pp. 77*, 111*, 125*.

11. For this argument see Newman, "Three-Part Invention" (n. 2 above), p. 196. For another study of Hildegard's memoir see Peter Dronke, *Women Writers of the Middle Ages: A Critical Study of Texts from Perpetua († 203) to Marguerite Porete († 1310)* (Cambridge: Cambridge University Press, 1984), pp. 144–71.

12. For *vitae* of this type see *Sainted Women of the Dark Ages* (n. 3 above). The biographies of these high-born abbesses are rich in visions, a motif especially prominent in the life of St. Aldegund, Abbess of Maubeuge (d. ca. 684).

13. Theoderic's outlook is not unlike the more fully developed view taken by Guibert of Gembloux in his extensive correspondence with and about Hildegard. I thank John Coakley for letting me read his stimulating unpublished essay, "Guibert of Gembloux and Hildegard of Bingen" (paper presented at the 30th International Congress on Medieval Studies, Kalamazoo, Michigan, May 1995).

14. *Vita* II.2, pp. 22–23.

15. *Vita* II.2, p. 24.

16. *Scivias* preface, quoted in *Vita* I.1, pp. 6–7.

17. *Vita* II.2, p. 24.

18. In order to authenticate her prophetic call, Hildegard seems to have exaggerated her educational deficiencies. A recently discovered *vita* of her teacher Jutta of Sponheim (d. 1136), commissioned by Hildegard and possibly written by Volmar, describes the aristocratic recluse as literate, intelligent, and a skillful teacher; it characterizes her repeatedly as a *magistra*, her nuns as *discipulae*, and their monastery as a *schola*. "Vita domnae Juttae inclusae," ed. Franz Staab, in *Reformidee und Reformpolitik im spätsalisch-frühstaufischen Reich*, ed. Stefan Weinfurter (Mainz: Gesellschaft für mittelrheinische Kirchengeschichte, 1992), pp. 172–87; translation in Silvas, *Jutta and Hildegard* (n. 1 above).

19. Ep. 1, in *Epistolarium*, 1: 3–7.

20. Hugo was cantor and *magister* at the cathedral of Mainz; it was he who educated Raoul of Zähringen, future bishop of Liège. After Gottfried's death in 1176 and shortly before his own, Hugo was pressed into service as provost at the Rupertsberg. Hildegard's acceptance in high ecclesiastical circles may have more connection than is usually recognized with the influence of her family.

21. "Hec ad audientiam Mogontine ecclesie allata cum essent et discussa, omnes ex Deo esse dixerunt et ex prophetia, quam olim prophete prophetaverant." *Vita* II.2, p. 24.

22. There seems to be no reason to doubt this statement, which is amplified

in Gottfried's account (*Vita* I.4), although the pope's original letter does not survive. The letter ostensibly from Eugene printed in *PL* 197: 145 has been exposed as a forgery (Marianna Schrader and Adelgundis Führkötter, *Die Echtheit des Schrifttums der heiligen Hildegard von Bingen* [Cologne: Böhlau, 1956], pp. 111–23). Four letters from Hildegard to Eugene are extant; the earliest (1148) refers to his prior approval of the *Scivias* and was sent as a cover letter with a further portion of that text (Ep. 2, *Epistolarium*, 1: 7–8). One authentic letter from Eugene to Hildegard survives (Ep. 4, *Epistolarium*, 1: 10–11), but it concerns the departure of her nun Richardis von Stade and dates from 1151, a few years after the pope's sojourn in Trier.

23. Hildegard's reliance on this prelate is also clear from his role in helping her secure permission to move (*Vita* II.5, p. 28), her insistence on having no other patron for the Rupertsberg, and her attempt to protect him by interceding with Pope Eugene at the time of his downfall in 1153 (Ep. 5, *Epistolarium*, 1: 11–13).

24. Cf. Barbara Newman, *Sister of Wisdom: St. Hildegard's Theology of the Feminine* (Berkeley: University of California Press, 1987), pp. 34–41.

25. "Sed et ego, que iaceo in pusillanimitate mentis mee . . . interdum sonans aliquantulum velut parvus sonus tube a vivente lumine": Ep. 201r to Elisabeth of Schönau, in *Epistolarium*, 2: 457.

26. Hildegard and Gottfried use identical words but not with identical meaning: she says that Volmar reported her visions to *his* abbot ("abbati suo," *Vita* II.2, p. 24), while Gottfried says that through Volmar she revealed them to *her own* abbot ("abbati suo," I.3, p. 8). The difference is a subtle one: the hagiographer, himself a monk of St. Disibod, emphasizes Hildegard's monastic obedience and the abbot's decisive role, whereas Hildegard—who was already *magistra* and would soon leave the Disibodenberg—recognizes the abbot's direct authority over Volmar but not over herself. Cf. Klaes, *Vita*, pp. 107*–108*.

27. Herbert Grundmann, "Zur Vita S. Gerlaci Eremitae," repr. in *Ausgewählte Aufsätze* (Stuttgart: Hiersemann, 1976), 1: 187–94.

28. For the council of Trier see Balderic, *Gesta Alberonis Archiepiscopi*, chap. 23, *MGH*, *SS* 8 (Hannover: Hahn, 1848), pp. 254–55, and *Sacrorum Conciliorum Nova et Amplissima Collectio*, ed. J. D. Mansi (repr. Graz: Akademische Druck, 1961), vol. 21, cols. 737–38, 743–46.

29. *Vita* I.4, pp. 9–10. See also Klaes, *Vita*, pp. 97*–99*, and n. 22 above.

30. For a detailed record of Bernard's movements in 1146–48 see "Tables chronologiques," Commission d'Histoire de l'Ordre de Cîteaux, *Bernard de Clairvaux* (Paris: Editions Alsatia, 1953), pp. 605–9.

31. Others were Gembloux, Villers, St. Eucharius in Trier, and of course the Rupertsberg; the commemoration did not spread to the Mainz cathedral. See Helmut Hinkel, "St. Hildegards Verehrung im Bistum Mainz," in *Hildegard von Bingen, 1179-1979: Festschrift zum 800. Todestag der Heiligen*, ed. Anton Brück (Mainz: Gesellschaft für mittelrheinische Kirchengeschichte, 1979), p. 388.

32. "Praeterea sciendum quod libri sanctae Hildegardis recepti et canonizati sunt a papa Eugenio in concilio Trevirensi, praesentibus multis episcopis tam Francorum quam Teutonicorum, et sancto Bernardo abbate Clarevallensi." Because of the vast number of manuscripts, Gebeno's influential work still remains unedited.

There is a very partial edition in *Analecta S. Hildegardis*, ed. J.-B. Pitra (Monte Cassino, 1882), pp. 483–88; quoted passage, p. 484.

33. ". . . cum nullis litteris nisi tantum psalmis Daviticis esset erudita, per Spiritum sanctum edocta de divinis oraculis et sacramentis sibi revelatis grandia edidit volumina, que ab Eugenio papa mediante sancto Bernardo Clarevallense abbate canonizata et inter sacras scripturas sunt connumerata." *Vita S. Gerlaci* 8.20, *AASS*, Jan., vol. 1 (Paris, 1863), p. 309. Cf. *Vita* I.1, p. 6: "Ceterum preter psalmorum simplicem noticiam nullam litteratorie vel musice artis ab homine percepit doctrinam, quamvis eius extent scripta non pauca et quedam non exigua volumina."

34. "Papa Eugenius scripta eius canonizavit in concilio Treverensi." Albert von Stade, *Annales Stadenses, MGH, SS* 16 (Hannover: Hahn, 1859), p. 330; Friedhelm Jürgensmeier, "St. Hildegard 'Prophetissa Teutonica,'" in *Hildegard von Bingen* (n. 31 above), pp. 286–87. William of St.-Amour is cited in *Sacrorum Conciliorum* 21 (n. 28 above), col. 738: "Vidimus etiam quemdam librum de archivo eodem [Claraevallensi] assumptum, quasdam prophetias dictae Hildegardis clarius exponentem, et inter cetera continentem, quod tempore B. Bernardi Claraevallensis, Eugenio papa libros ejusdem prophetissae canonizavit in concilio Trevirensi."

35. "Prophetias Hildegardis non multum pondero, sed magis eos arguo qui mulieris doctrinam in ecclesias introducunt, quam apostolus docere in ecclesia non permittit. . . . Ad quod dicunt quidam Bernardum prophetias Hildegardis collegisse, si verum est, huiusmodi prophetie auctoritatem non ostendit: collegit enim Bernardus quedam ad reprobandum sicut errores Abelardi. . . . Et quod dicunt papam Eugenium ea confirmasse, plane est mendacium, quia sedes apostolica non sole[t] dubia confirmare, maxime cum hec in aliis temeritatis sue scriptitationibus suis noscatur plura erronea reliquisse. Credo autem donec aliud mihi innotescat, prophetiam Hildegardis ex dyaboli astutia processisse." John Peckham, "Tractatus Pauperis," chap. 16, in *Tractatus Tres de Paupertate*, ed. C. L. Kingsford, A. G. Little, and F. Tocco (Manchester: Manchester University Press, 1910), p. 76. This passage represents the most scathing extant attack on Hildegard.

36. Newman, *Sister of Wisdom*, pp. 25–29; Christel Meier, "Prophetentum als literarische Existenz: Hildegard von Bingen (1098–1179), Ein Portrait," in *Deutsche Literatur von Frauen*, ed. Gisela Brinker-Gabler (Munich: C. H. Beck, 1988), 1: 76–87.

37. *Vita* II.7, p. 32 (Joshua and Joseph); II.9, p. 34 (Job and Jeremiah); II.12, p. 38 (Susanna); III.23, p. 66 (Jonah).

38. "Ego autem paupercula forma hos precipue dilexi et invocavi, qui carnem suam in spiritu afflixerunt, et ab his declinavi, qui se contra spiritum induraverunt et eum suffocaverunt." *Vita* II.14, p. 41.

39. *Vita* II.5, pp. 28–29.

40. *Vita* II.12, p. 37.

41. ". . . sed tantum in anima mea, apertis exterioribus oculis, ita ut numquam in eis defectum extasis patiar; sed vigilanter die ac nocte illa video." Ep. 103r to Guibert of Gembloux, in *Epistolarium*, 2: 261. Theoderic inserts this passage, with slight stylistic changes, in *Vita* I.8, p. 15.

42. *Vita* II.16, p. 43.

43. *Vita* II, prologue, p. 17.

44. The sole exception appears to have been St. Ursula. Cf. Newman, *Sister of Wisdom*, pp. 225–28, 246–47.

45. *Vita* II.5, p. 29.

46. *Vita* I.8, p. 14 (Leah and Rachel); II.6, p. 30 (Deborah); cf. Origen, *In librum Judicum*, Hom. 5.2. I accept Klaes's argument that it was Theoderic, not Gottfried, who wrote the last two chapters of Book I (pp. 92*–95*).

47. *Vita* II.1, p. 20; II.17, p. 45.

48. Klaes, *Vita*, p. 131*; Rupert of Deutz, *Comm. in Canticum canticorum* 5 and *Comm. super Matthaeum* 12 (*PL* 168: 914a, 1611c).

49. *Vita* II.3, pp. 24–25; cf. II.2, p. 21.

50. *Vita* II.15, pp. 41–42. On the benefits of obscurity see Augustine, *De doctrina christiana* II.7–8.

51. "Et nos igitur secundi libri termino hic fixo etiam canticum laudis Domino canamus, dum tam vastum pelagus visionum sancte virginis enavigamus." *Vita* II.17, p. 45. On the topos of brevity in saints' lives see Simone Roisin, *L'Hagiographie cistercienne dans le diocèse de Liège au XIIIe siècle* (Louvain: Bibliothèque de l'Université, 1947), pp. 225–26.

52. Klaes, *Vita*, p. 145*.

53. *Analecta S. Hildegardis*, ed. Pitra (n. 32 above), pp. 484–85.

54. Kathryn Kerby-Fulton, "Hildegard and the Male Reader: A Study in Insular Reception," in *Prophets Abroad: The Reception of Continental Holy Women in Late-Medieval England*, ed. Rosalynn Voaden (Cambridge: D. S. Brewer, 1996), p. 10.

55. Annotation in a manuscript of Hildegard's letters (London, BL Add. 15102, fol. iv), cited by Kerby-Fulton in ibid., p. 12. Cf. the similar comment in Trithemius's *Chronicon Hirsaugiense* ad 1149, in *Opera historica*, ed. Marquard Freher (1601; repr. Frankfurt: Minerva, 1966), p. 132; Newman, *Sister of Wisdom*, p. 22.

56. ". . . respondeo, me solum huius operis translatorem existere non auctorem; quippe qui de meo parum addidi vel mutavi; sed, prout in cedulis suscepi, oblata verba vulgaria latino tantum eloquio coloravi." *Vita Beatricis*, Prol. 4, ed. Léonce Reypens; Latin text reprinted on facing pages in Roger De Ganck, trans., *The Life of Beatrice of Nazareth, 1200–1268* (Kalamazoo, Mich.: Cistercian Publications, 1991); quoted passage, p. 4. For more on this text see Amy Hollywood, "Inside Out: Beatrice of Nazareth and Her Hagiographer," this volume, chap. 5.

57. *Vita Beatricis* III.275–76, in *Life of Beatrice*, pp. 342–45.

58. De Ganck, *Life of Beatrice*, p. xxix; Hadewijch, *Het Visioenenboek van Hadewijch*, ed. H. W. J. Vekeman (Nijmegen: Dekker and Van de Vegt, 1980); trans. Helen Rolfson, "The List of the Perfect," *Vox Benedictina* 5 (1988): 285.

59. Gilbert of Tournai, *Collectio de scandalis ecclesiae*, ed. Autpert Stroick, *AFH* 24 (1931): 33–62; trans. from Ernest McDonnell, *The Beguines and Beghards in Medieval Culture, with Special Emphasis on the Belgian Scene* (1954; repr. New York: Octagon, 1969), p. 366.

60. De Ganck, *Life of Beatrice*, pp. xxx–xxxii.

61. *Book of Blessed Angela of Foligno, Memorial*, chap. 2, trans. Paul Lachance in *Angela of Foligno: Complete Works* (New York: Paulist Press, 1993), pp. 137–38.

62. Catherine M. Mooney, "The Authorial Role of Brother A. in the Com-

position of Angela of Foligno's Revelations," in *Creative Women in Medieval and Early Modern Italy: A Religious and Artistic Renaissance*, ed. E. Ann Matter and John Coakley (Philadelphia: University of Pennsylvania Press, 1994), pp. 34–63; the passage from chap. 7 of the *Memorial* is quoted on p. 54.

63. Mooney, "Authorial Role," p. 52. It is also possible that, in stressing their own incomprehension, scribes like Angela's "Brother A." were protecting themselves in advance against possible accusations of heterodoxy.

64. Stephan Hilpisch, "Der Kult der heiligen Hildegard," *Pastor Bonus* 45 (1934): 118–33; Hinkel, "St. Hildegards Verehrung" (n. 31 above), pp. 385–411.

65. For the hymn, composed by the Cistercian monks of Villers in 1181, see *Analecta S. Hildegardis*, ed. Pitra (n. 32 above), pp. 439–40; for the *Octo lectiones* in prose, possibly compiled by Theoderic, see the edition by Klaes in *Vita*, pp. 75–80. The fragment of a rhymed office from Cologne can be found in *Analecta hymnica Medii Aevi* 28 (Leipzig, 1898), no. 115, pp. 299–300.

66. This was among the sources used by Theoderic for Book III; he specifically mentions the nuns' writing in *Vita* III.26, p. 68.

67. Hinkel, "St. Hildegards Verehrung" (n. 31 above). The altarcloth, woven ca. 1230 by the nuns, depicts Hildegard with SS. Rupert and Martin, patrons of the Rupertsberg church, as part of a *majestas Christi* composition. She is shown wearing the white silken veil that Rupertsberg nuns wore to receive communion rather than the standard black veil of the Benedictines. For the controversy provoked by this practice see Hildegard's correspondence with Tenxwindis, *magistra* of Andernach: Ep. 52–52r, *Epistolarium*, 1: 125–30. Hildegard's veil and the jeweled crown she wore for communion were among the relics included when the altar at St. Quirinus, Trier, was consecrated in 1287. Hilpisch, "Kult," p. 122.

68. Bull of 27 Jan. 1227: "Nos, qui de laudabili et sancta conversatione ipsius audierimus, dum in minori constituti officio . . . legatione in partibus Alemanniae fungeremur, deberemus nunc eam exaltare in terra, quam Dominus honoravit in coelis, canonizantes eam videlicet et sanctorum catalogo adscribentes." Hilpisch, "Kult," p. 120.

69. Kathryn Kerby-Fulton, "Hildegard of Bingen and Antimendicant Propaganda," *Traditio* 43 (1987): 386–99. Cf. the interest William of St.-Amour took in Hildegard, n. 34 above.

70. Vauchez, *Sainteté* (n. 3 above), pp. 295–300.

71. Vauchez, *Sainteté*, pp. 308, 316. Aviad Kleinberg stresses that papal canonization was not only rare, but of fairly limited importance: many late medieval saint cults arose and flourished with neither assistance nor interference from the papacy. *Prophets in Their Own Country* (n. 3 above), pp. 21–39.

72. Benedicta Ward, *Miracles and the Medieval Mind: Theory, Record, and Event 1000–1215* (Philadelphia: University of Pennsylvania Press, 1982), pp. 189–90; Adriaan Bredero, *Etudes sur la Vita Prima S. Bernardi* (Rome, 1950). For similar cases of papal objection to imprecise testimony in protocols, see Vauchez, *Sainteté*, pp. 60–64.

73. The commissioners, all clerics of Mainz, submitted their report on 16 December 1233; this is the *Acta inquisitionis de virtutibus et miraculis S. Hildegardis* published in *PL* 197: 131–40. On 6 May 1237 Gregory asked the same inquisitors

to prepare a revised version. As they never did so, Innocent IV attempted to revive the cause on 24 November 1243. The protocol of 1233 was in fact revised and corrected at this time. It is still extant in the Koblenz Staatsarchiv and reveals the requisite names, dates, and places inserted by a later hand, but was evidently never sent to Rome. Hilpisch, "Kult," pp. 119–21. For a translation of the *Acta* see Silvas, *Jutta and Hildegard* (n. 1 above).

74. *Acta inquisitionis* 10, *PL* 197: 138c; Conrad of Eberbach, *Exordium Magnum Cisterciense* 2.20, ed. Bruno Griesser, *CCCM* 138 (Turnhout: Brepols, 1994); Ward, *Miracles*, p. 180. The nuns were probably familiar with the *Exordium*; they maintained close ties with the monks of Eberbach, where it originated.

75. Klaes, *Vita*, pp. 157*–183*; a few unverifiable catalogue entries are also noted.

76. Brussels, BR 7917, from a house of Brethren of the Common Life in Utrecht, contains fifty female saints' lives, including an abridged version of Hildegard's *Vita*. I thank Jennifer Carpenter for allowing me to consult her extensive database on manuscripts of the *mulieres religiosae*.

77. Edouard de Moreau, *L'Abbaye de Villers-en-Brabant aux XIIe et XIIIe siècles* (Brussels: Albert Dewit, 1909), pp. 105–14; Simone Roisin, "L'Efflorescence cistercienne et le courant féminin de piété au XIIIe siècle," *Revue d'Histoire Ecclésiastique* 39 (1943): 342–78; McDonnell, *Beguines and Beghards* (n. 59 above), pp. 281–98.

78. Klaes, *Vita*, pp. 54*–56*, 178*–179*, 83–88 (text). This is the Utrecht MS. cited in n. 76 above.

79. "Vita Abbreviata Traiectensis," in Klaes, *Vita*, p. 83.

80. By contrast, the *Vita Abbreviata* stemming from Guibert's circle characterizes Hildegard's style as "simple": her books are "nec tamen propter stili simplicitatem viliora, ymmo forsitan digniora." Klaes, *Vita*, p. 85.

81. Gebeno, *Speculum futurorum temporum*, in *Analecta S. Hildegardis*, ed. Pitra (n. 32 above), p. 488.

82. Hadewijch, "List of the Perfect" (n. 58 above), p. 285.

83. Kerby-Fulton, "Hildegard and the Male Reader" (n. 54 above), pp. 4–5.

Chapter 3. Holy Woman or Unworthy Vessel? The Representations of Elisabeth of Schönau

I would like to thank Kevin Trainor, who read and thoughtfully commented on this essay, Diane Senior, who read a related essay and whose comments there helped clarify my argument here, and Catherine Mooney, for her encouragement, conversation along the way, and insights about the larger issues raised in this volume.

1. For Hildelin's preaching, see Elisabeth's letter to Hildegard of Bingen, in *Die Visionen der hl. Elisabeth und die Schriften der Aebte Ekbert und Emecho von Schönau*, ed. F. W. E. Roth (Brünn: Verlag der Studien aus dem Benedictiner- und Cistercienser-Orden, 1884), p. 73. Hereafter cited as *Visionen*.

2. This information comes from Ekbert's introduction to the collection of Elisabeth's letters, *Visionen*, p. 139.

3. Jean Beleth, *Rationale divinorum officiorum*, PL 202: 148.

4. See Ruth J. Dean, "Elizabeth, Abbess of Schönau, and Roger of Ford," *Modern Philology* 41 (1944): 209–20.

5. Alberic of Trois Fontaines, *Chronica*, MGH, SS 23, p. 843.

6. The manuscripts are catalogued in Kurt Köster, "Elisabeth von Schönau: Werk und Wirkung im Spiegel der mittelalterlichen handschriftlichen Überlieferung," *Archiv für Mittelrheinische Kirchengeschichte* 3 (1951): 243–315; and Köster, "Das visionäre Werk Elisabeths von Schönau: Studien zu Entstehung, Überlieferung und Wirkung in der mittelalterlichen Welt," *Archiv für Mittelrheinische Kirchengeschichte* 4 (1952): 114–19. To this list should be added Cologne, Stadtarchiv MS GB 8° 60; Cologne, Stadtarchiv MS W133; and Troyes, Bibliothèque Municipale MS 946; †Trier, St. Eucharius-Matthias Abbey MS 148 (D56); and †Trier, St. Eucharius-Matthias Abbey MS 524 (I66). From this list should be deleted Trier, Stadtbibliothek 646/869 8°, a manuscript in which letters of Hildegard of Bingen are ascribed to Elisabeth. The first edition of Elisabeth's visions is Jacques Lefèvre d'Etaples, *Liber trium virorum & trium spiritualium virginum* (Paris: Henri Estienne, 1513).

7. For Ekbert's study in Paris, see Kurt Köster, "Elisabeth von Schönau: Leben, Persönlichkeit und visionäres Werk," in *Schönauer Elisabeth Jubiläum 1965: Festschrift anlässlich des achthundert jährigen Todestages des heiligen Elisabeth von Schönau* (Limburg: Pallottiner Druckerei, 1965), p. 19; and Anne L. Clark, *Elisabeth of Schönau: A Twelfth-Century Visionary* (Philadelphia: University of Pennsylvania Press, 1992), pp. 15–16. For Ekbert's ecclesiastical ambitions and conversion to the monastic life, see Emecho of Schönau, *Vita Eckeberti*, ed. S. Widmann, *Neues Archiv der Gesellschaft für ältere deutsche Geschichtskunde* 11 (1886): 447–54. For Ekbert's connections to Rainald of Dassel, whom he appears to have met during his student life, see his letters to Rainald, PL 195: 11–14; and *Visionen*, pp. 310–17.

8. *Visionen*, pp. 3, 32–33. These texts were later used by Ekbert in his compilation of the visionary books. None of these records produced by the other nuns of Schönau are known to have survived independently of the collections he edited.

9. *Visionen*, p. 38.

10. See Elisabeth's letter to Hildegard of Bingen, *Visionen*, p. 73.

11. *Visionen*, p. 2.

12. For a more detailed analysis of how the social and cultural structures of male dominance shaped the relationship between Elisabeth and Ekbert, see Anne L. Clark, "Repression or Collaboration? The Case of Elisabeth and Ekbert of Schönau," in *Christendom and Its Discontents: Exclusion, Persecution, and Rebellion, 1000–1500*, ed. Scott L. Waugh and Peter D. Diehl (Cambridge: Cambridge University Press, 1996), pp. 151–67.

13. *Visionen*, pp. 2–3. My characterization of some parts of the visionary texts as reflecting Elisabeth's own sentiments is based on my earlier analysis disentangling the respective voices of Elisabeth and Ekbert. See Clark, *Elisabeth of Schönau*, esp. pp. 50–67.

14. *Visionen*, pp. 22, 26–27.

15. *Visionen*, p. 1.

16. *Visionen*, p. 318.

17. "Qui universa magnalia, que dominus noster cum ipsa operatus est, dili-

genter perscrutans, ea que fidelium utilitati congruere videbat, conscripsit, ea vero, que legentibus non prodesse sciebat, omnino reticuit." Emecho, *Vita Eckeberti*, pp. 448–49.

18. See Clark, *Elisabeth of Schönau*, pp. 46, 52–53.

19. *Visionen*, p. 54.

20. *Visionen*, pp. 60–61.

21. Cf. Lynn Staley Johnson, "The Trope of the Scribe and the Question of Literary Authority in the Works of Julian of Norwich and Margery Kempe," *Speculum* 66 (1991): 820–38.

22. Ekbert wrote a brief introduction to the first visionary diary which he expanded when he later expanded that text. He also wrote introductions to the second visionary diary and the collection of letters, and a general prologue to the whole collection of works. Except for the original introduction to the first visionary diary, all the introductory materials were published only after Elisabeth's death.

23. "Quam multa est dignatio tua super eos o zelator humani generis benigne Jhesu. Non enim vel etas, vel sexus, vel conditio, vel quicquam extrinsecus adiacens in eis despectum tibi est, sed solam devoti cordis humilitatem metuis." The prayer, known by its incipit as *Tua sunt*, is printed in *Visionen*, p. VI, n. 1. This printing is taken from Meerseburg, Dombibliothek 96. I have also consulted Trier, Dombibliothek 10, Halle, Universitätsbibliothek Yc quart 6, and Fulda, Landesbibliothek Aa96.

24. Ekbert seemed to have recognized the connection between this prayer and the introduction to the second visionary diary, for when he wrote the introduction to the second visionary diary, he moved this prayer into that text. (Typical of Roth's preference for following manuscripts of the later redactions, the prayer is edited as an annotation to Ekbert's introduction to the second visionary diary.) In his final redaction of the visionary works, Ekbert omitted the prayer altogether.

25. "Non enim cohibetur murmuratione eorum, qui magnos se estimantes et que videntur infirmiora spernentes, divitias bonitatis eius in illa subsannare non formidant. . . . Hoc illos scandalizat, quod in his diebus plurimum in sexu fragili misericordiam suam dominus magnificare dignatur. Sed cur in mentem non venit, quoniam simile factum est in diebus patrum nostrorum, quando viris socordie deditis, spiritu dei replete sunt mulieres sancte, ut prophetarent, populum dei strennue gubernarent, sive etiam de hostibus Israel gloriose triumpharent, quemadmodum Olda, Debora, Judith, Jahel, et huiusmodi?" *Visionen*, p. 40.

26. Elisabeth also complained about the skepticism of religious leaders: "those who walk in the habit of religion . . . mock the grace of the Lord in me" ("qui in habitu religionis ambulant . . . gratiam domini in me irrident"); and some "magistrates of the Church and religious men" concluded that her angelic informant was in fact a demonic force ("Hoc igitur sermone inductus dominus abbas, cepit divulgare verbum coram magistratibus ecclesie, et viris religiosis. Quorum quidam cum reverentia verbum exceperunt, quidam vero non sic, sed sinistre de angelo, qui familiaris mihi est, locuti sunt dicentes, eum esse illusorem spiritum, et in angelum lucis tranfiguratum"). *Visionen*, pp. 71–72.

27. ". . . stabam sola in oratorio, et eram intenta orationibus. Et ecce radius copiosi luminis repente de celo effusus est super me, faciens mihi estum, quemad-

modum sol, quando splendet in virtute sua. Et cecidi prona in terram cum impetu vehementi, et veni in mentis excessum. . . . Et post pusillum venit angelus domini, et erexit me velociter, et statuit me supra pedes meos dicens: O homo surge et sta supra pedes tuos, et loquar tecum, et noli timere, quia ego tecum sum omnibus diebus vite tue. Viriliter age et confortetur cor tuum, et sustine dominum. Et dices prevaricatoribus terre: Sicut olim gentes crucifixerunt me, sic cottidie crucifigor inter illos, qui prevaricati sunt me in cordibus suis." *Visionen*, p. 32.

28. "Et dixit angelus domini ad me: Et tu fili hominis dices ad eos, qui habitant in terra. Audite populi! Deus deorum locutus est: Penitentiam agite, prope est enim regnum dei. . . . Et dixi: Domine, nescio loqui, et tarda sum ad loquendum. Et dixit: Aperi os tuum, et ego dicam, et qui audit te, audit et me." *Visionen*, p. 33. The phrase *fili hominis*, traditionally rendered as "son of man," is here translated as "son of humanity." The word *homo* in this context emphasizes the humanity of the prophet being commissioned in contrast to the divinity of the one who commissions. See the many examples in the Book of Ezekiel, such as Ez. 2: 1.

29. ". . . die quadam, cum essem in spiritu, duxerat me quasi in pratum quoddam, in quo fixum erat tentorium, et introivimus illuc. Et ostendit mihi congeriem magnam librorum illic repositorum et ait: Vides libros istos? Omnes adhuc ante diem iudicii dictandi sunt. Elevans autem unum ex eis dixit: Hic est liber viarum dei, qui per te revelandus est, quando visitaveris sororem Hildigardim, et audieris eam. Et ita quidem impleri cepit, continuo cum ab ea redissem." *Visionen*, p. 91. For an assessment of the relationship between Hildegard and Elisabeth and Hildegard's influence on Elisabeth's visionary career, see Clark, *Elisabeth of Schönau*, pp. 14–15, 21–25, 34–36, 95, 134.

30. In defiance of the adjuration, Ekbert suppressed it in the final redaction of the visionary collection. For the text of the adjuration, see F. W. E. Roth, "Aus einer Handschrift der Schriften der heil. Elisabeth von Schönau," *Neues Archiv der Gesellschaft für Ältere Deutsche Geschichtskunde* 36 (1911): 221.

31. *Visionen*, p. 122.

32. In *Visionen*, p. 318.

33. See, e.g., Gratian, *Decretum*, C. I q. I c.79.

34. For the sanctification of people during their lifetime, see Aviad M. Kleinberg, *Prophets in Their Own Country: Living Saints and the Making of Sainthood in the Later Middle Ages* (Chicago: University of Chicago Press, 1992).

35. "En nostra Elisabeth, illa electa lampas celici luminis, virgo illustris et honorificata in habundanti gratia dei, splendida gemma cenobii nostri, dux nostri virginei cetus, heu, ante annos maturiores ex hac luce subtracta est." *Visionen*, p. 263.

36. The short version of *De Obitu* is transmitted only in Vienna, Österr. Nationalbibliothek Vindob. Pal. MS 488. The long form, transmitted in seven manuscripts, is edited in *Visionen*, pp. 263–78. Neither version can be dated precisely. The earlier version probably was written very soon after Elisabeth died. The longer version, which suggests a possible lapse of time from her death, may still have been written within a year of her death.

37. ". . . et super dolorem vulnerum, quem tibi infligebat manus eius, semper adiciebas sacrificium spontanee afflictionis." *Visionen*, p. 264.

38. For example, "May God, who raises up the humble, look upon and honor the humility of your spirit" is found in both versions. In the later version, Ekbert elaborated by adding, "May the divine kindness acknowledge the kindness which you were accustomed to show to those opposing you, and may He lead you to a just reward. Weary soul, contrite soul, soul soaked in the miseries of a life full of suffering, go now to the repose so long desired; may the bosom of eternal peace receive you" ("Humilitatem spiritus tui . . . respiciat et honorificet sublevator humilium deus. Benignitatem, quam erga adversantes tibi habere solebas, benignitas divina agnoscat, et ad condignam retributionem adducat. Anima lassa, anima contrita, et saturata miseriis erumnose vite, perge nunc in requiem diu desideratam, suscipiat te sinus pacis eterne"). *Visionen*, p. 265.

39. "Sermone precedenti ad finem deducto, distulit solito diutius visitare me angelus domini. Quod ego delictis meis imputans anxiabar intra me, ac diligentius lacrimis et orationibus operam dedi, et adiuvabat me conventus noster oratione communi. Et consummatis decem et septem diebus ab eo, quo iam dicta verba compleverat, stabam sola in oratorio circa horam terciam effundens coram domino cor meum ac dicens: Non mea merita domine aspexisti in omnibus, que hactenus mecum operatus es, sed in tua misericordia fecisti omnia hec. Propterea obsecro, ne compescaris delictis meis, aut cuiusquam alterius, quin hec, que nunc apud me iniciare dignatus es, propter bonitatem tuam ad bonam consummationem perducas." *Visionen*, p. 111.

40. *Visionen*, pp. 16, 96.

41. "Quia ecce in servicio eius tepida facta es, et debitum ei ministerium non, sicut solebas, impendis." *Visionen*, p. 44.

42. Elisabeth learns that the other nuns are to join in propitiating Mary for their communal negligence (*communi negligentia nostra*). *Visionen*, p. 45.

43. This theme emerges elsewhere in the second visionary diary. See Clark, *Elisabeth of Schönau*, pp. 114–17.

44. "Frequenter enim et quasi ex consuetudine in diebus dominicis aliisque festivitatibus circa horas, in quibus maxime fidelium fervet devotio, cecidit super eam passio quedam precordiorum" ("Frequently and indeed as if by habit, on Sundays and other feast days, around the hours in which the devotion of the faithful was especially inflamed, a certain affliction of the heart came over her"). *Visionen*, p. 1.

45. See also *Visionen*, pp. 7, 111, for other examples where Elisabeth describes the community praying for her.

46. ". . . si tot martirum honor aliquid incrementi acceperit ex his, que per meos labores dominus de eis revelare dignatur." *Visionen*, p. 123.

47. The connection between these two aspects of her power can be seen when Elisabeth recounts that she had been frequently asked to find out about Saint Gerasma, but for some odd reason, she always forgot to inquire about her. "At last it happened that he who had asked me to inquire about her sent to us three holy little bodies which were from the company of virgins" ("Tandem autem contigit, ut ipse, qui de ea interrogare me rogaverat, mitteret ad nos tria corpuscula sancta, que fuerant ex societate virginum prefatarum"). *Visionen*, p. 131. Her forgetfulness of someone's petition eventually led to Schönau's further acquisition of relics.

48. ". . . quam multe electorum anime desideratis consolationibus per tuam negotiationem potite sunt." *Visionen*, p. 264.

49. Ekbert's influence can be seen in the larger context of this passage, where Elisabeth is described as directed by a "more learned one" to question the angel about certain obscurities in Scripture, and the answer is recorded in a style of rhetorical questions and answers very foreign to the style of Elisabeth's narration in the earlier diary entries.

50. *Visionen*, p. 64.

51. Most extant manuscripts of this text transmit it as the final work in a collection of Elisabeth's visions. The only exception is †Wiesbaden, Nassauische Landesbibliothek MS 3, from Schönau, in which *De Obitu* is the penultimate item followed by a collection of Elisabeth's letters. Vienna, Österr. Nationalbibliothek Vindob. Pal. MS 488, which transmits the later version of *De Obitu* and represents what I have characterized as Ekbert's preparation of a final collection of the visionary texts for public circulation, transmits *De Obitu* as the final element. This order is also reproduced in a later Schönau manuscript, Wiesbaden, Nassauische Landesbibliothek MS 4.

52. Fulda, Landesbibliothek MS Aa96. This manuscript, dated to the second half of the fifteenth century, is from the Benedictine abbey of Blauberen. The Schönau material comprises the largest single entry in this collection, fols. 120v–169r. The final unpublished notice, found in no other manuscript, includes information about the monastery at Schönau and the following comment about Elisabeth: "Virgo sanctissime conversationis, que superscriptas revelationes divinitus acceperat, quas ad edificationem posteritatis litteris demandavit" ("A virgin of most holy life, who received the above written revelations from heaven, which she committed to writing for the edification of future generations.")

53. Peter Dinzelbacher, "Die 'Vita et Revelationes' der Wiener Begine Agnes Blannbekin († 1315) im Rahmen der Viten- und Offenbarungsliteratur ihrer Zeit," in *Frauenmystik im Mittelalter*, ed. Dinzelbacher and Dieter R. Bauer (Stuttgart: Schwabenverlag AG, 1985), pp. 152–78.

Chapter 4. Imitatio Christi *or* Imitatio Mariae?
Clare of Assisi and Her Interpreters

I wish to thank Caroline Walker Bynum and Francine Cardman for reading an earlier draft of this paper and offering many insightful suggestions.

1. "Il Processo di Canonizzazione di S. Chiara d'Assisi," ed. Zeffirino Lazzeri, *AFH* 13 (1920): 439–93.

2. Luke Wadding, *Annales Minorum seu trium ordinum a S. Francisco institutorum* (Quaracchi: Ad Claras Acquas, 1931), vol. 3, ad annum 1253, pp. 340–43.

3. Giovanni Boccali, "Testamento e benedizione di S. Chiara: Nuovo codice latino," *AFH* 82 (1989): 273–81.

4. *Escritos de Santa Clara y Documentos Contemporáneos*, ed. Ignacio Omaechevarría et al. (Madrid: Biblioteca de Autores Cristianos, 1970; rev. and enl. 1982).

5. Notably, *Textus opusculorum S. Francisci et S. Clarae Assisiensium* (Assisi: Ed. Portiunculae, 1976), ed. Giovanni M. Boccali; published with Italian translation as *Opuscula sancti Francisci et scripta sanctae Clarae Assisiensium*, trans. Luciano Canonici (Assisi: Ed. Porziuncola, 1978). The best edition at present of Clare's corpus in Latin, with concordances and indices, is *Concordantiae verbales opusculorum S. Francisci et S. Clarae Assisiensium*, ed. Boccali (Assisi: Edizioni Porziuncola, 1976; rev. and enl. 1995). A more accessible edition, with Latin and French on facing pages, is *Claire d'Assise: Ecrits* (Paris: Editions du Cerf, 1985), ed. and trans. Marie-France Becker, Jean-François Godet, and Thaddée Matura. An English translation of texts attributed to Clare and medieval texts about her is *Clare of Assisi: Early Documents*, ed. Regis J. Armstrong (New York: Paulist Press, 1988; rev. and enl. Saint Bonaventure, N.Y.: Franciscan Institute Publications, 1993); except when noted otherwise, all references to Armstrong's edition are to the 1993 edition.

6. For bibliography, see *Bibliografia di Santa Chiara di Assisi: 1930–1993*, ed. Isidoro de Villapadierna and Pietro Maranesi (Rome: Istituto Storico dei Cappuccini, 1994); *St. Clare of Assisi and Her Order: A Bibliographic Guide*, ed. Mary Frances Hone (St. Bonaventure, N.Y.: Franciscan Institute Publications, 1995).

7. Marianne Schlosser, "Mutter—Schwester—Braut: Zur Spiritualität der hl. Klara," *Laurentianum* 31 (1990): 176. All translations of primary and secondary sources throughout this essay are mine unless otherwise noted. Marie Aimèe du Christ, "Charism prophétique de Claire pour la femme de tous les temps," *Laurentianum* 26 (1985): 865–82, also considers Clare's use of these terms. See *Greyfriars Review* for English translations of these and some other foreign language essays about Clare.

8. Epistola ad fratrem Leonem 2, p. 109. All references to Francis's and Clare's writings are from *Concordantiae verbales*, cited in n. 5. Others who wrote about Francis also cite him as having spoken of himself as a mother and woman: Thomas of Celano, *Vita secunda* 16–17, 82, and see 180, in *AF* 10 (Quaracchi: Collegium S. Bonaventurae, 1926–41); *Legendum trium sociorum: Edition critique*, ed. Théophile Desbonnets, *AFH* 67 (1974) 51: 127; 63: 138. In 1219 Odo of Cheriton said that Francis referred to himself as a woman, impregnated by the Lord, who bore spiritual children; "S. Francisci parabola in sermonibus Odonis de Ceritonia," *AFH* 22 (1929): 585.

9. Regula non bullata 9, 14, p. 29; De religiosa habitatione in eremo 3, p. 73; 7, p. 73; 10, p. 74; 11, p. 74; 12, p. 74; and see Regula bullata 6, 10; Thomas of Celano, *Vita prima* 98, in *AF* 10; Celano, *Vita secunda* 164.

10. Epistola ad Fideles [recensio prior], p. 218d; Epistola omnibus fidelibus 10, 6, p. 84; 10, 9, pp. 84–85; see also Celano, *Vita prima* 74.

11. See, for example, Celano, *Vita prima* 60, 79, and see 61; Celano, *Vita secunda* 137; *Legendum trium sociorum* 50–51, pp. 126–27. Other descriptions of Francis as a woman or that employ feminine terms include Celano, *Vita secunda* 16–17, 82, 93, 164; Bonaventure, *Legenda maior* (in *AF* 10) VII, 6 (compare with III, 10); *Legenda minor* (in *AF* 10) III, 7, 8.

12. Celano, *Vita secunda* 94.

13. For example, *Legendum trium sociorum* 41, p. 121.

14. But see Caroline Walker Bynum's discussion of this in *Holy Feast and Holy*

Fast: The Religious Significance of Food to Medieval Women (Berkeley: University of California Press, 1987), pp. 94–102, 282–88; and Richard C. Trexler's discussion of gender boundaries breached in pictorial representations of Francis's renunciation in *Naked Before the Father: The Renunciation of Francis of Assisi* (New York: Peter Lang, 1989), esp. pp. 98–99, 101–2, 108–9.

15. *L'Osservatore Romano*, Eng. ed., no. 34 (1304), 25 August 1993, p. 1.

16. Chiara Augusta Lainati, "Santa Clara de Asís, Mujer Bella," trans. Juan Oliver, *Selecciones de Franciscanismo* 21 (1992): 369.

17. Susan Muto, "Clare of Assisi: A Woman of Spirit, a Model of Strength for Today's World," in *Clare of Assisi: A Medieval and Modern Woman*, ed. Ingrid Peterson (St. Bonaventure, N.Y.: Franciscan Institute Publications, 1996), p. 189.

18. "Claire et la vie au féminin: Symboles de femme dans ses Ecrits," *Laurentianum* 31 (1990): 150, 158, 161–68. Godet uses highly stereotyped understandings of femininity and masculinity to argue that both exist within Clare, but stresses above all her womanly/feminine qualities.

19. *Laurentianum* 31, 1–2 (1990); Lainati, "Mujer Bella," pp. 367, 369.

20. For example, Cettina Militello, "Chiara e il 'femminile'," *Laurentianum* 31, 1–2 (1990): 62–105; Davide Covi, "Il Femminile nel linguaggio morale di Chiara d'Assisi," *Laurentianum* 31, 1–2 (1990): 106–47. These and other essays appearing in the multi-lingual *Laurentianum* 31, 1–2 (1990) all appear in Italian in *Chiara: Francescanesimo al Femminile*, ed. Covi and Dino Dozzi (Rome: Edizioni Dehoniane; Edizioni Collegio S. Lorenzo, 1992).

21. For a thorough discussion of the theme and its various meanings from New Testament times through the late Middle Ages with abundant references to primary and secondary sources, see Giles Constable, "The Ideal of the Imitation of Christ," in *Three Studies in Medieval Religious and Social Thought* (Cambridge: Cambridge University Press, 1995), pp. 143–248. For twelfth-century treatments of this theme, see Inos Biffi, "Aspetti dell'imitazione di Cristo nella letteratura monastica del secolo XII," *La Scuola Cattolica* 96 (1968): 451–90; Erich Kleineidam, "Die Nachfolge Christi nach Bernhard von Clairvaux," in *Amt und Sendung: Beiträge zu seelsorglichen und religiösen Fragen*, ed. Kleineidam, Otto Kuss, and Erich Puzik (Freiburg: Herder, 1950), pp. 432–60.

22. On this theme, see Rosemary Hale, "*Imitatio Mariae*: Motherhood Motifs in Devotional Memoirs," *Mystics Quarterly* 16 (1990): 193–203; Martina Wehrli-Johns, "Haushälterin Gottes: Zur Mariennachfolge der Beginen," in *Maria, Abbild oder Vorbild? Zur Sozialgeschichte mittelalterlicher Marienverehrung*, ed. Hedwig Röckelein, Claudia Opitz, and Dieter R. Bauer (Tübingen: Diskord, 1990), pp. 147–67; Jeffrey F. Hamburger, *The Rothschild Canticles: Art and Mysticism in Flanders and the Rhineland Circa 1300* (New Haven, Conn.: Yale University Press, 1990), pp. 88–104. The impossibility of imitating Mary, both virgin and mother, is discussed by Marina Warner, an early proponent of this point, in *Alone of All Her Sex: The Myth and Cult of the Virgin Mary* (New York: Knopf, 1976), to be used with caution.

23. *Vita prima*, in *AF* 10, pp. 2–117.

24. Georges Mailleux, the compiler of the concordance of Celano's four works regarding Francis together with the *Legend of Saint Clare* remarks that if

the *Legend* is indeed by Celano, then it shows an astonishingly diverse vocabulary from the works he indisputably authored; *Thesaurus Celanensis, Vita prima, Legenda ad usum chori, Vita secunda, Tractatus de miraculis, Legenda sanctae Clarae virginis* (Louvain: CETEDOC, 1974), p. xi n. 11. Regis J. Armstrong reviews the debate regarding authorship in "Clare of Assisi, the Poor Ladies, and their Ecclesial Mission in the 'First Life' of Thomas of Celano," *Laurentianum* 32 (1991): 131–37, slightly expanding his remarks in *Early Documents*, pp. 246–49.

25. Henry of Avranches, "Legenda in versi del Beato Francesco," ed. and trans. Antonio Cristofani, *Il Più antico poema della vita di S. Francesco d'Assisi scritto innanzi all'anno 1230* (Prato: Ranieri Guasti, 1882); "Legenda Versificata S. Clarae Assisiensis, Saec. XIII," ed. Benvenutus Bughetti, in *AFH* 5 (1912): 237–60, 459–81; see 235–36, 621–31.

26. Although this document has traditionally been called a "rule" and is identified in the Latin text I employ as the "Regula S. Clarae," I join the recent practice of some scholars in identifying it in my own text as the "Form of Life" since the term *formula vivendi*, not *regula*, is employed within the document.

27. The animated scholarly debate regarding the Testament's authenticity, which began nearly a century ago, has recently been reignited by Werner Maleczek, "Das *Privilegium Paupertatis* Innocenz' III. und das Testament der Klara von Assisi. Überlegungen zur Frage ihrer Echtheit," *Collectanea Franciscana* 65 (1995): 5–82, esp. 41–75, who casts doubt on the document's authenticity; responding to Maleczek and arguing for authenticity is Niklaus Kuster, "Das Armutsprivileg Innozenz' III. und Klaras Testament: Echt oder raffinierte Fälschungen?" *Collectanea Franciscana* 66 (1996): 5–95.

28. See n. 3.

29. The Blessing of Clare is found in four of the manuscripts containing the Testament. On the doubtful authenticity of the Blessing, see Emore Paoli, in *Fontes franciscani*, ed. Enrico Menestò and Stefano Brufani (Assisi: Edizioni Porziuncola, 1995), pp. 2251–60.

30. The Regula bullata, pp. 55–62, written in 1223. An earlier rule written by Francis in 1221, the Regula non bullata, pp. 19–50, did not receive papal approbation.

31. Livarius Oliger, "De Origine Regularum Ordinis S. Clarae," *AFH* 5 (1912): 431–32.

32. For example, Lothar Hardick, *Spiritualité de Sainte Claire* (Paris: Editions Franciscaines, 1961), pp. 19, 34.

33. Such reasoning appears in both early and recent scholarship, for example, Paschal Robinson's comments regarding the Testament, "The Writings of St. Clare of Assisi," *AFH* 3 (1910): 443; and Godet's regarding the *formula vivendi*, "Claire et la vie au féminin," p. 158.

34. For example, Margaret Carney, *The First Franciscan Woman: Clare of Assisi and Her Form of Life* (Quincy, Ill.: Franciscan Press, 1993), pp. 65–97, esp. 77–97; Elizabeth Alvilda Petroff, "A Medieval Woman's Utopian Vision: The Rule of Clare of Assisi," in *Body and Soul: Essays on Medieval Women and Mysticism* (New York: Oxford University Press, 1994), pp. 66–79.

35. In the *Actus beati Francisci et sociorum eius: Nuova edizione postuma di Jacques Cambell*, ed. Marino Bigaroni and Giovanni Boccali (Assisi: Edizioni Porziuncola, 1988), chaps. 6.1, 18.27. Conceptually, the notion appears as early as the letter Elias wrote upon Francis's death: *Epistola encyclica de transitu S. Francisci*, in *AF* 10, pp. 525–28. On its gradual development from the official *vitae* of Celano and Bonaventure through unofficial Franciscan sources after the *Actus*, see Stanislao da Campagnola, *L'Angelo del sesto sigillo e l' "alter Christus": Genesi e sviluppo di due temi francescani nei secoli XIII–XIV* (Rome: Laurentianum; Antonianum, 1971). On its iconographic development, see ibid. pp. 284–92; H. W. van Os, "St. Francis of Assisi as a Second Christ in Early Italian Painting," *Simiolus* 7 (1974): 115–32; Anne Derbes, *Picturing the Passion in Late Medieval Italy: Narrative Painting, Franciscan Ideologies, and the Levant* (Cambridge: Cambridge University Press, 1996), esp. pp. 16–24.

36. *"Compilatio Assisiensis" dagli Scritti di fr. Leone e Compagni su s. Francesco d'Assisi*, ed. Marino Bigaroni, 2nd ed. (Assisi: Biblioteca Francescana di Chiesa Nuova, 1992), p. 13; *Le Speculum perfectionis ou Mémoires de frère Léon*, ed. Paul Sabatier, vol. 1 (Manchester: Manchester University Press, 1928), chap. 108, 1, p. 309 (*aemulatrix praecipua beati Francisci*). The *Speculum* has been dated to 1318. Scholars differ in dating the *Compilatio* but generally agree that significant portions of the text were first gathered in 1246. The *Compilatio* has been known by a variety of names, including *Legend of Perugia*, not to be confused with *Anonymous of Perugia*; and *I Fiori dei tre compagni* (ed. Jacques Cambell [Milan: Vita e pensiero, 1967]), not to be confused with the *Legendum trium sociorum* (ed. Desbonnets).

37. Marco Bartoli, *Clare of Assisi*, trans. Sister Frances Teresa (Quincy, Ill.: Franciscan Press, 1993) p. 132. Hardick, *Spiritualité de Sainte Claire*, p. 26, calls her a "deuxième François"; and see Daniel Elcid, *Clara de Asís: La hermana ideal de San Francisco*, 3rd ed. (Madrid: Biblioteca de Autores Cristianos, 1994), p. 113.

38. Much recent scholarship, alternatively, presents Clare as a spiritual leader in her own right whose insights, while complementary to Francis's, were also deeply original; see for example Patricia Ranft, "An Overturned Victory: Clare of Assisi and the Thirteenth-Century Church," *Journal of Medieval History* 17 (1991): 123–34; Carney, *The First Franciscan Woman*; Petroff, "A Medieval Woman's Utopian Vision: The Rule of Clare."

39. Hardick, *Spiritualité de Sainte Claire*, pp. 34–35.

40. "Latebat namque Clara, sed eius vita patebat; silebat Clara, sed sua fama clamabat; celabatur in cella, et in urbibus noscebatur." *Legenda* 3, in *Escritos*, p. 118.

41. *Sacrum Commercium s. Francisci cum Domina Paupertate* (Quaracchi: Collegium S. Bonaventurae, 1929), 4, 1; *Vita prima* 84, 6; *Vita secunda* 216, 3.

42. Testamentum 5, p. 185; 36, p. 188; *Legenda maior* XI, 2; XIII, 2; XIV, 4; *Le Speculum Perfectionis*, vol. 1: chap. 14, 1, p. 39; chap. 73, 1, p. 217; chap. 88, 6 (twice), p. 262; chap. 88, 9, p. 262. Imitation not only of Christ, but also of Francis and others were expanding notions in Franciscan literature.

43. Antiphona "Sanctae Maria Virgo" 2, p. 146 ("sponsa Spiritus Sancti"); Forma vivendi 1, p. 75 ("Quia divina inspiratione fecistis vos filias et ancillas altissimi summi Regis Patris caelestis et Spiritui Sancto vos desponsastis"). See Chiara

Augusta Lainati, in *Fonti francescane*, ed. Feliciano Olgiati (Assisi: Movimento Francescano, 1977), p. 2221; Optato van Asseldonk, *Una Spiritualità per domani: Maria, Francesco e Chiara* (Rome: Collegio s. Lorenzo da Brindis, 1989), pp. 32–34, 419–32; Oktavian Schmucki, "St. Francis's Devotion Toward the Blessed Virgin Mary," *Greyfriars Review* 5 (1991): 224–26.

44. "Processo di Canonizzazione" v.2; VII.11; XI.5.

45. "Benedecta allora Abbadessa, con le altre Monache del predicto monasterio de Sancto Damiano, dissero de una voluntà . . . che tucto quello che se trovava de sanctità in alcuna sancta che sia de po la Vergine Maria, se pò veramente dire et testificare de la sancta memoria de madonna Chiara." "Processo di Canonizzazione" XV.1[b]; trans. *Early Documents*, pp. 179–80.

46. To offer but one example: examination of the testimony of sisters other than the three noted above suggests that they too were asked, in more or less similar terms, if any human explanation was possible to account for Clare's virtue and holiness or if her goodness could be fully described; see, for example, III.2; VI.5; VIII.1; IX.1; X.2; XII.7; XIV.4; see also XIII.3. In keeping with canonization procedures of the time, the papacy had compiled a list of questions (*interrogatoria*) to be posed to the witnesses; see *Escritos*, p. 67, 5. This list did not survive and those interrogating the witnesses may have added questions of their own. On the format of canonization inquests and questions posed, see André Vauchez, *La Sainteté en Occident aux derniers siècles du moyen âge d'après les procès de canonisation et les documents hagiographiques*, Bibliothèque des Etudes Françaises d'Athènes et de Rome 241 (Rome: Ecole Française de Rome, 1988), pp. 50–60 and fig. 5. For a more detailed discussion of the implications of male clerical questioning, see Dyan Elliott's essay in this volume, chap. 9.

47. Lainati, *Fonti francescane*, p. 2393 n. 4, states that the sisters in the Process of Canonization spoke of Clare as a "perfect copy of the Mother of the Lord," but Lainati here misinterprets the Process in light of later documents; see below.

48. The terminology "following Christ" (*Christi sequela*) is applied to Clare once: *Legenda* 14, in *Escritos*, p. 149. Elsewhere, for example, she is depicted multiplying bread: 15, p. 150; or being joined to Christ by sharing his experiences: 31, pp. 166–67.

49. "Sequantur ergo viri viros Verbi incarnati novos discipulos; imitentur feminae Claram, Dei matris vestigium, novam capitaneam mulierum." *Legenda*, "Proemialis epistola," in *Escritos*, p. 134.

50. ". . . incessu proprio signat vestigia secuturis." *Legenda* 10, in *Escritos*, p. 143; see also 11, p. 145.

51. "[Ego] exhortans [dilectas filias] et inducans, ut beatissimae matris vestrae . . . virtutum vestigia sollicite comitantes," in *Escritos*, pp. 367–68, and see 366.

52. *Legenda* 8, in *Escritos*, p. 141.

53. ". . . ipsius Christi eiusque sanctissimae Matris sequentes vestigia." Prooemium 2, in *Escritos*, p. 267.

54. ". . . Matris Christi vestigium." "Concinat plebs fidelium," 1, in Sister Mary Immaculata Cashal, *Hymns in Honor of Saint Clare of Assisi: An Exhaustive Analysis of Their Contents and Structure* (Mohegan Lake, N.Y.: Ladycliff Academy, 1964), p. 292 (I thank Sister Mary Francis Hone, O.S.C. for this reference). On

thirteenth- through fifteenth-century hymns relating Clare to Mary see Cashal, "Hymns," pp. 136–37, 180, 200–210.

55. ". . . eius adhaesisti vestigiis, cuius meruisti connubio copulari." II Epistola 7, p. 203.

56. ". . . te novi et arbitror vestigiorum pauperis et humilis Iesu Christi tam in me quam in aliis ceteris sororibus imitationibus mirifice supplere defectum." III Epistola 4, p. 207.

57. "Et beatissimus pater noster Franciscus, eius vestigia imitatus, sanctam paupertatem suam, quam elegit per se et per suos fratres, exemplo suo et doctrina dum vixit ab ipsa nullatenus declinavit." Testamentum 36, p. 188.

58. The authenticity of the first of these, attributed to Pope Innocent III (1216), is still debated; see the authors cited in n. 27 above. The Privilege of Poverty attributed to Gregory IX (1228) is generally accepted as authentic.

59. ". . . nullas omnino possessiones habere proponitis, illius vestigiis per omnia inhaerentes, qui pro nobis factus est pauper, via, veritas, atque vita." "Privilegium paupertatis," in *Escritos*, p. 232.

60. *Early Documents*, 1988 ed., p. 13; and see 1993 ed., p. 13, for the virtually identical passage. Elcid, *Clara de Asís*, p. 200, calls Clare "another Mary" (*otra María*) in counterpoint to Francis, the *alter Christus*.

61. Regis J. Armstrong and Ignatius C. Brady, trans., *Francis and Clare: The Complete Works* (New York: Paulist Press, 1982), Letter 3, 24–25, p. 201. For the Latin, see n. 94.

62. *Early Documents*, 1988 ed., Letter 3, 24–25, p. 45; and also 1993 ed., p. 46.

63. 1 Peter 2: 21: "It was for this you were called, since Christ suffered for you in just this way and left you an example, to have you follow in his footsteps." Armstrong again employs this translation in a discussion of the image of Mary in Clare's letters, "Starting Points: Images of Women in the Letters of Clare," *Collectanea Franciscana* 62 (1992): 85–93, esp. 90; see also 99.

64. Ignatius Brady, *The Legend and Writings of Saint Clare of Assisi* (St. Bonaventure, N.Y.: Franciscan Institute, 1953), p. 94; Jan Kapistran Vyskocil, *The Legend of Blessed Agnes of Bohemia and the Four Letters of St. Clare*, trans. Vitus Buresh (Cleveland: Bell and Howell, 1963), p. 198. Translations into the romance languages are able to preserve the apparent ambiguity of the Latin: *Escritos*, ed. Omaechevarría, p. 391; *Ecrits*, ed. Becker, Godet, and Matura, p. 107; *Le Lettere di Santa Chiara d'Assisi* (Marigliano [Naples]: Scuola tipografica "Istituto Anselmi," 1975), p. 20.

65. Ranft, "An Overturned Victory," p. 130, also noted that Clare's association with *imitatio Mariae* originated in male-authored texts and differed from Clare's own insistence on *imitatio Christi*.

66. Regula non bullata 1, 2, p. 19 (associated with poverty); 22, 2, p. 40; Epistola omnibus fidelibus 2, 10, p. 80; Epistola capitulo generali 63, p. 97; Epistola ad fratrem Leonem 3, p. 109 (associated with poverty).

67. III Epistola 4, p. 207. See n. 56.

68. III Epistola 7, pp. 207–8, emphasis mine.

69. III Epistola 8, p. 208.

70. ". . . transforma te ipsam totam per contemplationem in imagine divinitatis ipsius. . . ." III Epistola 13, p. 208.

71. See, for Francis, *Verba admonitionis* 6, 2, p. 8; *Regula non bullata* 1, 3–4, pp. 19–20; 9, 1, p. 28; *Ultima voluntas* 1, p. 77 (as given in the 1253 Form of Life 6, 7, p. 175; this passage refers also to Mary, see below).

72. "Vide contemptibilem pro te factum et sequere, facta pro ipso contemptibilis in hoc mundo." II *Epistola* 19, p. 204.

73. ". . . et cum reliquis sanctissimis virginibus ante thronum Dei et Agni novum cantare canticum et quocumque ierit Agnum sequi," IV *Epistola* 3, p. 213. In *Epistola ad Ermentrudem* 9, p. 217, the letter of doubtful authenticity, Clare writes, "take up the cross and follow Christ who goes before us" (*tolle crucem et sequere Christum qui nos praecedit*); note also 12, p. 217, where Clare writes that Ermentrude should meditate on the mysteries of the cross and the agonies of Christ's mother.

74. See the critical apparatus for *Verba admonitionis* 6, 4, p. 8.

75. *Opuscula sancti Francisci; Scripta sanctae Clarae: Concordance, Index, Listes de fréquence, Tables comparatives*, ed. Jean-François Godet and Georges Mailleux (Louvain: CETEDOC, 1976), p. ix.

76. II *Epistola* 4, p. 203.

77. II *Epistola* 15, p. 204.

78. II *Epistola* 17, p. 204.

79. II *Epistola* 20, p. 205.

80. III *Epistola* 4, p. 207.

81. *Testamentum* 5, p. 185.

82. *Testamentum* 36, p. 188.

83. *Testamentum* 56–57, p. 191.

84. II *Epistola* 7, p. 203; III *Epistola* 4, p. 207; *Testamentum* 36, p. 188; 56, p. 191.

85. II *Epistola* 7, p. 203; III *Epistola* 4, p. 207; *Testamentum* 56, p. 191.

86. *Testamentum* 56, p. 191.

87. II *Epistola* 7, p. 203.

88. II *Epistola* 20, pp. 204–5.

89. "Et amore sanctissimi et dilectissimi pueri pauperculis panniculis involuti, in praesepio reclinati, et sanctissimae matris eius moneo, deprecor et exhortor sorores meas, ut vestimentis semper vilibus induantur." *Regula S. Clarae* 2, 25, p. 170.

90. "Sorores nihil sibi approprient, nec domum nec locum, nec aliquam rem; et tamquam peregrinae et advenae in hoc saeculo, in paupertate et humilitate Domino famulantes, mittant pro eleemosyna confidenter; nec oportet eas verecundari, quia Dominus pro nobis se fecit pauperem in hoc mundo." *Regula S. Clarae* 8, 1–3, p. 176.

91. "Et ut nusquam declinaremus a sanctissima paupertate quam cepimus, nec etiam quae post nos venturae essent, paulo ante obitum suum iterum scripsit nobis ultimam voluntatem suam dicens: Ego frater Franciscus parvulus volo sequi vitam et paupertatem altissimi Domini nostri Iesu Christi et eius sanctissimae matris, et perseverare in ea usque in finem. Et rogo vos, dominas meas, et consilium do vobis, ut in ista sanctissima vita et paupertate semper vivatis." *Regula S. Clarae* 6, 6–8, pp. 174–75.

92. "Quapropter flexis genibus et utroque homine inclinato, sanctae matri Ecclesiae Romanae, summo Pontifici et praecipue domino cardinali, qui religioni fratrum minorum et nobis fuerit deputatus, recommendo omnes sorores meas, quae sunt et quae venturae sunt, ut amore illius Dei, qui pauper positus est in praesepio, pauper vixit in saeculo et nudus remansit in patibulo, semper gregi suo pusillo, quem Dominus Pater genuit in Ecclesia sua sancta verbo et exemplo beatissimi patris nostri Francisci, insequendo paupertatem et humilitatem dilecti Filii sui et gloriosae virginis Matris suae, sanctam paupertatem, quam Domino et beatissimo patri nostro Francisco promisimus, faciat observari, et in ipsa dignetur favere ipsas semper et conservare." Testamentum 44–47, pp. 189–90.

93. It should be noted that the language in the Form of Life echoes language from Francis's own Regula bullata 12, 5, p. 62, but modifies it by the addition of Mary's name.

94. ". . . illum dico Altissimi Filium, quem Virgo peperit, et post cuius partum virgo permansit. Ipsius dulcissimae matri adhaereas, quae talem genuit Filium, quem caeli capere non poterant, et tamen ipsa parvulo claustro sacri uteri contulit et gremio puellari gestavit.

Quis non abhorreat humani hostis insidias, qui per fastum momentaneorum et fallacium gloriarum ad nihilum redigere cogit quod maius est caelo? Ecce iam liquet per Dei gratiam dignissimam creaturarum fidelis hominis animam maiorem esse quam caelum, cum caeli cum creaturis ceteris capere nequeant Creatorem, et sola fidelis anima ipsius mansio sit et sedes, et hoc solum per caritatem qua carent impii: Veritate dicente: Qui diligit me diligetur a Patre meo, et ego diligam eum, et ad eum veniemus et mansionem apud eum faciemus.

Sicut ergo Virgo virginum gloriosa materialiter, sic et tu, sequens eius vestigia, humilitatis praesertim et paupertatis, casto et virgineo corpore spiritualiter semper sine dubietate omni portare potes, illum continens, a quo et tu (et) omnia continentur." III Epistola 17–26, pp. 208–9.

95. The remarks of Godet, "Claire et la vie au féminin," pp. 171–72, 172 n. 96, suggest that he too interprets the passage's meaning in this sense.

96. Mother: I Epistola 24, p. 200; III Epistola 18, p. 208; Regula S. Clarae 2, 25, p. 170; 6, 7, p. 175; 8, 6, p. 176; 12, 13, p. 181; Testamentum 46, p. 190; 75, 77, p. 193; see also Epistola ad Ermentrudem 12, p. 217. God-birther: III Epistola 17, p. 208 (*Filium, quem Virgo peperit*); III Epistola 18, p. 208 (*quae talem genuit Filium*); Benedictio 7, p. 196 (*genitrix*). Christ-carrier: III Epistola 24, p. 209 (*Sicut ergo Virgo virginum gloriosa materialiter . . . portare*).

97. I Epistola 24, p. 200; III Epistola 17 (twice), p. 208; 24, p. 209; Testamentum 46, p. 190; 75, 77, p. 193.

98. Testamentum 77, p. 193; Benedictio 7, p. 196.

99. I Epistola 24, p. 200; III Epistola 17, p. 208; 18, p. 208; 24, p. 209; see also Epistola ad Ermentrudem 11–12, p. 217; Regula S. Clarae 2, 25, p. 170; 6, 7, p. 175; 8, 6, p. 176; 12, 13, p. 181; Benedictio 7, p. 196.

100. Regula S. Clarae 3, 14, p. 171.

101. Testamentum 46, p. 190; 75, 77, p. 193.

102. Mother: Regula non bullata 23, 12, p. 46; Epistola omnibus fidelibus 2, 3, p. 80; Salutatio beatae Virginis 6, p. 127; Antiphona "Sanctae Maria Virgo" 2,

p. 146; Ultima voluntas 1, p. 77 (as given in the 1253 Regula S. Clarae 6, 7, p. 175). God-birther: Regula non bullata 5, p. 45 (*verum Deum et verum hominem ex gloriosa semper Virgine beatissima sancta Maria nasci fecisti*); 23, 5, p. 45; Salutatio beatae Virginis 1, p. 127 (*genetrix*); Psalmus ad Vesperam in Nativitate Domini (V sch.) 3, p. 161 (*natus fuit de beata Virgine*). Christ-carrier: Verba admonitionis 1, 14, p. 4; Epistola omnibus fidelibus 2, 1–2, pp. 79–80; Epistola capitulo generali 26, p. 93; and see Epistola omnibus fidelibus 10, 6 and 9, pp. 84–85. For Francis's understanding of mother as one who carries and gives birth, see also Psalmus ad Matutinum (I sch.) 4–5, p. 147; Psalmus ad Nonum (III sch.) 5, p. 158.

103. Salutatio beatae Virginis 4–5, p. 127; see also Epistola capitulo generali 26, p. 93; Verba admonitionis 1, 16, p. 4; Epistola omnibus fidelibus 2, 1, p. 79.

104. *Vita secunda* 198; *Legenda maior* IX, 3.

105. Verba admonitionis 1, 16, p. 4; Regula non bullata 9, 6, p. 29; 23, 5, p. 45; 23, 12, p. 46; Epistola omnibus fidelibus 2, 1, p. 79; 2, 3, p. 80; Epistola capitulo generali 26, p. 93; 48, p. 96; Salutatio beatae Virginis 2, p. 127; Pater noster (Laudes ad omnes horas) 16, p. 142; Antiphona "Sancta Maria" 1, p. 146; Psalmus ad Vesperam in Nativitate Domini (V sch.) 3, p. 161.

106. Francis applies a variety of other descriptions, but they are scattered and mostly single instances: she is intercessor, queen, handmaid, spouse, daughter, and beggar; see Pater noster (Laudes ad omnes horas) 16, p. 142; Antiphona "Sancta Maria" 2–3, p. 146; Salutatio beatae Virginis 1, p. 127; 6, p. 127; Regula non bullata 9, 6, p. 29.

107. "Matres eius sumus quando portamus in corde et corpore nostro per amorem et puram et sinceram conscientiam et parturimus eum per sanctam operationem, quae lucere debet aliis in exemplum." Epistola omnibus fidelibus 10, 9, pp. 84–85; and see 10, 5–8, p. 84.

108. See nn. 49 and 54 above.

109. Hilda Graef, *Mary: A History of Doctrine and Devotion*, 2 pts. (Westminster: Christian Classics; London: Sheed and Ward, 1963, 1965), pt. 1, pp. 49, 100, 160, and on the general evolution of Marian theology in the eastern and western churches, pp. 48–161.

110. Ambrose, *Concerning Virgins*, in *Nicene and Post-Nicene Fathers of the Christian Church*, 2d ser., vol. 10, *Saint Ambrose: Letters and Select Works* (Grand Rapids, Mich.: Eerdmans, 1983), pp. 361–87; Jerome, "Liber adversus Helvidium de perpetua virginitate B. Mariae," *PL* 23: 183–206; *Paschasii Radberti: De partu virginis*, ed. E. Ann Matter, *CCCM* 56C (Turnhout: Brepols, 1985).

111. On Marian devotion in this period, see Elizabeth A. Johnson, "Marian Devotion in the Western Church," in *Christian Spirituality: High Middle Ages and Reformation*, ed. Jill Raitt (New York: Crossroad, 1987), pp. 392–414. On new uses of the Song of Songs to re-create the history of Mary's human life, see Rachel Fulton, "Mimetic Devotion, Marian Exegesis, and the Historical Sense of the Song of Songs," *Viator* 27 (1996): 85–116. On iconography, see Penny Schine Gold, *The Lady and the Virgin: Image, Attitude, and Experience in Twelfth-Century France* (Chicago: University of Chicago Press, 1985), pp. 43–75.

112. Jaroslav Pelikan, *The Growth of Medieval Theology (600–1300)*, vol. 3 of *The Christian Tradition: A History of the Development of Doctrine* (Chicago: University

of Chicago Press, 1978), p. 167; Graef, *Mary*, pt. 1, pp. 206–7, and on earlier theological speculations regarding the parallel, passim.

113. Fulton, "Mimetic Devotion," p. 106.

114. Pelikan, *Growth of Medieval Theology*, pp. 72, 171–73; Graef, *Mary*, passim.

115. "Ipsa est via, per quam Salvator advenit. . . . studeamus . . . ad ipsum, per eam ascendere, qui per ipsam ad nos descendit." Bernard of Clairvaux, "In adventu Domini: Sermo secundus," 5, in *Obras completas de San Bernardo*, ed. Cistercian Monks of Spain, 8 vols. (Madrid: Biblioteca de autores cristianos, 1983–93), 3:76; Pelikan, *Growth of Medieval Theology*, p. 165. On Mary as *mediatrix*, see Jaroslav Pelikan, *Mary Through the Centuries: Her Place in the History of Culture* (New Haven, Conn.: Yale University Press, 1996), pp. 125–36.

116. "De aquaeductu," in *Obras completas*, 4:418–38; for these points, pars. 3, 7; Johnson, "Marian Devotion," p. 401.

117. "Dominica infra octavam Assumptionis," 1–2, in *Obras completas*, 4:394–96; "De aqueductu," 7, in ibid., 4:424–26; Johnson, "Marian Devotion," pp. 401–2.

118. Catherine M. Mooney, "Women's Visions, Men's Words: The Portrayal of Holy Women and Men in Fourteenth-Century Italian Hagiography" (Ph.D. diss., Yale University, 1991).

119. "La Plus ancienne légende de la b. Marguerite de Città di Castello," ed. M.-Hyacinthe Laurent, *AFP* 10 (1940): chaps. 25–26, pp. 127–28 (both chapters are inadvertently designated as chap. 26); "Vita beatae Margaritae virginis de Civitate Castelli," ed. A. Poncelet, *AB* 19 (1900): chap. 8, pp. 27–28; Berengar of Sant'Africano, *Storia de S. Chiara da Montefalco secondo un antico documento dell'anno 1308*, ed. P. T. De Töth (Siena: Tipografia Pontificia S. Bernardino, 1908), pp. 97–103.

120. On women's and men's diverse perspectives on Mary, see also Bynum, *Holy Feast and Holy Fast*, pp. 261–69.

121. Bynum, *Holy Feast and Holy Fast*, p. 263; see also her study, "'. . . And Woman His Humanity': Female Imagery in the Religious Writing of the Later Middle Ages," in *Fragmentation and Redemption: Essays on Gender and the Human Body in Medieval Religion* (New York: Zone Books, 1991), pp. 151–79.

122. Bynum, *Holy Feast and Holy Fast*, p. 269.

123. "Similemente, la Madre di Cristo promise di rinnovare la sua purità verginale e la sua umiltà in una femmina, cioè in suora Chiara, per tale modo che per lo suo esempio ella trarrebbe molte migliaia di femmine delle nostre mani." *Le Considerazioni sulle Stimmate* 5, in *I Fioretti di San Francesco*, ed. Guido Davico Bonino (Turin: Einaudi, 1968). For a similar example of the Christ/Francis and Mary/Clare parallels in the late fifteenth century, see Lázaro Iriarte, "Clara de Asís en la tipología hagiográfica," *Laurentianum* 29 (1988): 459.

124. Male monks' and mendicants' reluctance to serve the spiritual needs of women is well documented: see John B. Freed, "Urban Development and the 'Cura Monialium' in Thirteenth-Century Germany," *Viator* 3 (1972): 311–27; Herbert Grundmann, *Religiöse Bewegungen im Mittelalter: Untersuchungen über die geschichtlichen Zusammenhänge zwischen der Ketzerei, den Bettelorden und der religiösen Frauenbewegung im 12. und 13. Jahrhundert und über die geschichtlichen Grundlagen der*

deutschen Mystik (1935; rpt. with additions, Hildesheim: Georg Olms, 1961; Eng. trans., 1995), passim. Less frequently cited are cases of collaboration: Penny Schine Gold, "Male/Female Cooperation: The Example of Fontevrault," in *Medieval Religious Women*, vol. 1, *Distant Echoes*, ed. John A. Nichols and Lillian Thomas Shank (Kalamazoo, Mich.: Cistercian Publications, 1984), pp. 151–68; Constance H. Berman, "Men's Houses, Women's Houses: The Relationship Between the Sexes in Twelfth-Century Monasticism," in *The Medieval Monastery*, ed. Andrew MacLeish (St. Cloud, Minn.: North Star Press, 1988), pp. 43–52.

125. See n. 23.

126. *Vita prima*, Prologus 1.

127. *Vita secunda*, in *AF* 10, pp. 127–268; *Chronica XXIV Generalium Ordinis Minorum*, in *AF* 3 (Quaracchi: Collegium S. Bonaventurae, 1897), p. 262.

128. "Hic est locus ille beatus et sanctus, in quo gloriosa religio et excellentissimus ordo pauperum Dominarum et sanctarum virginum . . . exordium sumpsit"; "Clara . . . lapis pretiosissimus atque fortissimus"; "pretiosissimarum margaritarum nobilis structura"; *Vita prima* 18–20.

129. *Vita prima* 116–17.

130. *Legenda* 37, in *Escritos*, pp. 171–72; Iriarte, "Clara en la tipología hagiográfica," pp. 444, 437.

131. ". . . licet pater illis paulatim suam praesentiam corporalem subduxerit, affectum tamen in Spiritu Sancto ad ipsarum curam extendit. . . . promisit eis et aliis paupertatem in simili conversatione profitentibus firmiter suum et fratrum suorum auxilium et consilium perpetuo exhibere. Haec semper, dum vixit, diligenter exsolvit, et fieri semper, cum morti proximus esset, non negligenter mandavit: unum atque eumdem spiritum, dicens, fratres et dominas illas paupperculas de hoc saeculo eduxisse.

Mirantibus quandoque fratribus, quod tam sanctas Christi famulas sua praesentia corporali non saepius visitaret, dicebat: 'Non credatis, carissimi, quod eas perfecte non diligam. Si enim crimen esset eas in Christo fovere, nonne maius fuisset eas Christo iunxisse? Et quidem non eas vocasse nulla fuisset iniuria, non curare vocatas summa est inclementia. Sed exemplum do vobis, ut quemadmodum ego facio ita et vos faciatis. Nolo quod aliquis ad visitandum eas spontaneum se offerat, sed invitos et plurimum renitentes iubeo ipsarum servitiis deputari'." *Vita secunda* 204–5; trans. Placid Hermann, in *St. Francis of Assisi, Writings and Early Biographies: English Omnibus of the Sources for the Life of St. Francis*, ed. Marion A. Habig, 4th rev. ed. (Chicago: Franciscan Herald Press, 1983), p. 526.

132. *Vita secunda* 206.

133. "Opere docuit illas se cinerem reputare, nihilque cordi eius aliud approximare de ipsis, nisi hac reputatione condignum. Haec erat conversatio eius cum feminis sanctis; haec visitatio illarum perutilis, coacta tamen et rara. Haec voluntas eius pro fratribus omnibus, quos eis ita pro Christo, cui serviunt, servire volebat, ut semper, velut animalia pennata, laqueos coram positos praecaverent." *Vita secunda* 207; trans. Hermann, in *Omnibus*, p. 528.

134. "Mellita toxica, familiaritates videlicet mulierum, quae in errorem inducunt etiam viros sanctos. . . . Harum contagionem evadere conversantem cum eis . . . tam facile dixit quam, iuxta Scripturam, in igne ambulare nec comburere plan-

tas. . . . Siquidem femina usque adeo molesta erat, ut non cautelam vel exemplum crederes, sed formidinem vel horrorem." *Vita secunda* 112; and see 113, 114; trans. Hermann, in *Omnibus*, pp. 454–55. On Francis's attitude toward Clare and Celano's *vitae*, see Jacques Dalarun, "Donne e Donna, femminile e femminizzazione negli scritti e le leggende di Francesco d'Assisi," in *Chiara di Assisi* (Spoleto: Centro Italiano di Studi sull'Alto Medioevo, 1993), pp. 237–67.

135. Vauchez, *La Sainteté*, p. 135, identifies the friar as Franciscan; Iriarte, "Clara en la tipología hagiográfica," p. 447, as Dominican.

136. Bartoli, *Clare of Assisi*, p. 199, notes her absence in Franciscan sources, although he incorrectly states that Bonaventure's biography failed to mention Clare (see *Legenda maior* IV, 6; XII, 2; XIII, 8; XV, 5) and that the laity of Assisi were inattentive to her cult; see Giovanna Casagrande, "Presenza di Chiara in Umbria nei Secoli XIII–XIV," *Collectanea Franciscana* 62 (1992): 481–505. On the friars' struggle during this period to be released from their responsibilities toward the Poor Ladies, see John Moorman, *A History of the Franciscan Order from Its Origins to the Year 1517* (Oxford: Clarendon Press, 1968), pp. 213–15.

137. Jeryldene M. Wood, *Women, Art, and Spirituality: The Poor Clares of Early Modern Italy* (Cambridge: Cambridge University Press, 1996), figs. 3, 9; and see eadem, "Perceptions of Holiness in Thirteenth-Century Italian Painting: Clare of Assisi," *Art History* 14 (1991): 301–28.

138. Wood, *Women, Art, and Spirituality*, p. 31.

139. William Cook, "The Early Images of St. Clare of Assisi," in *A Medieval and Modern Woman*, ed. Peterson, p. 20.

140. Wood, *Women, Art, and Spirituality*, figs. 12–16.

141. Cook, "Early Images of St. Clare," pp. 24, 26–27.

142. Cook, "Early Images of St. Clare," pp. 24, 26.

143. Wood, *Women, Art, and Spirituality*, pp. 31–32, fig. 17; Cook, "Early Images of St. Clare," pp. 16–17, 24–27. See Fabio Bisogni, "Per un census delle rappresentazioni di Santa Chiara nella pittura in Emilia, Romagna e Veneto sino alla fine del quattrocento," in *Movimento religioso femminile e francescanesimo nel secolo XIII* (Assisi: Società Internazionale di Studi Francescani, 1980) for some fourteenth-century images underlining Francis's likeness or proximity to Christ (figs. 4–5, 11, 14, 19, 26) and Clare's to Mary (fig. 14, and esp. figs. 19, 26; see commentary pp. 154–55, 157). Some other images from the region depict both saints with Mary or Christ.

144. Examples of studies addressing these issues include Caroline Walker Bynum, "'. . . And Woman His Humanity'"; Ute Stargardt, "Male Clerical Authority in the Spiritual (Auto)biographies of Medieval Holy Women," in *Women as Protagonists and Poets in the German Middle Ages*, ed. Albrecht Classen (Göppingen: Kummerle, 1991), pp. 209–38; John Coakley, "Friars, Sanctity, and Gender: Mendicant Encounters with Saints, 1250–1325," in *Medieval Masculinities: Regarding Men in the Middle Ages*, ed. Clare A. Lees (Minneapolis: University of Minnesota Press, 1994), pp. 91–110; Catherine M. Mooney, "The Authorial Role of Brother A. in the Composition of Angela of Foligno's Revelations," in *Creative Women in Medieval and Early Modern Italy: A Religious and Artistic Renaissance*, ed. E. Ann Matter and John Coakley (Philadelphia: University of Pennsylvania Press, 1994), pp. 34–63;

Anne L. Clark, "Repression or Collaboration? The Case of Elisabeth and Ekbert of Schönau," in *Christendom and Its Discontents: Exclusion, Persecution, and Rebellion, 1000–1500*, ed. Scott L. Waugh and Peter D. Diehl (Cambridge: Cambridge University Press, 1996), pp. 151–67.

145. Anonymous Augustinian canon, "De S. Bona Virgine," *AASS*, May, vol. 7 (Paris and Rome, 1866), May, pp. 142–60; Giovanni del Coppo, "De S. Fina Virgine," *AASS*, March, vol. 2 (Paris and Rome, 1865), pp. 232–38.

Chapter 5. Inside Out: Beatrice of Nazareth and Her Hagiographer

I would like to thank Ellen Armour, Dyan Elliott, John King, Cynthia Marshall, Catherine Mooney, Walter Simons, and Peter Travis for their helpful comments on this paper.

1. Talal Asad, *Genealogies of Religion: Discipline and Reasons of Power in Christianity and Islam* (Baltimore: Johns Hopkins University Press, 1993), p. 62.

2. Marcel Mauss, "Body Techniques," in *Sociology and Psychology: Essays*, trans. Ben Brewster (London: Routledge, 1979), pp. 97–135.

3. Pierre Bourdieu, *Outline of a Theory of Practice*, trans. Richard Nice (Cambridge: Cambridge University Press, 1977), p. 78.

4. As Louis Althusser argues, subjects are interpellated, called into being as subjects, by those who address them in the name of the law. As Judith Butler explains, "the call is formative, if not *per*formative, precisely because it initiates the individual into the subjected status of the subject." See Louis Althusser, "Ideology and the Ideological State Apparatuses," in *Lenin and Philosophy and Other Essays*, trans. Ben Brewster (New York: Monthly Review Press, 1971), pp. 170–86; and Judith Butler, *Bodies That Matter: On the Discursive Limits of "Sex"* (New York: Routledge, 1993), p. 121.

5. Asad, *Genealogies*, p. 77. Sarah Beckwith follows Althusser, Bourdieu, and Zizek in citing the famous lines from Pascal in which he claims that the habit of prayer gives rise to belief. See Blaise Pascal, *Pensées*, trans. A. J. Krailsheimer (Harmondsworth: Penguin, 1966), p. 152; Althusser, "Ideology," p. 158; Pierre Bourdieu, *The Logic of Practice*, trans. Richard Nice (Stanford, Calif.: Stanford University Press, 1990), p. 49; Slavoj Zizek, *The Sublime Object of Ideology* (New York: Routledge, 1989), pp. 38–40; and Sarah Beckwith, "Passionate Regulation: Enclosure, Ascesis, and the Feminist Imaginary," *South Atlantic Quarterly* 93 (1994): 811–12.

6. Beckwith, "Passionate Regulation," p. 819. Caroline Walker Bynum makes the same claim in different ways in "Introduction: The Complexity of Symbols," in *Gender and Religion: On the Complexity of Symbols*, ed. Bynum, Stevan Harrell, and Paula Richman (Boston: Beacon Press, 1986), pp. 1–20.

7. Yet while bringing together theories of bodily practice with psychoanalytic account, Beckwith does not theorize their relationship.

8. For another critique of some contemporary feminist work on mysticism and the body, see Amy Hollywood, "Beauvoir, Irigaray, and the Mystical," *Hypatia* 9 (1994): 158–85.

9. Beckwith, "Passionate Regulation," p. 818.

10. This claim does not require that we fall back on essentialized conceptions of sexual difference, but merely that we acknowledge the difference between those identified as women within the culture in which they lived and those identified as men. For more on the complexities of this issue, see Amy Hollywood, *The Soul as Virgin Wife: Mechthild of Magdeburg, Marguerite Porete, and Meister Eckhart* (Notre Dame, Ind.: University of Notre Dame Press, 1995), pp. 36–37.

11. I stress this approach to the material in the slightly different presentation given in Hollywood, *Virgin Wife*, pp. 27–30. There my concern is to show that women's relationship to embodiment is much more complex than modern associations of women with the body suggest. Hence my interest in Beckwith's parallel project. Here I hope to take the discussion a step further, demonstrating the tensions between medieval women's writings and twentieth-century materialist assumptions.

12. For this information and the text of the *vita* in Latin and English, see *The Life of Beatrice of Nazareth, 1200–1268*, trans. Roger De Ganck (Kalamazoo, Mich.: Cistercian Publications, 1991). For the treatise in Dutch, see L. Reypens and J. Van Mierlo, eds., *Seven Manieren van Minne* (Louvain: S. V. de Vlaamsche Boekenhalle, 1926).

13. On mystical hagiographies, see Simone Roisin, "L'Efflorescence cistercienne et le courant féminin de piété au XIIIe siècle," *Revue d'Histoire Ecclésiastique* 39 (1943): 342–78; Simone Roisin, *L'Hagiographie cistercienne dans le diocèse de Liège au XIIIe siècle* (Louvain: Bibliothèque de l'Université, 1947); Caroline Walker Bynum, *Holy Feast and Holy Fast: The Religious Significance of Food to Medieval Women* (Berkeley: University of California Press, 1987); and Caroline Walker Bynum, *Fragmentation and Redemption: Essays on Gender and the Human Body in Medieval Religion* (New York: Zone Books, 1991).

14. *Life of Beatrice*, pp. 340–41. Ursula Peters questions the attestation of "Seven Manners" to Beatrice of Nazareth, arguing that the differences between it and *Life*, bk. III, chap. 14 are too great for the latter to be a translation of the former. Yet the similarities in structure, metaphors, and images are exceptionally strong and clearly override their divergences. See Ursula Peters, *Religiöse Erfahrung als literarisches Faktum: Zur Vorgeschichte und Genese frauenmystischer Texte des 13. und 14. Jahrhunderts* (Tübingen: Niemeyer, 1988), pp. 32–33.

15. *Life of Beatrice*, pp. 338–39.

16. On the importance of these features to medieval Christian hagiographical literature, see Hippolyte Delehaye, *The Legends of the Saints*, trans. V. M. Crawford (Notre Dame, Ind.: University of Notre Dame Press, 1961); Thomas J. Heffernan, *Sacred Biography: Saints and Their Biographies in the Middle Ages* (Oxford: Oxford University Press, 1988); and Renate Blumenfeld-Kosinski and Timea Szell, eds., *Images of Sainthood in Medieval Europe* (Ithaca, N.Y.: Cornell University Press, 1991). On the mystical hagiographies of the thirteenth century, see Roisin, "L'Efflorescence"; and *L'Hagiographie cistercienne*. For the contested relationship between hagiography and historiography, see Felice Lifshitz, "Beyond Positivism and Genre: 'Hagiographical' Texts as Historical Narrative," *Viator* 25 (1994): 95–113.

17. "Mirentur forsan alij a sanctis antiqui temporis, in signis et virtutibus copiose satis superque patrata miracula; mirentur ab obsessis corporibus fugata demonia., et a morte resuscitata cadauera; necnon et alia quamplurima, vel hijs maiora vel horum similia:, de quibus loquitur in euangelio dominus dicens ita.: 'Qui credit in me opera que ergo facio et ipse faciet: et maiora horum faciet. Ego vero, pace sanctorum, beatricis caritatem multis miraculis et signis prefero; de quibus alibi dicitur.: 'signa data sunt non fidelibus sed infidelibus':, presertim cum absque signis ad regnum celorum multi perueniunt." *Life of Beatrice*, pp. 284–85.

18. The hagiographer's comments and his overall dilemma might also be understood within the context of changing attitudes toward supernaturalism and miracles. See Lifshitz, "Beyond Positivism," pp. 104–5; and Benedicta Ward, *Miracles and the Medieval Mind: Theory, Record, and Event, 1000–1215* (Philadelphia: University of Pennsylvania Press, 1982), pp. 1–24.

19. "Cum autem dicat in euangelio dominus 'Attendite ne iusticiam vestram faciatis coram hominibus vt videamini ab eis'., ⟨e⟩t rursus alibi 'Sic luceat lux vestra coram hominibus vt videant opera vestra bona [.] et glorificent patrem vestrum qui in celis est': huius vtriusque dominici precepti superficialem discordantiam sic in vnam obeditionis sentenciam concordauit, vt et hostis antiqui versutias, secretum suum intra se vigilanter occultando, deluderet., et rursus illud in palam opportuno tempore proferendo, proximorum necessitatibus erogaret." *Life of Beatrice*, pp. 4–7.

20. Compare *Life of Beatrice*, bk. 1, chap. 5, pp. 36–37 and *Vita Arnulfu*, in *AASS* (Antwerp, 1643; rpt. Brussels: Culture et Civilisation, 1965–70), June 30, vol. 24: 612–16. See *Life of Beatrice*, p. x (although the citation he gives there is incorrect).

21. On medieval women's asceticism, see Bynum, *Holy Feast*, pp. 82–87, 103–4, 237–44.

22. This might be understood as a function of the demand for humility, which would preclude the mystic describing her own ascetic heroics. Yet many thirteenth-century mystical writings, such as Beatrice's, take the form of treatises in which the experience of the soul is described in the third person. If ascetic activity beyond that demanded by monastic and other religious rules was seen as essential to the mystical life, it could certainly be described and prescribed within these kinds of texts. Women's writings after 1300 will begin to do so.

23. The exceptions are Angela of Foligno's *Book*, an early example of "auto-hagiography" and some hagiographies written by women. See Hollywood, *Virgin Wife*, pp. 36–38, 231 nn. 49–52.

24. ". . . quieuisset., magnoque conamine cor suum ad dominum eleuasset. . . . in excessu⟨m⟩ mentis sue continuo rapta prosilijt." *Life of Beatrice*, pp. 66–69.

25. "Crucem quippe ligneam, vnius palmi longitudinis, nodoso funiculo sibi stricte colligatam., die noctuque gestabat in pectore; cui tytulum dominice passionis., horrorem extremi iudicij., iudicisque seueritatem inscripserat:, et cetera que iugiter proponebat in memoria retinere. Aliud nichilominus dominice crucis signaculum, in pargameni cedula depictum, etiam gestabat in brachio colligatum:; tercium quoque coram se, cum scribendi vacabat officio, depictum habebat in assere:, quatenus ad quecumque loca se diuerteret., aut quidquid operis extrinsecus

actitaret:, omnis obliuionis effugata caligine, per dominice crucis signaculum, id, de cuius amissione timebat., impressum cordi suo in memoria firmiter retineret." *Life of Beatrice*, pp. 88–91.

26. ". . . ad pedes domini crucifixi, coram ipsius ymagine." *Life of Beatrice*, pp. 90–91.

27. "Exinde vero, per continuum ferme quinquennium, tam firmiter impressum habebat mentis intuitum in memoria dominice passionis., vt vix vmquam ab ⟨illius⟩ suaui meditatione recederet:; sed singulis que pro humana salute pati dignatus est, miro deuotionis affectu, iugique meditatione medullitus inhereret." *Life of Beatrice*, pp. 92–93.

28. The hagiographer does not explicitly compare Beatrice's suffering to that of Christ on the cross, yet the increasing emphasis on her suffering, bloody, and wrenched body suggests the identification. See, for example, *Life of Beatrice*, bk. III, chaps. 1, 2, 3, 4, 14.

29. "Unde frequenter accidit:, vt, vellet nollet, is quem tolerabat interius mentis iubilus, per aliqua demonstrationis indicia foris erumperet, et vel risu vel tripudio, gestu vel alio quovis indicio se prodendo, quid iubilantis mens pateretur interius, extrinsecus indicaret." *Life of Beatrice*, pp. 94–97.

30. See *Life of Beatrice*, bk. I, chaps. 11, 13–18; bk. II, chap. 16; bk. III, chaps. 2, 4–5, 14.

31. See *Life of Beatrice*, bk. I, chap. 18; bk. III, chap. 5.

32. *Life of Beatrice*, bk. III, chap. 8.

33. See *Life of Beatrice*, bk. I, chap. 11; bk. II, chap. 18; bk. III, chap. 1, 18.

34. "In qua liquefactione quid, quantumve spiritualis iocunditatis acceperit., quid senserit., quid gustauerit, et-si verbis explicari non valeat:, ex corporalium tamen defectione sensuum extrinsecus aliquantulum apparebat." *Life of Beatrice*, pp. 238–39.

35. Beckwith argues for the importance of metaphors of enclosure in the *Ancrene Wisse*. Here the desire to maintain the body's boundaries parallels the desire to maintain the boundaries of the cloister. Beckwith, "Passionate Regulation," pp. 808–12.

36. *Life of Beatrice*, bk. II, chaps. 7–9.

37. This imagery coincides with a cultural tendency to desire an "enclosed" body, one that does not menstruate or release other problematic fluids. Yet the presence of "good" emissions—like Beatrice's tears and blood—problematizes any use of Mikhail Bakhtin's distinction between the classical and the grotesque bodies. See Mikhail Bakhtin, *Rabelais and His World*, trans. Hélène Iswolsky (Bloomington: Indiana University Press, 1984). On good and bad emissions, see Claude Carozzi, "Douceline et les autres," in *La Religion populaire en Languedoc du XIIIe siècle à la moitié du XIVe siècle* (Toulouse: Privat, 1976), pp. 251–67.

38. *Life of Beatrice*, bk. II, chap. 16.

39. "Seuen manieren sijn van minnen, die comen vten hoegsten ende ⟨keren⟩ weder ten ouersten." *Seven Manieren*, p. 3; and "There Are Seven Manners of Loving," trans. Eric Colledge, in *Medieval Women's Visionary Literature*, ed. Elizabeth Alvilda Petroff (Oxford: Oxford University Press, 1986), p. 200.

40. "Sunt igitur hij dilectionis gradus siue status septem numero;, per quos ad dilectum suum, non equalibus quidem passibus., sed nunc vt pedibus incedendo., nunc cursu velocissimo properando., nonnumquam etiam, sumptis agilitatis pennis, pernicius euolando, peruenire promeruit." *Life of Beatrice*, pp. 288–89.

41. There is an implicit hierarchy among the manners, and Beatrice uses the metaphor of ascent, but the dialectic of presence and absence running through and between the seven manners disrupts any easily identified pattern. There is a parallel here with Marguerite Porete's seven states of the soul, which operate in a similarly dialectical manner. See Hollywood, *Virgin Wife*, pp. 87–119; and Michael Sells, *Mystical Languages of Unsaying* (Chicago: University of Chicago Press, 1994), pp. 116–45.

42. As Else Marie Wiberg Pedersen points out, these are the only two instances in which Beatrice uses female imagery to describe the soul. Else Marie Wiberg Pedersen, "Image of God—Image of Mary—Image of Woman: The Theology and Spirituality of Beatrice of Nazareth," paper presented at the 28th International Congress on Medieval Studies, Kalamazoo, Michigan, May 1993.

43. There is a similar theological movement in Mechthild of Magdeburg. See Hollywood, *Virgin Wife*, pp. 57–86.

44. ". . . te vercrigene ende te wesene in die puerheit ende in die vriheit ende in die edelheit daer si in ghemaket es van haren sceppere na sijn beelde ende na sijn ghelikenesse." *Seven Manieren*, p. 4; "Seven Manners," p. 201.

45. ". . . pro hac de qua mentionem fecimus libertate spiritus obtinenda." *Life of Beatrice*, pp. 290–93.

46. ". . . corporales etiam languores solebat incurrere.; quibus aliquotiens adeo grauabatur in corpore, quod mortem sibi ⟨crederet⟩ imminere." *Life of Beatrice*, pp. 292–93.

47. *Life of Beatrice*, pp. 294–97.

48. *Life of Beatrice*, pp. 298–99.

49. "Alse aldus har seluen gevuelt in die oueruloedicheit van waelheit ende in die grote volheit van herten, soe wert hare geest altemale in minnen versinkende ende hore lichame hare ontsinkende hare herte versmeltende, ende al hare macht verderuende. Ende ⟨so⟩ seere wert si verwonnen met minnen, datsi cumelike hare seluen can gedragen ende datsi dicwile ongeweldich wert haerre lede ende al hare sinne.

Ende also gelijc also .i. vat dat vol es, alsment ruret, haesteleke oueruloyt ende vut-welt also wert hi haestelec sere gerenen, ende al verwonnen // van der groter uolheit hars herten, so datsi dicwile hars ondanx vut moet breken." *Seven Manieren*, pp. 15–16; "Seven Manners," p. 202 (translation modified).

50. "Fuit etiam in hoc statu tam delicatus sancte mulieris affectus:, vt, liquefacto corde, frequentissime lacrimarum imbre madesceret., et, pre nimia spiritualis copia delectationis, interdum, virium deficiente presidio, languens et egrotans in lectulo decubaret.

. . . frequenter accidit vt, ad vasis similitudinem quod, cum plenum liquoris fuerit., impulsum vel modice, mox quod continet eiciendo refundit;, et ipsa, per plurima sancti amoris indicia, quod sentiebat intrinsecus, velut impulsa, refunderet:; aut certe paraliticum quodammodo tremorem incurreret., aut alia queque languoris incommoda sustineret." *Life of Beatrice*, pp. 304–7. The hagiographer here also follows a familiar topos of the genre, tears as a mark of compunction and mystical fervor. See, for example, Jacques de Vitry, *Vita Mariae Oignacensis*, in *AASS* (Antwerp, 1643; rpt. Brussels: Culture et Civilisation, 1965–70); June 4, vol. 23, par. 18.

51. "Ondertusschen so wert minne so onghemate ende so ouerbrekende in der sielen also har seluen so starkeleke ende so verwoedelike ⟨berurt⟩ int herte, dat hare dunct, dat har herte menichfoudeleke wert seere gewont ende dat die wonden dagelix veruerschet werden ende verseert, in smerteliker weelicheiden ende in nuer iegenwordicheiden. Ende so dunct hare. dat har adren ontpluken ende hare bloet verwalt ende hare march verswijnt ende hare been vercrencken, ende ⟨hare⟩ borst verbernt ende hare kele verdroget, so // dat hare anscijn ende al har ede gevuelen der hitten van binnen ende des orwoeds van minnen." *Seven Manieren*, pp. 19–20; "Seven Manners," p. 203 (translation modified). My thanks to Walter Simons for help with this difficult passage and other suggestions for reading the Dutch text.

52. This movement can be traced in texts involving the stigmata. While in the early texts describing this phenomenon the visibility of the markings was unimportant, in later ones it takes precedence. On this phenomenon, see Herbert Thurston, *The Physical Phenomenon of Mysticism* (Chicago: Regnery, 1952); and Antoine Imbert-Gourbeyre, *La Stigmatisation: L'Extase divine et les miracles de Lourdes: Réponse aux libres-penseurs*, 2 vols. (Clermont-Ferrand: Librairie Catholique, 1894).

53. "Siquidem ipsum cor, ad illius inuasionem viribus destitutum, frequenter, ipsa sentiente simul et a foris audiente, quasi vas quod // confringitur ⟨sonitum⟩ fractionis emisit:; ipse quoque sanguis, per corporalia membra diffusus, apertis venis exiliens., ebulliuit;, ossibusque contractis ipsa quoque medulla disparuit:, pectoris siccitas ipsius gutturis raucitatem induxit:, et, vt paucis multa concludam., ipse feruor sancti desiderij et amoris omnia membra corporea, mirum in modum sensibiliter estuanti., incendio conflagrauit." *Life of Beatrice*, pp. 308–11.

54. See *Life of Beatrice*, bk. II, chap. 16; bk. III, chap. 2.

55. On the relationship between the human body and divine presence, see Elaine Scarry, *The Body in Pain: The Making and Unmaking of the World* (Oxford: Oxford University Press, 1985), pp. 181–243; and Hollywood, *Virgin Wife*, pp. 1–25.

56. "Fuit enim huius desiderij tam vehemens insolentia:, quod, pre nimia importunitate ⟨vel sensum sui⟩ se putaret interdum amittere vel etiam vite sue dies, pre magna lesione vitalium et cordis angustia, breuiare." *Life of Beatrice*, pp. 324–25.

57. *Life of Beatrice*, bk. II, chap. 16; bk. III, chap. 8.

58. "Also ontsegt si allen troest dicwile van gode selue ende van sinen creaturen want alle die rasten die hare daer af mogen gescien dat sterket meer hare minne, ende trecket har begerte in een hoger wesen, ende dat uernuwet hare verlancnisse der minnen te plegene ende int gebruken der minnen te wesene ende sonder genuechte in ellenden te leuene. Ende so bliuet si ongesadet ende ongecosteghet in allen ghiften, om datsi noch daruen moet der iegenwordicheit hare minnen." *Seven Manieren*, pp. 34–35; "Seven Manners," p. 205 (translation modified).

59. ". . . sola mentis experientia, non autem verborum affluentia possunt concipi." *Life of Beatrice*, pp. 324–25.

60. Although there are important exceptions, asceticism and paramystical phenomena clearly are more prominent in the hagiographies of women than in those of men. See, for example, Bynum, *Holy Feast*, pp. 82–87, 103–4, 237–44; André Vauchez, *La Sainteté en Occident aux derniers siècles du moyen âge d'après les procès de canonisation et les documents hagiographiques*, Bibliothèque des Etudes Françaises d'Athenes et de Rome 241 (Rome: Ecole Française de Rome, 1988), pp. 450–55; and Donald Weinstein and Rudolph M. Bell, *Saints and Society: The Two Worlds of Western Christendom, 1000–1700* (Chicago: University of Chicago Press, 1982), pp. 123–27, 153–57, 236–37. Francis of Assisi and Henry Suso are two famous exceptions, but they remain just that—exceptional. The importance of this trend can be seen in Brenda Bolton's reading of the hagiographies of the *mulieres sanctae* as "desert mothers"—early Christian male models of ascetic heroism are transformed in the later Middle Ages into women. It is precisely the gap between the desert fathers and Beatrice's life and text that creates difficulties for her hagiographer. See Brenda Bolton, "Mulieres Sanctae," in *Women in Medieval Society*, ed. Susan Mosher Stuard (Philadelphia: University of Pennsylvania Press, 1976), pp. 141–58.

61. On the identification of women with the body, see Joan Ferrante, *Woman as Image in Medieval Literature* (New York: Columbia University Press, 1975), pp. 17–35; Vern Bullough, "Medieval Medical and Scientific Views of Women," *Viator* 4 (1973): 485–501; and Caroline Walker Bynum, "The Female Body and Religious Practice in the Later Middle Ages," in *Fragmentation*, pp. 181–238.

62. See Petroff, "Introduction," *Medieval Women's Visionary Literature*, pp. 3–86; and Caroline Walker Bynum, *Jesus as Mother: Studies in the Spirituality of the High Middle Ages* (Berkeley: University of California Press, 1982), pp. 247–62. For the authorizing function of visionary experience, see Thomas Aquinas, *Summa Theologiae*, ed. Blackfriars (New York: McGraw Hill, 1964–81), Pt. III, Supplement, q. 39, a. 1; and Barbara Newman, *Sister of Wisdom: Saint Hildegard's Theology of the Feminine* (Berkeley: University of California Press, 1987), pp. 34–41.

63. Elizabeth Castelli's comments about the movement between the visionary and object of vision in *The Martyrdom of Perpetua and Felicitas* helped me to clarify this point. See Elizabeth Castelli, "Mortifying the Body, Curing the Soul: Beyond Ascetic Dualism in *The Life of Saint Syncletica*," *differences* 4 (1992): 151 n. 17.

64. Bynum, *Holy Feast*, p. 151.

65. Mechthild of Magdeburg, *Mechthild von Magdeburg, "Das fleissende Licht der Gottheit": Nach der Einsiedler Handschrift in kritischem Vergleich mit der gesamten Überlieferung*, ed. Hans Neumann (Munich: Artemis Verlag, 1990), bk. 4, chap. 2. There are accounts within the beguine literature, however, that show a movement from spiritual exercise to visionary and ecstatic experience easily read in terms of bodily practice. See especially the visions of Hadewijch in Hadewijch, *The Complete Works*, trans. Mother Columba Hart (New York: Paulist Press, 1981).

66. Sigmund Freud, "The Ego and the Id," *The Standard Edition of the Complete Psychological Works of Sigmund Freud*, trans. and ed. James Strachey (London: Hogarth, 1953–74), 19: 25–26. On the bodily ego, see also Kaja Silverman, *The Threshold of the Visible World* (New York: Routledge, 1996), pp. 9–37; and Beckwith, "Passionate Regulation," p. 814.

67. Drew Leder, *The Absent Body* (Chicago: University of Chicago Press, 1990), pp. 69–99; and Scarry, *The Body in Pain*, pp. 27–59.

68. See Bynum, *Holy Feast*, pp. 261–76; Bynum, *Fragmentation*, pp. 181–238; Elizabeth Robertson, "The Corporeality of Female Sanctity in *The Life of Saint Margaret*," in *Images of Sainthood in Medieval Europe*, pp. 268–87; and Elizabeth Robertson, "Medieval Medical Views of Women and Female Spirituality in the *Ancrene Wisse* and Julian of Norwich's *Showings*," in *Feminist Approaches to the Body in Medieval Literature*, ed. Linda Lomperis and Sarah Stanbury (Philadelphia: University of Pennsylvania Press, 1993), pp. 142–67.

69. See Jacques Lacan, *Ecrits: A Selection*, trans. Alan Sheridan (New York: Norton, 1977), pp. 1–7. For more on psychoanalytic theories of identification, see Butler, *Bodies That Matter*, pp. 57–120; and Diana Fuss, *Identification Papers* (New York: Routledge, 1996), pp. 1–82.

70. Beckwith, "Passionate Regulation," p. 817.

71. Beckwith, "Passionate Regulation," p. 818.

72. "Hier omme es si in groet verlancnisse ende in starke begerte ute desen ellende te werdene uerledecht, ende van desen lichame ontbonden te sine ende so segtsie die wile met sereleken herten alse die apostel[en] dede die seide. 'Cupio dissolui et esse cum cristo.' Dat es Ic begere ontbonden te sine ende te wesene met kerste." *Seven Manieren*, p. 33; "Seven Manners," p. 205 (translation modified).

73. "ene salige passie ende .i. scarp torment / ende ene uerlange⟨n⟩ quale, ende ene mordeleke doet ende steruende leuen." *Seven Manieren*, p. 34; "Seven Manners," p. 205.

74. Beckwith uses Foucault's aphorism at the opening of her essay; "The soul is the prison of the body." See Beckwith, "Passionate Regulation," p. 803.

75. This use of hagiographies is made evident by the manuscript tradition for Beatrice's own *vita*. Of the four known manuscripts, one is contained in a collection of spiritual writings produced at the request of John of St. Trond, a monk in Villers, when he was the chaplain of the Cistercian convent at Vrouwenpark in Wezemaal. The manuscript, completed in 1320, was presumably collected for the edification of these Cistercian nuns. Examination of this and similar manuscript collections might further elucidate how hagiographies were read in relationship to other forms of religious writing. For the manuscript information, see *Life of Beatrice*, p. xxi. These practices are also suggested by the development of hagiographical and auto-hagiographical writings by women in the fourteenth century. When women's spirituality comes under more stringent ecclesiastical scrutiny, they repeat these hagiographical gestures in their own texts. See Hollywood, *Virgin Wife*, pp. 201–6.

76. It is worth mentioning that Beatrice had early contact with beguines, women who wished to live religious lives in the world. In the reaction against the beguines, their rejection of enclosure and destabilization of the boundaries between inside and outside played a key role. A comparison of the *Ancrene Wisse* with Julian of Norwich's *Showings* in light of Beckwith's reading of the former text would clarify to what extent the anchorite rule was enacted in the ways Beckwith suggests.

77. Butler, *Bodies That Matter*, p. 76; cited by Beckwith, "Passionate Regulation," p. 818.

78. Beckwith, "Passionate Regulation," pp. 818–19.

79. For an attempt to bring gender into the genealogy of mysticism, see

Grace Jantzen, *Gender, Authority and Christian Mysticism* (Cambridge: Cambridge University Press, 1996). For the other major genealogical study, see Michel de Certeau, *"Mystique* au XVIIe siècle: Le problème du langage mystique," in *L'Homme devant Dieu: Mélanges de Lubac,* 2 vols. (Paris: Aubier, 1964), 2: 267–91; and Michel de Certeau, *La Fable mystique, XVIe–XVIIe siècle* (Paris: Gallimard, 1982). For a representative and already highly influential attempt to write the history of the modern subject, see Charles Taylor, *Sources of the Self: The Making of Modern Identity* (Cambridge: Harvard University Press, 1989). Taylor mentions the work of two women in the text of the book: Hannah Arendt and Iris Murdoch. A few more appear in the notes, although self-consciously feminist scholarship has virtually no impact on his account. See also Michel Foucault, *The History of Sexuality,* vol. 1, *An Introduction,* trans. Robert Hurley (New York: Vintage, 1980) and the voluminous literature emerging from that work, much of it critical of his refusal to acknowledge sexual difference. For an introduction to the history of the subject in literary studies, see David Aers, "A Whisper in the Ear of Early Modernists: or, Reflections on Literary Critics Writing the 'History of the Subject'," in *Culture and History 1350–1600: Essays on English Communities, Identities and Writing,* ed. David Aers (Detroit: Wayne State University Press, 1992), pp. 177–202. For a brief response to Aers's argument and further literature on the topic, see Valerie Traub, M. Lindsay Kaplan, and Dympna Callaghan, "Introduction," in *Feminist Readings of Early Modern Culture: Emerging Subjects,* ed. Valeria Traub, M. Lindsay Kaplan, and Dympna Callaghan (Cambridge: Cambridge University Press, 1996), pp. 1–4.

80. Denys Turner, *The Darkness of God: Negativity in Christian Mysticism* (Cambridge: Cambridge University Press, 1995), p. 4.

81. For a better stated version of this argument, and one which does take into account women's texts, see Sells, *Languages of Unsaying,* pp. 1–13. Jantzen also argues convincingly for the role of modern western Protestant theology and philosophy of religion in shaping contemporary conceptions of mysticism. See Jantzen, *Power, Gender, and Authority,* pp. 304–21.

82. I cannot speak here to the situation of women south of the Alps. For the complexities of Northern Europe, see Hollywood, *Virgin Wife,* pp. 201–6.

83. The desire to free body and soul from the demands of corporal and spiritual exercises and the pain they engender is most explicit in Marguerite Porete. "And to the one who would ask them [simple and free souls] what was the greatest torment that a creature could suffer, they would say that it would be to dwell in Love and to be in obedience to the Virtues. For it is necessary to give to the Virtues all that they ask, whatever the cost to Nature. For it is thus that the Virtues demand honor and goods, heart and body and life." The interiorization and annihilation of the simple soul frees her from this torment. See Marguerite Porete, *Le Mirouer des simples ames anienties et qui seulement demourent en vouloir et desir d'amour,* ed. Romana Guarnieri and Paul Verdeyen, CCCM (Turnhout: Brepols, 1986), chap. 8, pp. 28–30.

In this view, a freely given experience of the divine other is the source of the soul's liberating movement. Yet if the experience of the divine other depends on bodily practice, freedom is constrained. And if the theories of Mauss and Asad are correct, without bodily and spiritual exercises, the divine other will not be encountered and unbelief ensues. All this suggests the mystic's movement may be self-defeating, although a careful reading of Porete and Eckhart on this issue may suggest another approach.

Chapter 6. A Marriage and Its Observer: Christine of Stommeln, the Heavenly Bridegroom, and Friar Peter of Dacia

1. On the events and chronology, see Jarl Gallén, *La Province de Dacie de l'Ordre des Frères Prècheurs* (Helsingfors: Soderstrom, 1946), pp. 225–44.

2. On the letters and particularly the distinction between Peter's edited collection and the remaining letters (Peter's exhibiting a more formal style and abstract theological content, less reflective of particular events), see Monika Asztalos, "Les Lettres de direction et les sermons épistolaires de Pierre de Dacie," in *The Editing of Theological and Philosophical Texts from the Middle Ages*, ed. Asztalos (Stockholm: Almqvist and Wiksell International, 1986), pp. 161–84.

3. The manuscript has three parts, edited as follows. The first part, containing the poem and its commentary: Peter of Dacia, *De Gratia naturam ditante sive de virtutibus Christinae Stumbelensis*, ed. Monika Asztalos (Stockholm: Almqvist and Wiksell International, 1982); the second, comprising Peter's narratives and the collection of letters (within which the *quaternus* is included): Peter of Dacia, *Vita Christinae Stumbelensis*, ed. Johannes Paulson (Göteborg: Wettergren and Kerber, 1896; hereafter cited as *Vita*), which supersedes the seventeenth-century edition of Daniel Papenbroek in *AASS*, June, vol. 5 (Paris, 1867), pp. 236–94, 348–62; the third, consisting of John the schoolmaster's narratives of Christine's sufferings: *AASS*, June 5: 294–348, containing portions only, completed by Johannes Paulson, *In Tertiam Partem Libri Juliacensis Annotationes* (Göteborg: Wettergren and Kerber, 1896). For descriptions of the manuscript and its contents see Asztalos, "Introduction," in Peter of Dacia, *De Gratia*, pp. 16–27, and Peter Nieveler, *Codex Iuliacensis: Christina von Stommeln und Petrus von Dacien, ihr Leben und Nachleben in Geschichte, Kunst und Literatur* (Mönchengladbach: Kuhlen, 1975), pp. 13–28.

4. Aviad M. Kleinberg, *Prophets in Their Own Country: Living Saints and the Making of Sainthood in the Later Middle Ages* (Chicago: University of Chicago Press, 1992), p. 71.

5. Christine Ruhrberg, *Der Literarische Körper der Heiligen: Leben und Viten der Christina von Stommeln (1242–1312)* (Tübingen and Basel: Francke Verlag, 1995), pp. 203–13.

6. Here I agree, in essentials, with the approach of Ruhrberg to these texts; see her discussion of these issues in *Der Literarische Körper*, pp. 262–90. Aviad Kleinberg takes a different approach, considering the voice of Christine in the letters and narratives more or less straightforwardly as that of the saint herself: Kleinberg, *Prophets*, pp. 84–95. Kleinberg rightly objects to "the dismissal of all saints' *Lives* as untrustworthy and stereotypical" (p. 3), and he presents an attractive argument for Peter's dependability as a witness to events (pp. 50–70). But in the case of the putative writings of Christine, their apparently composite authorship and their

evident aim—to establish her sanctity—tend to undermine efforts to read them as the woman's personal self-revelation.

7. *De Gratia* I, l. 2, p. 83.

8. *De Gratia* I, ll. 25–28, p. 84.

9. There is a large lacuna in the text of the commentary; twenty-two leaves—more than half of the original thirty-nine leaves in the first part—are missing. Asztalos, "Introduction," pp. 41–42.

10. Asztalos, "Introduction," p. 42; chaps. 3–9 of the commentary explicate the first part of the couplet, p. 52.

11. Asztalos, "Introduction," pp. 9, 53, 51.

12. *De Gratia* I, ll. 29–32, p. 84.

13. On the term *gracia privilegiata*: Asztalos, "Introduction," pp. 49–50.

14. On rapture: *De Gratia* 13.1, p. 169. Cf. 11.26, p. 151: "And although no one can achieve perfect beatitude in this life, it is given however to some by privileged grace to perceive something of it through rapture" ("Et licet ad perfectam beatitudinem in hac vita nullus possit pervenire, datur tamen aliquibus per graciam privilegiatam ut per raptum de ea aliquid presenciant").

15. ". . . creauit deus spiritum racionalem ad sui ymaginem et similitudinem, et eum tante amicicie federe limo terre copulauit, ut nec sub quantacumque miseria ab eo uelit separari; et nunc, quasi oblitus preteritorum operum, eundem spiritum tanta dulcedine allicit ad se et se ipso afficit et illicit, ut non solum limi, sed et sui obliuiscatur, omniaque reputat ut stercora, ut cristum lucrifaciat. o dulcissime ihesu! o uiolentissime amor et amator! numquid dissoluere uis, quod bona racione conpactum est? 'non' ait; 'sed uolo hac arte corpus, cuius sensus in malum ab adolescencia sua proni sunt, per spiritum sic affectum ad me conuertere et attrahere, ut meo degustato spiritu desipiat omnis caro. quod ex eo manifestissime conprobabo, si eciam in uita presenti alicui tantam contulero mee beatitudinis et dulcedinis exuberanciam, ut mente excedat propriam naturam, ut magis uelit esse mecum quam secum, cupiatque a se et in se dissolui, ut me possit perfrui. Tali enim arte ad me traham spiritum, mea ymagine insignatum, et per eum lucrabor limum ex omni elementorum genere conpositum, ut, sicut a me creata sunt corporalia et spiritualia, sic utraque secundum modum sibi possibilem pro me et in me beatificentur et a se quodammodo alienentur, ut in me transformentur." *Vita*, pp. 94–95 (Letter 10).

16. *Vita*, pp. 11–12 (second visit), pp. 25–26 (fifth visit), pp. 26–27 (sixth visit), pp. 35–36 (seventh visit), pp. 37–38 (eighth visit), pp. 47–48 (ninth visit), pp. 56–57 (eleventh visit), pp. 59–64 (twelfth visit).

17. ". . . et rapta est predicta puella in tantum mentis excessum, ut in omnibus sensibus inmobilis facta et toto corpore indurata nullum uite sensibilis preferret indicium, et—quod plus addidit stuporis—nec perpendi poterat, quod attraheret spiritum. fateor: dum hec fierent, pre gaudio flebam et pro miraculo stupebam et pro tanto diuine influencie dono gracias largitori referebam; nichil enim de hiis nature uel humane industrie attribuebam, sed divinam presenciam in hoc facto sum ueneratus . . . cum ergo talem disposicionem in homine mortali numquam uidissem, putabam hoc esse, quod in apostolo legi: 'siue mente excedimus,' nulli enim alii rei michi, quod uidi, uidebatur esse similius cepique tanto solicicius cuncta considerare facta, ascultare uerba, motus et gestus ponderare et memorie alcius

recommendare, quia priuilegio gracie singularis omnia esse iudicaui attribuenda." *Vita*, pp. 11–12 (first visit).

18. *Vita*, p. 25 (fifth visit).

19. *Vita*, pp. 35–36 (seventh visit).

20. ". . . ut aliquem seruorum suorum michi ostenderet, in quo conuersacionem sanctorum suorum non solum uerbis sed factis et exemplis secure et plane addiscerem; cui caritate ex corde coniungerer et consociarer; cuius moribus informarer; cuius deuocione inflammarer et ab accidia, que me a puericia depresserat, excitarer; cuius collocucione illuminarer; cuius familiaritate consolarer; cuius exemplis de omnibus certificarer dubiis, maxime que ad conuersacionem pertinent sanctorum." *Vita*, p. 2 (first visit).

21. ". . . hec nox est, in qua domini mei sponsam primo uidere merui." *Vita*, p. 8 (first visit).

22. ". . . et rem uidi ab infancia desideratam." *Vita*, p. 16.

23. *Vita*, p. 75 (Letter 5); p. 70 (Letter 4).

24. "Quomodo enim non letificarer in bono eius, quem sicut me diligebam?" *Vita*, p. 76 (Letter 5).

25. "Dicit quidam, quod amicus sponsi gaudio gaudet propter uocem sponsi. Et quid, queso, faceret, si ipsius quoque sponse interdum uocem audiret, de qua dicitur: Vox tua dulcis et facies tua decora; sponsus enim et sponsa dicunt, ueni. qui, inquam, audiret, numquid non gauderet? audeo dicere: non solum gauderet, sed et iubilaret, sed et uerbum bonum eructaret, quia et qui audit dicat: ueni! Maxime certe, si ei daretur interdum preuento dilectione, inbuto deuocione, induto cognicione, talibus nupciis interesse, thalamum cum obsequio et reuerencia introire, epithalamium intente et deuote audire." *Vita*, p. 76 (Letter 5).

26. Jordan of Saxony, *Epistolae*, ed. Angelus Walz (Rome: Institutum Historicum Fratrum Praedicatorum, 1951), p. 13. See also John Coakley, "Gender and the Authority of Friars: The Significance of Holy Women for Thirteenth-Century Franciscans and Dominicans," *Church History* 60 (1991): 450–52.

27. *Vita*, p. 80 (Letter 5).

28. Ibid.

29. ". . . ex uerbis tamen uel responsis sponse, que pluries audiui, dicta eius uel promissa conieci." *Vita*, p. 80 (Letter 5).

30. ". . . quam affectuose congratularer de uestro et uestri dilecti concursu et conuictu, coniunctione et coniocundacione duorum michi tam dilectorum et desideratorum, sibi inuicem karissimorum, cum ex parte uestra audirem uota deuocionis, uerba dilectionis, sonos obedicionis, preces expectacionis, gaudia suscepcionis, exultacionis, perfruicionis, desideria remansionis, suspiria separacionis et fletus desolacionis!" *Vita*, p. 96 (Letter 10).

31. Ruhrberg discusses the passage but, without noting the allusion to Rachel and Leah, suggests an allusion to the brother of the bride in Cant. 8: 8. *Der Literarische Körper*, p. 246. There is no clear verbal reminiscence of that verse, however, and Peter is clearly making himself out as sister, not brother.

32. "Quid igitur michi restat, qui annis antiquior, nupciis iam factus inepcior —quia corde frigidior, facie rugosior, mercede pauperior, fetu sterilior, superductione iunioris sororis despectior—nisi ut, qui in me placere non merui, saltem

caueam displicere? Scio, quid faciam. exhibebo me sorori mee familiarem et sponso eius deuotum et obsequiosum, ut et hec michi saltem de effluencia gaudiorum et sciencia secretorum aliquid communicet, et ille eo libencius, frequencius, festiuius et familiarius ueniat, dum in una sororum paratum inueniat thalamum cordis et in alia promtum reperiat obsequium corporis, in utraque autem desiderium deuote expectacionis. sic igitur placabo sponsum precibus, placabo muneribus, placabo obsequiosis operibus; et dicam, ut facilius alliciam, efficacius suadeam et forcius traham: habeo sororem iuniorem, uenustiorem; ad illam ingredere, illi coniungere, illam amplectere, ut uel sic memoria mei ab affectu eius non deleatur." *Vita*, p. 97 (Letter 10).

33. *Vita*, 88 (Letter 8). It is true that in recounting his 1279 visit to Christine, Peter will say, "I will hope, and I hope already, to be able to obtain, through Christine the friend of Christ, not only forgiveness of sins but also the grace to do good works" ("sperabam tamen et adhuc spero per cristinam cristi amicam posse optinere et ueniam peccatorum et graciam exercicii bonorum operum"). *Vita*, p. 108 (fifteenth visit). But these are the only examples I find in which Peter ascribes even an implied intercessory role to Christine. Ruhrberg, quoting this passage as evidence that Christine fulfilled, in Peter's view, the obligatory saintly role of intercessor, does not remark on the paucity of the evidence. Ruhrberg, *Der Literarische Körper*, p. 253.

34. In Letter 15, *Vita*, pp. 104–5, he complains of his torpor and lack of devotion at Paris, and solicits her prayers. Moreover, there is at least some suggestion that he may associate his deficiency of devotion with his corresponding proficiency in what we would call cognitive skills; in two instances in the narrative of his fifth visit, at any rate, he seems to be suggesting a contrast between Christine's devotion and his own learning, as he pictures displays of her ecstatic behavior precisely at moments when he himself was giving public learned discourses. *Vita*, pp. 24–26; see John Coakley, "Friars as Confidants of Holy Women in Medieval Dominican Hagiography," in *Images of Sainthood in Medieval Europe*, ed. Renate Blumenfeld-Kosinski and Timea Szell (Ithaca, N.Y.: Cornell University Press, 1991), p. 231.

35. On the concept of love in these texts, see Friedrich Ochsner, *Petrus de Dacia Gothensis: Mystiker der Freundschaft* (Visby: Barry Press Verlag, 1975), esp. pp. 89–97; Ruhrberg, *Der Literarische Körper*, pp. 122–36.

36. "karissima, quamuis plurima solacia michi deus dederit in hac uia . . . unum tamen est, quod pre omnibus me letificat, quia uidelicet datum est michi intelligere, quid sit dictum: 'Despondi enim uos uni uiro uirginem castam exhibere cristo.' . . . Rogate autem dominum, karissima et per amorem diuinum deo et anime mee desponsata, ut huius, desponsacionis fidem seruemus intemeratam et arram amoris senciamus incontaminatam." *Vita*, pp. 227–28 (Letter 39), 12 November 1279. In this and other dating of the letters, I follow Gallén, *La Province de Dacie* (see n. 1), pp. 240–44.

37. ". . . vasculum . . . divine habitacionis," *Vita*, p. 229 (Letter 39); p. 159 (Letter 33), 24 November 1279.

38. ". . . similitudinem quandam in nobis video eternis societatis et intime sanctorum caritatis." *Vita*, p. 190 (Letter 27), November–December 1280.

39. ". . . ipse eciam nos, distantes loco, dispares merito et dissimiles coti-diano exercicio, in unum fedus amicicie adunauit." *Vita*, pp. 246–47 (Letter 55), of uncertain date between 1280 and 1286.

40. *Vita*, p. 162 (Letter 24).

41. "clamet ergo mundus, irrideat, detrahat, irascatur et dehortetur: spon-sam tamen domini mei ex intimo corde meo diligam propter sponsum ipsum." *Vita*, p. 165 (Letter 24).

42. Aviad Kleinberg in his discussion of Christine rightly notes the promi-nence of strife and demons in these texts, but goes, I believe, too far in saying that "good is secondary and posterior to evil in Christina's world." Kleinberg, *Prophets*, p. 92.

43. The vexations' prevention of her partaking of communion is itself a con-stant theme. Examples: her obsessive thought that her food turned into repulsive animals applied to the Eucharist, and so kept her from partaking, *Vita*, pp. 112–14; a fire would arise in her sight, apparently to distract and terrify her, not only when she confessed to the priest but also when she communicated, *Vita*, p. 121.

44. "postea non delectabar audire missam nec uerbum dei, nec loqui de deo nec orare ullo modo potui sine terrore ferri igniti." *Vita*, p. 71 (Letter 4).

45. *Vita*, p. 84 (Letter 7).

46. Is the connection between Christine and the texts written down by the schoolmaster more tenuous than the connection between her and those written down by the parish priest? The weight of recent scholarship suggests that it prob-ably was not. It is true that the scenes the schoolmaster describes are more spec-tacularly unlikely. Also in Letter 25, in an aside to Peter, the schoolmaster writes that the things he has reported "are not given to me from a human but from God" ("mihi not ab homine, sed diuinitus sunt manifestata") and that in fact Christine forgets her experiences after she has had them; and he implies that she reported them involuntarily therefore while she was in a trance: "Christine, your daugh-ter did not by her own power relate any of the things that are written, except a few things about her sufferings" ("cristina, uestra filia, sui conpos, nichil horum, que scripta sunt, preter pauca de passionibus michi retulit"). *Vita*, p. 181 (Letter 25). The passage raises the suspicion that the schoolmaster took liberties with the material. The early twentieth-century Jesuit Herbert Thurston, who at any rate viewed Christine as a suggestible "hysterical case," concluded that John would have had to "fill in the gaps" in whatever she actually involuntarily said. Thurston, "The Case of Blessed Christina of Stommeln," *The Month* 152 (1928): 191. More recently Anna J. Martin has written of a "strong mixing of Christine's experiences and Mas-ter John's fantasy" in these texts. Martin, "Christina von Stommeln," *Mediaevistik* 4 (1991): 191. Ruhrberg however points out that Letter 25 is in the collection Peter edited, and that there is another version of the letter in the third part of the *Codex Iuliacensis* (text in *In Tertiam Partem* [see n. 3 above], p. 55), in which the pas-sage in question is missing—which suggests that, for whatever reason, Peter may have wished to cast doubt upon the narrative of the schoolmaster, who, it must be remembered, "was sitting right next to his source"—unlike Peter. Ruhrberg, *Der Literarische Körper*, p. 295. See also Kleinberg, *Prophets*, p. 81, who finds the school-

master's narratives "entirely consistent" with those written down by the priest. It is certainly clear, as Ruhrberg's impressive work shows, that the priest was no less a part of the hagiographical enterprise than was the schoolmaster.

47. ". . . in quibus nupciis tantis mirabilibus gaudiis et deliciis affluebat. quod usque ad diem tercium nullius rei discrecionem habebat." *Vita*, p. 172 (Letter 25).

48. ". . . in amplexus sui sponsi rapitur et ibidem ineffabiliter consolatur." *Vita*, p. 175 (Letter 25).

49. "ille dulcissimus sponsus, beatam eius animam rapiens, in archanum sui dilectissimi cordis thalamum hanc transuexit; vbi secundum multitudinem dolorum precedencium diuine consolaciones eius animam ineffabiliter letificaverunt." *Vita*, p. 202 (Letter 29).

50. It is in Letter 10, written in February 1270, that Peter requests her to produce the *quaternus* (*Vita*, p. 100), she promises it in Letter 13, in March (*Vita*, p. 101), and in the account of his sixteenth visit he reports receiving it from her on his final departure from Stommeln for Sweden on 30 September (*Vita*, p. 108).

51. *Vita*, pp. 109–12 (narrative of early life), pp. 112–30 (vexation accounts; hiatus, p. 115); pp. 130–31 (concluding vision and ravaging by serpent).

52. ". . . karissima filia, ecce ihesus cristus sum; promitte michi fidem tuam, ita quod semper michi seruias. Siquis de cetero te de altera fide requisierit, dicas: quia ihesu cristo eam promisisti in suas manus—in quas igitur promisit—cum beginis manebis." *Vita*, pp. 109–10 (*quaternus*).

53. ". . . cui fidem promiserat." *Vita*, p. 110, pp. 111–12 (*quaternus*). The beguines derided her as someone who was feigning sanctity. *Vita*, p. 114 (*quaternus*).

54. *Vita*, p. 112 (*quaternus*).

55. *Vita*, p. 113 (*quaternus*).

56. "statim audiuit uocem optimam de deo psallentem, et uenit in cor eius gaudium, quale de cantu numquam habuit." *Vita*, p. 119 (*quaternus*).

57. ". . . nec eciam in oracione suum dilectum omnino sentire potuit." *Vita*, p. 122 (*quaternus*).

58. *Vita*, p. 122 (*quaternus*).

59. "Religiosi et clerici et omnes continentes decepti sunt, quia heresis est sic uiuere, quia deus a principio sic ordinauit, ut omnes uiuerent in matrimonio." *Vita*, p. 124 (*quaternus*).

60. *Vita*, pp. 123–25 (*quaternus*).

61. *Vita*, p. 125 (*quaternus*).

62. *Vita*, p. 129 (*quaternus*).

63. *Vita*, p. 131 (*quaternus*).

64. Trials that appear to end without resolution include: an obsession that her food has turned into snakes, spiders, etc. (*Vita*, p. 114), an episode of muteness (in which she, at any rate, could not voice a response to the demon, p. 119), a series of experiences in which, when she tried to pray or confess, her prayerbook or her confessor would appear to break into flames (p. 120), and the demon's criticism of her for being too lax in her discipline (p. 125). Trials that end when she dispels the demon include a temptation to suicide by starvation (p. 115) and a temptation to wound herself with thorns (p. 116).

65. See n. 52.

66. *Vita*, p. 110 (*quaternus*).

67. *Vita*, pp. 111–12.

68. Ruhrberg, *Der Literarische Körper*, pp. 155–56, 100–22.

Chapter 7. Henry Suso and Elsbeth Stagel: Was the Vita a Cooperative Effort?

1. *Das Leben der Schwestern zu Töss beschrieben von Elsbet Stagel samt der Vorrede von Johannes Meier und dem Leben der Prinzessin Elisabet von Ungarn*, ed. Ferdinand Vetter (Berlin: Weidmann, 1906).

2. Heinrich Seuse, *Deutsche Schriften*, ed. Karl Bihlmeyer (Stuttgart: Kohlhammer, 1907). This is the standard edition of all German writings, including the *Exemplar*, authored by or attributed to Suso. All quotations from and references to Suso's German works are from this edition and are cited by page and line.

3. Lichtenberger, "Inauthenticité de la Vie de Suso," *Revue des Cours et Conférences* 19, 1 (1910–1911): 203–28.

4. See, however, Jeanne Ancelet-Hustache, "Le Problème de l'authenticité de la Vie de Suso," *La Mystique Rhénane* (Paris: Presses Universitaires de France, 1963), pp. 193–205.

5. Schwietering, "Zur Autorschaft von Seuses Vita," first published in 1953; cited here from the revised version in *Altdeutsche und altniederländische Mystik*, ed. Kurt Ruh (Darmstadt: Wissenschaftliche Buchgesellschaft, 1964), pp. 311–12, 317.

6. Schwietering, "Zur Autorschaft," pp. 312–13.

7. Bihlmeyer, "Einleitung," the introduction to Seuse's *Deutsche Schriften* (n. 2 above), pp. 132*–136*. Page numbers followed by asterisks refer to Bihlmeyer's introduction (*Einleitung*).

8. Bihlmeyer, "Einleitung," p. 133* n. 2.

9. Ibid.

10. ". . . do braht si zuo . . . ein vil guot buoch" (97, 2–3). Translations are from *Henry Suso: The Exemplar with Two German Sermons*, trans., ed., and intro. Frank Tobin (New York: Paulist Press, 1989), here, p. 132. In passing it should be noted, as Klaus Grubmüller, "Die Viten der Schwestern von Töss und Elsbeth Stagel," *Zeitschrift für deutsches Altertum und deutsche Literatur* 98 (1969): 201 n. 2 points out, the word Suso uses here for "complete" (*zuobringen*) can mean "bring to completion" and does not necessarily attribute the entire book to Stagel's authorship.

11. *Henry Suso*, p. 132. "Si zoh im us verborgenlich die wise sines durpruches zuo gote und screib es an, als es da vor und hie na stet geschriben" (97, 8–9).

12. For example, "the naked Godhead," "the nothingness of all things," "losing oneself in the nothingness [of God]," "the inadequacy of all images" (*von aller bilden bildlosekeit*; 97, 13). *Henry Suso*, p. 133.

13. *Henry Suso*, p. 141. "got der hat nút allein dich dur mit getrofen, er hat och mich in dir gelezzet, wan ich nieman me hab, der mir mit soelichem flisse und

goetlichen trúwen behulfen sie minú buechlú ze volbringen, als du tet, die wil du gesund werd" (109, 5–8).

14. Cf. chap. 33 (98, 9–16); and chap. 53 (190, 24–191, 2).

15. ". . . mit glichnusgebender wise von mengerley hailigen werken, dú in der warheit also geschahen" (3, 8–10).

16. This event is related in chap. 23 of the *Vita*.

17. *Heinrich Seuses Horologium Sapientiae*, ed. Pius Künzle, O.P. (Freiburg: Universitätsverlag, 1977). The passage discussed here is from the prologue, pp. 366, 20–367, 14.

18. Cf. 2 Sam. 12: 1–7.

19. Cf. 2 Sam. 14: 1–22.

20. Cf. Tob. 5.

21. Though these remarks are directed to *visiones* in the *Horologium*, Bihlmeyer, "Einleitung" (p. 84*) says one is justified in applying them to the visions in the *Vita* as well. And we are certainly justified in applying them also to incidents not formally labeled visions.

22. See the prologue to the *Vita* (7, 5–8, 3).

23. Most likely chaps. 1–32 of the *Vita*.

24. Ruh, "Altdeutsche Mystik: Ein Forschungsbericht," *Wirkendes Wort* 7 (1957): 222.

25. Ruh, *Geschichte der abendländischen Mystik*, vol. 3, *Die Mystik des deutschen Predigerordens und ihre Grundlegung durch die Hochscholastik* (Munich: Beck, 1996), p. 445.

26. Grubmüller, "Die Viten der Schwestern von Töss," see esp. pp. 187–204. Actually, in a dissertation written much earlier Otto Loewe, *Das Tösser Schwesternbuch* (Münster, 1921), pp. 20–37 had expressed serious doubts about whether Stagel could have been the author of more than small parts of this sister-book. However, Loewe does not seem to have had much impact on subsequent scholarship. For more on the sister-books, see the excellent study by Gertrud Jaron Lewis, *By Women, for Women, About Women: The Sister-Books of Fourteenth-Century Germany* (Toronto: Pontifical Institute of Medieval Studies, 1996). For the Töss sister-book, see esp. pp. 21–25.

27. *Das Leben der Schwestern zu Töss* (cf. n. 1 above), here Prologue, pp. 12–16; and the life of Elsbeth Bechlin, pp. 86–90.

28. Grubmüller, "Die Viten der Schwestern von Töss," p. 202.

29. Peters, *Religiöse Erfahrung als literarisches Faktum: Zur Vorgeschichte und Genese frauenmystischer Texte des 13. und 14. Jahrhunderts* (Tübingen: Niemeyer, 1988); see esp. pp. 133–42.

30. *Das Leben der Schwestern zu Töss*, p. 93, 5.

31. In the prologues to the *Exemplar* and *Vita*, she remains an unnamed "spiritual daughter" (4, 9) and a "holy enlightened person" (7, 5).

32. Peters, *Religiöse Erfahrung*, p. 140.

33. The main literature to be consulted: Ringler, *Viten- und Offenbarungsliteratur in Frauenklöstern des Mittelalters* (Munich: Artemis, 1980); Dinzelbacher, *Vision und Visionsliteratur im Mittelalter* (Stuttgart: Hiersemann, 1981); Dinzelbacher, review of Ringler, *Viten- und Offebarungsliteratur, Anzeiger für deutsches*

Altertum und deutsche Literatur 93 (1982): 63–71; Ringler, "Die Rezeption mittel-alterlicher Frauenmystik als wissenschaftliches Problem, dargestellt am Werk der Christine Ebner," *Frauenmystik im Mittelalter*, ed. Dinzelbacher and Dieter R. Bauer (Ostfildern bei Stuttgart: Schwabenverlag, 1985), pp. 178–200; Dinzelbacher, "Zur Interpretation erlebnismystischer Texte des Mittelalters," *Zeitschrift für deutsches Altertum und deutsche Literatur* 117 (1988): 1–23. Some reviews of Peters, *Religiöse Erfahrung*, are also relevant: Frank Tobin in *Colloquia Germanica* 23 (1990): 177–78; Martina Wehrli-Johns in *Beiträge zur deutschen Sprache und Literatur* 112 (1990): 326–32; Urban Küsters und Otto Langer in *Arbitrium* 9 (1991): 37–41; Rosemary Hale in *Speculum* 68 (1993): 239–40. See also Tobin, *Mechthild von Magdeburg: A Medieval Mystic in Modern Eyes* (Columbia, S.C.: Camden House, 1995), pp. 115–22.

34. ". . . man könne nur über den Text sprechen und nicht darüber, welche Art von Erfahrung diesem zugrundeliege." In Klaus Kirchert's "Diskussionsbe-richt" of the Weingarten Conference published as *Abendländische Mystik im Mittel-alter* (Stuttgart: Metzler, 1986), p. 472.

35. Kieckhefer, *Unquiet Souls: Fourteenth-Century Saints and Their Religious Milieu* (Chicago: University of Chicago Press, 1984), p. 5.

36. See n. 8 above.

37. ". . . mit bedahten worten." *Das Leben der Schwestern zu Töss*, p. 87, 3–4, just as Suso was questioned "surreptitiously" (*verstoln*; 7, 14).

38. Grubmüller, "Die Viten der Schwestern von Töss," pp. 197–98. One could counter all this, of course, by saying that most of the similarities are based on the fictitious Stagel, and not on the actual one.

39. For example, within three pages (87–89) we find: *mineklich* (three times), *zartlich, hertzliebes, kintliches hertz, hertzlich, mineriches hertz*.

40. Schwietering, "Zur Autorschaft," pp. 313–22.

41. Ruh, "Altdeutsche Mystik," p. 222; and Grubmüller, "Die Viten der Schwestern von Töss," p. 196.

42. Haas, "Heinrich Seuse," *Die deutsche Literatur des Mittelalters: Verfasser-lexikon*, 2nd ed. Kurt Ruh (Berlin: de Gruyter), vol. 8 (1992), p. 1118. The *doppelter Kursus* structure, common to most knightly romances, is one in which the hero pursues a course of action culminating in a climax that then turns out to be a false resolution of the struggle based on the hero's misunderstanding of what his goal should be. The re-oriented hero is then required to embark on a second path of con-flict at the culmination of which he attains his goal. Because he has now exercised true insight and solid knightly virtue, he is raised to the status of an ideal. The turn-ing point for Suso occurs in chap. 20 when he realizes the insubstantiality of the goal he has achieved through self-imposed ascetical practices and the necessity of embarking on a new path: that of enduring suffering which God chooses for him.

43. Ruh, *Geschichte der Abendländische Mystik*, 3: 445.

44. Two pertinent studies on the *Vita* that make a much more thorough case for the *Vita* as autobiography than can be attempted here are Georg Misch, *Geschichte der Autobiographie*, vol. 4, pt. 1 (Frankfurt am Main: Schulte-Bulmke, 1967); and Christine Pleuser, "Tradition und Ursprünglichkeit in der Vita Seuses," *Heinrich Seuse: Studien zum 600. Todestag, 1366–1966*, ed. E. M. Filthaut, O.P. (Co-logne: Albertus Magnus Verlag, 1966), pp. 135–60.

45. Schwietering, "Zur Autorschaft," pp. 319, 322.

46. At the beginning of chap. 3, Suso himself refers to both the *Little Book of Eternal Wisdom* and the *Horologium Sapientiae* as the sources for much of what he is about to write. This admitted inclusion in the first part of the *Vita* of revised passages from other of his works serves as a warning that we are not to take his statements in the prologue to the *Vita* (8, 1–2) to mean that the first part relies entirely on Stagel's notes.

47. For the letters, see Walter Blank, "Zum Stilwandel in Seuses Briefbüchern," *Seuse: Studien*, pp. 171–90; Debra Stoudt, *The Vernacular Letters of Heinrich von Nördlingen and Heinrich Seuse* (Ph.D. diss., University of North Carolina, 1986); and Stoudt, "The Structure and Style of Seuse's *Großes Briefbuch*," *Neuphilologische Mitteilungen* 90 (1989): 359–67. For chap. 3 of the *Vita*, see Paul Michel, "Stilwandel bei Heinrich Seuse," *Verborum Amor. Studien zur Geschichte und Kunst der deutschen Sprache*, Festschrift für Stefan Sonderegger zum 65. Geburtstag, ed. Harald Burger, Alois M. Haas, and Peter von Matt (Berlin: de Gruyter, 1992), esp. pp. 320–41.

48. Pleuser, "Tradition und Ursprünglichkeit," p. 149.

49. These are listed in Tobin, "Introduction," *Henry Suso*, pp. 44–47.

50. Chap. 9, which resembles a homily, could be based on notes from a colloquium delivered to a religious community.

51. Schwietering, considering such claims to reflect badly on Suso, finds it necessary to defend his manliness. "Zur Autorschaft," p. 313.

52. Pleuser, "Tradition und Ursprünglichkeit," p. 149.

53. In the later chapters Suso replaces "spiritual daughter" with "holy daughter" as his preferred epithet for Stagel.

54. ". . . der aller nehsten blossen warheit" (194, 8).

55. "Si trat hin zuo ime und zogte ime, wie adellich si in die blossen gotheit vergangen were" (194, 26–27).

Chapter 8. Mystical Death, Bodily Death: Catherine of Siena and Raymond of Capua on the Mystic's Encounter with God

The author wishes to thank her friends and colleagues for their encouragement and help on this essay, and particularly Caroline Walker Bynum, John Coakley, Geneviève James, Catherine Mooney, and Augustine Thompson.

1. *Le Lettere di S. Caterina da Siena*, ed. Piero Misciattelli (Florence: Giunti, 1940), 6 vols.: hereafter cited as *Lettere*. A critical edition exists for the earliest eighty-eight letters: S. Caterina da Siena, *Epistolario*, ed. Eugenio Dupré Theseider (Rome: Tipografia del Senato, 1940), vol. 1. This volume has been translated into English: *The Letters of Catherine of Siena*, trans. Suzanne Noffke, O.P. (Binghamton, N.Y.: Center for Medieval and Early Renaissance Studies, 1988), vol. 1. Other selections of St. Catherine's letters in translation can be found in *Saint Catherine of Siena as Seen in Her Letters*, trans. Vida Scudder (New York: Dent and Sons, 1905); and *I Catherine: Selected Writings of Catherine of Siena*, trans. Kenelm

Foster and Mary John Ronayne (London: Collins, 1980). A recent general bibliography of works by and about St. Catherine in English is included in Suzanne Noffke, O.P., *Catherine of Siena: Vision Through a Distant Eye* (Collegeville, Minn.: Liturgical Press, 1996), pp. 233–67. For a study of Catherine's correspondence, see Karen Scott, "'*Io Catarina*': Ecclesiastical Politics and Oral Culture in the Letters of Catherine of Siena," in *Dear Sister: Medieval Women and the Epistolary Genre*, ed. Karen Cherewatuk and Ulrike Wiethaus (Philadelphia: University of Pennsylvania Press, 1993), pp. 87–121. All translations for this essay are my own.

2. S. Caterina da Siena, *Le Orazioni*, ed. Giuliana Cavallini (Rome: Edizioni Cateriniane, 1978). The recent English translation is *The Prayers of Catherine of Siena*, trans. Suzanne Noffke, O.P. (New York: Paulist Press, 1983).

3. S. Caterina da Siena, *Il Dialogo della divina provvidenza ovvero Libro della divina dottrina*, ed. Giuliana Cavallini (Rome: Edizioni Cateriniane, 1980). The recent English translation is *The Dialogue*, trans. Suzanne Noffke, O.P. (New York: Paulist Press, 1980). The *Dialogo* expands on Letter 272, located in *Lettere*, 4: 158–72.

4. Raymond of Capua's Life of Catherine, called *Legenda Major*, is published as "De S. Catharina Senensi virgine de poenitentia S. Dominici," in *AASS*, April, vol. 3 (Paris, 1866), pp. 862–967 (hereafter cited as *Legenda*; first number cited refers to paragraphs). For a recent English translation of the *Legenda*, see *The Life of St. Catherine of Siena*, trans. Conleth Kearns (Wilmington, Del.: Glazier, 1980). See the "Introduction" to this volume, pp. xiii–lxxxix, for an extended treatment of Raymond and his work, and A. W. Van Ree, "Raymond de Capoue: Eléments biographiques," *AFP* 33 (1963): 159–241. Other recent studies of the *Legenda* include Sofia Boesch Gajano and Odile Redon, "La *Legenda Major* di Raimondo da Capua, costruzione di una santa," in *Atti del Simposio Internazionale Cateriniano-Bernardiniano: Siena, 17–20 aprile 1980*, ed. Domenico Maffei and Paolo Nardi (Siena: Accademia Senese degli Intronati, 1982), pp. 279–94 (hereafter cited as *Atti del Simposio*); and John Coakley, "Friars as Confidants of Holy Women in Medieval Dominican Hagiography," in *Images of Sainthood in Medieval Europe*, ed. Renate Blumenfeld-Kosinski and Timea Szell (Ithaca, N.Y.: Cornell University Press, 1991), pp. 222–46, esp. pp. 234–38.

5. For a readable presentation and critique of postmodernist approaches to history, see Joyce Appleby, Lynn Hunt, and Margaret Jacob, *Telling the Truth About History* (New York: Norton, 1994), esp. chaps. 6, 7, and 8.

6. Many biographies of Catherine were written in the late nineteenth and early twentieth centuries, for example: Augusta Theodosia Drane, *History of St. Catherine of Siena and Her Companions* (London, 1880); Edmund Gardner, *Saint Catherine of Siena: A Study in the Religion, Literature, and History of the Fourteenth Century in Italy* (New York: Dutton, 1907); Johannes Jörgensen, *Saint Catherine of Siena*, trans. Ingeborg Lund (New York: Longmans, 1938); Arrigo Levasti, *S. Caterina da Siena* (Turin: U.T.E.T., 1947).

7. For the debates concerning the Catherinian manuscripts, see Robert Fawtier, *Sainte Catherine de Sienne, essai de critique des sources*, 2 vols. (Paris: E. De Boccard, 1921–30); R. R. Motzo, "Per una edizione critica delle opere di S. Caterina

da Siena," in *Annali della Facoltà di filosofia e lettere della R. Università di Cagliari* (Rome: L'Universale Tipografia Poliglotta, 1931), pp. 111–41. And by Eugenio Dupré-Theseider: "Un Codice inedito dell'Epistolario di Santa Caterina da Siena," *Bullettino dell'Istituto Storico Italiano* 48 (1932): 17–56; "Il Problema critico delle lettere di Santa Caterina da Siena," *Bullettino dell'Istituto Storico Italiano* 49 (1933): 117–278.

8. Insightful treatments of these themes are found in Caroline Walker Bynum, " '. . . And Woman His Humanity': Female Imagery in the Religious Writing of the Later Middle Ages," in *Gender and Religion: On the Complexity of Symbols*, ed. Caroline Walker Bynum, Stevan Harrell, and Paula Richman (Boston: Beacon Press, 1986), pp. 257–88; Bynum, "Presidential Address: Wonder," *American Historical Review* 102 (1997): 1–26, esp. 10–12; Coakley, "Friars as Confidants"; Amy Hollywood, *The Soul as Virgin Wife: Mechthild of Magdeburg, Marguerite Porete, and Meister Eckhart* (Notre Dame, Ind.: University of Notre Dame Press, 1995).

9. Karen Scott, "St. Catherine of Siena, 'Apostola'," *Church History* 61 (1992): 34–46.

10. Karen Scott, "Urban Spaces, Women's Networks, and the Lay Apostolate in the Siena of Catherine Benincasa," in *Creative Women in Medieval and Early Modern Italy: A Religious and Artistic Renaissance*, ed. E. Ann Matter and John Coakley (Philadelphia: University of Pennsylvania Press, 1994), pp. 105–16.

11. *Legenda*: 152, 289.

12. For example: *Legenda*: 172, 365; Letters 92, 93, 117, 118, 240, 250.

13. Catherine's references to herself in her correspondence usually involved short notes at the end of her letters informing her friends of her whereabouts, asking for favors, or defending herself against criticism. In contrast, her letters to Raymond usually combine general spiritual teaching, personal advice and reproof, and long accounts of significant spiritual events in her own life. For her habit of confiding personal matters to her confessors, see also her example of personal confession in Letter 41 to Tommaso della Fonte, in *Lettere*, 1: 168–71.

14. For example, see L. 295, in *Lettere*, 4: 243: "Io vorrei poi venire costà a . . . ritrovarmi con voi a narrare gli ammirabili misteri che Dio in questo tempo ha adoperati, con allegrezza di mente e con giocondità di cuore, e con accrescimento di speranza, col lume della santissima fede." In Letter 373 sent to Raymond several months before she died, Catherine recounted saying to God, "Tu hai permesso che io sia sola in questa battaglia, senza il refrigerio del padre dell'anima mia" (*Lettere*, 5: 288).

15. *Legenda*: 154–64; 179–81; 194–98.

16. References to Tommaso's notebooks can be found in *Legenda*: 113, 142, 162, 167, 181, 186, 189, 199, 202.

17. L. 273, in *Lettere*, 4: 173–78.

18. Tommaso Caffarini identified the executed man with Niccolò di Toldo in both his *Legenda Minor*, a hagiographical narrative, and in his testimony at the *Processo Castellano* in the early fifteenth century. See Anna Imelde Galletti, " 'Uno capo nelle mani mie': Niccolò di Toldo, perugino," in *Atti del simposio*, pp. 121–27.

19. L. 219, in *Lettere*, 3: 266–70: " 'Di' a loro: io vi annunzio gaudio magno.' Allora l'anima mia più s'empiva; annegata era co'veri gustatori della divina Essen-

zia per unione e affetto d'amore." For an analysis of this letter, see Scott, "Catherine of Siena, 'Apostola'," pp. 37–38.

20. L. 226, in *Lettere*, 3: 294–301. In particular, Catherine said that on " 'l dì poi che fui partita da voi," " 'l Verbo, somma eterna e alta Deità, . . . mi donò tanta letizia, che eziandio le membra del corpo si sentivano dissolvere, disfare, come la cera nel fuoco" (p. 294). "[Io] dimandando voi, [Dio] mi diè [sè] medesimo, ed egli mi fece l'assoluzione e la remissione de'peccati miei e vostri, . . . obumbrandomi d'uno grande fuoco d'amore, con una sicurtà sì grande e purità di mente, che la lingua non è sufficiente a poterlo dire" (pp. 299–300). God's final words to her were the following: "Confortati dunque, e sia buono istrumento e virile ad annunziare la verità: che sempre sarò con voi" (p. 300). Catherine concluded that this experience "mi faceva stare, e gustare, nella vita durabile co' veri gustatori" (p. 301).

21. L. 272, in *Lettere*, 4: 158–72.

22. Ibid., p. 160: "E speculando con l'occhio dell'intelletto nella Verità eterna, dimandava ine quattro petizioni, tenendo sè e il padre suo dinanzi alla sposa della Verità."

23. Ibid., p. 161: "E a questo vi chiamava e allegava la Verità eterna, rispondendo alla terza petizione, ciò era la fame della vostra salute, dicendo: 'Figliuola, questo voglio ch'egli cerchi con ogni sollicitudine. Ma questo non potrebbe nè egli nè tu, nè alcuno altro avere senza le molte persecuzioni; secondo che io ve le concederò. Digli: come egli desidera il mio onore nella santa Chiesa, così concepi amore a volere sostenere con vera pazienzia. . . . E allora sarà il carissimo figliuolo, e riposerassi sopra il petto dell'unigenito mio Figliuolo; del quale ho fatto ponte perchè tutti possiate giungere a gustare e ricevere il frutto delle vostre fadighe.' " Toward the end of the letter Catherine addressed Raymond again directly: "Padre dolce, rallegratevi, poichè tanto dolcemente sete chiamato; e sostenete con grande allegrezza e pazienzia": Ibid., p. 171.

24. Ibid., p. 171: "O carissimo e dolcissimo padre, allora, vedendo e udendo dalla dolce prima Verità, 'l cuore per mezzo pareva che si partisse. Io muoio e non posso morire. Abbiate compassione della miserabile figliuola."

25. Ibid., p. 172: "Questa lettera, e un'altra ch'io vi mandai, ho scritte di mia mano. . . . [Dio] m'aveva dato, e proveduto con darmi l'attitudine dello scrivere; acciocchè discendendo dall'altezza, avessi un poco con chi sfogare 'l cuore, perchè non scoppiasse."

26. *Legenda*: 349–59.

27. Fawtier, *Sainte Catherine de Sienne*, 1: 169–71; and 2: 321–30.

28. L. 371, in *Lettere*, 5: 273–78. This letter is not complete in any of the available editions. The Tommaseo edition of Catherine's correspondence identified Urban VI as the recipient of this letter, but modern scholars disagree. Internal evidence shows that it was addressed to Raymond and was closely connected to Letter 373. For Misciattelli's view, see *Lettere*, 6: 142, n. 1. More recently, Suzanne Noffke concurs: see *Vision Through a Distant Eye*, p. 33 n. 38.

29. L. 373, in *Lettere*, 5: 284–92. A further text by Catherine documenting this stage of her life is Prayer XXVI, uttered at about the same time and containing much of the same imagery and sentiments: see *Orazioni*, pp. 282–85.

30. L. 371, in *Lettere*, 5: 277: "E con tanto lume si speculava questa Verità, che

in quello abisso allora si rinfrescarono i misterii della santa Chiesa, e tutte le grazie ricevute nella vita mia, passate e presenti; e il dì che in sè fu sposata l'anima mia."

31. Ibid., p. 276: "sentendo venire quella disposizione che fu al tempo della morte."

32. Ibid., p. 277: "Dio posemi dinanzi a sè, benchè io gli sia sempre presente, perchè contiene in sè ogni cosa; ma per uno nuovo modo, come se la memoria, lo intelletto e la volontà non avessero a fare cavelle col corpo mio."

33. L. 373, in *Lettere*, 5: 286: "Ma subito fui io gittata giù: ed essendo gittata, parbe a me, come se l'anima si fusse partita dal corpo; non per quello modo come quando se ne partì, perocchè allora l'anima mia gustò il bene degl'Immortali, ricevendo quello sommo bene con loro insieme: ma ora pareva come una cosa riservata; perocchè nel corpo a me non pareva essere, ma vedevo il corpo mio come se fussi stata un altro."

34. For a collection of essays on the Schism, several of which deal with St. Catherine's role in trying to end it, see *Genèse et débuts du Grand Schisme d'Occident, Avignon, 25–28 septembre 1978*, ed. Jean Favier et al. (Paris: Editions du Centre National de la Recherche Scientifique, 1980).

35. L. 371, in *Lettere*, 5: 274: "'Ragguarda dunque con dolore e amaritudine, e vedrai che a questa Sposa non si va se non per lo vestimento di fuore, cioè per la sustanzia temporale. Ma tu la vedi bene vota di quelli che cerchino il mirollo d'essa, cioè il frutto del sangue. . . . Ma io mi dolgo che io non trovo chi ci ministri. Anco, pare che ognuno l'abbia abandonata. Ma io sarò remediatore.'"

36. Ibid., p. 275: "E crescendo il dolore e il fuoco del desiderio, gridava nel cospetto di Dio dicendo: 'Che posso fare, o inestimabile fuoco?' E la sua benignità rispondeva: 'Che tu di nuovo offeri la vita tua.'"

37. Ibid., pp. 275–76.

38. Ibid., p. 277: "E attendevo pure a quello che si poteva fare, che io facessi sacrifizio di me a Dio per la santa Chiesa, e per tollere la ignoranzia e la negligenzia a quelli che Dio m'aveva messi nelle mani."

39. Ibid.: "'O Dio eterno, ricevi il sacrifizio della vita mia in questo corpo mistico della santa Chiesa. Io non ho che dare altro se non quello che tu hai dato a me. Tolli il cuore dunque, e premilo sopra la faccia di questa Sposa.'"

40. Ibid.: "Allora Dio eterno, vollendo l'occhio della clemenzia sua, divelleva il cuore, e premevalo nella santa Chiesa. E con tanta forza l'aveva tratto a sè, che, se non che subito (non volendo che 'l vasello del corpo mio fusse rotto) il ricerchiò della fortezza sua, ne sarebbe andata la vita."

41. Ibid., p. 278.

42. Ibid.: "Non è dunque nè sarà sconfitto il dimonio per lo patire dei corpi nostri, ma nella virtù del fuoco della divina ardentissima e inestimabile carità." See *Dialogo*, chaps. 5 and 12, pp. 12, 31.

43. Two recent studies connecting medieval discussions of the heart with spirituality and iconography are Eric Jager, "The Book of the Heart: Reading and Writing the Medieval Subject," *Speculum* 71 (1996): 1–26; and Jeffrey F. Hamburger, *Nuns as Artists: The Visual Culture of a Medieval Convent* (Berkeley: University of California Press, 1997), pp. 137–75.

44. *Legenda*: 179–80.

45. *Dialogo*, chap. 15, p. 44.

46. L. 373, in *Lettere*, 5: 286.

47. Ibid., p. 285: "O padre dolcissimo, io non vi tacerò i misteri grandi di Dio; ma narrerogli il più breve che si potrà, secondo che la fragile lingua potrà narrando esprimere . . . ; io non so quello che la divina bontà si farà di me, o del farmi rimanere, o del chiamarmi a sè."

48. Ibid., p. 287: "E stando così per grandissimo spazio, tanto che la famiglia mi piangeva come morta; in questo, tutto il terrore delle dimonia era andato via. Poi venne la presenza dell'umile Agnello dinanzi all'anima mia, dicendo: 'Non dubitare; chè io compirò i desiderii tuoi e degli altri servi miei. Io voglio che tu vegga che io sono maestro buono, che fa il vasellaio, il quale disfà e rifà i vaselli, come è di suo piacere. Questi miei vaselli io li so disfare e rifare: e però io piglio il vasello del corpo tuo, e rifollo nel giardino della santa Chiesa, con altro modo che per lo tempo passato?'"

49. Ibid., p. 289: "Quando egli è l'ora della terza, e io mi levo dalla messa, e voi vedreste andare una morta a Santo Pietro; ed entro di nuovo a lavorare nella navicella della santa Chiesa."

50. Ibid., pp. 289–90: "Mi pare che questo tempo io il debba confermare con uno nuovo martirio nella dolcezza dell'anima mia, cioè nella santa Chiesa: poi, forse che mi farà resuscitare con lui; porrà fine e termine sì alle mie miserie e sì a'crociati desiderii. O egli terrà i suoi modi usati, di ricerchiare il corpo mio."

51. This is Pt. 3, chap. 2 of the *Legenda*: 345–48, pp. 948–49.

52. *Legenda*: 345, p. 948 col. 2: "Ut ipsa mihi scripsit per quamdam suam epistolam, vidit in spiritu totam urbem plenam daemonibus, qui undique incitabant ad parricidii scelus, et contra orantem virginem horribiles dabant clamores."

53. *Legenda*: 246, p. 949 col. 1: "In hac disputatione, si non male recolo, plures occupavit dies ac noctes, cum magna corpusculi sui afflictione pariter et labore; illa semper orante, Dominoque suam justitiam allegante: ac daemonibus contra eam clamantibus, ut est scriptum, tantus fervor erat orantis, quod, sicut ipsa tunc mihi scripsit, nisi Dominus (ut modo ejus loquar) circulasset fortitudine corpus ejus, sicut veges solet circulis roborari et stringi, absque dubio corpusculum totaliter defecisset et concrepuisset."

54. Ibid.: ". . . quicquid poenalitatis debetur super hunc populum, fiat supra corpus meum: libentissime namque, pro tui nominis honore ac pro Ecclesia tua sancta, bibam hunc calicem passionis et mortis. . . . Factumque est, quod ex illa hora cessavit primo paulatim et tandem totaliter murmur in populo illo: sed totam passionem virgo virtutibus plena portavit. Nam infernales illi serpentes super virginale corpusculum licentia obtenta, ex divina permissione, tanta cum crudelitate suum ostenderunt furorem."

55. Raymond's relative discretion about Catherine's apostolates has caused some recent commentators not to focus on the relatively few passages where he does mention them, and to portray the *Legenda* Catherine (and the historical Catherine in general) almost exclusively as an ascetic and mystical holy woman. See, for example, Rudolph M. Bell, *Holy Anorexia* (Chicago: University of Chicago

Press, 1985), pp. 22–53; Caroline Walker Bynum, *Holy Feast and Holy Fast: The Religious Significance of Food to Medieval Women* (Berkeley: University of California Press, 1987), pp. 165–80.

56. *Legenda*: 178, p. 907 col. 1: "Tanta superabundavit in ea gratiae plenitudo, quod quasi continue in actuali contemplatione occupabatur; et spiritus ejus tam fixe suo inhaerebat et omnium Conditori, quod partem inferiorem et sensitivam, pro majori parte temporis, relinquebat absque actibus sensitivis . . . dum illi contemplationi actuali vacabat. Oculi clausi erant ex toto, aures nullum quantumcumque magnum sonum percipiebant, et omnes sensus corporei proprio actu pro tunc erant privati."

57. *Legenda*: 180.

58. *Legenda*: 182, p. 908 col. 1: "Unde dicebat Fratri Thomae Confessori suo: Non videtis vos, Pater, quod non sum illa quae fui, sed mutata sum in aliam personam? . . . Tantum gaudium tantaque jubilatio possidet mentem meam, quod grandis est mihi admiratio, qualiter anima potest stare in corpore."

59. *Legenda*: 184–87.

60. *Legenda*: 190–91.

61. *Legenda*: 192–93.

62. *Legenda*: 194–95. For the iconographic tradition used by Raymond, see Chiara Frugoni, "Des Stigmates," in *Catherine de Sienne: Grande Chapelle du Palais des Papes, Avignon, 1992* (Avignon: Imprimerie Laffont, 1992), pp. 57–71.

63. *Legenda*: 196–98.

64. *Legenda*: 206.

65. *Legenda*: 207, 212.

66. *Legenda*: 212–13, p. 914 col. 2: "Experta namque fuerat experimento sensibili, quantum eam Salvator simul et humanum genus dilexerat, sustinendo tam acerbissimam passionem: ex quo fiebat in corde suo tanta violentia caritativa et amorosa, quod fas non erat cor illud in sua integritate manere, quin scinderetur ex toto. Sic enim contingit cum vas aliquod continet liquorem magnae virtutis sive vigoris virtualiter excellentis, quod ex vi contenti frangitur continens; et virtus arctata, dissipato arctante, diffunditur; quia non erat inter locum et locatum aequa proportio. . . . Tanta fuit vis amoris illius, quod cor virginis scissum est a summo usque deorsum."

67. *Legenda*: 213–16.

68. *Legenda*: 216, p. 915 col. 2: "Multarum animarum salus requirit ut redeas, nec amplius modum vivendi tenebis, quem tenuisti huc usque, nec cellam pro habitaculo habebis de cetero: quin potius et urbem te propriam egredi oportebit pro animarum salute. Ego autem semper tecum ero, et ducam et reducam: portabisque nominis mei honorem et spiritalia documenta coram parvis et magnis, tam laicis quam clericis et religiosis: ego enim tibi dabo os et sapientiam, cui nullus resistere poterit. Adducam etiam te coram Pontificibus et Rectoribus Ecclesiarum ac populi Christiani, ut consueto meo modo, per infirma fortiorum confundam superbiam."

69. See Karen Scott, " 'This is why I have put you among your neighbors': St. Bernard's and St. Catherine's Understanding of the Love of God and Neighbor," in *Atti del Simposio*, pp. 279–94.

Chapter 9. Authorizing a Life: The Collaboration of Dorothea of Montau and John Marienwerder

1. *Vita Dorotheae Montoviensis Magistri Johannis Marienwerder* 1.6.m; ed. Hans Westpfahl (hereafter cited as *Vita latina*), Forschungen und Quellen zur Kirchen- und Kulturgeschichte Ostdeutschlands, vol. 1 (Cologne and Graz: Böhlau, 1964), p. 44.

2. Occasionally, scholars have tried to argue in favor of Dorothea's literacy, at least in the vernacular. See especially Richard Stachnik, ed., "Die Geistliche Lehre der Frau Dorothea von Montau an ihre Tochter im Frauenkloster zu Kulm," *Zeitschrift für Ostforschung* 3 (1954): 589–90. John Marienwerder, however, draws attention to Dorothea's illiteracy many times, and certain testimonies at her process for canonization seem to concur with this assessment. See in particular Bishop John Mönch's questioning of Dorothea when he saw her holding one of the pages on which her revelations had been recorded. Thus the bishop asked if she had ever learned her letters, all the time knowing her to be illiterate ("cum tamen ipse deponens sciret ipsam esse sine literis et ydeotam"). This provoked her celebrated answer that God had taught her to read three letters: the first concerned the multitude of her sins; the second, the pain of Christ's passion; the third, the rejoicing of the blessed (Richard Stachnik, ed., *Die Akten des Kanonisationsprozesses Dorotheas von Montau von 1394 bis 1521* [Cologne and Vienna: Böhlau, 1978], pp. 418–19). A version of this story was incorporated into the *Vita latina* (1.2.a–d, pp. 32–33). There were in total three sets of articles drawn up for purposes of interrogation, although most witnesses responded to the third and most comprehensive set. The pertinent set of articles in any given testimony is represented by the Roman numeral prefix. Though John Mönch responded to the third set, his comment was not made in response to any particular article, but appended to his testimony.

3. See particularly the work of John Coakley on this subject: "Friars as Confidants of Holy Women in Medieval Dominican Hagiography," in *Images of Sainthood in Medieval Europe*, ed. Renate Blumenfeld-Kosinski and Timea Szell (Ithaca, N.Y.: Cornell University Press, 1991), pp. 222–46; idem, "Gender and the Authority of Friars: The Significance of Holy Women for Thirteenth-Century Fransciscans and Dominicans," *Church History* 60 (1991): 445–60. Also see Janette Dillon, "Holy Women and Their Confessors or Confessors and Their Holy Women? Margery Kempe and the Continental Tradition," in *Prophets Abroad: The Reception of Continental Holy Women in Late-Medieval England*, ed. Rosalynn Voaden (Cambridge: D. S. Brewer, 1996), pp. 115–40; Elizabeth Avilda Petroff, "Male Confessors and Female Penitents: Possibilities for Dialogue," in *Body and Soul: Essays on Medieval Women and Mysticism* (New York and Oxford: Oxford University Press, 1994), pp. 139–60. Dyan Elliott, "*Dominae* or *Dominatae*? Female Mysticism and the Trauma of Textuality," in *Women, Marriage, and Family in Medieval Christendom: Essays in Memory of Michael M. Sheehan*, ed. Joel Rosenthal and Constance Rousseau (Kalamazoo, Mich.: Medieval Institute Publications, 1998), pp. 47–77. For the later period, see Jodi Bilinkoff, "Confessors, Penitents, and the Construction of Identities in Early Modern Avila," in *Culture and Identity in Early Modern*

Europe (1500–1800), ed. Barbara B. Diefendorf and Carla Hesse (Ann Arbor: University of Michigan Press, 1994), pp. 83–100.

4. On John's academic career before his move to Marienwerder, see Franz Hipler's article (as revised by Hans Westpfahl), "Johannes Marienwerder, der Beichtvater der seligen Dorothea von Montau," *Zeitschrift für die Geschichte und Altertumskunde Ermlands* 29, 1 (1956): 6–14, 27–32; Heribert Rossmann, "Johannes Marienwerder O.T., ein ostdeutscher Theologe des späten Mittelalters," in *Sacrum Pragense Millennium, 973–1973*, ed. Augustinus Kurt Huber, Archiv für Kirchengeschichte von Böhmen-Mähren-Schlesien, 3 (Königstein: Königsteiner Institut für Kirchen- und Geistesgeschichte der Sudetenländer, 1973), pp. 221–33. On her background and her arrival in Marienwerder, see Hipler, "Johannes Marienwerder," pp. 36–42. For Dorothea's pre-Marienwerder days, see Hans Westpfahl, "Beiträge zur Dorotheenforschung," *Zeitschrift für die Geschichte und Altertumskunde Ermlands* 27 (1939): 123–76.

5. Dorothea represented something of an unlikely choice, however, since according to Hipler, John was hitherto sceptical about mystical spirituality, as is evident from his earlier works ("Johannes Marienwerder," pp. 15–26).

6. Michel de Certeau is certainly the most original and eloquent spokesperson on the authorization of mystic speech. See his *Mystic Fable*, vol. 1, *The Sixteenth and Seventeenth Centuries*, trans. Michael B. Smith (Chicago and London: University of Chicago Press, 1992), esp. section 3, "The Circumstances of the Mystic Utterance," pp. 153–200; idem, "Discourse Disturbed: The Sorcerer's Speech," in *The Writing of History*, trans. Tom Conley (New York: Columbia University Press, 1988), pp. 244–68, esp. 246–48.

7. This examination is described in *Vita Lindana* chap. 56, in *AASS*, October, vol. 13 (Paris, 1883), p. 530 (note that the chapter references in this essay refer to the original numbering, which appears in the margins of the Bollandist edition). The later *Vita latina*, moreover, makes it clear that she was examined at the beginning of her relationship with John as well as before her enclosure as an anchoress (3.28.e, g, pp. 150, 151). Cf. article III, 18 in the process of canonization (*Akten des Kanonisationsprozesses*, pp. 21–22). On John Reyman, see Hipler, "Johannes Marienwerder," p. 42; and the entry in *Altpreussische Biographie*, ed. Christian Krollmann (Marburg and Lahn: N. G. Elwert, 1974), 1: 307. John Reyman was made head of the cathedral chapter at Marienwerder in 1388, and became bishop of Pomerania in 1409. Throughout the Dorothean corpus, Reyman is referred to as the *Praepositus*, while Marienwerder is called the *Confessor*.

8. This is only conjecture based on the fact that Mönch seemed to have also conducted his own, somewhat informal, examination of Dorothea, as aspects of his testimony in the process of canonization suggest (see *Akten des Kanonisationsprozesses*, III, ad 5, p. 413; III, ad 22, p. 417; III, ad 26, p. 418). In one of Dorothea's visions, for example, Christ mystically sent her before the bishop, who had told Dorothea earlier that he wanted a vision revealed to him (*Liber de festis* chap. 92, in *AASS*, October, 13: 582). Also, note that Dorothea's enclosure as an anchoress would require the bishop's cooperation and presence. On Mönch, see *Altpreussische Biographie*, 1: 306.

9. I am adopting the titles used by modern scholars to designate these

works. The *Vita prima* and the *Vita Lindana* (the latter so-named for its eighteenth-century editor) are both printed in *AASS*, October, 13: 493–99, 499–560. The full title of the *Liber de festis* is *Apparitiones venerabilis dominae Dorotheae seu Liber de festis*. It is still unedited. See MS Theol. Lat. fol. 207, Universitätsbibliothek, Tübingen, fols. 142v–217v; and MS Mar. F. 260, Stadtbibliothek, Danzig. I have only been able to consult the excerpts included in *AASS*, October, 13: 579–84 as well as in the *Scriptores rerum Prussicarum*, ed. Max Töppen (Leipzig: S. Hirzel, 1863), 2: 367–74. The citation for the *Vita latina* is given in n. 1 above. It incorporates most of the *Vita Lindana* verbatim. The *Septililium* was edited by Franz Hipler and printed in *AB* 2 (1883): 381–472 (treatise 1); 3 (1884): 113–40, 408–48 (treatises 2–3); 4 (1885): 207–51 (treatises 4–7). Some of Dorothea's confessions in the vernacular are appended to the conclusion of the work. They are edited by Franz Hipler as "Die Beichten der seligen Dorothea von Montau," *Zeitschrift für die Geschichte und Altertumskunde Ermlands* 6 (1877): 147–83. The *Vita germanica*, entitled *Des Leben der zeligen Frawen Dorothee Clewsenerynne in der Thumkyrchen czu Marienwerdir des Landes czu Prewszen*, is edited by Töppen in *Scriptores rerum Prussicarum*, 2: 197–350. In addition, there is also a short rule of life that Dorothea intended for her only surviving child, Gertrude, who became a nun ("Die Geistliche Lehre," pp. 589–96. For full reference, see n. 1 above). In addition to these major works, there is also the *Libellus de vita*—a short treatise summarizing Dorothea's virtues that was written for inclusion in Dorothea's process (*Akten des Kanonisationsprozesses*, pp. 297–327). For John's literary production on Dorothea, see Hipler, "Johannes Marienwerder," pp. 62–73; Richard Stachnik, "Zur Veröffentlichung der grossen Lebensbeschreibung Dorotheas von Montau von Johannes Marienwerder," *Zeitschrift für Ostforschung* 17 (1968): 713–17.

For an analysis of the *Vita germanica*, see Ute Stargardt, "Male Clerical Authority in the Spiritual (Auto)biographies of Medieval Holy Women," in *Women as Protagonists and Poets in the German Middle Ages*, ed. Albrecht Classen (Göppingen: Kümmerle, 1991), pp. 209–38, esp. 214ff.

10. For Nicholas, see *Altpreussische Biographie*, 2: 470.

11. This chronology for Dorothea's life is based on the appendix in Stachnik's edition of the *Vita latina*, pp. 409–18. Note, however, that Stachnik's reconstruction was facilitated by John Marienwerder's great attention to chronology, indicating precise dates for various revelations (usually via feast days) as well as noting the time elapsed between major spiritual events in Dorothea's life.

12. On the penitential movement and the gradual change in previous views of the incompatibility of marriage and sanctity, see André Vauchez, *La Sainteté en Occident aux derniers siècles du moyen âge d'après les procès de canonisation et les documents hagiographiques*, Bibliothèque des Etudes Françaises d'Athènes et de Rome 241 (Rome: Ecole Française de Rome, 1981), pp. 316–18, 412–13; Dyan Elliott, *Spiritual Marriage: Sexual Abstinence in Medieval Wedlock* (Princeton, N.J.: Princeton University Press, 1993), pp. 195–205. On Bridget of Sweden and her influence on Dorothea, see Clarissa Atkinson, *Mystic and Pilgrim: The Book and the World of Margery Kempe* (Ithaca, N.Y.: Cornell University Press, 1983), pp. 168–81. Atkinson also demonstrates the way in which the models of these two holy matrons were, in turn, used by Margery Kempe.

13. Birgitta and Ulf also delayed the consummation of their marriage, which adds approximately a year to the total number of years of chastity. On Birgitta's and Dorothea's marriages in the context of their respective spiritualities, see Elliott, *Spiritual Marriage*, pp. 224–45.

14. For a discussion of Dorothea's spirituality within its contemporary religious context, see Richard Kieckhefer, *Unquiet Souls: Fourteenth-Century Saints and Their Religious Milieu* (Chicago and London: University of Chicago Press, 1984), esp. pp. 22–33, 117–18, 127–29.

15. This chronology emerges in Nicholas's testimony at the proceedings for canonization. See *Akten des Kanonisationsprozesses*, I, ad 5, p. 80; III, ad 11, p. 83.

16. See *Vita Lindana* chap. 13, *AASS*, October, 13: 506; *Vita latina* 2.22.b, p. 84. On the early assertion of women's spiritual vocation, see Donald Weinstein and Rudolph M. Bell, *Saints and Society: The Two Worlds of Western Christendom, 1000–1700* (Chicago and London: University of Chicago Press, 1982), pp. 42–44, 234–35.

17. For Dorothea's raptures in marriage and Adalbert's averse reactions, see esp. *Vita latina* 2.39–42, pp. 105–8; *Vita Lindana* chaps. 26–29, *AASS*, October, 13: 513–14. On Adalbert's abuse of Dorothea, see Elliott, *Spiritual Marriage*, pp. 230–31. Ute Stargardt argues that John deliberately falsified his portrait of Adalbert by demonizing him ("Male Clerical Authority," pp. 227, 231–32).

18. On the extraction of her heart and its spiritual consequences, see *Vita latina* 3.1–2, pp. 112–16; *Vita Lindana* chap. 35, *AASS*, October, 13: 517–18.

19. *Vita latina* 3.26.c, p. 147; *Vita Lindana* chap. 55, *AASS*, October, 13: 529.

20. *Vita latina* 3.27.e, p. 149; this is almost verbatim from *Vita Lindana* chap. 56, *AASS*, October, 13: 530.

21. *Vita latina* 2.14.a, p. 77; *Vita Lindana* chap. 1, *AASS*, October, 13: 504.

22. On Dorothea's wounds, see *Vita latina* 2.24, pp. 86–87; *Vita Lindana* chap. 17, *AASS*, October, 13: 508; and Kieckhefer, *Unquiet Souls*, p. 27.

23. Raymond of Peñafort seemed to have introduced the concept of the penitential forum. See Pierre Michaud-Quantin, "A propros des prèmieres *Summae confessorum*," *Recherches de Théologie Ancienne et Médiévale* 26 (1959): 305.

24. *Vita latina* 3.28.h, p. 151; *Vita Lindana* chap. 56, *AASS*, October, 13: 530. There is considerable consensus on the necessity for Dorothea's stabilization from surprisingly different quarters. Christ glossed his desire to stabilize Dorothea in one fixed location, asserting that she was too often in a state of flux ("qui interdum fluctuabat"). Christ's rationale actually evokes the devil's ridicule of Dorothea, who often accused Dorothea of crazily running around from church to church in search of indulgences—thus tempting her to the sin of diffidence (*Vita latina* 2.34.n, p. 98; *Vita Lindana* chap. 20, *AASS*, October, 13: 209). The devil's charge is echoed by Adalbert who, interestingly, chained Dorothea up for several days in an effort to prevent her from running around and thereby neglecting her domestic duties (*Vita latina* 2.41.b, p. 107; *Vita Lindana* chap. 28, *AASS*, October, 13: 514). Note that the depth of Dorothea's feeling for John was apparently reciprocated as the tenth of the twenty-four proofs concerning the authenticity of her visions was her miraculous intuition that John loved her more than any of his other spiritual daughters or even more than his own brother—as did John Reyman (*Vita latina*

1.6.l, pp. 43–44). In the *Vita Lindana*, where only three proofs of visionary authenticity are given, John Marienwerder's love for Dorothea still figures as the third (see chap. 56, *AASS*, October, 13: 531). John's love for Dorothea is also an aspect of article III, 18 in her process (*Akten des Kanonisationsprozesses*, pp. 21–22).

25. *Vita latina* 3.28.i, p. 151; *Vita Lindana* chap. 56, *AASS*, October, 13: 530.

26. On the particular obedience to confessors that characterizes the spirituality of many pious laywomen, see Elliott, *Spiritual Marriage*, pp. 261–64.

27. *Vita latina* 4.19.d, p. 177.

28. *Vita latina* 5.4.b, p. 216.

29. *Vita Lindana* chap. 69, *AASS*, October, 13: 540. The *Vita latina* goes into considerable detail about Dorothea's life in the *reclusorium* (5.6, pp. 218–20). Her confessor's absolute control over her movements is also the substance of article III, 19 of her process (*Akten des Kanonisationsprozesses*, p. 22).

30. *Vita latina* 1.6.s, p. 46. This is part of the sixteenth proof concerning the authenticity of her visions. Cf. the incident in which God suggests that John should be absolved from all jobs except writing Dorothea's visions—a portion of the last of these twenty-four proofs (1.6.z, p. 49). Similarly, when John Reyman began to spend more time with Dorothea toward the end of her life, Christ mystically articulated his approval, commenting favorably on the presence of both confessors since later they would be able "to testify" (7.19.g, p. 356).

31. *Vita latina* 5.15.f, p. 235.

32. *Vita latina* 1.6.n, p. 44.

33. "Confessio autem ejus fuit discreta, recollecta; festina, voluntaria, lacrimosa, integra, indivisa, propria, vera, nuda et bene circumstantionata" (*Septililium* 7.2, *AB* 4 (1885): 244. Raymond states that a true confession should be bitter, speedy (i.e., not delayed), entire, and frequent. Each of these categories was, in turn, subdivided. A bitter confession required shame, humility, tears (*lacrimae*), fortitude in conquering embarrassment, and the inclination of obedience. There are four reasons for a speedy (*festina*) confession: that the hour of death is uncertain, that sin accumulates in the course of delay, that accumulation of sin distances one from God, that in extreme sickness penance (and sometimes even thought) is impossible, and that communication with God in this life strengthens our position in the next. An entire (*integra*) confession means that an individual's confession in its entirety should be made to one priest, and not divided among several. Such a confession has nine characteristics: it should be orthodox, personal (*propria*, i.e., only implicating oneself), self-accusing, true (*vera*), naked (*nuda*, i.e., in person and not by proxy—detailing all of the circumstances), pure (in intention), and morose (i.e., dwelling on one's own sins in order to kindle greater contrition and devotion). Finally, the term "frequent" can be understood in two ways. The first denotes that an individual who frequently falls by sin can be frequently raised through penance. The second interpretation implies that a person should frequently confess the same sins, although he or she is only bound to do so in certain cases (Raymond of Peñafort, *Summa de paenitentia* ed. Xavier Ochoa and Aloisius Diez, Universa Bibliotheca Iuris, vol. 1, pt. B (Rome: Commentarium pro religiosis, 1976), 3.34.23–29, cols. 817–26.

The categories for which I have provided the Latin adjectives correspond directly with John's description of Dorothea's confessional practice. John also adds *recollecta, indivisa,* and *bene circumstantionata.* All these are simply glosses on the category immediately preceding: that is, *discreta, integra,* and *nuda* respectively. On the preeminent significance of Raymond's *Summa* and his importance in the development of auricular confession in the high and later Middle Ages, see Amadeus Teetaert, "La doctrine pénitentielle de Saint Raymond de Penyafort, O.P.," *Analecta Sacra Tarraconensia* 5 (1929): 121–82, esp. 145ff.

34. Raymond of Peñafort, *Summa de paenitentia* 3.34.21, cols. 816–17.

35. *Vita latina* 2.20.b, p. 81; 7.6.g, p. 336.

36. *Vita latina* 7.26.f, p. 366. On women's eucharistic devotion, see Caroline Walker Bynum, *Holy Feast and Holy Fast: The Religious Significance of Food to Medieval Women* (Berkeley and Los Angeles: University of California Press, 1987), esp. pp. 136–37, where Dorothea's case is discussed.

37. Jacques de Vitry, *Vita B. Mariae Oigniacensis* 1.2.6, *AASS,* June, vol. 5 (Paris and Rome, 1867), p. 551. Also see Dillon, "Holy Women and Their Confessors," pp. 119–22 (see n. 3 above).

38. *Vita latina* 2.7.b, p. 73; *Vita Lindana* chap. 7, *AASS,* October, 13: 505.

39. The confessor is described as doctor in the same constitution which mandated annual confession at Lateran IV (const. 21, *Decrees of the Ecumenical Councils,* ed. and trans. Norman Tanner et al. [London: Sheed and Ward; Washington, D.C.: Georgetown University Press, 1990], 1: 245); cf. Raymond of Peñafort's evocation and discussion of this text (*Summa paenitentia* 3.34.29, cols. 826–27).

40. *Vita latina* 3.19.d–e, p. 138; *Vita Lindana* chap. 51, *AASS,* October, 13: 527.

41. *Vita latina* 3.19.f, p. 138; cf. *Vita Lindana* chap. 51, *AASS,* October, 13: 527. The long duration alludes to the fact that Dorothea had to wait for a number of hours before John arrived. For a lengthy discussion of the impact of the wounds of sin on the soul, see *Septililium* 7.3, *AB* 4 (1885): 245–47; also see 7.1, p. 243.

42. *Vita latina* 2.7.b, p. 73; *Vita Lindana* chap. 7, *AASS,* October, 13: 505.

43. *Vita latina* 3.2.a–b, p. 114; 3.2.m, p. 115; *Vita Lindana* chap. 35, *AASS,* October, 13: 517–18.

44. *Vita latina* 3.2.e–g, pp. 114–15; almost verbatim in *Vita Lindana* chap. 35, *AASS,* October, 13: 518.

45. *Vita latina* 3.2.l, p. 115; *Vita Lindana* chap. 35, *AASS,* October, 13: 518.

46. *Vita latina* 3.2.h–i, p. 115; *Vita Lindana* chap. 35, *AASS,* October, 13: 518.

47. When Dorothea demurred slightly, saying that she no longer had sufficient sorrow over these sins since they had been forgiven, she was told that if she could not confess from compunction she should confess from love (*Septililium* 7.6, *AB* 4 [1885]: 251).

48. Raymond of Peñafort, *Summa paenitentiae* 3.34.29, col. 826. Note, however, that a person is only bound to do this in certain special cases: if, for instance, the priest was inexperienced; or if penance had been ignored; or if the sin was so grievous that it was redirected to the priest's superior (3.34.56, cols. 858–59). Penance must also be repeated when either the penitent relapsed or never reformed in the first place (3.34.53, col. 854). Also see John of Freiburg, *Summa confessorum* 3.34.70 (Rome: s.n., 1518), fols. 191r–v.

49. John of Freiburg, *Summa confessorum* 3.34.85, fol. 193v.

50. *Vita Lindana* chap. 40, *AASS*, October, 13: 520; cf. *Septililium* 7.2, *AB* 4 (1885): 245.

51. See Bynum, *Holy Feast*, pp. 227–37; Coakley, "Friars as Confidants," pp. 236–38; Dillon, "Holy Women and Their Confessors," pp. 128–31. Also note that Dorothea manages to solicit God's cooperation in healing the wounds in the soul of another (presumably John). See *Septililium* 7.3, *AB* 4 (1885): 246.

52. Thus Francis writes in his *Testament*: "I am determined to reverence, love and honour priests. . . . I refuse to consider their sins, because I see the Son of God in them and they are better than I. I do this because in this world I cannot see the most high Son of God with my own eyes, except for his most holy Body and Blood which they receive and alone administer to others," in *St. Francis of Assisi, Writings and Early Biographies: English Omnibus of the Sources for the Life of St. Francis*, ed. Marion A. Habig (Chicago: Franciscan Herald Press, 1973), p. 67. Also see Bynum, *Holy Feast*, pp. 57, 99.

53. John of Freiburg, *Summa confessorum* 3.34.91, fol. 194r.

54. *Vita latina* 6.4.a–b, pp. 293–94.

55. *Septililium* 7.2, *AB* 4 (1885): 244–45. See Raymond of Peñafort, *Summa de paenitentia* 3.34.12, cols. 809–10.

56. Raymond of Peñafort, *Summa de paenitentia* 3.34.31, col. 828. Cf. John of Freiburg, *Summa confessorum* 3.34.82–83, fols. 192v–93r.

57. Raymond of Peñafort, *Summa de paenitentia* 3.34.30, col. 827. On the importance and widespread use of interrogation in confession, see Thomas N. Tentler, *Sin and Confession on the Eve of the Reformation* (Princeton, N.J.: Princeton University Press, 1977), pp. 88–95.

58. See Esther N. Goody's "Towards a Theory of Questions," in *Questions and Politeness: Strategies in Social Interaction*, ed. Esther N. Goody (Cambridge: Cambridge University Press, 1978), pp. 17–43, esp. 39–43.

59. *Septililium* 7.4, *AB* 4 (1885): 247–48. Similarly, Jean Gerson associates the interrogatory method with the more difficult cases, since the prepared penitent—if not suffused with modesty—is ready to "vomit forth his virus" unassisted (*De cognitione castitatis*, in *Oeuvres complètes*, ed. M. Glorieux [Paris: Desclée and Cie, 1973]), 9: 63.

60. With regard to confession, the Lord urged Dorothea to examine her life carefully, her body, and her soul—using the analogy of a rich man doing a meticulous inventory of his house. She should, in turn, gather the resulting reflections into an appropriate confession (*Septililium* 7.2, *AB* 4 [1885]: 244).

61. *Vita latina* 1.7.g, p. 51.

62. *Vita latina* 1.1.f, p. 31.

63. *Vita latina* 1.6.b, p. 41.

64. *Vita latina* 2.14.c, p. 77; *Vita Lindana* chap. 14, *AASS*, October, 13: 507.

65. *Vita Lindana* chap. 59, *AASS*, October, 13: 538.

66. See *Septililium* 3.7–26, *AB* 3 (1884): 410–48. These chapters loosely correspond to *Vita Lindana* chaps. 58–68, *AASS*, October, 13: 535–40. As is clear from Catherine Mooney's analysis, the scribe-confessor to Angela of Foligno has a parallel function in shaping Angela's revelations. He also makes similar efforts to efface his endeavors. See "The Authorial Role of Brother A. in the Composition of Angela of Foligno's Revelations," in *Creative Women in Medieval and Early Mod-*

ern Italy: A Religious and Artistic Renaissance, ed. E. Ann Matter and John Coakley (Philadelphia: University of Pennsylvania Press, 1994), pp. 34–63.

67. Gerson, *De probatione spirituum* chap. 11, in *Oeuvres complètes*, 9: 184.

68. *Liber de festis* chap. 125, *AASS*, October, 13: 583. The name of the damned soul is represented as G., though John adds that this was not his real name (chap. 126, p. 584). There is little doubt that the unhappy soul was Konrad von Wallenrodt (d. 1393), former master of the Teutonic Order, whom Dorothea had criticized and who resisted Dorothea's growing reputation for sanctity. See Anneliese Triller, "Häresien in Altpreussen um 1390?" in *Studien zur Geschichte des Preussenlandes: Festschrift für Erich Keyser zu seinem 70. Geburtstag dargebracht von Freunden und Schülern*, ed. Ernst Bahr (Marburg: N. G. Elwert, 1963), p. 403; Ute Stargardt, "The Political and Social Backgrounds of the Canonization of Dorothea von Montau," *Mystics Quarterly* 11 (1985): 112–15. On Konrad, see *Altpreussische Biographie*, 2: 772.

69. *Liber de festis* chap. 92, *AASS*, October, 13: 583.

70. *Septililium* 7.6, *AB* 4 (1885): 251. The German confessions are edited separately by Hipler, as cited above in n. 9.

71. *Vita latina* 1.7.l, p. 52. I discuss some of the technicalities of the actual writing process in "*Dominae* or *Dominatae?*" pp. 57–60 (full citation in n. 3).

72. *Vita Lindana* chap. 84, *AASS*, October, 13: 553; *Septililium* 3.12, *AB* 3 (1884): 431–32.

73. *Septililium* 2.11, *AB* 3 (1884): 132.

74. *Vita latina* 1.6.u, pp. 46–47; 1.6.x, p. 48. Claims of divine censorship constitute the eighteenth and the twenty-first proofs of authenticity. For further discussion, see Elliott, "*Dominae* or *Dominatae?*" pp. 62–63.

75. *Vita latina* 1.6.t, p. 46; 1.6.z, p. 49. Also see God's requirement that Dorothea's revelation of the feast of the Virgin's conception be written in a new and beautiful script (*Liber de festis* chap. 92, *AASS*, October, 13: 583).

76. Certeau, "Discourse Disturbed," in *The Writing of History*, pp. 250, 254–55.

77. *Vita latina* 7.19.b, p. 354; *Vita Lindana* chap. 86, *AASS*, October, 13: 551.

78. *Vita latina* 4.20.a, p. 179.

79. See *Septililium* 3.12, 3.13, *AB* 3 (1884): 427, 434. John mentions in the latter citation that other "sentiments" are recorded in the *Liber de festis*. The "sentiments" in the *Vita Lindana* are discussed above in the context of John's subtle interrogatory.

80. *Vita latina* 4.2.b, p. 179; 1.7.k, p. 51; 1.6.s, p. 46 (the third reference constitutes the sixteenth proof of the visions' veracity); *Vita Lindana* chap. 79, *AASS*, October, 13: 551. Christ likewise claims that even if Dorothea could write, this ability would not avail her in expressing his mysteries. Dorothea seconds this, thinking to herself that the marvels she was experiencing were so inexhaustible that if all the world took up writing about her, this would still prove inadequate (*Septililium* 1.32, *AB* 2 [1883]: 465–66).

81. When this change came about is not entirely clear, but it is described in the eighteenth proof of the visions' authenticity (*Vita latina* 1.6.u, p. 46). God's

recommendation that she appeal directly to him for the words may be John's safer alternative to the suppressed interrogatory mode discussed with respect to the *Vita Lindana*.

82. This is the nineteenth of the twenty-four proofs of authenticity (*Vita latina* 1.6.v, p. 47). Cf. the sixteenth such proof, in which the same idiom is used (1.6.s, p. 45). With respect to the caresses that Dorothea receives from God (and which John wants to know more about), God tells Dorothea to explain to her confessor that the caresses are too fast and sweet. It would be impossible for her to explain them in words, unless God provided the words (*Vita latina* 4.35.c–d, p. 202).

83. *Vita Lindana* chap. 86, *AASS*, October, 13: 557; also see *Vita latina* 7.20.c, p. 357. On heaven as an image of stability, see *Vita Lindana* chap. 40, *AASS*, October, 13: 520.

84. Cf. Certeau's remark: "Possessed women's texts do not provide the skeleton key for their language, for it remains undecipherable even to themselves" ("Discourse Disturbed," in *The Writing of History*, p. 257).

85. *Septililium*, prologue, *AB* 2 (1883): 393–94; *Vita latina* 7.29.b, p. 371. According to John Marienwerder's testimony at the process of canonization, formerly there was yet another person privy to Dorothea's revelations—John Lubicz, the head of the cathedral chapter. But he was dead by the time of the canonization proceedings, being replaced by John Reyman (*Akten des Kanonisationsprozesses*, III, ad 8, p. 265).

86. *Vita latina* 4.10.e, pp. 166–67; *Septililium* 4.5, *AB* 4 (1885): 217. Also see *Vita latina* 2.19.d, p. 81, in which Dorothea also alludes to the many things she could express that she does not.

87. *Vita latina* 7.25.a, p. 363.

88. *Vita latina* 4.10.e, p. 167. Later in the same work, the Lord tells Dorothea that a person would die were he or she aware of all the good that was done to him or herself in the course of rapture (4.35.e, p. 203). This is, perhaps, consonant with the biblical injunction "no one may see God and live" (Ex. 33.20). See Dyan Elliott, "The Physiology of Rapture and Female Spirituality," in *Medieval Theology and the Natural Body*, ed. Peter Biller and A. J. Minnis (Woodbridge, Suffolk: York Medieval Press in association with Boydell and Brewer, 1997), p. 144.

89. *Vita latina* 4.20.f, p. 180; *Vita Lindana* chap. 26, *AASS*, October, 13: 513; also see *Septililium* 3.26, *AB* 3 (1884): 444.

90. *Vita latina* 2.15.a, p. 77.

91. *Vita latina* 2.19.a, p. 80; also see 2.19.d, p. 81.

92. *Vita latina* 2.17.d, pp. 79–80. Dorothea then understands that the part of her life that she is attempting to apprehend is God, but that her humanity is not strong enough to retain the divine presence for comprehension.

93. *Vita latina* 2.14.a–b, p. 77.

94. *Vita latina* 2.15.b, p. 78.

95. Thus the prologue of the *Vita latina* aligns Dorothea's life with the seven seals of the Apocalypse (chaps. 2–8, pp. 16–29). In the *Septililium*, by way of contrast, John attempts to place Dorothea's mystical experiences in the framework of other authorities such as Richard of St. Victor, as well as to justify any deviations

from earlier celebrated models (prologue, chap. 2, *AB* 1 [1883]: 394–98). John is careful to note, however, that any such alignment is his own doing, not Dorothea's (chap. 3, pp. 398–99).

96. *Vita latina* 1.6.y, p. 49.

97. *Septililium*, prologue, *AB* 2 (1883): 392–93. Later in the same work, Christ explicitly confirms John's qualms that a person who has not experienced divine charity is incapable of expressing it adequately (*Septililium* 1.34, *AB* 2 [1883]: 469).

98. On John's efforts for Dorothea's canonization, see Hipler, "Johannes Marienwerder," pp. 60–62; also see Stargardt, "The Political and Social Backgrounds," pp. 110–12, 115–18 (full citations in nn. 4 and 68, above, respectively). On the procedures for canonization in this period, see Vauchez, *La Saintéte*, pp. 39–67; Aviad M. Kleinberg, "Proving Sanctity: Selection and Authentication of Saints in the Later Middle Ages," *Viator* 20 (1989): 183–205, esp. 190ff; idem, *Prophets in Their Own Country: Living Saints and the Making of Sainthood in the Later Middle Ages* (Chicago: University of Chicago Press, 1992), pp. 26–32.

99. Stargardt, "The Social and Political Backgrounds," pp. 111–12; eadem, "Male Clerical Authority," p. 216 (full citations in nn. 68 and 9 above respectively).

100. *Vita latina* 7.25.f, p. 364; *Vita Lindana* chap. 87, *AASS*, October, 13: 557.

101. See, for example, the testimony of Cristanus Coslaw who was one such scribe (*Akten des Kanonisationsprozesses*, pp. 241–44, esp. III, ad 20, p. 243. Coslaw's miracle book is included in the process after his testimony (pp. 244–50).

102. In his testimony, John mentions the scribes by name, along with the fact that they publish the miracles daily in the church (*Akten des Kanonisationsprozesses*, III, ad 20, p. 283).

103. See Stachnik's introductory remarks to the third set of articles (*Akten des Kanonisationsprozesses*, p. 18).

104. See *Akten des Kanonisationsprozesses*, pp. 297–327.

105. *Akten des Kanonisationsprozesses*, III, ad 25, p. 287.

106. *Akten des Kanonisationsprozesses*, III, ad 25, p. 118.

107. See Triller, "Häresien in Altpreussen um 1390?" pp. 400–401; Stargardt, "Male Clerical Authority," p. 226 (full citations in nn. 68 and 9, above).

108. *Akten des Kanonisationsprozesses*, III, ad 20, p. 84.

109. *Akten des Kanonisationsprozesses*, III, ad 11, p. 107.

110. *Akten des Kanonisationsprozesses*, III, ad 20, p. 108. When Metza confessed to Dorothea that she had recently been avoiding her due to the suspicions of heresy, Dorothea gave the unsettling response that she was incapable of erring because she had one doctor and magistrate who teaches her, and all people, lovingly. Dorothea also said that she would gladly burn for her beliefs (p. 109). On these charges, also see Katherina Seveldische's testimony (III, ad 20, p. 117). The story of the heresy charges became known to the sacristan (*custos*) of the church of Pomerania as well, who heard it from one of her persecutors—a priest named Cristanus (III, ad 14, pp. 473–74). Dorothea's belief that she was incapable of erring could be construed as the kind of antinomian beliefs associated with the so-called Free Spirit movement of the early fourteenth century. See Robert E. Lerner, *The Heresy of the Free Spirit in the Later Middle Ages* (Berkeley and Los Angeles: University

of California Press, 1972). On Dorothea's possible susceptibility to this movement, see Triller, "Häresien in Altpreussen um 1390?" p. 399.

111. This impression is further solidified by Nicholas of Hohenstein, who learned of the extraction of Dorothea's heart in the course of confession (*Akten des Kanonisationsprozesses*, III, ad 21, p. 84).

112. The more punitive canonical view is articulated by Raymond of Peña-fort (*Summa de paenitentia* 3.34.62, cols. 866–67). Raymond was, significantly, at one time an inquisitor himself. But the more theologically inflected counsel, represented by John of Freiburg who upholds the position of Thomas Aquinas, entirely rejects any such pretext for disclosure, including heresy (*Summa confessorum* 3.34.91, fol. 194r).

113. *Vita latina* 3.9.a, p. 123; almost verbatim in *Vita Lindana* chap. 41, *AASS*, October, 13: 520.

114. *Vita latina* 3.26.b, p. 147; *Vita Lindana* chap. 55, p. 529.

115. *Akten des Kanonisationsprozesses*, III, ad 6, p. 96. Cf. Dorothea's similar disclosures to other witnesses: III, ad 8, p. 106; III, ad 5, p. 114; III, ad 5, pp. 138–39; III, ad 3, p. 141; III, ad 14, pp. 355–56.

116. *Akten des Kanonisationsprozesses*, chap. 4, p. 300.

117. *Akten des Kanonisationsprozesses*, III, ad 8, p. 83; III, ad 22, p. 84.

118. *Akten des Kanonisationsprozesses*, III, ad 17, p. 275; III, ad 17, p. 83. Although Nicholas apparently learned about the extraction of the heart from Dorothea herself (see n. 111 above), he only mentions this source after testifying to John's preaching on the event (III, ad 21, p. 84). Some of the other evocations of John's authority by Nicholas are: III, ad 6, p. 82; III, ad 18, pp. 83–84; III, ad 23, p. 85; III, ad 24, p. 85 (in which he mentions that he had read the *Vita Lindana*); III, ad 27, p. 85; III, ad 28, p. 85.

119. See the report for the proceedings on 27 June 1404 (*Akten des Kanonisationsprozesses*, p. 87).

120. As Stachnik's notes indicate, Reyman's answers are verbatim or almost verbatim in many places. Some of the most striking concurrences are: *Akten des Kanonisationsprozesses*, Reyman, III, ad 21, pp. 211–16, compared with *Libellus de vita* chaps. 25–30, 33, 34, pp. 313–15, 319; Reyman, III, ad 20, pp. 206–9, compared with *Libellus de vita* chaps. 37, 39, 40, pp. 320–22. The information flow seems to work both ways, however. Thus Reyman tells of an incident he witnessed which testified to the intensity of Dorothea's prayer life (III, ad 20, p. 210). John Marien-werder incorporates the anecdote almost verbatim into the *Libellus de vita* with the preface that he heard this "from a notable man" (chap. 45, p. 325).

121. Stargardt, "The Social and Political Backgrounds," pp. 118–19.

122. Gerson, *De probatione spirituum*, in *Oeuvres complètes*, 9: 177–85; trans. Paschal Boland, in *The Concept of "Discretio Spirituum" in John Gerson's "De probatione spirituum" and "De distinctione verarum visionum a falsis"* (Washington, D.C.: Catholic University of America, 1959), pp. 25–38. See especially, *Oeuvres complètes* chap. 5, 9: 179ff; trans. Boland, pp. 28ff. On Gerson's attack as well as the work of Birgitta's supporters, see Eric Colledge, "*Epistola solitarii ad reges*: Alphonse of Pecha as Organizer of Birgittine and Urbanist Propaganda," *Mediaeval Studies* 18 (1956): 19–49. Also see Jo Ann McNamara, "The Rhetoric of Orthodoxy: Clerical

Authority and Female Innovation in the Struggle with Heresy," in *Maps of Flesh and Light: The Religious Experience of Medieval Women Mystics*, ed. Ulrike Wiethaus (Syracuse, N.Y.: Syracuse University Press, 1993), pp. 24–27; Vauchez, *La Sainteté*, pp. 473–74.

123. Gerson, *De examinatione doctrinarum* 2.3, in *Oeuvres complètes*, 9: 469.

124. Gerson, *De distinctione revelationum*, in *Oeuvres complètes*, 3 (1963): 43. This woman, however, was not under the direction of any spiritual adviser and had not confessed for over a year. Even so, Gerson would have found Dorothea's divinely inspired taciturnity about aspects of her visions highly suspect.

The Saints and Their Interpreters

Selected Primary Sources in Original Languages

BEATRICE OF NAZARETH AND HER HAGIOGRAPHER

Beatrice of Nazareth. *Seven Manieren van Minne*. Ed. L. Reypens and J. Van Mierlo. Louvain: S. V. de Vlaamsche Boekenhalle, 1926.
The Life of Beatrice of Nazareth, 1200–1268. Ed. Léonce Reypens. Trans. Roger De Ganck. Kalamazoo, Mich.: Cistercian Publications, 1991. This gives the Latin text as well as an English translation.

CATHERINE OF SIENA AND RAYMOND OF CAPUA

Catherine of Siena. *Il Dialogo della divina provvidenza, ovvero Libro della divina dottrina*. Ed. Giuliana Cavallini. Rome: Edizioni Cateriniane, 1980.
———. *Le Lettere di S. Caterina da Siena*. 6 vols. Ed. Piero Misciattelli. Florence: Giunti, 1940.
———. *Le Orazioni*. Ed. Giuliana Cavallini. Rome: Edizioni Cateriniane, 1978.
Raymond of Capua. *Legenda Major: De S. Catharina Senensi virgine de poenitentia S. Dominici*. In *AASS*, April, 3: 862–967. Paris, 1866.

CHRISTINE OF STOMMELN AND PETER OF DACIA

Peter of Dacia. *De Gratia naturam ditante sive de virtutibus Christinae Stumbelensis*. Ed. Monika Asztalos. Stockholm: Almqvist and Wiksell, 1982.
———. *Vita Christinae Stumbelensis*. Ed. Johannes Paulson. Scriptores Latini Medii Aevi Suecani l. Göteborg: Wettergren and Kerber, 1896.

CLARE OF ASSISI, FRANCIS OF ASSISI, AND THEIR INTERPRETERS

Clare of Assisi et al. *Escritos de Santa Clara y Documentos Contemporáneos*. Ed. Ignacio Omaechevarría et al. Madrid: Biblioteca de Autores Cristianos, 1970; rev.

and enl., 1982. This contains Clare's corpus and key documents such as the *Legend*, the Process of Canonization, papal letters, and legislative texts, primarily in their original languages with Spanish translation.

Clare of Assisi and Francis of Assisi. *Concordantiae verbales opusculorum S. Francisci et S. Clarae Assisiensium*. Ed. Giovanni M. Boccali. Assisi: Edizioni Porziuncola, 1976; rev. and enl., 1995.

Clare of Assisi, Francis of Assisi, Thomas of Celano, Bonaventure, et al. *Fontes franciscani*. Ed. Enrico Menestò and Stefano Brufani. Assisi: Edizioni Porziuncola, 1995. This contains the writings of Clare of Assisi and Francis of Assisi, eighteen major texts about Francis, and two legends and the process of canonization for Clare.

DOROTHEA OF MONTAU AND JOHN MARIENWERDER

Die Akten des Kanonisationsprozesses Dorotheas von Montau von 1394 bis 1521 (= Vita latina). Ed. Richard Stachnik. Cologne and Vienna: Böhlau, 1978.

John Marienwerder. *Des Leben der zeligen Frawen Dorothee Clewsenerynne in der Thumkyrchen czu Marienwerdir des Landes czu Prewszen (= Vita germanica)*. Ed. Max Töppen. In *Scriptores rerum Prussicarum* 2: 197–350. Leipzig: S. Hirzel, 1863.

———. *Vita B. Dorotheae Lindana*. In *AASS*, October, 13: 499–560. Paris, 1883.

———. *Vita prima B. Dorotheae*. In *AASS*, October, 13: 493–99. Paris, 1883.

John Marienwerder and Dorothea of Montau. *Apparitiones venerabilis dominae Dorotheae seu Liber de festis (= Liber de festis)*. MS Theol. Lat. fol. 207, Universitätsbibliothek, Tübingen; and MS Mar. F. 260, Stadtbibliothek, Danzig. Excerpts in *AASS*, October, 13: 579–84. Paris, 1883. Excerpts in *Scriptores rerum Prussicarum* 2: 367–74. Ed. Max Töppen. Leipzig: S. Hirzel, 1863.

———. "Die Beichten der seligen Dorothea von Montau," ed. Franz Hipler. (Confessions in German appended to the *Septililium*.) *Zeitschrift für die Geschichte und Altertumskunde Ermlands* 6 (1877): 147–83.

———. "Die Geistliche Lehre der Frau Dorothea von Montau an ihre Tochter im Frauenkloster zu Kulm," ed. Richard Stachnik. *Zeitschrift für Ostforschung* 3 (1954): 589–96.

———. *Septililium*. Ed. Franz Hipler. *AB* 2 (1883): 381–472; 3 (1884): 113–40, 408–48; 4 (1885): 207–51.

ELISABETH OF SCHÖNAU, EKBERT OF SCHÖNAU, AND EMECHO OF SCHÖNAU

Ekbert of Schönau. *De Obitu Elisabeth*. Vienna, Österreische Nationalbibliothek Vindob. Pal. MS 488, fol. 166r–72r.

Ekbert of Schönau and Elisabeth of Schönau. "Aus einer Handschrift der Schriften der heil. Elisabeth von Schönau," ed. F. W. E. Roth. *Neues Archiv der Gesellschaft für ältere deutsche Geschichtskunde* 36 (1911): 221.

Ekbert of Schönau, Elisabeth of Schönau, and Emecho of Schönau. *Die Visionen der hl. Elisabeth und die Schriften der Aebte Ekbert und Emecho von Schönau.* Ed. F. W. E. Roth. Brünn: Verlag der Studien aus dem Benedictiner- und Cistercienser-Orden, 1884.

Emecho of Schönau. *Vita Eckeberti.* Ed. S. Widmann. *Neues Archiv der Gesellschaft für ältere deutsche Geschichtskunde* 11 (1886): 447–54.

HENRY SUSO AND ELSBETH STAGEL

Stagel, Elsbeth. *Das Leben der Schwestern zu Töss beschrieben von Elsbet Stagel samt der Vorrede von Johannes Meier und dem Leben der Prinzessin Elisabet von Ungarn.* Ed. Ferdinand Vetter. Berlin: Weidmann, 1906.

Suso, Henry. *Deutsche Schriften.* Ed. Karl Bihlmeyer. Stuttgart: Kohlhammer, 1907.

———. *Heinrich Seuse's Horologium sapientiae.* Ed. Pius Künzle, O.P. Freiburg: Universitätsverlag, 1977.

HILDEGARD OF BINGEN AND HER HAGIOGRAPHERS

Acta inquisitionis de virtutibus et miraculis S. Hildegardis. PL 197: 131–40.

Gottfried of St. Disibod, Theoderic of Echternach, and Hildegard. *Vita Sanctae Hildegardis.* Ed. Monika Klaes. *CCCM* 126. Turnhout: Brepols, 1993.

Guibert of Gembloux. *Epistolae.* Ed. Albert Derolez. *CCCM* 66–66A. Turnhout: Brepols, 1988, 1989.

Hildegard of Bingen. *Epistolarium.* Ed. Lieven Van Acker. *CCCM* 91–91A. Turnhout: Brepols, 1991, 1993.

Contributors

CAROLINE WALKER BYNUM is Morris A. and Alma Schapiro Professor of History at Columbia University. She is author of *Docere Verbo et Exemplo*; *Jesus as Mother: Studies in the Spirituality of the High Middle Ages*; *Holy Feast and Holy Fast: The Religious Significance of Food to Medieval Women*; *Fragmentation and Redemption: Essays on Gender and the Human Body in Medieval Religion*; and *The Resurrection of the Body in Western Christianity, 200–1336*, which was awarded the Ralph Waldo Emerson prize of Phi Beta Kappa and the Jacques Barzun prize of the American Philosophical Society.

ANNE L. CLARK is Associate Professor of Religion at the University of Vermont. She is author of *Elisabeth of Schönau: A Twelfth-Century Visionary* (University of Pennsylvania Press); "Repression or Collaboration? The Case of Elisabeth and Ekbert of Schönau," in *Christendom and Its Discontents: Exclusion, Persecution, and Rebellion, 1000–1500*, ed. Scott L. Waugh and Peter D. Diehl; and editor and translator of forthcoming *The Complete Works of Elisabeth of Schönau*.

JOHN COAKLEY is L. Russell Feakes Memorial Professor of Church History at New Brunswick Theological Seminary. He is coeditor, with E. Ann Matter, of *Creative Women in Medieval and Early Modern Italy: A Religious and Artistic Renaissance* (University of Pennsylvania Press) and author of "Friars as Confidants of Holy Women in Medieval Dominican Hagiography," in *Images of Sainthood in Medieval Europe*, ed. Renate Blumenfeld-Kosinski and Timea Szell; "Gender and the Authority of Friars: The Significance of Holy Women for Thirteenth-Century Franciscans and Dominicans," *Church History* 60 (1991); and "Friars, Sanctity, and Gender: Mendicant Encounters with Saints, 1250–1325," in *Medieval Masculinities: Regarding Men in the Middle Ages*, ed. Clare A. Lees.

DYAN ELLIOTT is Associate Professor of History and Adjunct of Religious Studies at Indiana University, Bloomington. She is author of *Spiritual Marriage: Sexual Abstinence in Medieval Wedlock*; and *Fallen Bodies:*

Pollution, Sexuality, and Demonology in the Middle Ages (University of Pennsylvania Press).

AMY HOLLYWOOD is Assistant Professor of Religion at Dartmouth College. She is author of *The Soul as Virgin Wife: Mechthild of Magdeburg, Marguerite Porete, and Meister Eckhart*; "Bataille and Mysticism: A 'Dazzling Dissolution,'" *Diacritics* 26 (1996); and "Deconstructing Belief: Irigaray and the Philosophy of Religion," *Journal of Religion* 78 (1998).

CATHERINE M. MOONEY is Assistant Professor of History at Virginia Commonwealth University. She is author of *Philippine Duchesne: A Woman with the Poor*; "The Authorial Role of Brother A. in the Composition of Angela of Foligno's Revelations," in *Creative Women in Medieval and Early Modern Italy: A Religious and Artistic Renaissance*, ed. E. Ann Matter and John Coakley (University of Pennsylvania Press); and "Authority and Inspiration in the *Vitae* and Sermons of Humility of Faenza," in *Medieval Monastic Preaching*, ed. Carolyn Muessig.

BARBARA NEWMAN is Professor of English and Religion at Northwestern University. She is author of *Sister of Wisdom: St. Hildegard's Theology of the Feminine*; editor and translator of Hildegard of Bingen, *Symphonia*; translator of *The Life of Juliana of Mont-Cornillon*; author of *From Virile Woman to WomanChrist: Studies in Medieval Religion and Literature* (University of Pennsylvania Press); and editor of *Voice of the Living Light: Hildegard of Bingen and Her World*.

KAREN SCOTT is Associate Professor of History at De Paul University. She is author of "Saint Catherine of Siena, 'Apostola,'" *Church History* 61 (1992); "'Io Catarina': Ecclesiastical Politics and Oral Culture in the Letters of Catherine of Siena," in *Dear Sister: Medieval Women and the Epistolary Genre*, ed. Karen Cherewatuk and Ulrike Wiethaus (University of Pennsylvania Press), "Urban Spaces, Women's Networks, and the Lay Apostolate in the Siena of Catherine Benincasa," in *Creative Women in Medieval and Early Modern Italy: A Religious and Artistic Renaissance*, ed. E. Ann Matter and John Coakley (University of Pennsylvania Press); and "Candied Oranges, Vinegar, and Dawn: The Imagery of Conversion in the Letters of Caterina of Siena," in *Women Mystic Writers*, ed. Dino S. Cervigni.

FRANK TOBIN is Professor of German at the University of Nevada, Reno. He is author of *Gregorius and Der arme Heinrich: Hartmann's Dualistic and Gradualistic Views of Reality*; *Meister Eckhart: Thought and*

Language (University of Pennsylvania Press); and translator, with Bernard McGinn and Elvira Borgstadt, of *Meister Eckhart, Teacher and Preacher: Selections*; editor and translator of *Henry Suso: The Exemplar with Two German Sermons*; author of *Mechthild von Magdeburg: A Medieval Mystic in Modern Eyes*; and editor and translator of *The Flowing Light of the Godhead*.

Index of Modern Authors

Editors' names are indexed only for the first citation of their works in each essay, unless the citations are to their contributions as authors within those works.

General Index

References to major entries are printed in boldface.

Acknowledgments

For their expert advice regarding particular details involved in planning, overseeing, and completing a volume of collected essays, I wish to thank Caroline Walker Bynum, E. Ann Matter, and Barbara Newman. I am especially grateful to Francine Cardman and M. Brinton Lykes for their insightful comments and support.

I thank also the Women's Studies in Religion Program of the Harvard Divinity School where, as a Research Associate, I first grappled with many of the methodological issues involved in comparing women's and men's hagiographical texts and first conceived of a volume of essays dedicated to this topic.